The "Bergson Boys" and the Origins of Contemporary Zionist Militancy

JUDITH TYDOR BAUMEL

Translated from the Hebrew by Dena Ordan

With a Foreword by Moshe Arens

SYRACUSE UNIVERSITY PRESS

First Edition 2005
05   06   07   08   09   10   6   5   4   3   2   1

Previously published in Hebrew by Magnes Press of Jerusalem in 1999.

The paper used in this publication meets the minimum requirements of
American National Standard for Information Sciences—Permanence of
Paper for Printed Library Materials, ANSI Z39.48–1984.∞™

Library of Congress Cataloging-in-Publication Data

Baumel, Judith Tydor, 1959–
[English]
The "Bergson Boys" and the origins of contemporary Zionist militancy / Judith Tydor
Baumel ; translated from the Hebrew by Dena Ordan.— 1st ed.
p. cm.—(Modern Jewish history)
Includes bibliographical references and index.
ISBN 0–8156–3063–8 (hardcover (cloth) : alk. paper)
1. Irgun tseva'i le'umi. 2. Jews—Palestine—Politics and government—20th century.
3. Palestine—Politics and government—1917–1948. 4. Revisionist Zionism—United
States. I. Title. II. Series.
DS126.B3413 2005
320.54'092'3924—dc22   2005018496

Manufactured in the United States of America

To Yoav

Judith Tydor Baumel is chair of the graduate program in Contemporary Jewry at Bar Ilan University in Ramat-Gan, Israel, and teaches in the Department of Jewish History, specializing in twentieth-century Jewish history with emphasis on the Holocaust, the State of Israel, women's studies, and historical memory. She is the author of numerous articles and books on these subjects. Born in New York, Professor Baumel moved to Israel in 1974, where she completed her studies.

Contents

Illustrations

Foreword

MOSHE ARENS

On 1 February 1944, the Irgun Zva'i Leumi (IZL), the dissident underground force led by Menahem Begin, issued "The Proclamation of the Revolt" against British rule in Palestine. The call to action included a demand that rule over Palestine should immediately be transferred to a provisional Hebrew government. The proclamation was shortly followed by Irgun attacks against the British government immigration offices in Jerusalem, Tel Aviv, and Haifa. In their wake came almost four years of armed struggle against British rule in Palestine, the imprisonment of hundreds of IZL fighters in Palestine, the expulsion by the British of 251 underground members to prison camps in Africa, and the execution on the gallows of IZL fighters who were sentenced to death by British courts. The struggle of the underground finally led to Britain's decision to relinquish the mandate over Palestine granted it by the League of Nations and the evacuation of its forces from there on 15 May 1948—the day of the proclamation of the Jewish State, Israel.

At the time the revolt was proclaimed the IZL counted no more than a few hundred combatants. Vladimir Zeev Jabotinsky, the ideological mentor of the IZL, had died in New York three and one-half years earlier, and no one had as yet risen to take his place at the head of the movement he had founded.

At the time of Jabotinsky's death in 1940 the main areas of support for the movement that he had founded and led, as well as the reservoir of recruits for the IZL in Eastern Europe, had been destroyed by the German conquest of western Poland and the Soviet occupation of eastern Poland

and the Baltic countries. It was around this time that a small group of IZL emissaries came to the United States on a mission to mobilize support for the IZL, only to find themselves essentially cut off from their home base and leaderless, faced with the challenge of how to fulfill the task they had been assigned by their superiors in the IZL in British-occupied Palestine. It was a time when the American Jewish community and its leadership, in awe of President Franklin Roosevelt, were reticent in making their voices heard. Most of the leaders of the American Zionist movement backed the Zionist establishment in Palestine that was fiercely opposed to the Irgun's struggle against the British there. They played no part on the political scene and had little influence in Washington. Even after the news of the destruction of European Jewry reached America, the Jewish leadership there, beholden to President Roosevelt and reluctant to be accused of interfering in any way with the war effort, did not manage to make its voice heard. The IZL emissaries, many of whom had to master the English language before they could become active, burst on the scene with single-minded devotion to their cause, and in short order, despite the opposition of the American Jewish and Zionist establishment, succeeded in attaining unparalleled influence in many circles of American society as well as in the U.S. administration and Congress.

At first, they campaigned for the establishment of a Jewish army to fight Hitler on the side of the Allies, a campaign that contributed to the eventual establishment of the Jewish Brigade that fought the German army in Italy. Thereafter, they campaigned to arouse U.S. public opinion against the tragic fate of European Jewry, a campaign that resulted toward the end of the war in the establishment by the U.S. government of the War Refugee Board, the only attempt of any significance by the United States to assist European Jewry during the years of the Holocaust. And finally, through the American League for a Free Palestine and the Hebrew Committee of National Liberation, they mobilized political and financial support for the struggle of the IZL against British rule in Palestine.

Their success in lobbying for their cause in Washington, in arousing public support for the Jewish struggle for independence in Palestine, and in raising substantial funds in support of that struggle stands to this day as a unique achievement of a handful of talented men, strangers to the United States, completely devoted to their cause. Their contribution to the victory of the Jewish underground over British occupation in Palestine and to the establishment of the State of Israel in May 1948 was significant. In defending the right of the Jewish people to their own country and the justice of the Zionist cause before the American public, the administration, and Congress they were the precursors of Israel's present diplomatic mission in the United States. To this day they have been denied the recognition they so richly deserve for their Herculean efforts.

This book helps to set the record straight.

Preface to the English Edition

In late autumn the Talbiyeh neighborhood of Jerusalem becomes a kaleidoscope of changing colors. During the afternoon a chill breeze blows through the narrow tree-lined streets, making the falling leaves dance between the old stone buildings. There, in an old house at the top of the hill, I met for almost a decade with one of the neighborhood's longtime residents, a man whose study was filled with pictures and artifacts from his long and colorful life. His name was Alexander Rafaeli.

My first meeting with Dr. Rafaeli took place in that same study in the autumn of 1990, overlooking a view in which time seemed to have stood still. Sitting on one of the long sofas under the glaring visages of a dozen African masks that peered down at me from the ceiling, I learned about a most fascinating period of his life—the years when he was a member of the Irgun Delegation in the United States. "Imagine that I was once considered a terrorist, a 'gangster,' " said the octogenarian Rafaeli, his green eyes dancing and a half-smile on his face, remembering days long gone. "Beware of me," he joked at another opportunity, "I might still remember some of the techniques that the 'boys' we worked with in Hollywood taught me in the forties!"

These meetings with Rafaeli were my introduction to the saga of the "Irgun Delegation in the United States"—a Revisionist-Zionist organization that was active between 1939 and 1948 until it disbanded when the last of its founders returned to Palestine with the establishment of the State of Israel. Rafaeli's stories sent me to a variety of documentation found in archives throughout the world describing the delegation's inception and activities. The correspondence, pamphlets, reports, and newspaper articles that I perused portrayed a plethora of Jewish and Zionist activity during a watershed period of history. To these I added oral documentation: interviews with Zionist activists and with the delegation's remaining members. The result is a study of the activities and inner world of the Irgun Delegation in the United States during the 1940s, as its members saw themselves both then and in retrospect.

◆ ◆ ◆

Our saga of the Irgun Delegation begins in the late 1930s when the Irgun Zeva'i Leumi (IZL, or national military organization, hereafter also referred to as Irgun) was formed out of the remnants of the Hagana B defense organization in Palestine. Within months of its inception the Irgun had become the military arm of the Revisionist-Zionist movement, with its members involved in various undertakings including opposition to British Mandate policy and organizing illegal immigration from Europe. Both the Anschluss (the German "unification" with Austria) and Kristallnacht (the Night of Broken Glass) heightened the need for a rapid solution to the refugee problem, which in the eyes of Revisionist-Zionists meant illegal immigration to Palestine. Consequently, several Irgun activists were temporarily posted to the United States in order to raise funds to cover the costs of these undertakings. Within a short time the original group disbanded and the remaining activist in America was joined by five additional comrades from Europe. These six young men, almost all of whom were connected to the militant wing of the Revisionist-Zionist movement, were to become the nucleus of the Irgun Delegation.

To call the group a "delegation" is, in fact, a misnomer as its members never received an organizational mandate to work together in the United States. Nevertheless, because they saw themselves as such and functioned accordingly, most studies have adopted the term in reference to the half-dozen young activists who are the subject of this book. Within a short time the group decided to expand its activities in the United States, first to spearhead the fight for a Jewish army and later to promote the rescue of European Jewry. Later, it attempted to organize illegal immigration of Holocaust survivors to Palestine after World War II, promote public support for the establishment of an independent Jewish State in Palestine, and raise funds in order to secure arms for the fight to come. During its ten years of activity this "undelegated delegation" changed its name and form several times, each time announcing a different set of goals. However, throughout each of these metamorphoses three factors remained constant: the makeup of the group's nucleus, headed by Hillel Kook, who was better known by his pseudonym Peter Bergson; the unique (and, according to their opponents, hyperactive) techniques of the bodies they established; and the complex and problematic relationship that they maintained with the Zionist establishment—Revisionist-Zionist inclusive—both in the United States and in Palestine.

The unique dynamics that ensued from these factors are a central point in numerous studies that mention the delegation and examine its successes. Such studies usually fall into one of three categories: Revisionist-Zionist hagiography such as the movement's official publications and activists' memoirs; literature written by the movement's opponents; research literature published since the 1960s dealing with the delegation's activities, particularly from the American viewpoint. With few exceptions, however, none of the historical studies has focused upon the delegation from the viewpoint of its members, nor charted the long-term innovations that it introduced into the American and American Jewish world. Furthermore, in spite of the numerous studies dealing with the delegation's "glorious period"—1943 and 1944—none has attempted to deal with its entire ten-year working life from 1939 to 1948. *The "Bergson Boys" and the Origins of Contemporary Jewish Militancy* attempts to rectify this lacuna by portraying and analyzing several neglected aspects of the delegation's story and legacy.

In a book dealing with what many consider to be a contentious subject, it is imperative to state clearly what I intend to cover and what lies outside its scope. Much has been written about the development and activities of both the American Zionist movement and Revisionist-Zionism in the United States, particularly during the 1930s and 1940s. These subjects have been covered in depth in pathbreaking and compelling studies such as those of Samuel Halperin, who examines the political world of American Zionism; Menachem Kaufman, in his exploration of the interaction between non-Zionist and Zionist organizations in America during the immediate pre-State era; David H. Shpiro, who analyzes the political transformation of American Zionism during the Holocaust; and Aaron Berman, in his discussion of the American Zionist understanding of the Holocaust. Other studies have exhausted the collective diplomatic and organizational efforts of American Jewish and Zionist organizations to rescue European Jewry during the Holocaust. These include Henry L. Feingold's examination of the politics of rescue during the Roosevelt era; Rafael Medoff's exposé of the American Jewish leadership during the Holocaust; Saul Friedmann's exploration of U.S. policy toward refugees from Europe; Monty N. Penkower's studies of rescue, Zionism, and American Jewry; Yehuda Bauer's analysis of the activities of the American Joint Distribution Committee during the Second World War; and David S. Wyman's indictment of the Roosevelt administration during the war years.[1] This literature has spawned a long-lasting polemical debate focusing on appropriating responsibility and guilt for the paucity of American, American Jewish, and American Zionist rescue efforts during the Holocaust.

Several of these studies—particularly those by Shpiro, Berman, Penkower, and Wyman—have assessed the political impact of the Bergson group during and subsequent to the period of its activities, particularly in the field of rescue. Some, such as Shpiro, Berman, and, to a much greater extent, Penkower, see them as little more than a catalyst on the American Jewish organizational scene with little or no practical success. Wyman's study portrays their political impact as being much greater, a factor that I discuss in chapter 4. These and other historians such as Feingold and Kaufman have also documented American Jewish and Zionist organizational attitudes toward the Bergson Boys during the 1940s, which became a predictable and rather unremarkable factor throughout the delegation's history. In brief, it appears that most Jewish or Zionist bodies in the United States viewed the delegation either as an annoying insect whose buzzing was distracting but of negligible consequence, or as a tantalizing Siren whose initial attraction of the uninitiated could ultimately endanger or even destroy the efforts of the Jewish and Zionist establishment. Their arguments against the delegation ranged from ideological attacks centering upon the group's "fascist" leanings to practical arguments focusing upon their success in fund-raising and public relations. A wealth of documentation about these attitudes may be found in the Central Zionist Archives in Jerusalem (such as the files of the American office of the Jewish Agency and material on the activities of the American Zionist Emergency Council), in the New York Zionist Archives, and in the papers of personages such as Rabbi Stephen S. Wise (American Jewish Historical Archives, Waltham, Massachusetts) and those of Rabbi Abba Hillel Silver

(The Temple, Cleveland). However, as the main thrust of the American Jewish and Zionist arguments against the delegation, summarized above, are well known, well documented, and repetitive, I will refer to them only briefly in order to avoid duplication of effort.

Furthermore, as the delegation was an offshoot of the right-wing militant Zionist Irgun, Revisionist-Zionist historians and activists such as David Niv, Eli Tavin, and Shmuel Katz have tended to analyze it as a Zionist organization and to focus upon its interaction with other Zionist bodies. Their studies, similar to those mentioned above, ultimately return to the polemical debate that punctuates most of the research literature dealing with the delegation and concentrate either upon a balance sheet of successes and failures or upon Zionist-delegation interaction.

Instead of entering this well-populated and exhausting battleground, my intention is more modest: I explore several largely neglected aspects of the delegation's nature and legacy. The first deals with the group's self-image; the second, with its internal activity patterns; the third—and most important—with its tactical legacy in the sphere of public relations, something that I see as deriving from its nature as a cultural and ideological hybrid: a prototype of an ethnic interest/protest group, headed in the United States by a half-dozen Palestinian Jews of Revisionist-Zionist persuasion, who had received their training in prewar Europe and were attempting to understand the workings of the American mind.[2]

Several reasons led me to concentrate upon the delegation's public relations efforts. First, because of the centrality of publicity and public relations in American political life. Public mood, molded to a large extent by propaganda and public relations, has long been accepted as a dominant force in the American system of direct representation, limiting governmental actions and guiding those in positions of power. Rapidly grasping the dynamics of this mechanism, the Bergson Boys made an almost seamless transition from European-style diplomacy to American-style media manipulation, integrating themselves into the social and political culture of their temporary home. In her study of the American press during the Holocaust, Deborah Lipstadt has shown how American officials used the press as a barometer and cultivator of American public sentiment, particularly during wartime. By utilizing the press and other public relations tactics to their fullest during and after the Second World War, delegation members became the first Jewish organization in the United States to attempt to sway American government policy primarily by influencing the public mind.[3]

Second, because I believe that public relations efforts symbolize the essence of most of the American Jewish and particularly Zionist organizational activities of the 1940s. With few exceptions, most of the time and efforts of the American Jewish and Zionist organizations was not taken up with direct political activity but either with their never-ending internal deliberations and infighting, or with various forms of public relations, propaganda, and the like. Of all the issues with which the delegation and other American Jewish or Zionist organizations dealt—the creation of a Jewish army, the rescue of European Jewry, the establishment of a Jewish State—in practice, their independent efforts resolved none of the above, and in most cases they were barely a contributory factor. A Jewish army was never created, and it is difficult to draw a direct connection between the British establishment of the Jewish Brigade in 1944 and the activities of any one specific group. As for the rescue issue, even taking into account David Wyman's claims regarding the impact of the delegation's activities on the establishment of the War Refugee Board, there is little debate that the remnants of European Jewry were ultimately rescued by the advancing Allied armies and not by any American Jewish or Zionist organization. Finally, as Menachem Kaufman states, although it had the support of most of Diaspora Jewry, "the State of Israel came into being primarily because of the decisiveness of its leaders and the fighting spirit of the Yishuv" and not because of any concrete activities of an American Zionist organization, delegation-sponsored group, or other Diaspora Jewish entity.[4] The contribution of American Jewish and Zionist organizations in almost all these spheres was to generate positive public opinion using various organizational and tactical methods. Consequently, I examine the unique methods used by the delegation, which took the issue of American Jewish public relations to a new zenith.

The centrality of public relations in the Bergson Boys internal world and self-image is yet another reason for concentrating primarily upon the group's tactical aspect. Within a year of the delegation's inception its modus operandi had metamorphosed into its entire essence, overshadowing organizational norms, party loyalty, and even ideological leanings. Ultimately the delegation's tactics became the main cause of its notoriety in American and American Jewish circles.

A final reason that draws my focus to the delegation's public relations activities is the fact that I believe them to be the group's longest lasting legacy. In many ways, the Irgun Delegation was an organization active before its time. In the latter part of this book I develop the theory that the delegation acted as a prototype of an American ethnic interest/protest group, combining and perfecting tactics used by organizations preceding them and passing on a tactical legacy to those that followed. Indeed, during the last years of its existence delegation members were approached by representatives of other national groups in the United States attempting to learn more about their modus operandi. As historian Yonah Ferman noted, even a decade and a half after the delegation was dissolved its activities during 1943 and 1944 were serving as a model for foreign-policy-oriented ethnic protest groups in the United States such as the Cuban National Liberation Movement. A deeper examination of the delegation's activities shows it to be a model for many ethnopolitical groups in the United States, including those that were domestically oriented. Consequently, I examine the delegation's tactics in detail, focusing upon factors that would later be adopted by a number of successful groups as the mechanism of protest.

One of the best known of these groups was active in the Jewish and later the Israeli sphere. More than twenty years after the delegation had dissolved, the Bergson Boys' tactical patterns acted as a beacon lighting the path of an American Jewish rabbi—Meir (Martin David) Kahane—who was to found two controversial, and in the eyes of many infamously dangerous, organizations: the Jewish Defense League in the United States and the "Kach" political movement in Israel. Paying lip service to Revisionist-Zionist ideology and militancy as the ideological roots of his organizational creations, from the late 1960s onward Kahane honed the delegation's tactical patterns of hyperactive and bombastic public relations down to a fine science that was a far cry from the wildest dreams of the delegation members in the 1940s. Only by examining the Bergson Boys' original tactical patterns can one understand their later metamorphosis within these two organizations, which would affect the American Jewish and later the world Jewish discourse of power and protest.

The Bergson Boys' public relations efforts were intrinsically connected with the first two topics that I discuss: group introspection and organizational interaction. How did the group view itself? Almost all existing research literature, even that which makes use of the delegation's papers or interviews with one or two of the founders, concentrates primarily upon how they were seen by others and not on how they saw themselves. This focus is true for both those who mention the Bergson Boys in passing such as Feingold or Shpiro and those who concentrate upon their activity in depth such as Penkower and Wyman. As I believe that self-image is an important factor in determining the nature and thrust of one's activities, I focus upon how the delegation members saw themselves, both during their period of activity in the United States and in retrospect. In order to examine their self-image during the 1940s I make extensive use of documentation found in the Jabotinsky Archives in Israel (JAI), which also contains copies of the delegation's papers found in the Yale archives. To chart their self-image in retrospect, I have used autobiographies and biographies of four of the six delegation's founding members, and their personal papers. As delegation member Samuel Merlin's papers have become unavailable since his death in 1994, I have used copies of many of his papers located in Alex Rafaeli's personal collection. Similarly, copies of many of Hillel Kook's papers may be found in the JAI collection in Tel Aviv. Finally, this book was written at the eleventh hour, when three of the six delegation founders were still alive and two could still be interviewed. By the time this book was completed, all but one had passed away. Apart from interviews that I conducted, three delegation members had left extensive interviews at the repository of the Oral Documentation Center at the Hebrew University in Jerusalem, an unrivaled source for examining how they viewed themselves and their activities in retrospect.

My second topic of interest, which has received almost no attention in the existing literature, is organizational: the group's internal activity patterns, which derived, at least in part, from its members' self-image. An analysis of the group's internal interaction sheds light upon the mechanism allowing six young men, working in a foreign environment and speaking a foreign language, to create an apparatus that made those around it stand up and take notice, irrespective of whether it succeeded in its stated goals. Similar patterns were later adopted by ethnic protest and interest groups in the United States, some of which had been in touch with delegation members during their final years in America. Material about this topic may be found not only in the JAI collection but in the National Archives in Washington, D.C., the Public Record Office (PRO) in

London, and the Morgenthau Papers and Documents of the War Refugee
Board in Hyde Park, New York. These shed light not only upon the delegation's relationship with other groups but also upon its internal workings
and modus operandi. Unfortunately, almost six years after being submitted, my access of information request to view the Department of Justice
documents pertaining to an FBI investigation of the group and particularly its leader, Hillel Kook (Peter Bergson), is still being processed. I have
therefore had to avail myself of the information contained in those files
only second hand, using references found in David S. Wyman's comprehensive analysis of America and the Holocaust and Joanna M. Saidel's recent study of the Revisionist-Zionism in America.[5]

This operational apparatus is the third and central topic upon which I
focus: the group's modus operandi, particularly in the field of public relations. The topic's centrality was expressed in the Hebrew title of the original study upon which this book was based: *From Ideology to Propaganda.*
Whether or not the Bergson Boys adhered to Revisionist-Zionist ideology
became a moot point during the 1940s; their main thrust was not in the
ideological or diplomatic spheres but in that of propaganda and public
relations.

The importance of the group's operational aspect in the field of public
relations has been mentioned by almost all historians who refer to the delegation, both those who view them as having a certain impact, such as
David Wyman and Monty Penkower, and those who consider them a
more negligible force on the American Jewish scene, like Henry Feingold,
David Shpiro, and others. More than one historian has claimed that the
entire American Jewish establishment was influenced directly or indirectly
by the delegation's public relations and propaganda tactics. For example,
in his study of the political transformation of American Zionism during
the Holocaust, David Shpiro states categorically that after 1944, the Bergson Boys' tactics in the field of public relations were a catalyst for similar
activity carried out by the American Zionist Emergency Council headed
by Abba Hillel Silver and his chief adviser, Emmanuel Neumann.[6] Nevertheless, none of the existing studies has examined the delegation's operational aspect in depth.

By focusing upon these three issues—self-image, organizational dynamics, and tactical legacy in the field of public relations—I shift this study
from a particularistic Zionist and Jewish context into a much broader one

of ethnic protest groups. By so doing, this study charts the delegation's development, ideological shifts, and activity patterns without sinking into the particularistic format that characterizes many, if not most, of the studies dealing with Jewish and Zionist organizations.

The first part of this study describes the organizational and institutional background of the delegation and the history of its members. In addition it provides the reader with a concise description of the Zionist-Revisionist and the American Jewish contexts into which it was born. Each of the remaining chapters is devoted to analyzing the delegation members' self-image, intraorganizational activity, and tactical patterns as connected with one of the organizations that the group founded during its ten-year existence: the American Friends of a Jewish Palestine, the Committee for a Jewish Army of Palestinian and Stateless Jews, the Emergency Committee to Save European Jewry, the Hebrew Committee for National Liberation, and the League for a Free Palestine. The book's final chapter probes the delegation's right-wing character and elaborates upon its long-term tactical legacy among other organizations, particularly ethnic interest/protest groups in the United States and the American Jewish militant right, from the 1940s up to the present.

This portrait of the Irgun Delegation has significance for Jewish and Zionist historiography on two planes. On the one hand, this is an anthropological, sociological, and conceptual study of an intimate group of activists, strangers in their geographical arena of activity, who took upon themselves a variety of goals that they tried to promote in the public sphere. On the other hand, this study examines the conceptual and tactical roots of the militant right wing in the United States, and also of the Israeli right wing in some respects. In his pioneering work Joseph Heller presented the Lohamei Herut Yisrael (LHI)—a militant right-wing offshoot of the Irgun that will be discussed later—as an entity whose activity encapsulates an extremist ideology. Similarly, the Irgun Delegation may be viewed as a group that pioneered modern propagandizing. Learning to utilize newspaper ads and public displays in the America of the 1940s, before almost any of its American Jewish contemporaries, the delegation's methods left their mark on coming generations of political followers.

The group's intimate nature should not detract from its broader implications in mass political terms. An anecdote relates that four of the founders of Russian social democracy were sailing on Lake Geneva when a storm broke. One said, "Let us return to shore before Russian social democracy drowns in the lake." This small group, which lived far from Russian shores, sparked the ten-day revolution that changed the face of history and was responsible for the founding of a world power whose rise and fall mark the boundaries of what historian Eric Hobsbawm has termed the "short twentieth century." Similarly, the small Irgun Delegation, whose detractors claim that it did no more than electrify the American public, must be credited with giving birth to the operational and propagandizing patterns utilized by many Jewish and Zionist organizations in Israel and the United States to the present.

Acknowledgments

It is my great pleasure to thank all those who assisted me during the researching and writing of this study. First and foremost the late Alex Rafaeli, who was the driving force behind both the Hebrew and English editions of this book, and who was taken from all those who admired and respected him before he could see the English edition in print. I hope that this volume will be a fitting tribute to his memory.

I would like to thank the archivists who assisted me in locating the documentation upon which this study is based, and particularly the archival staff of the Jabotinsky Institute in Israel and its director, Amira Stern. To my colleagues at the Department of Jewish History and the Interdisciplinary Graduate Program in Contemporary Jewry at Bar-Ilan University, especially Professor Joshua Schwartz, dean of the faculty of Jewish Studies; and to the staff of the Herzl Institute for the Study of Zionism at the University of Haifa, under whose auspices this book was written, go my gratitude for academic support and personal friendship during an academically turbulent time in my life. To the Herzl Institute also go my heartfelt thanks for supporting the translation of the Hebrew edition of this volume upon which this English adaptation is based.

I am indebted to many friends and colleagues who assisted me at various junctures while I was preparing this study. In particular, I wish to thank several individuals who gave of their time and assistance: Professor Walter Laqueur, whose patience and advice know no bounds; Professor Yechiam Weitz, whose knowledge of the political machinations within the Yishuv and the Zionist movement saved me many hours of library work; Professor Joseph Heller, who provided me with guidance about the book's focus; the late Professor Charles Liebman and Professor Jonathan

Sarna for their insightful comments about the introduction; Dr. Eli Tzur, whose vast knowledge of the Zionist left wing was surpassed only by his unstinting willingness to read draft after draft of this manuscript, always lifting my flagging spirits with his unique sense of humor and never-ending enthusiasm.

I am also grateful to my family, who shared with me the ups and downs that go along with every book, for their patience with what often appeared to be an endless research project; to my friend and colleague Dena Ordan, whose outstanding translating skills turned the Hebrew version of this volume into a coherent English edition; to the staff of the Magnes Press in Jerusalem, and particularly its director, Dan Benovici, who published the original Hebrew edition; and to Syracuse University Press for supporting the idea of this book and producing the English edition.

Finally I wish to express special thanks to Professor Yoav Gelber, director of the Herzl Institute for the Study of Zionism at the University of Haifa, who made the initial suggestion to examine the history of the Irgun Delegation in the United States. Throughout the research and writing of this book, he provided me with historical guidance, institutional assistance, and the type of friendship and moral support that kept me from throwing in the towel (or rather, trashing the word processor) during those moments when difficulties seemed overwhelming. No words can express what I owe such a unique person, and I dedicate this book to him with friendship and gratitude.

Abbreviations

AECZA	American Emergency Committee for Zionist Affairs
AFL	American Federation of Labor
AFJP	American Friends of a Jewish Palestine
AJC	American Jewish Congress
AZEC	American Zionist Emergency Council
CO	Colonial Office
CR	Congressional Record
CZA	Central Zionist Archives
DP	Displaced Person
DWRB	Documents of the War Refugee Board, Roosevelt Library
FAZ	Federation of American Zionists
FO	Foreign Office
FRUS	Foreign Relations of the United States
HCNL	Hebrew Committee of National Liberation
IDF	Israel Defense Forces
IZL	Irgun Zeva'i Leumi
JAI	Jabotinsky Archives in Israel
JDC	Joint Distribution Committee (also Joint)
JDL	Jewish Defense League
LHI	Lohamei Herut Yisrael
LST	Landing ship tanks
MP	Member of Parliament
NZF	New Zionist Federation
NZO	New Zionist Organization
OHD	Oral History Documentation Center, Institute for Contemporary Jewry, Hebrew University
OSS	Office of Strategic Services
PRO	Public Record Office

Abbreviations

UJA	United Jewish Appeal
WO	War Office
WRB	War Refugee Board
ZOA	Zionist Organization of America

The "Bergson Boys" and the Origins
of Contemporary Zionist Militancy

What Was the Irgun Delegation?

"It all began with our political activity in Europe in the thirties," said Alexander Rafaeli.

> Our roots must be sought there, in the place where we became acquainted and had our first experience of how to coordinate our activities under conditions of pressure. That was where our ties to Jabotinsky were institutionalized; but that was also where the initial rifts in our complex and convoluted relationship with him emerged. It was in [the] Europe of those days that the idea of transferring the focal point of our activity to the United States was born, and it was from there that we left on a mission that lasted far longer than originally planned, in the course of which we became the "cutoff battalion"—one without a superior commander that is therefore forced to act independently.[1]

Thus, in a single paragraph, did Rafaeli (Sasha to his friends) sum up the birth of the Irgun Delegation: the European political and institutional genesis of its members, the idea to move their sphere of activity to the United States, and the delegation's ultimate sense of independence from Zionist norms, both those of the Zionist establishment and those of the Revisionist-Zionist movement.

At first reading, Rafaeli's remarks seem crystal clear, but closer examination reveals that they are open to a number of synchronous multilayered significations with distinctive associations. The terminology as employed necessitates reference to a specific set of codes without which neither the relevant *texts* nor their concomitant *contexts* can be deciphered. *We* refers here to the small group of young men who manned the Irgun Delegation

1. Irgun Delegation member Alexander Rafaeli. Courtesy of Judith Tydor Baumel.

in the United States from the late 1930s until the founding of the State of Israel, while *Europe* includes Paris and Vienna, but refers primarily to Poland and the Balkans—the arena where these activists undertook Betar and Irgun organizational tasks from the mid-1930s until their departure for the United States. Next we come to the more tangled term *political activity,* often found in the memoirs of the delegation's members, which refers not just to the political sphere but also to the organizational one. "By this we meant our inherently military patterns of activity," Rafaeli noted in an aside. "During our entire period of service our behavior was not that of a group attached to a political body but that of members of a military organization. We were not Revisionists but members of the IZL; we were not subject to the authority of the [Revisionist] movement either in the United States or in Palestine, but to its commander and its leaders."[2] Finally, *our complex relationship with Jabotinsky* encompasses a virtual realm, one that gives us insight into the dynamic underlying the delegation's founding and early activities. On the one hand, this relationship embodied the exiled and aging leader's innermost aspirations for his ideological offspring's chosen path; on the other, it also embodied his disappointment with their autonomous impulses that time and again sparked an almost inevitable process of division within the Revisionist movement and its branches, some of which Vladimir Zeev Jabotinsky (generally known as Zeev Jabotinsky) viewed as his personal demesne.

It is interesting to note that all of the delegation's members devoted an inordinate amount of time in their interviews and a great deal of space in their autobiographies to discussion of what they called "political activity." This catchall phrase takes on various meanings at various times. On the one hand, they often refer thusly to the diplomatic efforts that were undertaken during the 1940s; on the other hand, it is usually used in describing the field that was, in fact, the group's only forte: public relations. Indeed the use of the term "political" contrasts sharply with the reality of the Irgun Delegation's existence, which centered less around diplomatic efforts than around one main field of expression: propaganda, fanfare, and show.

This volume examines the history, internal dynamics, and activity patterns of a group that emerged against the ideological context of the Revisionist movement during the 1940s. Within its framework, the main elements explicitly and implicitly cited by Rafaeli—the personalities involved, its arena of activity, organizational patterns, motives, goals, and inter—and intra-organizational relationships—conjoined to create one of the more fascinating episodes in the pre-State decade of Zionist history. A handful of Palestinian "boys" who came to New York to raise funds for Irgun activities in Palestine and abroad formed a half-dozen entities that fomented a minor revolution in the American Jewish and American Zionist tactical patterns. Shaped by the needs of the hour and their leaders' inclinations, these entities reflect the central processes affecting both world and American Jewry. Analysis of their organizational metamorphoses and activity patterns as seen through their own eyes affords us insight into both the workings of an ethnic protest group and the turbulent American Jewish world of the 1940s.

The story of the Bergson Boys begins at the intersection among three circles—alternately concentric, parallel, or tangential—that shaped both the nature of the group and its members' behavioral patterns. One circle targets the fiber of internal group relations and focuses on both the delegation's internal hierarchy and the temper of intragroup interaction. The other two circles relate to external factors: one demarcates the divisions within the Revisionist-Zionist movement both in Palestine and abroad; the other maps the American Jewish and American Zionist organizational divisions. The remainder of this chapter will therefore concentrate upon the inner dynamics within each of these circles during the 1930s—a time when they were essentially parallel but began to overlap—focusing upon the two main arenas of delegation activity: the Revisionist movement and the American scene.

Founders of the Irgun Delegation

How can we account for the success of action groups? What enables certain groups to function in difficult circumstances and to accomplish their goals, whereas other groups disintegrate without attaining their aims? Group theory cites a number of factors that facilitate the creation of an active and cohesive group capable of achieving success under pressure; among them are a shared definition of goals, the desire to continue to act in concert, an attempt to preserve group cohesion at all costs, and fear of internal or external sanctions for divergence from accepted group norms.[3]

Another factor determining group character and survival potential—in small groups in particular—is role delegation. In addition to the group leader (whether overt or covert), group task roles often include the coordinator, the evaluator-critic, the elaborator, the information giver, and the initiator-contributor, among others. A clearly delineated consistent division of these roles creates a cohesive atmosphere and sense of continuity that significantly boost group success in implementing its goals.[4]

Many factors contributed to the singularity of the Irgun Delegation in the United States, first and foremost the character of its founding nucleus and hard core. This nucleus, which set the tone for the various group-created entities and also absorbed new members during the war years in answer to its needs, was essentially comprised of six young men, almost all Irgun or Betar activists, who in the early 1940s took it upon themselves to raise money in the United States to fund Irgun activity in Europe and Palestine.

All members of this core group were already acquainted with each other before late December 1938, when the idea of a delegation was first raised. In the wake of the sharp deterioration in the status of Reich Jews after Kristallnacht and of Austrian Jews in the months after the Anschluss, most Irgun emissaries in Europe were intensely involved in organizing Revisionist-sponsored illegal immigration to Palestine. According to several delegation members, the idea to send an Irgun delegation to the United States in order to raise funds for illegal immigration was originally that of Yitzhak Ben-Ami, the Irgun emissary to Vienna. Yitzhak, or "Mike," Ben-Ami (Rosen, 1912–1983) was one of the first children born in the new Hebrew city of Tel Aviv. Initially active in left-wing political circles, he subsequently moved to the right, joining Betar and becoming a member of the Irgun. Recalling his first meetings with Ben-Ami, Alex Rafaeli described him as "a typical sabra. Nice, friendly, helpful when possible. He was also the only one who had a car in those days, and we, the members of the Irgun, treated it as our national car." [5]

In 1937 Ben-Ami was dispatched to Vienna, Poland, and Prague, where he engaged in organizing illegal immigration under the pseudonym "Ben-Menachem." This activity climaxed in fall 1938 when he escorted a group of illegal immigrants from Vienna to Romania. These immigrants underwent a particularly traumatic experience before being allowed to depart: Gestapo officers searched their baggage for hours, tore their clothes off, and subjected them to verbal and physical abuse. But this experience by no means concluded their suffering: only after each and every one of these 550 Viennese refugees had passed individual inspection by Adolf Eichmann himself and received his permission to leave Austria were they allowed to board ship and sail down the Danube.[6]

Upon its arrival in Budapest some two weeks later, the group learned that, on the previous night, 9 November, unrestrained outbreaks of anti-Jewish violence had taken place throughout Germany and Austria. At that moment Ben-Ami fully grasped the significance of having snatched this particular group of Jews from its threatened expulsion to the Mathausen concentration camp; simultaneously, fears lest Revisionist-sponsored illegal immigration cease because of severe lack of funding for Irgun activities burdened his thoughts. "I stood at the rail on the upper deck of the *Melk* and watched the lights of Vienna disappear," Ben-Ami wrote some forty-five years later. "What would have happened to these people on board, I wondered, if they had remained in Austria? And what would happen to

2. Irgun Delegation member Yitzhak Ben-Ami. Courtesy of Judith Tydor Baumel.

thousands of Jews in the near future if we could not expand our work? The Zionist establishment still fought us at every turn and we never knew from one day to the next where we could get funds to expand our activities."[7]

A new problem awaited Ben-Ami upon his return to Vienna, where the young Irgun activist received orders to report to Eichmann's assistants at Gestapo headquarters in the Metropole Hotel. A short businesslike conversation ensued. Despite German willingness to assist Jewish emigration, it was suggested that Ben-Ami close the Revisionist emigration office in Vienna and relocate elsewhere. Vienna "was now dead for its Jews," he recalled. "The one hotel still available to them, the Hotel de France, had its own café and a few Jews still dropped in for coffee and the latest rumors. But it was not safe—a Gestapo raid could take place at any time and the Jews sat on the edge of their chairs, their eyes on the door ready to grab their coats and run."[8]

Ben-Ami needed no further invitations to Gestapo headquarters in order to recognize the full gravity of the situation. In coordination with other Irgun activists in Europe he began to dismantle his office, arranging for the transfer of illegal immigration activity to Warsaw, Bucharest, and Prague. But logistical problems were not Ben-Ami's sole concern; he faced financial worries as well. For some time Revisionist activists had discussed the vital need to raise funds for illegal immigration. One as yet unimplemented proposal suggested dispatching several activists from Britain to the United States for a short period of time, and it now occurred to Ben-Ami that he might volunteer to join this group, since the New Zionist Organization (NZO; that is, the Revisionist movement), Betar, and the Irgun had recently begun acting in concert on matters of illegal immigration. In the course of his meetings with leading Irgun members in late 1938, Ben-Ami had put forth this proposal, even going so far as to suggest that the Irgun send an independent delegation to the United States. His repeated pleas finally evoked a positive response: the Irgun high command agreed to seriously consider sending such a delegation to the United States in order to raise funds for the European arena. Thus, according to Yitzhak Ben-Ami, the idea of an Irgun Delegation was born.

It is hard to know how much of this description, penned by Ben-Ami three decades after the events in question took place, actually represents the dynamics of that time. On the one hand, the general tone of Ben-Ami's story is echoed in Alex Rafaeli's memoirs. In a series of interviews granted in the 1970s, however, delegation leader Hillel Kook was surprisingly reticent about Ben-Ami's involvement. Ben-Ami's Viennese activities in the sphere of illegal immigration are documented in the Jabotinsky Archives and elsewhere; nevertheless we have only his story—and the fact that he was the first of the delegation's members to reach the United States—as proof that his proposal was the catalyst for the formation of the Irgun Delegation.

In winter 1938 most of the "boys" who would eventually form the future nucleus of the Irgun Delegation were scattered throughout Europe, engaging in political activity or in organizing illegal immigration to Palestine. Most had originally been sent overseas as Revisionist movement or

Irgun emissaries, but their missions shifted in response to changing conditions in Europe. Even Ben-Ami did not proceed immediately to his chosen destination. Rather, he was first dispatched to Zurich to determine the feasibility of opening a bureau there in the event that the military situation in central Europe deteriorated. From Zurich he traveled to Poland, where he again placed the idea of a delegation before the senior Irgun officer in the Diaspora, Hillel Kook. Kook (b. 1915), who was later to serve on the delegation under the pseudonym Peter Bergson (after his father, Dov Ber), came to Palestine from Lithuania in 1924. A member of a prominent rabbinic family—the Palestinian chief rabbi, Abraham Isaac ha-Kohen Kook, was his uncle—Kook joined the Hagana B, an organizational predecessor of the Irgun, in 1931 as a result of his friendship with David Raziel, a fellow student at the Merkaz ha-Rav Yeshivah in Jerusalem who would later command the Irgun. Kook worked at Hadassah Hospital until 1937, when he became a member of the Irgun high command and was sent to Poland. It was there that, according to Ben-Ami, he first heard of the delegation proposal to form, and he reacted with some skepticism. Ben-Ami claims that at that time the tall, handsome Irgun officer remained unconvinced of the need to send an independent delegation to the United States and decided to put off a final decision on this matter until after meeting with his longtime friend and military superior, Irgun commander David Raziel. In early February 1938, the two men met in Paris at a trilateral conference between the Irgun, NZO, and Betar leaders convened to set guidelines for cooperation between the three right-wing Zionist organizations.[9]

This three-way conclave established a blueprint for a cooperative partnership between the various Revisionist bodies. One practical outcome of this meeting relevant to our study was the decision to send a four-person delegation to the United States for a short period of time in order to raise funds for continued Revisionist-sponsored illegal immigration to Palestine. Three of this delegation's members—Colonel John Henry Patterson (1867–1947), who had commanded the Zion Mule Corps and the Jewish Legion during World War I; Robert Briscoe, the only Jewish member of the Irish parliament; and Haim Lubinsky, a young Palestinian lawyer who was an active rank-and-file member of the Irgun—were asked to leave for the United States immediately to lay the initial groundwork. A month later they were joined by Yitzhak Ben-Ami, the only one of the four slated to remain in America in order—again according to Ben-Ami and Rafaeli,

3. Hillel Kook, more commonly known as Peter Bergson, became the leader of the Irgun Delegation after Zeev Jabotinsky's death. Courtesy of Judith Tydor Baumel.

but with little documented verification from elsewhere—to oversee the formation of the permanent delegation.

Despite their constant talk of the need for fund-raising, not one of the four men slated to travel to the United States had the vaguest notion of how this task was to be accomplished. Haim Lubinsky traveled to Washington, D.C., with Colonel Patterson in the hope of obtaining an audience with congressmen or other influential personages. Their only success was to make contact with several wealthy Jewish families who provided them with home hospitality and to whom they made their first "sales pitch" regarding the need for money to continue their work in illegal immigration.[10] Describing his own shock upon reaching the United States several months later, Hillel Kook recalled the confrontation with the new mentality, so different from the European one with which they were familiar. "The Irgun in the Diaspora, which I commanded, was comprised of people . . . with classic Zionist backgrounds, education, and beliefs. At that point, we saw no great difference between an American Jew and a Polish Jew. . . . We had no exact plans regarding what we were going to do there [in the United States]; our stated purpose was to gain entré into American Jewish public and national life."[11]

Patterson and Briscoe's return to Britain in late spring 1939 and Lubinsky's ultimate return to Palestine forced the Irgun leadership to address the question of whether and how to staff the permanent delegation. Despite the ready availability of potential candidates, in the final analysis the person found most suited for the job, Arieh Ben-Eliezer, lacked some of the essential prerequisites, specifically, command of the relevant languages. Ben-Eliezer (1913–1970), who later became one of the Irgun commanders in Palestine, was born to an Orthodox family in Vilna and came to Palestine at the age of seven. In his youth he joined the Irgun; at the same time he earned a living as a truck driver. From 1937 his biography followed a route similar to that of the other delegation members: missions to Eastern Europe; organizing Revisionist-sponsored illegal immigration; and, in July 1939, transfer to the United States following a short stay in Palestine. Two outstanding characteristics assisted Ben-Eliezer in his role as a delegation member: his uncanny resemblance to the French actor Charles Boyer, and his superb command of Yiddish. Indeed, when he arrived in New York, Ben-Eliezer spoke only two languages: Hebrew and Yiddish. Alex Rafaeli recalled their initial hesitation as to the wisdom of sending someone with no English skills to the United States. "I sat with him and inquired whether he spoke English. His answer was negative. French?—No. German?—No. 'I speak Yiddish,' he said. 'But I'll manage.' " The Irgun leadership decided to gamble on the spirited young man and sent him overseas. The gamble paid off. A combination of youth and piquant Yiddish entranced his audience, and within a few weeks Ben-Eliezer was a sought-after speaker in the Jewish quarters of Brooklyn and the Bronx. The young Irgun activist soon learned English on the job, and after six months in America spoke it almost like a native.[12]

In the course of 1940 Ben-Ami and Ben-Eliezer were joined by another four young men, of whom one was Alexander Rafaeli (Rafaelovitch; 1910–1999). Like Ben-Ami, as a youth Rafaeli had moved from the left-wing Hashomer Hatsair movement to Betar ranks. A native of Riga who studied at Heidelberg University, Rafaeli came to Palestine as a student in 1933. After an unsuccessful attempt at agricultural work, he joined the staff of the newspaper *Hadoar Hakalkali (Economic News)*, ultimately spreading his energies on a number of fronts. In addition to serving as the economic editor of the daily newspaper *Haboker (The Morning)* and as the representative for a number of Tel Aviv insurance firms, he was also active in the Hagana B (National Hagana) defense organization, which he joined

4. Irgun Delegation member Arieh Ben-Eliezer. Courtesy of Judith Tydor Baumel.

in 1934. This organization, which had broken away from the Hagana after the 1929 Arab riots in order to serve as a nucleus for a standing army, drew many Betar members who felt that it actualized Betar's platform espousing national activism through "militarism." Because it was removed from the centers of power in the Yishuv, the new organization failed, however, to develop at the desired pace. Consequently, and against the background of the intensification of the Arab uprising and the July 1937 partition plan, Hagana B commander-in-chief Abraham Tehomi decided to return to the Hagana mother organization, a step many organization members opposed. After Tehomi and his faction returned to the ranks of the Hagana, these remaining opposition members formed the Irgun Zeva'i Leumi, the underground military arm of the Revisionist movement. Although not bound by formal ties, in actuality the Irgun and the Revisionist movement had shared ideological, organizational, and political affinities.[13]

Following the reunification of the National Hagana with the Hagana mother organization in 1937, Rafaeli and other Betar members, along with supporters of the activist Revisionist line, joined the new Irgun Zeva'i Leumi organization that, for them, embodied the National Hagana's original ideals. Rafaeli's friendship with Irgun commander David Raziel deepened. "I often walked with Razi through the streets of Jerusalem and we talked at length of our commitment to military action. Our conversations would begin in the early evening and continue through the night," Rafaeli recalled. One evening Raziel revealed to Rafaeli the approximate size of the Irgun membership and attempted to persuade him to leave his jobs and become a full-time Irgun activist. "It took me some time to come to a decision," Rafaeli continued. "I was twenty-seven years old, earning well by local standards and economically independent. I was being asked to renounce this and embark on an adventure. . . . Finally, one early morning, standing on Jerusalem's Jaffa Street after a night-long walk with Raziel, I agreed to become a full-time revolutionary." [14]

Rafaeli's willingness to become a "full-time revolutionary" also meant that he had to be prepared to leave for Europe almost immediately as an Irgun emissary. In 1938 and 1939 Rafaeli moved among Paris, Vienna, and Budapest, engaging in what he termed "political activity," which meant primarily establishing Irgun offices and organizing illegal immigration to Palestine. With the outbreak of war Rafaeli tried to reach London; however, the British ban on landing at Dover forced him to return to France. He then crossed the Pyrenees toward Spain and Portugal and sailed for Palestine, where the Irgun high command posted him temporarily to Eastern Europe to coordinate illegal immigration. Rafaeli was also assigned the task of withdrawing Irgun funds from a bank account in the Geneva branch of Lloyd's Bank, lest these assets be frozen during wartime. Only after successfully completing this mission at considerable personal risk did Rafaeli set out for his chosen destination: New York. He made passage to New York on an Italian ship, the last such Italian vessel to sail to the United States before Italy's entry in the war as a belligerent in May 1940. [15]

In late spring 1940, Hillel Kook left London to join Ben-Ami, Ben-Eliezer, and Rafaeli in the United States. Kook's charismatic personality, his standing as the senior Irgun officer in the Diaspora, and his "annexation" to the NZO presidium the previous year made him the group's undisputed leader during its early years. Not only did this organizational step confer the group with enhanced internal strength, it was doubly important given the complicated relationship between the delegation and American Zionist bodies that blocked the Irgun members at almost every turn. In Hillel Kook's eyes the attitude of Revisionist Zionists in the

United States toward the group was the final blow. "Even the Revision-ists, like all the Zionists, always opposed us," Kook commented acidly on more than one occasion. "Upon my arrival in America one of the first things I was told of was difficulties with the Revisionists. What did diffi-culty with the Revisionists mean? That whatever we tried to do they found undesirable."[16]

Kook's simplistic statement does not do justice to the complexity of both the American Zionist and American Revisionist-Zionist establish-ment attitude toward the delegation throughout its existence. In none of the memoirs, interviews, or correspondence of delegation members can one find anything more detailed regarding their relationships with these organizations than a statement or two similar to that of Kook's above. Few if any of these introspective statements attempt to understand the full complexity of the relationship between the Irgun Delegation and the Re-visionist-Zionists in America before and shortly after Zeev Jabotinsky's death in the summer of 1940; none attempts to explain the abortive at-tempt at cooperation in 1942 between American Zionist groups and the Irgun Delegation regarding the Jewish army issue. It is difficult to deter-mine whether this reticence stems from a need to justify the delegation members' decision to strike out on their own and ignore Jabotinsky's or-ganizational direction and the attempts of the American Revisionst-Zionists to co-opt the group; similarly, it may be their only means of self-justification in the face of the never-ending criticism of the American Zionist establishment. In any event, Kook's statement to the effect that no matter what the Irgun Delegation did, Revisionist-Zionists—and later the American Zionist establishment—would never be pleased, is echoed by Rafaeli and Merlin in their later papers, but more importantly is also found in much of the group's wartime correspondence, showing how early this attitude became entrenched in the group's collective mode of thought.

Kook's undisputed position as leader in the delegation hierarchy re-mained unchallenged even after the arrival of two men who had not been sent by anyone as delegation members but who joined the group, also during 1940, on their own initiative: Samuel Merlin (1910–1994) and Zeev Jabotinsky's son, Eri Jabotinsky (1910–1969). Merlin, a Sorbonne-educated native of Kishinev, was former secretary to Zeev Jabotinsky and served as executive head of the World Union of Zionists-Revisionists from 1933 to 1938. He later edited the Warsaw Irgun mouthpiece in conjunc-

5. Irgun Delegation member Samuel Merlin. Courtesy of
Judith Tydor Baumel.

tion with Nathan Friedman-Yellin (Yellin-Mor). Merlin left Poland just
three days before the outbreak of the Second World War and made his way
to Paris on the last train to cross Germany, remaining there for six months
until April 1940, when he traveled to New York as part of a French diplomatic mission aimed at initiating an anti-German boycott. "Merlin always
looked like a typical Russian student," Alex Rafaeli recalled. "His hair was
never combed, he dressed sloppily, and he took an inordinate interest in
society and girls. At the same time he had a superlative intellectual life. In
every conversation he spoke last and his comments were always sharp,
well-considered, and well-analyzed, presented so that a third party could
always follow his argument." It was only natural that when group tasks
were assigned, Merlin was chosen to serve as one of the two group "states-
men" alongside leader Hillel Kook.[17]

The delegation's final member was Eri Jabotinsky, whose father, Zeev
Jabotinsky, had founded the Revisionist movement. Born in Odessa, the
Paris-educated Eri Jabotinsky came to Palestine in 1935, where he was ap-

pointed Netziv Betar (Betar commander) a year later. Eri Jabotinsky was imprisoned by the British on several occasions as a result of his activities, and upon his release from prison in 1939 he traveled to Europe in order to organize IZL-sponsored illegal immigration. The apex of this activity was the *Sakarya* expedition, in which Eri Jabotinsky personally brought 2,350 illegal immigrants to Palestine on a Revisionist-sponsored boat (see chapter 2). Immediately after disembarking in Palestine he was again jailed by the British, but was released following his father's death in August 1940. Finding it politic to leave the country at that time, he proceeded to the United States in order to join his friends in the delegation. Because the younger Jabotinsky was not an official Irgun member, his job remained undefined; however, he served essentially as informal adviser to Hillel Kook. Existing evidence indicates that Eri Jabotinsky's patrimony strongly affected his behavior. "He was extremely intelligent but he suffered from an inferiority complex—how could he not, being the son of such a father?" Rafaeli commented. "Consequently, he always tried to be demonstrative without a political agenda, as by speaking French from the Knesset podium." [18]

Even a cursory glance confirms the degree to which the Irgun Delegation's core group satisfies scholarly criteria for effective, productive activist group cooperation. [19] The first criterion is a shared goal, usually anchored in a particular ideology. All the delegation's members, drawn from Irgun and Betar ranks, were clearly motivated by the desire to strengthen Revisionist-sponsored rescue operations in Europe. Even after apparent shifts in the delegation's goals and the emergence of its various offshoots, its core nucleus remained consistently united by a shared ideology and by full military discipline. A second scholarly criterion for group success, collective recognition of group parameters, relates to the interaction between its members. As we shall see, both the identity of the founding nucleus and its intergroup relationships were clearly defined. Third is the group's ability to expand or contract without modifying its essential character, an ability that came to the fore during the initial period of delegation activity when its members gathered in the United States over an eighteen-month period, as well as during the war years when two of its members were drafted into the American army and another two were sent overseas, one to join the Irgun high command in Palestine and the other as a special emissary to Istanbul. As it had no internal subdivisions, the delegation also fulfills a fourth scholarly condition: the absence of subgroups within the main group. A fifth criterion, that each member of the group stand on his own individual merit, was intrinsically linked with their earlier experience in organizing rescue missions before their arrival in the United States. The sixth and final condition, which calls for ways and means of handling internal differences and tensions, is the most difficult to fulfill. In the delegation's case, this criterion found expression in elections held at the end of World War II, intended to allow members the opportunity to set new group principles if they so desired.

It is no simple matter to draw a collective representative sociological profile of the delegation's members. However, certain shared features in their biographies enable us to sketch a model of the person likely to be attracted to the operational sector of an elite entity associated with the militant Zionist right wing. First we must note their socioeconomic background. Generally speaking, all the delegation's members came from at least a middle-class background, and several, such as Yitzhak Ben-Ami, even came from wealthy families. A second characteristic relates to their education: the majority possessed either a broad Jewish or secular education, and three members—Rafaeli, Merlin, and Eri Jabotinsky—had university degrees. This finding fits Ya'acov Shavit's profile of the Revisionist elite as consisting of "the intelligentsia, the quasi-intelligentsia, high school and university graduates, and professionals."[20] With the exception of Eri Jabotinsky, whose father, Zeev Jabotinsky, had founded the Revisionist movement, the delegation's members came to the Zionist right wing either as a result of intellectual or emotional conviction but not through family ties; that is, not through parental affiliation with the movement. This finding also fits Shavit's observation that apart from those drawn to the Revisionist movement by family ties, the movement primarily attracted young activists opposed to current Yishuv leadership policies.[21]

During the decade of delegation activity in the United States various individuals affiliated themselves with this core group, in some cases without outwardly professing military allegiance to the Irgun. Others either assisted the delegation temporarily or acted outside the American arena. To the first category belong individuals such as the journalist John Gunther and his Jewish wife, Frances, who played an instrumental role in assisting the delegation and its members from the group's inception until its disbandment. The second category included individuals such as the Jewish playwright Ben Hecht. During the mid-1940s Hecht was fascinated by the delegation's nucleus, which he perceived as a blend of activity and mystique; however, he subsequently became disillusioned with the group. In the third category we find individuals such as Yirmiyahu (Irma) Helpern (1901–1962), a leading Betar activist who pioneered the Hebrew navy. Helpern spent time in America during the early 1940s before going on to found the London branch of the Jewish Army Committee (an offshoot of the Irgun Delegation) in 1942. Despite the fact that several of the six individuals singled out above left the United States during or at the end of the war in order to engage in Irgun activity in the European or in the Yishuv arena, they alone can be termed the delegation's "hard core" or "founding nucleus."

The Revisionist-Zionist Movement During the 1930s

The preceding biographical sketch of the delegation's members has laid the groundwork for examining its first circle of activity: the dynamic that governed intergroup patterns of interaction throughout the 1940s (treated in the next chapter). But this dynamic emerges in its full significance only when viewed against the context of the two external circles mentioned earlier. To recall, the first of these circles circumscribes the state of the Revisionist-Zionist movement with its branches in the Yishuv and abroad, and primarily the organization that was to serve as the Irgun Delegation's central axis for more than a decade: the Irgun Zeva'i Leumi.

Three entities thought to be the mainstays of the Zionist political "right" in the thirties and forties form the base of this circle: the New Zionist Organization (NZO), Betar, and the Irgun. We start with the NZO, which was a spin-off of the Union of Zionists-Revisionists founded in 1925 in Paris by Zeev Jabotinsky. His choice of *revisionist* as a defining term epitomizes the movement's ideological platform, which called for revision of existing Zionist policy and for a return to so-called "Herzlian Zionism," actually their view of the original Zionist ideology created by Zionist movement founder Theodor Herzl, which was a far cry from the socialist-Zionist policies of the 1920s and 1930s. In 1933 the Union of Zionists-Revisionists seceded from the Zionist Federation, and two years later the New Zionist Organization was founded, intended as an alliance of all Zionist parties not affiliated with the existing Zionist Federation.

From the start, however, the Union and the NZO were virtually identical, this because the Union of Zionist-Revisionists was the sole party in the New Zionist Organization. Nor were the two organizations distinct in personnel or ideology: both were headed by Zeev Jabotinsky, their founder; and Union and later NZO policy was grounded in two shared principles to which they showed unswerving allegiance: unequivocal and absolute preservation of the territorial integrity of Eretz-Israel, and a declared intention of founding a sovereign Jewish state in this territory by political or military means.[22]

The second mainstay of Revisionist activity during that period was the Revisionist youth movement Betar, founded in Riga in 1923, two years before the Union of Zionists-Revisionists was established in Paris's Latin Quarter. Indeed, as Ch. Ben Yerucham noted in the beginning of *Sepher Betar*, his history of the Betar movement, 1923 was a fateful year, "a year of sobering up from socialist-communist dreams; a year of disappointment with the national regimes founded in the new states; and a year of confusion, wondering, and pain concerning the state of Zionism and of Palestine following Churchill's White Paper."[23] The new movement set the study of Hebrew, activity on behalf of the Jewish National Fund, and collective reading in the writings of Zeev Jabotinsky as its initial goals; however, its activity actually focused on military training provided under the tutelage of a former Russian officer. Based on their shared ideological and practical affinities, over time Betar became the Union of Zionists-Revisionists' youth movement, developing into an international movement that exercised its greatest attraction in those lands where the biggest Jewish concentrations were to be found. It should therefore not surprise us to learn that it was Poland that constituted the Betar movement's largest membership reserves.[24]

In the Yishuv as well, the Revisionist youth movement developed along military lines, with its members playing a central role in the Hagana. As a means of institutionalizing Betar military training, the well-known naval officer Yirmiyahu Helpern founded a school for Betar counselors where they received military training, political-ideological indoctrination, and character training. The Betar guard that emerged from this training school then entered Hagana ranks. Following the split in the Hagana in the wake of the 1929 Arab uprising, Betar members joined Abraham Tehomi's new organization, known as Hagana B or the National Hagana, later forming the nucleus for the third mainstay of the "right-wing" camp in the thirties and forties: the Irgun Zeva'i Leumi.[25]

From its inception the National Hagana—and later the Irgun—was distinguished by three somewhat innovative features: its clearly defined military character, its unswerving allegiance to the political goal of making Palestine a sovereign Jewish state, and the apolitical and classless nature of its Hebrew armed forces, which it viewed as a national army—as opposed to the Hagana, which was an arm of the Histadrut, a class-defined organization. This overt activist line not only determined both groups' operational nature but also the type of person they attracted. This was doubly true for the Irgun as for the National Hagana, as the latter was to become the Revisionist movement's underground activist arm. Four of the six delegation's hard-core members—young, energetic, extroverted militants—belonged to the Irgun.[26]

Students of activist movements maintain that a crucial determinant of movement strength lies in a group's ability to build an effective network of relationships or, at the very least, in its ability to arrive at a modus vivendi with kindred movements.[27] A focal issue on the political-organizational scene of the Revisionist movement then—and a constant undercurrent in the delegation's later work—revolved around the nature of the Irgun's relationship with other Revisionist entities. Who had the ultimate authority to make policy decisions? Was it the veteran political movement with its founder's rights, the new military organization representing the Revisionist movement's radical activist line, or the Revisionist youth federation, the military organization's main and perhaps only future reserves?

Based on their obvious ideological affinity, within a short time the Irgun and Betar worked out a practical understanding. In accord with this understanding Betar pledged to provide the Irgun with most of its military personnel, and the World Betar organization adopted the Irgun as an affiliated military entity on ideological, spiritual, and practical grounds. For its part, the Irgun initially agreed to accept Zeev Jabotinsky as its commander in chief and to coordinate its activity with the Betar Council and the Yishuv's Netziv Betar, Eri Jabotinsky. Practically speaking, however, difficulties arose in implementing this Betar-Irgun cooperation, because the Betar representatives, in particular Eri Jabotinsky, who also sat on the Irgun high command, did not take part in the day-to-day planning and command of the Irgun. It took an entire year from the Irgun's founding for the three bodies to establish formal patterns of cooperation at the February 1938 Paris summit, mentioned above.[28]

The atmosphere at the three-way conclave was tense. Time and again the Irgun representatives (who included Haim Lubinsky and Hillel Kook) asserted that the Irgun was an army and, as such, should not be affiliated with any political party. In line with this position, they requested permission to assume policy-making and propaganda tasks in the Yishuv and abroad, a request Zeev Jabotinsky refused. Despite this seemingly insurmountable impasse, a compromise was ultimately reached at a special meeting between Zeev Jabotinsky and Raziel. This was also the first face-to-face conversation between Jabotinsky, as the Irgun's military commander who resided in the Diaspora, and Irgun commander-in-chief Raziel, who had come especially from Palestine for this purpose. The meeting between the two was characterized by an atmosphere of mutual respect and in the final analysis led to a comprehensive agreement between the participants, known as the Paris Accord.

The Paris Accord, which set future patterns of NZO-Irgun-Betar cooperation, marked a turning point in the trifold relationship. It was resolved that in the Diaspora the Irgun and Betar would merge under the Betar aegis, and that an Irgun officer would be annexed to the Betar executive and would also head a special division for military training. In addition, the oldest division in Betar would now assume the name IZL and in the Yishuv the same person would serve as both Irgun commander and Netziv Betar. Thus, in Palestine Yishuv, Netziv Betar David Raziel now assumed command of both the Irgun and Betar. Furthermore, the accord stipulated cooperation on matters related to Revisionist-sponsored illegal immigration, known as *Af al-pi* (nevertheless) immigration, a project in which five future delegation members took part during the 1930s.[29]

The Paris Accord marked the successful mediation of a potentially divisive rift precipitated by pressure from a maximalist group seeking to set new norms for internal cooperation within the right-wing camp. This was, however, neither the first nor the last occasion on which Zeev Jabotinsky faced a struggle for hegemony within his own movement. A brief survey of Revisionist movement history in the thirties and forties reveals a series of conflicts, with both maximalists and minimalists challenging Jabotinsky's platform. Some of these groups undeniably left their imprint both ideologically and operatively on the formation of the Irgun Delegation to the United States.

The first challenge to Zeev Jabotinsky's hegemony came from the writer and publicist Abba Achimeir (1898–1962) in the early 1930s, when Achimeir founded Brit HaBiryonim, backed by a small contingent of maximalists critical of the official Revisionist platform and its implementation.[30] Self-styled as heirs to the ancient Hebrew zealots who defied Rome, Brit HaBiryonim was a gang of thugs that openly engaged in public protest against the British mandate, German-Nazi forces, and what they perceived as Jewish elements hostile to Zionism. At its height, Brit HaBiryonim's membership numbered several dozen activists, drawn primarily from Union of Zionists-Revisionists and Betar ranks. On more than one occasion, the group's public statements were censured by the Revisionist party center in Palestine, and Zeev Jabotinsky totally dissociated himself from its members' antidemocratic remarks. At the 1932 World Conference of the Union of Zionists-Revisionists held in Vienna, Zeev Jabotinsky admonished the maximalists for seeking to undermine the Revisionist party's democratic structure to suit the emergency needs of the Zionist struggle. When Brit HaBiryonim spokesmen refused to alter their policy, Jabotinsky penned the following to them: "There is no room in a single camp for you and for me. . . . If these views were to prevail, I would leave the party."[31] An open rift never developed, perhaps because in the wake of Chaim Arlosoroff's murder, Achimeir was imprisoned on charges of conspiracy and membership in a terrorist organization. Nevertheless, in spirit, Achimeir's declarations undoubtedly left a material impression on the ideological foundations of the two underground movements that emerged from the Revisionist ranks: the IZL and the LHI (Lohamei Herut Israel [Freedom Fighters of Israel]).

Another attempt to undermine Zeev Jabotinsky's leadership, made while Achimeir was jailed, came from the minimalist camp, from Jabotinsky's close intimate Meir Grossman (1888–1964). Grossman, a journalist, had taken an active role in the Revisionist movement from its founding, culminating with his assumption of the top post of London bureau chief of the Union of Zionists-Revisionists in 1929. By the early 1930s, though, his relationship with Jabotinsky had shifted to one characterized by sharp differences of opinion regarding the party program, and Grossman bitterly opposed Jabotinsky's 1933 decision to secede from the Zionist Federation. Despite Jabotinsky's efforts to preserve party unity, Grossman and his supporters elected to remain in the Zionist Federation as the newly founded Hebrew State Party. In the late 1930s Grossman emigrated to the United States and remained there until the end of World War II. Later we shall examine his unsuccessful attempt during the forties to participate in delegation activities.[32]

Achimeir's maximalist position again raised its head in the guise of another group that attempted to shake Zeev Jabotinsky's hegemony: the "Sadan" (Anvil) contingent founded by A. Selman in 1937. Dubbed the Faction for Ideological Criticism, Selmen and his backers accused the Union of Zionists-Revisionists of national vacuity and attacked Jabotinsky's ideology of restraint. The Sadan contingent espoused a militant anti-Marxist approach, arguing that by its neglect of the National Workers' Federation the Union of Zionists-Revisionists had failed to fulfill its assigned role. Essentially, the Sadan faction's maximalist platform focused on the obligation to foster revolutionary spiritual values in all areas. LHI historian Joseph Heller argues that Sadan was actually a permutation of Brit HaBiryonim in terms of both membership and ideology. It sought no less than to totally revolutionize the NZO. In the final analysis, the Sadan faction did not jeopardize Jabotinsky's position because it was expelled from the Union of Zionists-Revisionists, leaving Jabotinsky's authority intact. Nonetheless, the events of summer 1937, and particularly the publication of the Peel Commission Report, gave rise to a new revolutionary ideological-operative trend that would later find full expression in the two extreme underground groups that emerged from the right-wing camp: the IZL and the LHI.[33]

A further attempt to foment an ideological revolution in the Union of Zionists-Revisionists was made by Uriel Heilperin (Yonathan Ratosh), one of the founders of the Canaanite school of thought that attempted to historically and culturally merge the Jews of Palestine into a pan-Middle Eastern framework. Shortly after the publication of the Peel Commission Report, Heilperin argued that the twenty-year period of grace during which it would have been possible to found a state without the opposition of the "natives" had ended. A return to force, the method most commonly employed to achieve national liberation, would now be necessary. Heilperin's critique came at a time of pronounced disparity between declared Revisionist policy and reality; this after members of the NZO leadership had been arrested in the wake of the Irgun's violation of the policy of "restraint." Heilperin's revolutionary bent was not confined to a rhetorical attempt to sway NZO policymaking; at that time he enjoyed the support of Union of Zionists-Revisionists activist circles in Poland that published an open letter criticizing what they termed "the Revisionist Union's secret diplomatic policy." Encouraged by this backing, Heilperin attempted to raise his proposals at the 1938 NZO Convention, but his sole backer was Menachem Begin, Netziv Betar in Poland. Heilperin's bid to change Zeev Jabotinsky's declared pro-English orientation—an integral part of Jabotinsky's platform from the Revisionist movement's inception—failed. Nevertheless, he was to make his mark on the delegation after 1944 when its members adopted a policy that distinguished between "Jews" and "Hebrews," a Canaanite-style concept discussed in exchanges between Merlin and Heilperin during the duo's stay in Paris.[34]

But the struggle for hegemony was not limited to the Yishuv arena. As noted above, criticism of Zeev Jabotinsky also came from Poland, home to the largest human reserves of the world Revisionist movement. At the Third International Betar Convention held in 1938, Menachem Begin, Netziv Betar in Poland, raised principled objections to the main points of Jabotinsky's policies. According to Begin, the mainstays of Revisionist policy had collapsed, and accordingly he called for the adoption of a maximalist approach in order to achieve the movement's stated aims. The high point of the convention was a confrontation between Begin, who saw Betar as the actualization of militant Zionism, and those who viewed militarism as one aspect of the total complex of movement values. Notwithstanding the learned, polite debate between Jabotinsky and Begin in the latter's home court, Jabotinsky recognized the essential truth of Begin's concluding statement that "there are millions with nothing more to lose" and the emergence of a new militaristic spirit among Betar youth. A focal point in this ideological-rhetorical dispute revolved around a proposed change in the Betar pledge: to replace the phrase "defense of my people" with the more activist formula "conquest of my homeland." Despite the apologetic tone of the explanations in official Betar history regarding Jabotinsky's willingness to endorse this change, it appears that Jabotinsky's acquiescence more strongly reflected his capitulation to an irreversible dynamic within party ranks rather than his actual opinion. We can surmise that both this episode and the concurrent emergence of the maximalist IZL faction raised doubts in the aging Revisionist leader's mind as to his unquestioned control of the party.[35]

Although the Irgun-Betar relationship had been formalized in the

Paris Accord, one Irgun faction continued to exhibit separatist tendencies. Headed by Abraham Stern—code name "Yair"—this faction subsequently withdrew from the Irgun to found the "IZL in Israel." The ideas of the brilliant student who came to Palestine in 1925 closely resembled Achimeir's; if however, we classify Achimeir as an intellectual revolutionary, then, as Shavit suggests, Stern must be regarded as a charismatic revolutionary.[36] As early as 1937, when he was dispatched to Poland by the Irgun, Yair utilized the Betar framework to set up independent Irgun cells as a first stage in building a new organization that would not be answerable to Zeev Jabotinsky. Somewhat later he led an Irgun officer's training course without Jabotinsky's knowledge, a step that led the aging leader to comment acidly: "Are these our people?"[37] Stern, who was greatly influenced by Achimeir and Heilperin's maximalist theories, belonged to the faction of the Irgun that derogated statesmanship and favored the transformation of Betar ideology into a military program. During that early period Stern came in close contact with future members of the Irgun Delegation: he was jailed with Eri Jabotinsky in Palestine, and worked alongside Samuel Merlin and Hillel Kook in Poland. When he split off from the IZL in 1940, Stern turned to these prior acquaintances in an attempt to draft the members of the Irgun Delegation to his militant maximalist anti-British organization based on shared ideology and personal friendship. These overtures and their results are examined in the next chapter.

To the observer, Revisionist movement history in the 1930s appears as a series of bids to reshape the Zionist right wing—primarily in a maximalist direction—and to force its leader to face the reality of growing radicalization. This tendency was an important factor that shaped the inner world of the Irgun Delegation members during their sojourn in the United States, along with their hope that they, too, would play a role in reshaping their mother organization, the IZL. This intention appears in their papers—both those of the period in question and their later memoirs—which hint at a hope that their separatist tendencies would ultimately enable them to set the tone for the entire movement. Particularly during the 1930s and 1940s, the factionalism and hegemony challenges that characterized the Zionist right wing could be attributed to several factors, primarily the unique character of the Zionist right wing and the deterioration in the British mandatory attitude toward the Jewish Yishuv in

Palestine. It is against this background of attempts to recast the Zionist right wing and of the maximalist precedent of breakaway groups that we must consider the decision on the part of the Irgun Delegation's core members to act independently as early as 1940. It should not surprise us that although Kook and his coterie evinced a formal bond to the traditions of the Zionist right wing, in practical terms they acted on their autonomous grasp of "current needs."

What was Zeev Jabotinsky's response to these growing attempts to change the character of the movement he had founded? At a certain stage it seems that Jabotinsky came to terms with this trend on pragmatic grounds: his apprehension of the irreversible shift toward maximalism. Another factor was perhaps the physical weakness that eventually led to his death in New York at the age of sixty. "After all, they are all my sons," he was heard to say from late 1938 on.[38] Nonetheless, as we shall see, upon his arrival in the United States in spring 1940, Zeev Jabotinsky experienced a rekindled desire to impose his will on his wayward children, abandoning his former almost forgiving bent in dealing with what he interpreted as separationist tendencies on the part of the Irgun Delegation and using all the means at his disposal in an attempt to bend it to his will. Did Jabotinsky fear that Hillel Kook would be revealed as a "Yair" in American guise who would engage the hearts of the NZO membership in the United States? Or was it a final attempt to impose his will on what was to become the "cutoff battalion," the sole body on the American Zionist scene that answered neither to an American institution nor to an externally-based Yishuv one?

American Jewry and American Zionism During the 1930s

We now come to the third circle that had a hand in shaping the character of the Irgun Delegation: the American Jewish and American Zionist establishment in all its configurations. Upon their arrival in New York, the delegation's members found an American Jewish population of some five million in number, approximately 30 percent of the then current world Jewish population. American Jewry—because of its organizational nature it is difficult to speak of one American Jewish "community"—had been built by three main waves of immigration. The first wave of Jewish settlers to reach American shores in the mid-seventeenth century were descen-

dants of Spanish and Portuguese *conversos* who sought refuge from the Inquisition in the New World. During the next 150 years they were joined
by Jews from other European lands; nevertheless Jewish immigration to
America until the early 1800s was known as the "Spanish Wave," a tribute
to the ethnic composition of the earliest Jewish settlers.

The mid-1800s were punctuated by a second wave of Jewish immigrants known as the "German immigration," composed of poor, largely
uneducated German-speaking Jews from small villages in Bavaria, Posen,
Bohemia, and Hungary. A variety of factors motivated their migration:
their failure to gain entré into European national movements, the edict
that allowed only firstborn sons to marry, anti-Jewish discrimination and
persecution in their lands of origin, and the desire to ameliorate their economic condition. These Jews usually underwent a rapid process of Ameri-
canization; nevertheless they often maintained their German culture as
well while achieving social and economic security. One of their major contributions to American Jewry was the establishment of the first American
Jewish national organizations, some of which would later clash swords
with the delegation.[39]

The 1880s initiated the third and largest wave of Jewish immigration
to the United States, this time from Eastern Europe. Some 2,100,000
Jews from all over Eastern Europe came to the United States in what is
called the Great Migration, part of a much larger wave that brought
22,000,000 immigrants to American shores in less than thirty-three years
and irrevocably altered the shape of American and of American Jewish society. From 1881 until the Great Migration ended with the outbreak of
the First World War, the number of American Jews increased elevenfold:
from 280,000 to 3,000,000. For the majority of these Jewish immigrants
America was the Promised Land, for not only did the United States provide a refuge, it had all the requisites of modern Jewish life: freedom of religion, the chance for economic advancement, and equality before the law.
These qualities captivated Jews who had become disenchanted with growing European anti-Semitism or who had abandoned their hopes of being
accepted to Old World national movements, and young people seeking to
break out of the cycle of poverty that was the lot of many Jews in the Haps-
burg Empire and under the Russian czarist regime. More so than the first
two Jewish waves of immigration, the Eastern European immigrants left
their indelible stamp on American Jewish society. Not only did they lay the

foundation for a new American Jewish cultural base, they founded some of the pacesetting Jewish organizations in twentieth-century American Jewish life.

Upon the Irgun Delegation's arrival in New York, some 70 percent of American Jews were native born, descendants of Jews who had arrived during the Great Migration before its reduction to a trickle with the passage of restrictive immigration laws in the 1920s. Largely urban in nature, some 80 percent of the American Jewish population was concentrated in the fourteen largest cities, including two million in the New York City area alone.[40]

Organized American Jewry encompassed a variety of organizational structures, subsuming dozens of social, philanthropic, cultural, and religious associations. A substantial number were Zionist in nature; others, which defined themselves as non-Zionist, rejected Zionism in principle but nonetheless supported Zionist activity. Jewish organizations that openly espoused an anti-Zionist stance were in the minority.[41]

The first national American Jewish organization, Bnai Brith, a Jewish equivalent of Freemasonry, was founded in 1843 by members of the German wave. Evidently the combination of ceremony and philanthropy appealed to American Jews, and for decades this social-philanthropic organization remained one of the largest non-Zionist organizations in the United States. Another important non-Zionist organization, founded by central European immigrants in 1906 after the outbreak of anti-Jewish pogroms in Russia, was the American Jewish Committee, which sought to defend Jewish rights worldwide. A handful of prominent American Jews held the reins of leadership, relying primarily on behind-the-scenes diplomacy to achieve their political aims, as befit, in their opinion, an elitist organization. The Irgun Delegation's operative principles, which stood in diametric opposition to American Jewish Committee tactics, generated constant tension over the "damage" the delegation caused to the image of American Jewry.[42]

Another national American Jewish body that took a non-Zionist stance, at least during the period when the Irgun Delegation was active in the United States, was the Reform movement. From the 1880s the Reform movement espoused a negative attitude toward the Zionist idea as counteracting one of its cardinal principles: full national identification of American Jews with the United States. This doctrine was recast during the interwar period, and especially after 1937, when the movement reworded its theological platform and adopted a more favorable view of the Zionist movement, a shift attributable to several factors related to demography, leadership, and contemporary realia. The Reform movement had found itself in a minority position vis-à-vis the ever-increasing power of the Jews of Eastern European origins, who were largely pro-Zionist. Furthermore, we must note the impact of young charismatic leaders from within the movement, particularly the efforts of the pro-Zionist Reform rabbis Stephen S. Wise (1874–1949) and Abba Hillel Silver (1893–1949) that bore fruit in the mid-1930s. Finally, we must consider the emergence of Jewish solidarity in times of distress. Confronted with the ever-growing Jewish refugee problem during that period, world Jewry sought solutions of which Palestine was promoted as a viable one. In combination, these factors brought about mitigation of the Reform leadership's hard-line anti-Zionist attitude.

Despite this shift in attitude, the Reform leadership's behind-the-scenes elitist operational patterns, which closely resembled those of the American Jewish Committee administration, remained unchanged. Indeed, the Supreme Council of the Reform Movement and Committee activists were drawn from the same socioeconomic stratum, by and large, descendants of the German wave of immigration, longtime American residents who saw themselves as American in all respects. It is not surprising that this leadership barred synagogue and community center doors to what they termed the "hyperactive" members of the Irgun Delegation, who sought to use these forums to publicize their message and to raise funds for Irgun activity in Europe.[43]

Additional noteworthy non-Zionist organizations included the Jewish Labor Committee—an umbrella organization founded in 1934 to support Jewish workers' organizations in Europe, to foster anti-Nazi activity, to fight anti-Semitism, and to fight antidemocratic forces in cooperation with American labor organizations—and the National Council of Jewish Women, founded in 1893 by Jewish women of central European background in order to help the female immigrants of the Great Migration. Last among the large non-Zionist organizations was the Joint Distribution Committee, a welfare organization founded in 1914 for the purpose of assisting European Jewry. Its leadership too derived from the same circles as that of the American Jewish Committee, the Reform movement, and the National Council of Jewish Women.[44]

The early twentieth century also saw the emergence of many pro-Zionist organizations on the American scene of which the largest was the Zionist Organization of America (ZOA). Founded as an umbrella organization in 1918, the ZOA succeeded the first national Zionist organization in the United States, the Federation of American Zionists (FAZ), which was established twenty years earlier, soon after the first Zionist Congress. Up until the First World War the FAZ's membership remained small; among a Jewish population of three million, there were only twelve thousand registered Zionists and most FAZ members were recent immigrants who had not yet become integrated into local American Jewish life. However, it was the incompatibility of the Zionist idea with the prevailing weltanschauung of the major contemporary Jewish circles in the United States—Reform Judaism, socialist circles, and ultra-Orthodox Jewry (each of which opposed the Zionist idea for its own reasons)—that can be cited as the main factor for the FAZ's limited success.

With the entry of a young American Jewish lawyer, Louis Dembitz Brandeis, on the scene, American Zionism came into its own. Brandeis defined Zionism in harmony with his liberal American outlook, adopting a pluralistic cultural approach that placed American Zionism squarely in the American context. He solved the problem of dual loyalty by establishing the intrinsic compatibility of Zionism with American democratic ideals. In his effort to rejuvenate American Zionism, Brandeis brought a number of activists to the Zionist movement from the legal and political spheres, and even from the Reform movement, which then still embraced an anti-Zionist bent. Membership in the Zionist organization multiplied significantly during the First World War, bringing new American blood into the Zionist movement. The founding of the ZOA in 1918 bore a Brandeisian stamp as it called for all American Zionist activity and organizations to be united under the aegis of a single umbrella organization. Similarly, the establishment of the pro-Zionist American Jewish Congress at the end of the First World War was yet another Brandeisian achievement.

Brandeis's new orientation quickly placed him at odds with the established Zionist leadership. In 1921 a severe rift developed between Brandeis and Chaim Weizmann and his coterie, which was reluctant to relinquish its emphasis on Zionist ideology for the pursuit of practical goals. A contemporary American Jewish journalist went so far as to characterize Brandeis's version of Zionism as inherently non-Jewish: "His entire conception of Zionism was Goyish [gentile] and not Jewish, and this goyish conception of Zionism he wanted to impose upon American Jewry."[45] During the 1920s the American Jewish Zionist movement became factionalized, ultimately reaching its final form as a fund-raising entity entirely divorced from Zionist policymaking.

Like the world Zionist movement, the American Zionist movement was composed of three camps, of which only the centrist camp belonged to the ZOA from its inception. The centrist camp was represented mainly by the general Zionist organizations: Young Judea (founded 1908), the Order of Bnai Zion (1908), and Hadassah Women, which, owing to its size, enjoyed an almost autonomous status within the ZOA. On the American Zionist left we find circles allied with Poalei Zion (1905–21), and on the Zionist right we find the religious Zionists: Mizrachi (1911), which joined the ZOA at a later date, and the two Revisionist movements: Brit Trumpeldor (1929; Betar from 1944) and the New Zionist Federation (NZF; 1926). Because of its disorganization, the NZF failed to attract many sympathizers among American Jewry, and at the outbreak of World War II its membership numbered only several thousand.[46]

The thirties were a transitional period for American Zionism, during which the movement faced two issues that would later be the cause of many a clash with the Irgun Delegation. The first was the question of fund-raising and distribution of funds by the American Zionist movement, a clear indicator of Zionist strength and influence among American Jewry; the second was the organized Zionist reaction to the Nazi rise to power and the resulting refugee problem.

The beginning of the Great Depression in 1929 dealt a nearly fatal blow to the local American Zionist movement. In the days that followed Black Monday millions of Americans found themselves jobless and their savings lost. As the days turned into weeks and months with no amelioration in the economic crisis, the panic of the early days first turned into despair and then acceptance, bringing with it a substantially changed lifestyle. The impact of the Great Depression on American Jewry was not confined to the personal or familial level; its effects were felt on the communal and organizational level as well. Many American Jewish Zionist sympathizers found themselves unable to pay membership dues to the Zionist organizations with which they still identified ideologically. The number of registered members of Zionist organizations saw a drastic decline during the 1930s, a trend that continued into the second half of the decade despite Zionist membership drives.

During that decade, however, American Zionist youth movements showed a gain in strength, providing American Jewish youth with a socio-cultural focus and a heightened sense of Jewish identity and Jewish national consciousness. Moreover, during the thirties the Zionist movement attracted sympathizers from among the ranks of the Conservative and Orthodox Jews in the United States, and, as we have seen, even the Reform movement muted its objections to the national movement. In 1939 signs of recovery were apparent in the American Zionist movement, and by the early forties the Zionist organizations in the United States numbered hundreds of thousands of members, many of them new. The growing awareness among American Jews of the increased influence of anti-Semitic groups in the United States also contributed to the Zionist movement's enhanced strength.[47]

These new members comprised the base for the fund-raising apparatus of the American Zionist movement. At times during the 1930s this apparatus functioned in conjunction with the fund-raising divisions of the American non-Zionist organizations; at times it functioned at cross-purposes with them. Five attempts at joint fund-raising were made during this decade, culminating in the 1939 merger of the fund-raising apparatuses of the United Palestine Appeal and the American Joint Distribution Committee that created the United Jewish Appeal (UJA). Nonetheless, in 1941, intraorganizational tensions led to a rupture that necessitated renegotiation of the agreement governing the distribution of funds. The new criterion established called for at least 37 percent of the funds collected by the UJA to be handed over to the Zionist cause.[48]

The struggle for the Jewish donor's pocket was bitter, at times even deteriorating to mutual mudslinging in the attempt to win control of the American Jewish philanthropic network. Class aspects of the division between Zionists and non-Zionists also had a bearing on the financial issue: whereas most Zionist supporters came from the middle and lower classes, support for non-Zionist organizations derived from the more prosperous classes. The so-called philanthropic oligarchy that comprised the American Jewish communal leadership was also largely drawn from the upper-class non-Zionist ranks. Later we shall see how members of the Irgun Delegation, who rapidly put their finger on the financial pulse of American Jewry, used this philanthropic differentiation to create an independent fund-raising apparatus that competed successfully with the more established American Jewish and American Zionist networks.[49]

Hitler's rise to power and the ensuing refugee problem served as a test case for Jewish and Zionist organizations alike. The need to raise funds in order to assist the refugees was self-evident, and the question of interorganizational cooperation was raised at each meeting held for this purpose. Results were not long in coming. The ZOA-sponsored National Conference for Palestine, held in 1935, which promoted Palestine as a solution to the ever-increasing refugee problem, was attended for the first time by non-Zionist organizations like Bnai Brith and the Central Conference of American Rabbis, the supreme body of the Reform movement, thus laying the foundation for future organizational cooperation with the Zionists.

The thirties saw the formation of a number of organizations on which representatives of Zionist and non-Zionist bodies served jointly. Among these entities was the National Emergency Committee for Palestine, founded in early October 1938 in response to Chaim Weizmann's impassioned plea to American Zionist leaders to attempt to move the British government to rescind its harsh mandatory policy toward the Yishuv. The committee—instituted by the heads of the ZOA, Hadassah, Hamizrachi, and Poalei Zion—recruited an impressive list of Jewish organizations to its ranks, including the pro-Zionist American Jewish Congress (AJC) and representatives from non-Zionist organizations like the American Jewish Committee and the Jewish Labor Committee. With the British announcement of the St. James Conference, however, the Emergency Committee canceled its plans to lobby the British. Fear of evoking an anti-Semitic response in the United States also deterred the committee from implementing its plans.[50]

Disappointment with the results of the Round Table Conference was not long in coming. In early January 1939 David Ben-Gurion arrived in the United States for the purpose of galvanizing American Jewry to protest on behalf of the Zionist cause, bringing a renewed awareness of the American potential to influence British policy on the Palestine question. Following consultations with Ben-Gurion, the heads of the American Zionist organizations decided to set up a coordinating desk intended to enhance the Zionist movement's standing in the American public's eye. The Washington-based American Zionist Bureau was established in March 1939, after Hitler's forces had finished swallowing what remained of the Czech Republic. Two of its main objectives were to represent Zionist interests to the American government and to make the American public aware of the Yishuv's accomplishments and aspirations. But good intentions aside, this Zionist lobby folded but a year later because of a constant lack of funding. In contrast, the Irgun Delegation's success in fund-raising would all the more become a bone of contention between its members and the American Zionist establishment.

With the outbreak of World War II yet another coordinating body was founded: the American Emergency Committee for Zionist Affairs. This entity, initiated under the aegis of the outstanding American Jewish leader Rabbi Stephen Wise, was formed in order to amalgamate the activity of the large American Zionist organizations, including the ZOA, Hadassah, Poalei Zion, and HaMizrachi. Activists from non-Zionist organizations such as the American Jewish Committee and Bnai Brith were invited to the initial meeting; these invitations were issued, however, on the personal and not on the organizational level. This fact highlights an outstanding feature of American Jewish public life: the simultaneous association of many of its central figures with both Zionist and non-Zionist organizations did not interfere with the coordinating bodies' primarily Zionist aims. By way of example, one of the Emergency Committee's chief objectives was to explore the question of a Jewish army, an issue that subsequently played a major role in Irgun Delegation activity during 1941 and 1942. In 1943 the Emergency Committee changed its name to the American Zionist Emergency Council and turned to the leadership of the "activist" Rabbi Abba Hillel Silver, who took it upon himself to spearhead the American Zionist efforts to realize a Jewish commonwealth in Palestine and to lead the Zionist movement into a new era. Both the Emergency Council and the Emergency Committee would spend a great deal of time discussing ways to combat the delegation's activities in the United States, while ultimately—both subliminally and overtly—adopting many of their tactical patterns.

Two additional Zionist bodies active in the United States during the 1940s were the American Office of the Jewish Agency for Palestine and the American Jewish Conference, established in the summer of 1943, originally as an umbrella organization for over thirty American Jewish organizations, to formulate a program of action to meet world Jewry's postwar needs. Ultimately adopting a maximalist-Zionist stand, the conference catapulted the Zionist movement to the forefront of American Jewish life in the middle of the Second World War. Each of these organizations in turn would clash with delegation members in a struggle for hegemony over American Jewish affairs.

The state of the American Zionist movement in the late 1930s serves as a fascinating barometer of the contemporary circumstances of the American Jewish public. On the one hand, signs of the severe economic depression and the slow recovery that followed were still in evidence. On the other, we find unflagging efforts to meet current challenges: the Nazi danger, which gave rise to a variety of organizational responses that combined indigenous Jewish activity with appeals to external, including government, forces; the need to promote Palestine as a practical solution to the refugee problem; and internal American problems such as growing anti-Semitism and the first signs of assimilation. As we near the decade's end, a picture of enhanced activity on all fronts emerges, one exemplified by intensified fund-raising to implement their plans and also by constant airing of the need to engage public sympathy for the Zionist idea. The latter aim, however, was as yet not being pursued intensively. One thing was clear. Despite the established German-Jewish element's initial opposition to the Zionist idea, a shift in attitude occurred during the 1930s, and by the outbreak of the Second World War almost no significant anti-Zionist forces remained in the American Jewish public arena. Thus the Irgun Delegation began to function in the United States at a time when the Zionist movement was organizationally, practically, and emotionally anchored in the lives of American Jews.

◆   ◆   ◆

This survey has sketched a brief portrait of the two arenas in which the Irgun Delegation was to function. To recall, one arena encompassed the tangled web of factional interrelationships within the Revisionist movement in the 1930s; the other included the organizational structure of American Jewry in general and of American Zionism in particular on the eve of the Second World War. Despite unmistakable differences between these two arenas, impartial observation elicits two shared characteristics: first, the tendency toward factionalism that characterizes every organizational arena but that seems to reach new heights in Jewish organizations; second, the transition from an initial attitude of mutual suspicion that characterized contacts between entities in each of the two arenas in their early stages to one of varying degrees of cooperation with the deteriorating European situation before the American entry into the war. The hazy yet alarming reports from Europe from September 1939 onward dwarfed internal rivalries, sparking cooperation in the shared task of assisting European Jewry and later their rescue. This increased cooperation was true for most bodies but not all—some were to remain pariahs in the eyes of the Zionist establishment evermore.

Shortly before the outbreak of war the first members of the Irgun reached the United States in the hope of creating some sort of temporary organizational framework to raise funds for their efforts in Europe and Palestine. With the Nazi invasion of Poland it appeared that this effort had come too late. Forty-five years later, Yitzhak Ben-Ami recalled his feelings upon first learning of the fate of European Jewry in fall 1939: "Watching events in eastern Europe I knew that my worst fears were being borne out. I had to battle with myself not to be paralyzed. Though I managed to carry on my work, I was torn two ways at once. My pessimism told me that we had already lost the battle; yet somehow I continued to function, performing to the best of my ability, hoping against hope that some Jews could still be saved." [51]

Ben-Ami's intuitions were being echoed by others in the Irgun, including Hillel Kook, who now looked very favorably at broadening the delegation's budding power base in the United States. However, there appears to be a gap between Ben-Ami's assertion that the outbreak of war prodded Irgun leaders to already then designate the nucleus of the delegation and the slow gravitation of the four additional right-wing Zionist activists—of whom only two were Irgun members—who would ultimately act as the delegation's hard core to the United States. Did the distance between Ben-Ami's portrayal and historical reality stem from his need to claim total historical legitimacy for the delegation from an early date, or was this just another one of the *"rashomons"* punctuating the delegation members' individual interpretations of their collective history? Our search for the answer to this question begins in the next chapter, which covers the first period of delegation activity in the United States, 1939 to 1940.

A Time to Learn

The Irgun Delegation's Formative Years, 1939–1940

May 1940. The first spring of the Second World War brought with it new developments on the war front, first and foremost the German invasion of Western Europe. A month earlier Hitler had abandoned the *Sitzkrieg*— the tiresome deployment opposite the French Maginot Line—as having outlived its strategic usefulness and had initiated an all-out attack on. northern and western Europe. Within the space of a few days Denmark and Norway fell into German hands, leaving Holland, Belgium, and France facing the threat of a German invasion. Italy now joined the Axis powers with an eye to realizing Mussolini's dreams of colonizing North Africa, dominating the Balkans, and attaining sole hegemony over Mediterranean shores. In conquered Poland the Germans sealed the Lodz ghetto and founded the Auschwitz concentration camp in a remote swamp in Lower Silesia. May 1940 was marked by political changes as well: in Britain Prime Minister Neville Chamberlain stepped down and was replaced by Winston Churchill, sparking Jewish hopes for a shift in British policy toward the Yishuv.

The early war years, like the immediate postwar period, often seem to be the "forgotten" period of Irgun Delegation history. These formative years, during which the Irgun emissaries created operative, instrumental, and integrative activity patterns that would serve them throughout their organizational metamorphoses, have been little studied by historians of the group. Scholarly treatment of the delegation usually takes either the 1941 campaign for a Jewish army or the 1943 campaign to rescue European Jewry as its starting point, whereas the delegation's first offshoot, the

American Friends of a Jewish Palestine, receives mention only in passing. Apparently, for most historians, these campaigns dwarfed earlier delegation efforts to fund illegal aliyah and to create independent organizational machinery on American soil in order to serve Irgun interests in the Yishuv and abroad.

Closer examination of the Irgun Delegation's formative period reveals the critical importance of these years as a crucial link in its future development. Not only were the foundations for the group's public relations efforts laid during 1939–40, we can also trace the paradigms for intragroup relationships and the hierarchy of command maintained for its entire existence back to these years. If historians term the post-1942 period a "time for action," then I define the preceding two years as "a time to learn." During this so-called training period, the delegation's members underwent their initial trial by fire in the American public arena and used their experiences to identify the weaknesses of the indigenous Jewish organizations, Zionist and non-Zionist alike, in the public relations and fundraising spheres. Equally important, they learned to see themselves as an integrated group whose members performed together under pressure, shared an accepted leadership, and worked toward common goals.

This learning was particularly true regarding the make-or-break issue of authority and leadership, which, as we will see, underwent a generational transformation during 1940. Alex Rafaeli's description of his private odyssey in Irgun ranks epitomizes this change: "My first year in America was a crucial one with regard to all aspects of delegation activity. Our organization and implementation, arguments, relationships, our unending financial difficulties—all set the future pattern that would be repeated time and again in each of the entities we founded in the United States." In that year, Zeev Jabotinsky's death and the subsequent lack of clarity regarding the state of the Revisionist movement in Palestine allowed the delegation freedom to develop in a different direction than originally intended. Rafaeli recalled: "Hillel took charge upon his arrival, and we—like good soldiers—unquestioningly accepted his authority. Self-discipline, military organization, absolute obedience, and a shared dream—that was the key to our success in those years."[1] Finally, it was during this period that the delegation became an autonomous entity, owing to the convergence of a series of scattered events: the outbreak of war in Europe, Jabotinsky's sudden death in New York, and the split in Irgun ranks in Palestine. The interaction between the operative, introspective, and autonomous lines along which the delegation developed during its first two years sheds light on its initial steps and on its members' singular behavior shortly after their arrival in America.

Forming the "American Friends of a Jewish Palestine"

Members of the Irgun Delegation were often plunged directly into the unfamiliar American scene with little or no preparation. Yitzhak Ben-Ami had arrived with a number of other activists and had a month's grace before being left on his own to complete the groundwork for a delegation; Arieh Ben-Eliezer was taken under Ben-Ami's wing in his early days, particularly because of his lack of English. However Kook, Rafaeli, and Merlin were plunged directly into an unfamiliar scene, and it was expected that they "perform" within hours of their arrival. Alex Rafaeli recalled the day of his arrival in New York. After disembarking he was taken directly from the boat to a press conference Zeev Jabotinsky was holding at the Astor Hotel on Times Square. "There must have been about one hundred journalists in the audience. The war was then in its eighth month, and as I was coming from Eastern Europe they asked me to tell them about my first-hand experiences." Whispering in Russian, Jabotinsky asked Rafaeli how he wished to be introduced. "I could not use my real name and on the spur of the moment I thought of 'Hadani,' a name which stuck with me for many years." Knowing little English, Rafaeli spoke in German to his audience while Jabotinsky translated. "I reported on the state of refugees in Romania and Turkey, who were anxious to reach Palestine and were being kept away both by the local governments and by the British. I told them of our underground activities, of *Aliyah Bet,* of the boats we had managed to lease in Greece and Romania, of the political and technical obstacles blocking entrance into Palestine and of the few boats that had reached Palestinian shores successfully."[2]

Rafaeli's description summarized the basic issue that the Irgun Delegation would address during its first year of activity in the United States: raising financial and political support for illegal immigration to Palestine. At the time of his arrival the organizational mechanism that would deal with this issue had scarcely been put into motion, and the public relations techniques that the delegation members would adopt in order to achieve their goal were not even in the planning stages. Yet the initial step had been taken: Rafaeli's appearance before five-score journalists marks the first press conference that any delegation member had held in the United States, the first of many appearances before the press that he and the other members would make during the next eight years in order to bring word of their goal to the American and American Jewish public.

An initial delegation nucleus was already functioning when Rafaeli arrived in New York in May 1940. From the previous summer Yitzhak Ben-Ami and Arieh Ben-Eliezer had been raising money for the aliyah bet activities described by Rafaeli at the aforementioned press conference at the Astor Hotel. In fact, delegation efforts on the American scene had begun as early as March 1939 with the arrival of the vanguard: Lubinsky, Patterson, and Briscoe. There were two main tasks on their agenda: one financial, the other operational-diplomatic. Although their chief aim was to raise money, at the same time the group's members, particularly Robert Briscoe, also sought to promote a political cause. At Zeev Jabotinsky's personal request, the Irish parliamentarian was supposed to spark President Roosevelt's interest in an emergency program to evacuate two million Jews from eastern and central Europe to a safe haven, but these efforts met with failure.[3] Briscoe, later to serve as mayor of Dublin, found his access to the White House barred.

Both the complexity of the internal Jewish communal structure and the problematic contemporary public status of American Jewry contributed to this diplomatic failure. Ben-Ami recalled his initial inability to understand the divisions among American Jews and the nature of the barriers that had been erected against the Zionist right wing. He recalled in his memoirs how he spent his first evening in America listening to Lubinsky and Patterson recount their lack of progress in obtaining American Jewish support and their disappointment in the meager number of followers that Jabotinsky and the Revisionists had among American Jews. As for the other American Jewish organizations, Lubinsky and Patterson explained to him that the two leading Jewish organizations—the American Jewish Committee and the Jewish Labor Committee—were virtually "anti-Zionist" and that most American Zionist organizations were under the sway of the charismatic Rabbi Stephen S. Wise, the prominent Zionist leader associated with American President Franklin Delano Roosevelt and a man who made no secret of his aversion for Revisionists. Finally, those

American Jewish leaders who were favorably disposed to the Revisionist movement were in either in retirement or dead. Ben-Ami had initially relied upon the letters of introduction that he received from two prominent figures in Palestine, Professor Joseph Klausner and chief rabbi of Tel Aviv Moshe Avigdor Amiel, to grant him entry into American Jewish society, but he soon learned that they opened the doors to a very limited sector of American Jewry. The Reform movement, the socioeconomic bastion of the American Jewish upper crust, which provided the demographic pool for several American Jewish national organizations, was virtually closed to the delegation. Only one Reform leader, Rabbi Louis I. Newman of New York, was willing to assist Ben-Ami and Ben-Eliezer in organizing meetings in synagogues and private homes, where they attempted to garner support for illegal immigration to Palestine. Years later, Ben-Ami maintained that even as early as 1939 the American Jewish and Zionist establishment sabotaged their potentially successful efforts: "They went back to their homes and offices, called their rabbis or heads of their fraternal lodges and asked if they should help us. Who are these people? they asked. Who is Jabotinsky? What is the *Irgun*? And the answer was always the same: 'Don't touch them.' "[4]

Ben-Ami's claims take us back to the position held by all delegation members, both during their period of activity in the United States and in retrospect, regarding the attitude of the American Jewish establishment toward their efforts. It is interesting to note how much of the group's wartime correspondence, even as early as 1939–40, deals with the negative attitudes they encountered among American Jewish and Zionist organizations. Similarly, it is interesting to note how during this early period mention of the group rarely appears in the files of those whom they considered their antagonists—among them the American Jewish Committee, the American Zionist Emergency Fund, and the Jewish Agency office in New York. It therefore appears that, at least circumstantially, delegation members were more involved with anticipating their antagonists during the years 1939 and 1940 than was the American Jewish establishment in anticipating the moves of what they initially considered to be an insignificant body. As we shall see, by 1943 this situation would undergo a complete turnabout. By the time the American Jewish establishment became well aware of the activities of a group that they now considered a threat, and dealt with it on a regular basis in their internal meetings, the delegation had gone far beyond devoting time and effort to its antagonists and announced itself to be concentrating, as Samuel Merlin wrote in those days, "much more on action than on reaction."[5]

Having met with no success on the diplomatic front, from late 1939 onward the vanguard directed its steps to amassing public support. Ben-Ami recalled his initial efforts to win over two groups of Jews: the non-Zionists and the assimilated Americanized Jews. Indeed, over time these two groups, "along with a smattering of observant, Orthodox Jews, some recent immigrants from eastern Europe and a few warm-hearted non-Jews," became the mainstays of the delegation's offshoots.[6]

Who were the Irgun Delegation's activists and sympathizers? None of the aforementioned groups was part of the mainstream of activist American Jewry. In fact, it appears that the delegation actively sought public support among the unaffiliated Jews or those, such as the Orthodox, who had not found a home within the American Jewish establishment. Furthermore, the delegation appears to be the first Jewish group of that time functioning in the United States that actively made overtures to the non-Jewish public. Finally, the delegation's apparent policy of sidestepping the American Jewish establishment in order to gather grassroots support pointed to one of the main difficulties facing the other Zionist entities in America up to that time: their reluctance to actively recruit ad hoc adherents for special projects among those groups that either declared themselves opposed to the broad principles of Zionism or that were not connected with the Jewish world.

These non-Zionists, assimilated Americanized Jews, and warm-hearted non-Jews who evinced an interest in the delegation included a married couple slated to play a central role in drafting funds and sympathizers alike—John and Frances Gunther. Gunther, a noted journalist, and his Jewish wife, Frances, were two of the outstanding intellectuals who donated their time and energy to promoting delegation goals, opening their home to its members for the duration of its activity. Frances, a tiny fragile woman with a languid, hesitant voice, was a one-woman dynamo when it came to amassing support for the Irgun members, and she worked non-stop to persuade American Jews and Gentiles of the justice of the delegation's cause. The Gunthers were joined by another activist, a young Jewish lawyer named Harry Louis Selden, who assisted the delegation throughout the 1940s. Shortly after his arrival in New York the Gunther-Selden trio gave Ben-Ami a lesson on the growing anti-Semitism in the United States. Their analysis identified several contributory factors: the Great Depression; traditional American political isolationism and heightened nationalism; social and religious trends; and American concern lest a wave of European Jewish refugees flood their shores in the wake of Hitler's rise to power.[7] Ben-Ami quickly grasped that America of the late 1930s was far from being the pluralistic haven he had studied about in Jerusalem. Furthermore, he soon learned that the American Jewish establishment's antagonism toward Revisionist activity was serious enough to bar his entry into most temples, community centers, or organizational gatherings where he wished to promote his version of Jewish rescue.

The reasons for the American Jewish establishment's wariness toward Ben-Ami and Ben-Eliezer's nascent efforts and the explanations for the longstanding alienation between the American Jewish establishment and the Revisionist activists in the United States were both political and organizational. Apart from their reluctance to have anything to do with a group that they considered to have "fascist" leanings, and their desire to retain a monopoly over presenting Zionist and Jewish issues to the American public, it can be seen as part and parcel of the ingroup-outgroup dynamics punctuating American Jewish organizational history.

Much has been written about the inner dynamic of American Jewry from the early twentieth century to the present, about the reasons for the never-ending factionalization and varying degrees of cooperation among different bodies ostensibly working toward the same general goal. In his study of the American Jewish organizational dynamic, Daniel Judah Elazar notes the diversity, the mutual suspicion, and the unceasing controversy that characterized interorganizational relationships within the American Jewish polity, a polity that in his view has always been composed of scores of particularistic entities. Many of these organizations—including some promoting distinct and even opposing causes—billed themselves as representing the interests of the American Jewish public as a whole. It also happened that, whereas the specific goal was acceptable to all, it was the means to the end or the underlying issues that were subject to debate. This attitude emerges clearly, for example, with regard to the specific goal of the American Friends of a Jewish Palestine—aid for European Jewry—which enjoyed a broad consensus among American Jewish organizations. But this was not true for either the means to this end—the organization of illegal immigration—or for the broader issues—militarism and the question of British policy on Palestine.[8] This ends-means dichotomy was certainly not unique to American Jewry; it was also a characteristic feature of other minority groups active on the twentieth-century American scene, of which the Irish are a prime example.[9] Indeed, Irgun Delegation members drew inspiration from Irish militants thanks to links created during Briscoe's American tour.[10] Irish militants were among the few groups that had attempted to harness American public opinion before the Second World War in their attempt to solve the Irish question, utilizing not only the Irish diaspora but various alliances in the United States in order to further their cause. As we will see, their various activities—attempting to influence American foreign policy, creating a working relationship with other minority groups in America, supporting Irish cultural movements, and forming minor political organizations during the first two decades of the twentieth century—acted as a blueprint for delegation members and greatly influenced their public relations activities during the 1940s. This was but one of the ways in which they differed from the American Jewish establishment, which, until the mid-war years, preferred to take their cue from those bodies that had adopted less militant and more established European-style diplomacy.[11]

The various delegation members' initial period in the United States—their "baptism of fire"—is invariably dealt with in depth in their memoirs and interviews. Ben-Ami characterized his first weeks in New York as a crash course on the facts of life in the American Jewish public arena. During their eight-week stay in the city with the largest Jewish population in the United States, Lubinsky, Briscoe, and Patterson had not even succeeded in raising enough money to cover operating expenses. They encountered stiff establishment opposition from Zionists and non-Zionists alike, who opposed the activity of a group they identified as Revisionist, or "fascist," in their words. On his trips to Washington, Lubinsky went begging for home hospitality while attempting to make connections with individuals who could provide him with either financial support or political introductions. After learning about his political affiliation, few Zionists were willing to host the Irgun activist. Even the American branch of the NZO, an ephemeral movement that had barely attracted any followers during its brief existence and that remained outside the Zionist establishment, kept a close watch on the group. As Patterson and Lubinsky's stay in

the States drew to a close, they, along with Ben-Ami and Briscoe, concluded that the sole effective means of bringing the Revisionist point of
view on the Jewish-Zionist problem to the attention of the American Jewish public was to create an autonomous organizational entity. Indeed, in
his memoirs Ben-Ami emphasizes that before leaving the United States,
Patterson and Lubinsky had already set the groundwork for the formation
of the American Friends of a Jewish Palestine into motion. This was envisioned as an activist group that would meet the needs of all right-wing
Zionist activists in the United States. Intending that the group would be
unique among existing American Jewish organizations for openly declaring its intention of forwarding its aims at the expense of the "united Jewish organizational front" generally presented to the American public, the
American Friends of a Jewish Palestine was at that time the sole body on
the American Zionist scene to openly embrace militant opposition to
British immigration restrictions and to promote illegal aliyah to Palestine
as a partial solution to the European Jewish refugee problem.

It is interesting to note Ben-Ami's insistence that not he but Lubinsky
and Patterson laid the groundwork for the American Friends of a Jewish
Palestine, something that no correspondence from the period corrobo-
rates. Did this insistence have to do with the fact that delegation members
later took over the organization in its entirety, explaining the necessity for
this step by stating that Lubinsky and Patterson's original inclusion of Revisionists and not only Irgun members had laid at the basis for the organization's later impotence? There is no way of knowing whether Ben-Ami's
later recollections were a precise description of events or a deliberate reconstruction structured to legitimate the group's organizational coup;
however, in view of the lack of any other documentation that backs up his
description, and the Revisionists' claim that Ben-Ami initially used them
as a front in the American Friends, never intending to have them play a
major role, this remains an open question.[12]

In order to understand the history of the American Friends of a Jewish
Palestine (AFJP), we must examine four stories that evolved in tandem.
The first story is an operational one—the initial efforts that went into creating an organization capable of implementing three immediate aims:
fund-raising for Revisionist-sponsored illegal aliyah, drafting public American opinion in favor of Irgun-style Zionist activism, and fostering diplomatic activity to further the first two goals. For the second story we turn to

internal developments within the delegation itself, to the division of labor and activity patterns then determined that continued to function throughout the delegation's metamorphoses. Simultaneously, delegation members were forced to respond to internal divisions in the Irgun and to the overtures of Abraham "Yair" Stern, founder of the secessionist IZL in Israel. The third scenario took place within the context of the Revisionist movement and centers on power and supremacy issues among the various entities that shared the AFJP framework, in particular the relationship between the members of the Irgun Delegation and Revisionist movement president Zeev Jabotinsky. Our fourth story, upon which we will touch only in brief, belongs to the internal Zionist arena and analyzes the American Zionist movement's attitude toward AFJP activities in general and the efforts of the Irgun Delegation's members in particular during their first year of operations in the United States.

The sociologist Cecil A. Gibb has identified four sets of variables that determine the elements of intragroup interaction: "(1) the *leader*, with his characteristics of ability and personality and his 'resources relevant to goal attainment'; (2) the *followers*, who also have relevant abilities, personality characteristics, and resources; (3) the *situation* within which the relationship occurs; and (4) the *task* with which the interacting individuals are confronted." [13] Reams of paper have been devoted to the attempt to define a typology of leadership. One classic model is that proposed by sociologist Max Weber, who distinguishes between three broad categories of leadership: charismatic-demagogic, traditional-patriarchal or monarchic, and legal—head of a bureaucratic network. An alternative model also speaks of three leadership types: the responsible leader officially awarded the title "leader"; the effective leader who actually makes the decisions; and the psychological leader, perceived as such in group consciousness. We can also cite the existence of localized leaders: persistent momentary problem-solvers who address technical problems; salient leaders who exercise influence in specific situations; sociometric leaders who are personally accepted by the group; as well as elected leaders who derive their authority from formal elections. [14] These different types of leaders share certain characteristics: a high degree of adaptability, a dominant extroverted personality, and high intelligence in comparison to their followers. [15]

Throughout the history of the delegation, leadership was a major issue determining not only the relationship between group members but their organizational focus and operational tactics. This issue is readily apparent in the history of the American Friends of a Jewish Palestine, with May 1940 serving as the watershed between the organization's two historical periods. In his memoirs, Ben-Ami claims that during the AFJP's initial period, he and Ben-Eliezer (who had arrived in New York in the meantime) decided to downplay their role and functioned as behind-the-scenes advisers. Although this decision has no corroboration in the duo's correspondence from that period, their behavior from that period backs up Ben-Ami's assertion. This differed from their future policy: throughout the 1940s delegation members assumed a leading role in succeeding offshoots. Hillel Kook's arrival in New York in May 1940 marks the turning point when the group's operational patterns and leadership hierarchy achieved the characteristic form maintained throughout the war years.[16]

The official head of the American Friends of a Jewish Palestine was New York rabbi Louis I. Newman (1893–1972) of Temple Rodeph Shalom, the only member of the American Reform rabbinate then willing to cooperate with the Irgun representatives. Although ordained by the dean of Reform rabbis, Stephen S. Wise, who was an ardent opponent of the Revisionists in general and of the Irgun Delegation in particular, Newman nonetheless displayed sympathy for the delegation's aims and backed its members' modus operandi for the entire decade of its existence. Despite his assistance and involvement, however, Newman never became the group's official leader, nor did he even penetrate the delegation's inner circle.

It was Hillel Kook who became the Irgun Delegation's acknowledged leader even before Zeev Jabotinsky's death, both on counts of military discipline and on personal grounds. Not only was he the most senior Irgun officer then in the Diaspora, Kook was also endowed with natural leadership abilities. In their memoirs, delegation members were adamant about this point and expressed their complete obedience to Kook and the laws that he laid down: "We accepted his suggestions as the next things to commands," Ben-Ami recalled, "though we were on a civilian mission involving public relations and political activities, we still considered ourselves a unit of a liberation army, and we kept a strict hierarchical discipline within our ranks just as we had in Eretz-Israel. It was the ultimate source of our strength. Our attitude was the same as that of all nations in time of war—accept discipline or accept defeat."[17] Samuel Merlin's correspondence with Rafaeli on this matter provides us with a similar picture: "Hillel was boss and we all accepted his decisions as law."[18]

At first glance it appears that group cohesion was fostered by a common denominator of shared characteristics. All were youthful members of a military organization, adherents of a joint ideological-political path, and foreigners in the United States. This final factor in particular contributed not only to group cohesion but to an enhanced sense of mission and a lack of responsibility toward long-established American Jewish traditional attitudes and actions. The common denominator of shared characteristics had an additional effect of reducing internal tensions among group members—each an individualist, an activist, and a visionary in his own right—within the organizational pressure-cooker in which they now found themselves. Moreover, the unique circumstances of wartime furthered group cohesion just as they contributed to the organizational closing of ranks within the Jewish community at large.

A closer examination of the group's organizational dynamics shows that the members' idyllic memoirs did not always mirror reality. In truth, intragroup life rarely proceeded without turmoil. "We never lacked for arguments," Ben-Ami noted in his memoirs. "We disagreed, sometimes vehemently, about each other's analyses of events, about policies, tactics, and specific courses of action. But eventually a consensus always emerged, and when it did, we all adhered to it regardless of whether or not it led to bruised egos. It enabled our small disciplined group to achieve the impact we eventually had."[19]

But we must ask ourselves whether this idyllic description of patterns of bowing to authority within the group actually conforms to contemporary group reality. Can we perhaps detect the seeds of discontent that led to the postwar election of Samuel Merlin as group leader? In order to answer this question it is necessary to examine the group's wartime documentation and not only to rely on nostalgic memoirs usually written decades after the fact. Closer examination of the delegation's wartime documentation found in the Jabotinsky Archives and private collections, along with an analysis of its intragroup history, enables us to explore this issue. All sources point to three factors that allowed Kook both to concentrate the reins of decision-making power in his hands between 1940 and 1943, and to simultaneously endow his fellow members with a sense of freedom of action: a clear-cut division of tasks, delegation of authority, and geographical distance. Within the context of our earlier discussion of leadership types, it appears that Kook fulfilled a number of leadership functions concurrently. Undoubtedly a charismatic leader, he also served as the group's responsible and psychological leader. At the same time, by granting other members freedom of action, he engaged them in leadership on the operational level as well.

This behavioral pattern fits Barker's analysis of small-group interaction, in which he suggests that in addition to each group's main leader, or as a substitute for him, we find individuals taking responsibility for specific areas of group functioning. Among them we must note the *encourager,* who provides support or shows acceptance of another member's idea or statement; the *compromiser,* who arbitrates intragroup disagreements; the *standard setter,* who sets standards for the entire group; and the *gatekeeper,* who opens intermember channels of communication.[20]

Each member within the Irgun Delegation framework had his own niche, an area of responsibility for which he was uniquely suited and which also met the needs of the group as a whole. One specialized in diplomatic efforts, another in fund-raising, a third in communications and public relations, a fourth acted as general adviser, and so on. Although ultimate authority officially rested with Kook, he was receptive to each member's ideas with regard to his particular field of expertise. Finally, the fact that its members were geographically separated—one was located in New York, another on the West Coast, a third in the Midwest, while the others were in Washington—also enhanced their sense of autonomy. We must note here, however, that the original core group functioned concurrently in the United States for only a limited three-year period: in 1943 Ben-Eliezer was dispatched to Palestine, in 1944 Ben-Ami and Rafaeli were drafted into the American army and Eri Jabotinsky traveled to Turkey as delegation liaison to the War Refugee Board. It was not until late 1945 that four of the six original members joined forces once more, albeit reactivating the established pattern of clearly defined task roles and separate geographical arenas. Finally, Hillel Kook suffered poor health and was hospitalized for part of this period, which allowed delegation members full autonomy with regard to decision-making and implementation.

Another factor that enabled delegation members to initially accept Hillel Kook's authority was their total agreement over what form their lifestyle should take. Norms governing the delegation members' characteristically modest personal lifestyle regarding housing, apparel, and food were all set during this initial period. Salaries were fixed at a weekly rate of $25, but in actual fact each individual received considerably less. Even when the group experienced fund-raising success, its members continued to adhere to this modest standard of living. "We had a two-room office on Madison Avenue. All our costs were covered by two old friends of the movement," Ben-Ami wrote. "We were always on the verge of bankruptcy. Every ad was paid for with whatever the preceding one generated, and our small offices were maintained on a shoestring budget. I remember coming to the office early one morning and finding Arieh Ben-Eliezer there—he had arrived from out of town the day before and was too embarrassed to mention to the secretary that he had no money for a hotel room. He had slept on a desk."[21] Rafaeli corroborated this description with his own: "In the early days I had to hope that people would invite us for dinner, otherwise we wouldn't have anything to eat."[22] Similar descriptions may be found in Samuel Merlin's and Hillel Kook's recollections of the period.[23] Descriptions of the delegation's spartan living conditions and lifestyle play an important role not only in its members' memoirs but in their wartime correspondence as well. This lifestyle takes on an added significance in view of delegation associate Ben Hecht's pointed description of American Zionist leader Rabbi Stephen Wise's personal financial considerations resulting in his refusal to bury Hecht's mother for a less than significant sum.[24] However it becomes even more striking in view of various historians' indictment of certain American Jewish leaders of the period for their expansive lifestyle and two-hour lunches during the war years. It therefore appears that the group's insistence on emphasizing their financial plight and spartan living standards was a deliberate attempt to point to what they saw as a major shortcoming of the American Jewish and even Zionist establishment.

As we have seen, the delegation's self-image was a major factor in determining its organizational interaction. Subsequently, both provided the framework for the delegation's public relations tactics, which would become their calling card among American Jewish organizations. Only a few months after its formation, the American Friends of a Jewish Palestine was already engaged in a variety of seemingly eclectic activities. Initially, the group concentrated on organizing meetings in private homes, holding lotteries, and opportunistic dissemination of publications. The first issue of the *Bulletin,* which became its official organ, appeared in early October. Generally speaking, the skimpy coverage that appeared in the *Bulletin* can be broadly assigned to three categories: proposals, preaching, and pronouncements. In line with the best American tradition their proposals called for fund-raising lotteries and balls; their preaching was directed at the Jewish Agency and the UJA for their failure to fund illegal immigration to Palestine; and their pronouncements, which emanated from the Yishuv, contained reports on current Irgun activity.[25]

By what means did association members hope to influence American Jewry? An internal memo, probably written in 1940, addressed the major issues and proposed directions for action. The memo's author, William Stanton, who played a central role in the AFJP as well as in other delegation offshoots, isolated what he identified as American Jewry's most compelling concern: fear of accusations of disloyalty to the United States. In order to address this concern, he proposed a series of counter-steps simultaneously aimed at both furthering organizational goals and reassuring the American Jewish public, assigning top priority to a propaganda campaign to provide maximum exposure for the organization's goals. Its focal theme would promote the view that support for a Jewish entity in Palestine by no means represented a betrayal of the United States or its ideals. Once the American Jewish public had been convinced that the question of their loyalty was not at stake, it would then be possible to draft their support for Irgun aims: for both illegal immigration and other political causes. Stanton took his suggestions for eliciting public support and exercising political influence a step further, strongly recommending that substantial funding be directed to the public relations arena and that the public relations methods employed by local non-Jewish organizations be immediately adopted. As the Irgun Delegation's publicity campaigns attest, his recommendations fell on fertile soil.[26]

It was during the years of AFJP activity that the delegation developed the tactical patterns that would have both a short-term and a long-term effect on the American scene. Four aspects of the delegation's public relations tactics were already in evidence at this stage. First we note its employment of current American trends, like anticommunism and antifascism, to forward its aims. The opening lines of a public plea made in a 1940 issue of the association's official publication *Aims and Achievements,* which addressed the European Jewish refugee problem, appealed to anti-

Nazi and anti-Bolshevik sentiments commonly held by the American public: "We believe that if these refugees are to be supported by money from abroad, it is better to support them in Palestine than in Eastern Europe, controlled by the Nazis and the Bolsheviks, who in the end profit by the money sent by brother-Jews from free countries." [27] By utilizing preexisting sentiments among the American public the delegation would be able to link up with a body of fears and hopes, inserting its personal message into a more general American framework. This technique would place the delegation in a central, nonparticularistic Jewish area on the broad map of American wartime action.

A second facet of Ben-Ami and Ben-Eliezer's modus operandi was the maintenance of a low political profile: the association deliberately refrained from calling attention to its members' and supporters' Revisionist ties. References to Revisionist policy remained subliminal; witness the wording of the central aims of the American Friends of a Jewish Palestine, which spoke of assistance to Jewish refugees wishing to immigrate to "the territory comprised within the Palestine Mandate of 1922," a veiled allusion to Revisionist maximalist demands on territorial matters. [28] This indirection was particularly important in view of the tendency to equate Revisionist-Zionist with fascist, something that could sound the death knell for delegation activities during wartime.

Third, the American Friends of a Jewish Palestine made widespread use of at-homes and publications to disseminate its ideology and draft supporters to its ranks. This tactic was extremely important in view of the fact that almost all synagogues, community centers, and organizational halls were closed to the group because of the antagonism of the American Jewish establishment. Consequently, it was necessary to rely upon word of mouth, a group of dedicated volunteers, and the possibility of utilizing private establishments as an operational base of action. Three such volunteers were the Gunthers and Harry Selden, who worked tirelessly to bring the group's message before a broad public. With the arrival of the delegation's remaining members in the United States in spring and summer 1940, all shared in this public relations task, each according to his area of expertise and abilities: Ben-Eliezer's piquant Yiddish won fans in New York's Jewish neighborhoods; Hillel Kook's intriguingly dramatic personality met with success in New York's salons; and Alex Rafaeli would later take on public relations in Chicago and in Hollywood, where he won over "gangsters and filmmakers."[29] Rafaeli described his efforts on this front, stating that the delegation was probably the first Zionist group that sought to address a broader public. "We presented the Jewish plight as primarily an international problem and, therefore, one affecting America, which should be lending us a helping hand, in line with its traditions and interests." Although the Jews had already assimilated into the American culture and had shown deep loyalty to American interests, he saw them as being in "a political ghetto" as far as Palestine and Zionist aims were concerned, talking primarily to themselves. Rafaeli was convinced that the delegation's early activities initiated a new phase in the attitude of the American public to the Jewish problem. "Within less than two years we grew into a broad influential force sponsored by prominent figures that included senators, Christian dignitaries, labor leaders and academics."[30] Rafaeli's description, corroborated by those of other delegation members, pinpoints one of the important public relations tactics that the group employed: attempting to create a broad—and non-Jewish—power base and ultimately a series of alliances with groups that could further their cause. This was a tactic rarely used by other Jewish and Zionist groups in the United States at that time, and appears to have been copied from the Irish militants active in the United States before the Second World War.

Rafaeli's description leads us to the fourth facet of the delegation's operative pattern: the decision to found a nonsectarian entity, as opposed to a parallel organization for non-Jewish supporters similar to the Christian American Palestine Committee, which worked in tandem with American Zionist organizations. From the outset the delegation resolved in principle to integrate Christian sympathizers, Protestants and Catholics alike, into the Revisionist entity, and as we shall see, some of these non-Jewish figures filled key roles at the operational and representational levels. In this respect the American Friends of a Jewish Palestine more closely resembled other, often nonsectarian, refugee organizations then active in the States than the existing ones in the American Zionist organizational arena.[31] In comparison, American Zionist organizations preferred to keep their boards almost all Jewish, preferring to work with separate Christian organizations that supported their cause. It is difficult to know if this preference stemmed from their sincere belief that maintaining an all-Jewish administration would limit intraorganizational strife, or whether this was an overt expression of Jewish separatism. In either case, the delegation apparently considered these to be secondary problems and usually preferred to place prominent Gentiles in places of authority on their various organizational boards.

Organizational composition aside, the make-or-break issue was how to make contact with as broad a public as possible, encourage sympathizers as fast as possible, and reach as many potential adherents as possible. Delegation members employed a variety of means to reach out to potential sympathizers. "We followed the opinions of prominent Jews . . . as well as of prominent non-Jews, and we tried by various means to gain their ear and to interest them in our work," Samuel Merlin recalled.[32] Alex Rafaeli elaborated further: "We acted on the assumption that there was a large reserve of 'good will' within the United States which could be channeled to the right causes if these were presented to the public in the proper light, and indeed, over time, we found that the general American public showed sensitivity to just causes even when these were not directly related to its 'pocket.' "[33]

In this fashion the delegation shaped its public relations tactics in a fashion radically different from the existing operational patterns employed by American Jewish and American Zionist organizations. With few exceptions, these were based on behind-the-scenes diplomacy, creating ad hoc and often unsuccessful boards such as the American Zionist Bureau in Washington, and, in the case of Zionist activities, presenting their issues as a particularistic Jewish and/or Zionist cause. In comparison, the delegation's operational patterns were characterized by extroverted, ostensibly nonsectarian efforts, in order to solve what they presented to the public as a human and not particularly Jewish or Zionist problem. The initial success of these tactics may be gauged by examining the delegation's financial intake in the sphere of fund-raising. During the brief period from its founding until mid-1940 the AFJP raised more than $33,000 to fund illegal Revisionist-sponsored aliyah. Palestine-bound ships that sailed from Danzig, Salonika, Marseille, Fiume (Italy), and Constanta were partially supported by AFJP donations, thereby making a central contribution to the Revisionist solution for the refugee problem.[34]

Financial success was but one facet of what Alex Rafaeli had previously called the group's "political work." Another aspect was the group's efforts in the diplomatic sphere. Here, too, the American Friends of a Jewish Palestine sought to make an impact, as may be seen by three of their activities in 1939 and 1940. In September 1939 the AFJP presented a memorandum to the British ambassador in Washington, Lord Lothian (Philip Carr), who as private secretary to Lloyd George had assisted Zeev Jabotinsky and Chaim Weizmann in their negotiations for a Jewish battalion and for the Balfour Declaration, which suggested that given developments on the international scene, Britain should grant legal recognition to the Irgun, supply it with weapons, and allow it to take part in the defense of Palestine. A second attempt was the protest delivered to the British ambassador to the United States in late 1940 regarding the deportation of some seventeen hundred illegal Palestine-bound immigrants to Mauritius. A final diplomatic activity was the petition that was to be presented to Congress and to the American president in an attempt to enhance political support for the founding of a Jewish state in Palestine. An essential element of this third example was the group's utilization of a time-honored Revisionist tactic: the petition. As opposed to its success in molding public opinion and fund-raising, the diplomatic initiatives of the American Friends of a Jewish Palestine had no lasting influence.[35] It appears, therefore, that success in the diplomatic arena would require a change in the delegation's tactics in this sphere as well.

The *Sakarya* Expedition

If a key aim of the American Friends of a Jewish Palestine was the promotion of illegal aliyah to Palestine, then their efforts on this front reached their acme in the funding of the *Sakarya* Expedition, which proceeded by stages along the Danube during winter 1939–40. Three delegation members—Ben-Ami, Ben-Eliezer, and Eri Jabotinsky—dealt with the expedition in practice, leaving us a plethora of correspondence from the period; Ben-Ami and Eri Jabotinsky also dealt with it in depth after the war. It is therefore interesting to compare the various wartime and postwar versions in order to see how even within such a small Irgun Delegation there would always be room for different versions of the same events.

Even before the war, the Danube had served as a main escape route for the Jewish masses wishing to leave Europe for Palestine. "The river provides the sole egress from Germany, Slovakia, and Hungary to the sea," Eri Jabotinsky wrote in his postwar description of the expedition. "The boats that pass through this river faithfully reflect the region's political confusion. In the waters of the Danube all nations' flags can be seen . . . each type of ship adheres to its own rules. This makes using the river exceedingly difficult but also enhances the sporting chances of all the smugglers, pirates, and organizers of convoys of illegal immigrants." [36]

For the year-long period after the spring 1939 German takeover of Prague, Revisionist aliyah bet activists stationed in Vienna, Prague, Zurich, and Bucharest dispatched fourteen ships to Palestine, mainly via the Danube, with a total of 12,000 Jewish passengers on board. European-based aliyah activists looked to the AFJP for funding to cover the costs of these voyages. [37]

The 1 September 1939 German invasion of Poland and its subsequent dismemberment by Germany and the Soviet Union gave Polish Jews added impetus to evade the German approach by fleeing east toward the Soviet border. Concurrently, the Jews of the Third Reich—Germany, Austria, and the Czech Protectorate—continued their efforts to escape the German pincers either via legal emigration to Latin America and the United States or via illegal aliyah to Palestine.

The *Sakarya* Expedition began in the autumn of 1939 when a group of five hundred Jews left Prague for Romania. These illegal immigrants to Palestine had spent the preceding six months in a Prague transit camp living at subsistence level while waiting for news that a suitable vessel had been found either in Romania or Greece. With the outbreak of war on 1 September, the race against time began in an all-out effort to find a boat to transport them to their next port of call before their limited funds ran out. The situation was further exacerbated by the fact that, unless the group could prove to the Gestapo that a boat had already been contracted for, the Germans would not release foreign currency funds to pay for the sailing. Eri Jabotinsky, who was then stationed in Bucharest, managed to convince the Romanian Tourist Bureau that a small tramper had been chartered for the immigrants and this information satisfied the Gestapo as well. No one bothered to inform either the Romanians or the Germans that a final agreement had yet to be reached with the owners. Now a new complication arose. Even before the German release of foreign currency funds to pay for the sailing, the Vienna Betar representative informed the Bucharest activists that he had chartered two small Yugoslavian boats on his own initiative in order to transport the immigrants to the Romanian border port of Moldova Veche. Recognizing the hand of the Gestapo in this hasty departure from Prague, Bucharest headquarters nevertheless informed the Vienna activist that if he left Prague without first forwarding the necessary funds, he would spend the winter marooned on the frozen river, and in such an event, they stressed, Betar headquarters would wash its hands of him. The activist's reply was conveyed via a telephone call from his father: on 1 October the Vienna activist and his group were already underway.

Both wartime correspondence and postwar memoirs show that it was at this point that Eri Jabotinsky stepped in and assumed a central role in this affair. Despite efforts by his colleague, a Revisionist activist named Franco who was well acquainted with the Danube, to dissuade him, Jabotinsky decided to intervene personally in this matter and made plans to proceed to the port city of Moldova Veche. In his memoirs Jabotinsky emphasizes his decision to play a major role in this unfolding drama, attempting, possibly, to stress what he had been willing to sacrifice on the personal level in order to insure the group's rescue. Before his departure, he and Franco had sat drinking coffee in Bucharest's Majestic Hotel. Despite Franco's repeated pleas to abandon this plan, Jabotinsky was determined to show him that nothing would deter him from attempting to assist the group. "I said to him, 'Franco, do you know me to be a quiet person?' He answered, 'Yes.' I then said, 'Look,' and threw my coffee cup at the wall opposite with all my strength. The cup shattered and a large black stain slowly spread over the painted wallpaper. I said, 'Now stop.' "[38] Franco evidently found this overt display convincing and proceeded to purchase Jabotinsky's train ticket.

In Moldova Veche Eri Jabotinsky was joined by a number of additional activists, but they soon learned that the group had been detained in Yugoslavia. Primed by a generous "tip" from Jabotinsky, the local chief customs officer promised to assist the group upon its arrival. Impressed either by the group's daring or by the size of the "tip," this official even paid the immigrants a visit. "The chief customs' officer visited them on the night of their arrival," Jabotinsky wrote in his memoirs. "They staged a 'Viennese Cabaret' in his honor; they sang songs, plied him with alcohol, and taught him to shout 'Tel-Chai!' Late at night he boarded the skiff to return to shore. The Betar members cheered in his honor. He straightened up and stood in the boat, saluted them and yelled 'Tel-Chai'!—and fell into the water. It was only with great difficulty that he was rescued from the swift current."[39]

None of the wartime correspondence within Irgun ranks, whether to other European activists or to those in the United States, includes any of these details. Instead the letters that appear in the Revisionist-Zionist archives concentrate almost solely on the bureaucratic/financial aspects of the venture. A richer, though not necessarily totally accurate, picture appears in the postwar descriptions of the operation, found in Ben-Ami's and Jabotinsky's memoirs. According to Jabotinsky, at this juncture a Romanian barge, the *Spyroula*, was hired to bring the group of five hundred illegal immigrants to Giurgiu. "Picture a very large raft with two holds, each two and half meters deep," he wrote. "In these holds there are wooden platforms built three high. The lowest lies close to the floor, and the highest about seventy-five centimeters from the tin roof that serves as the barge's deck. In each hold about 250 people slept on these platforms. In the middle of the room there were desks; above—the kitchen, the dispensary, the dentist's office, the secretariat, and the bathrooms, all constructed by the convoy's work crew from boards they received in Moldova." [40]

October 1939: the "General Government" was initiated in Poland, groups of Jews from Vienna and the Protectorate were transferred to the Nisko region, and Polish Jews were forced to wear a badge distinguishing them from the surrounding population. Against the background of this deteriorating situation, the illegal immigrants continued their journey in late October, and as the barge, or so-called singing raft, docked along the Danube, scores of additional young Jewish passengers boarded the ship illegally at night. Several days later it reached Sulina, the last port on the Danube, where it docked to await a seagoing vessel.

The five hundred Jews from Prague now waiting in Sulina formed the nucleus of the full complement of illegal immigrants who were eventually to board the *Sakarya*. They were joined by a second group of several hundred Betar members who had gathered in that city in fall 1939 to await transport to Palestine. With the assistance of Revisionist immigration activist Dr. William R. Perl and the cooperation of Irgun activists in Vienna, some eight hundred illegal immigrants looking to make their way to the Danube delta congregated in Vienna. Despite the attendant risks and uncertainty, they opted to try their luck and make for Palestine rather than remain under Nazi occupation.

The five hundred Jews from Prague and the eight hundred from Vienna were joined by two additional groups: two hundred more Jews from

Vienna and four hundred from Hungary. These two latter groups had been organized in conjunction with Agudath Israel by the Irgun activist Reuven (Rudi) Hecht. Hecht, a member of a wealthy Swiss family, had become acquainted with several Irgun Delegation members as a student in Heidelberg and maintained close ties with the Irgun for many years. From 1939, at David Raziel's express request, Hecht had operated on matters of illegal Revisionist aliyah from Europe under the code name "Yerushalmi," since as a Swiss national Hecht enjoyed freedom of movement in Europe others lacked. Hecht's role in the rescue missions came to the fore in another sphere: the handsome young doctor's widespread popularity among Revisionist circles enabled him to mediate between the various factions involved in this joint venture.[41]

The nineteen hundred Jews already waiting in Sulina were complemented by several hundred illegal immigrants who had come from Poland via Romania and now wanted to join them. Threats of deportation by the Romanians if they did not find a ship within a month, and the unnerving rumors then current in the Balkans, pushed the search for a ship into high gear. Spokesmen for Perl and the Bucharest Betarites finally ironed out an agreement: Perl's representatives would take charge of finding a boat and the Betar activists would be responsible for getting everyone ashore in Palestine. Intensive efforts finally located a Turkish ship, the *Sakarya*, and arrangements were made for it to arrive in Sulina during the third week of November. The ship failed to meet this timetable, and potential immigrants and organizers alike hovered between hope and despair during the three-week delay.

But finding a ship by no means eliminated the logistical and financial problems facing the expedition's organizers. First and foremost, it was necessary to convert the Turkish coal ship into one suitable for transporting illegal immigrants. On the financial front, it was necessary to negotiate the price of the lease with the ship's owners, who now demanded thousands of pounds sterling, far beyond the original price. The two owners, dubbed "Laurel and Hardy" by Jabotinsky, were prepared for prolonged negotiations, and even brought along an attractive blond polyglot "cousin" to run the talks. For their part, the expedition's organizers sought to wrap up the negotiations with due speed. Overseas, the American Friends of a Jewish Palestine also stepped up the pace. As the money already donated by the South African NZO and the Bucharest Jewish

Council now proved insufficient, Hecht forwarded a request to Yitzhak Ben-Ami and Arieh Ben-Eliezer to immediately raise $10,000 to cover costs. Motivated by the urgency of the request, Ben-Ami and Ben-Eliezer took a daring step: they appealed to two wealthy anti-Zionist Jews, Lucius Littauer and David Donneger, for assistance. "We pleaded with them for help, asking them to forget their prejudices and react as if the people on our boats actually were en route to Paraguay. 'Please!' we implored, 'just help them out of Europe.' "[42] After a brief consultation with Rabbi Newman, who assured the two donors that the funds were earmarked for Romania, Ben-Ami and Ben-Eliezer claimed that they had succeeded in raising even more than the required amount, which they dispatched immediately to Hecht, who used it to pay the *Sakarya*'s owners.

Regarding this series of events there is an interesting difference between the Ben-Ami/Eri Jabotinsky postwar description of the operation and that appearing in Willy Perl's memoirs. While Ben-Ami and Jabotinsky claim that the money provided by the American Friends played a central role in the operation, Perl states that of the 13,200 English pounds paid to the ship owners, only 500 were provided by the American Friends. This statement is corroborated by delegation correspondence from the period. It appears, therefore, that delegation members felt a need to stress the importance of the American Friends rescue activities somewhat beyond their actual scope.[43]

It now remained to prepare the ship for sailing. In early February 1940, under cloudy skies and a biting wind, the *Sakarya* lifted anchor and sailed for Istanbul with twenty-three hundred Jews on deck. The thirteen-day sailing did not pass uneventfully. Upon reaching the Aegean Sea mechanical problems forced the ship to dock at a small port near Gallipoli where Jewish soldiers had fought under Colonel John Patterson during World War One. The immigrants' shipboard command decided to utilize this opportunity to honor the memory of the Jewish soldiers who had served there twenty-five years earlier. In his description, Eri Jabotinsky highlighted the ceremony's paradoxical nature: "Here were Jews escaping on a Turkish ship from Germany, honoring the memory of their brothers who died in British uniforms fighting the Turks; and now going to Palestine with the help of Germany, against the will of Britain, with the intention of joining the British army to fight against Germany. But at the time this seemed natural."[44]

Willy Perl provides us with a similar description: "On ships of neutral countries, young Jews of many nationalities were traveling with our organization to British-held Palestine, where they would undoubtedly join the British forces to fight the Nazis. The British tried to prevent this. The Germans not only permitted it; they aided the undertaking of providing the British with young soldiers who were doubtlessly well motivated to fight the Nazis."[45]

On the first sunny day of the voyage thirty-seven shipboard marriages were performed by the ship's captain. Each couple received an official marriage certificate, and that evening a celebration was held for all the passengers. The final stage of their journey began on 10 February when the *Sakarya* was accosted and boarded by a British warship. The trip to Haifa under armed British escort proceeded without incident. "When one of the British sailors asked Eri [Jabotinsky] what his function was on the vessel, Eri said he was a journalist traveling to gather material for a book. 'What is the title?' he was asked. '*Mare Nostrum*,' [our sea—the ancient Roman name for the Mediterranean] he replied."[46]

On 13 February 1940, four and one-half months after embarkation, the *Sakarya*'s passengers arrived at Haifa port. Eri Jabotinsky, the sole Palestinian national on board, was immediately placed under arrest on charges of assisting illegal Jewish immigration. Initially imprisoned in Acre and afterwards in the Mizra detention camp, Jabotinsky was released in early August 1940 following the death of his father. Of the 2,300 illegal immigrants on board the *Sakarya,* six Hungarian Jews who, contrary to the organizers' instructions, refused to relinquish their Hungarian passports were deported back to Hungary. The remaining passengers were placed under British arrest and some spent several months in the Sarafand and Atlit detention camps. They were released in August 1940. Seven years later one of their number was again placed under British arrest and executed on charges of Irgun activity. His name: Dov Gruner.

Wartime and postwar depictions of the *Sakarya* Expedition differ in several respects, as do the accounts by the delegation members and by outsiders such as Willy Perl. As previously stated, the first difference involved the extent of the American Friends' financial contribution, described by Perl—and backed up by wartime documentation—as being less central than the delegation members portrayed in their memoirs. This discrepancy may stem either from an honest difference in interpretation of what the term "central contribution" involved, or from a deliberate postwar attempt to emphasize the role that the American Friends played in financing illegal immigration to Palestine. The second dichotomy pertains to the form of cooperation between the various groups involved in planning the operation on the European scene. In this case the almost seamless cooperation described by Perl is not totally backed up by Jabotinsky's and Ben-Ami's descriptions, nor by wartime correspondence, something that may stem from the problematic Perl's psychological necessity to view himself as belonging to a collective Revisionist-Irgun operation. The final dichotomy centers around the extent to which the American Friends' organizational machinery became involved in this particular case of illegal immigration to Palestine. Almost all the postwar memoirs give the impression that the entire mechanism of the American Friends was galvanized into action when the desperate need for funds was communicated to New York from Europe. However, contemporary documentation shows that only the two delegation members, Ben-Ami and Ben-Eliezer—with Rabbi Newman acting as a catalyst—were involved in raising the necessary funds in this case. Could this difference stem from the delegation members' desire to draw attention away from the fact that even before the elder Jabotinsky's death in mid-1940, they were already taking over the activity within the American Friends? Was it not more politic for them to maintain the postwar assertion that it was Jabotinsky's death that paralyzed the Revisionist-Zionists in America, leaving a vacuum that delegation members were then forced to fill, and not their own desire to run the organization as they saw fit long before that date?

The *Sakarya* Expedition was but one of the expeditions partially funded by the American Friends of a Jewish Palestine. During the two-year period from 1939 to 1940, the association funded several successful aliyah bet expeditions, including the sailing of the *Parita* and the *Naomi Julia* in August and September 1939 with 850 and 1,130 passengers on board respectively. In October 1940, however, the voyage of another vessel, the *Pencho*, nearly ended in tragedy. The ship ran aground, and when it began to sink the passengers made landfall on a deserted island where they remained for ten days, subsisting on meager rations. Eventually rescued by an Italian warship, the group was taken to southern Italy, where it remained for the duration of the war.[47]

The tragedy of the *Pencho*, which followed five anxiety-filled months of traveling for its prospective passengers during which they endured hunger, internal discord, a sense of isolation, and external hostility, symbolizes the end of Revisionist-sponsored illegal aliyah during the early wartime years. Simultaneously, the last Revisionist aliyah office functioning in Europe, located in Romania, disbanded. Two additional tragedies—the detonation of the deportation ship *Patria* in Haifa harbor (1940) and the explosion and subsequent sinking of the aliyah bet ship *Struma* in Istanbul harbor (1942; Revisionist activists were involved in organizing this sailing)—ended the cooperative Irgun-NZO-Betar efforts to organize aliyah. These efforts were renewed only in 1944, made possible by changed conditions in the Balkans and southern Europe as the Allies advanced.[48]

The Irgun Delegation and the Revisionist-Zionist Movement

Apart from its declared goal of assisting illegal immigration to Palestine, the founding of the AFJP was supposed to usher in an era of cooperation between the Irgun members in the United States and the American Revisionist-Zionist movement. However, just as the sums raised by the AFJP to fund illegal aliyah sparked the rancor of the American Zionist establishment, its autonomous activity patterns fanned the flames of rivalry between leaders of the Irgun Delegation and the NZO in the United States, particularly Revisionist movement leader Zeev Jabotinsky.

Initially, delegation members Yitzhak Ben-Ami and Arieh Ben-Eliezer cooperated fully with their NZO partners in the context of the American Friends of a Jewish Palestine. According to Ben-Ami's memoir, in which the ex post facto narrative of events appears to be heavily weighted by the ultimate outcome, this apparent willingness on their part to accede to the authority of the veteran but anemic Revisionist body was essentially grounded in the brevity of their time in America and their numerical inferiority. Accordingly, he claimed, they limited their role in the joint association to a behind-the-scenes advisory capacity. But spring 1940 saw the introduction of two new factors that both changed the power balance and also marked the introduction of the growing NZO-IZL rift on the European and Palestinian fronts to the American arena: Zeev Jabotinsky's arrival in the United States to lobby for the creation of a Jewish army (see chapter 3) and the arrival of three additional Irgun activists—Alex Rafaeli,

Samuel Merlin, and Hillel Kook—to man the delegation. Inasmuch as Zeev Jabotinsky's arrival strengthened the status of the NZO members in the American Friends of a Jewish Palestine partnership, the arrival of the three Irgun activists transformed the delegation into a cohesive, active, but above all autonomous entity.

All Revisionist sources and documentation of the period—Zeev Jabotinsky's personal correspondence, delegation members' memoirs, and so forth—agree that tension between the Irgun Delegation and the NZO erupted immediately after Jabotinsky's arrival in the United States in March 1940, when he initiated a joint meeting between the American leaders of the NZO and AFJP activists in order to clarify the extent of the new entity's bent toward autonomy. Although his report to his wife in London reflected what he saw as a successful outcome to the meeting, Jabotinsky did however express concern regarding the intentions of Irgun activists who were then engaged in organizing the *Sakarya* expedition, that is, Eri Jabotinsky's coterie in Romania.[49] It is difficult to determine whether these fears were for Jabotinsky senior, the movement, or care for his son. However, with the arrival of Rafaeli, Kook, and Merlin in the United States two months later these concerns became a reality.

The addition of three more Irgun members opened a new page in delegation history. Rafaeli had only been in America for a few days when the issue of hegemony raised its head. In his memoirs Rafaeli recalls how two days later Jabotinsky asked him to discuss practical matters with Eliahu Ben-Horin. Ben-Horin was then an active party man whom Rafaeli had previously known as an Irgun officer. "He wanted facts and figures, numbers of people and details of the *Irgun* budget. This information was not available to me. . . . Had I known all these facts, however, I would have reported them only to my direct commander." Rafaeli had given Jabotinsky a general description but refused to reveal any further details to Ben-Horin. Ben-Horin and Jabotinsky reacted swiftly in turn. According to Rafaeli, Ben-Horin became incensed and forced Jabotinsky to write an official letter to Rafaeli in his capacity as an Irgun representative in the United States. "In the letter he demanded that I submit to his office full reports about all our work, in writing, and that I undertake not to initiate any political activities without his permission. I did not react. We did not enter into any further discussions, and the *Irgun* continued its political activities in the U.S. without any partisan or organisational affiliations."[50]

Rafaeli's description far from encompasses the total picture of the tension-laden interaction between himself and Zeev Jabotinsky. A more complex story emerges if we examine Jabotinsky's personal correspondence from that period. On 24 May Jabotinsky informed Yitzhak Ben-Ami in writing: "Henceforth all your activity in the United States will take place under my supervision."[51] When the delegation's members made no move toward accepting his authority, Jabotinsky even tried to block their activity by entreating his colleagues not to cooperate with the American Friends of a Jewish Palestine. "I have learned that the 'American Friends' have invited you to speak at their convention," Jabotinsky wrote to John Patterson in early June. "I sincerely hope you won't. They are not behaving as they should. Neither I nor any of my colleagues have been invited to that convention, nor to the dinner to which they have sent out dozens of invitations. . . . I have no desire for any of them to find out that I have written this to you, but imagine the position in which I will be placed if you attend their meeting. . . . I don't wish to harm them, just to larn 'em."[52] As no dinner was then planned by the American Friends of a Jewish Palestine, Jabotinsky's anger was evidently unfounded. Nonetheless, his plea to Patterson is indicative of his distressed state of mind with regard to the Irgun Delegation.

What was it about the Irgun Delegation that so pained Jabotinsky, prompting him to send a letter to a longstanding friend like Patterson in which he admitted that the Irgun arm in the United States was ignoring his very existence? Shmuel Katz has suggested that although not fully aware of the American Friends of a Jewish Palestine's true nature upon his arrival in the United States, the aged and sick Revisionist leader quickly discerned several troubling aspects. First of all, they did not submit reports of ongoing activity. It was only through a query addressed to him from London that Jabotinsky learned that he had been circumvented, that the association had forwarded suggestions concerning its relationship to the presidium without his knowledge. Furthermore, he rapidly reached the conclusion that the AFJP was not willing to promote his propaganda campaign on behalf of a Jewish army, the object of his trip to America. The association's efforts were then primarily directed to internal organization and fund-raising for Revisionist-sponsored illegal aliyah. For the AFJP, the issue of a Jewish army, which they themselves would promote strongly eighteen months later, had a low group priority in summer 1940.[53]

6. Alexander Rafaeli (left) and Vladimir Zeev Jabotinsky (right), founder of the Revisionist movement, and his wife Joanna Jabotinsky. Courtesy of Judith Tydor Baumel.

It appears that although Jabotinsky ceased to express his bitterness toward his wayward children in the United States in writing after dispatching his letter to Patterson, those feelings persisted nevertheless. In June 1940 Rafaeli went to take leave of Jabotinsky before proceeding to Chicago in order to open a delegation office there. He sought Jabotinsky out before the latter's planned appearance at a convention in New York to campaign for a Jewish army. "I went in and told him that I wanted to say goodbye as I was going away for a time. 'Where are you going?' the president asked. 'To Chicago.' 'For what?' " Rafaeli replied that a decision had been reached to open an Irgun bureau in Chicago and that he was going there to set it up. " 'Who gave you the order to go to Chicago?' the president inquired. I explained to him that it was an order, a collective decision by the Irgun members in New York in line with plans made in the Yishuv. The president became agitated and raised his voice. He began to shout . . . that it was impossible for us to do whatever we saw fit, that he was responsible for us, that we were his children and he would crush us if we refused to obey. I felt that my trip had a deleterious influence on the president, that he was very agitated, and I regretted this."[54] As we have no documentation from Jabotinsky regarding this meeting it is impossible to corroborate Rafaeli's interpretation of the events. Nevertheless, it appears that delegation members had come to a decision regarding their attitude toward the issue of Jabotinsky's authority. Notwithstanding his regrets, which troubled Rafaeli for years, they did not prevent him from carrying out his mission, just as they did not prevent Kook and the others from acting independently in New York, for all practical purposes ignoring Jabotinsky's orders.

Shortly thereafter Jabotinsky went to spend a weekend at Camp Betar in Hunter, New York, in order to more closely examine the work of the youth movement, but he collapsed upon his arrival and died several hours later. No family members were at his side: his wife, Anna, was alone in London because she had been unable to obtain an American visa, and his son, Eri, was under arrest in Palestine because of his part in the *Sakarya* Expedition. Jabotinsky's sudden death and his failure to name an heir left the Revisionist movement in shock. This disarray was even evident at Jabotinsky's funeral, which, according to some participants, showed signs of hasty organization. "I found Jabotinsky's funeral extremely depressing," one unidentified participant wrote. "Where were the Revisionists? All they do is make a lot of noise, nothing more. They blew rams' horns for 'Brit Trumpeldor' but no more than sixty or seventy people in brown shirts actually attended the funeral. . . . Even more heartbreaking was the procession to the cemetery: only seven cars and two buses accompanied the great leader in his last moments on this earth. Without counting the cantors and the discharged soldiers, there were maybe twenty participants."[55]

And how did the members of the Irgun Delegation react to Jabotinsky's death? No documentation from the period exists in order to assist us in sketching a picture of their immediate reaction in 1940, and only Alex Rafaeli referred to the issue in retrospect. "He was our leader, our spiritual father," Rafaeli remarked, "but from the moment of his death we knew that no other outsider would try to bend us to his will. The Revisionists in America were also aware of this and realized that there was now nothing to prevent us from acting as we pleased."[56] Rafaeli's remarks allude not only to the effect of the delegation's autonomous bent on its relationship with Jabotinsky, but also to its effect on the delegation's relationship with the American branch of the NZO. I have already noted the initial NZO-Irgun

Delegation cooperation within the AFJP framework, a state of affairs that changed following Jabotinsky's arrival and the addition of three members to the delegation. The Irgun representatives now felt a need to stress their independent chain of command and their idea of how public relations activities should be run, in order to highlight for their audience the distinction between them and the American Revisionists. Hillel Kook recalled their initial difficulty in expressing themselves as an independent entity: "It was not easy to come to a new country without any rearguard and to be taken under the wing or have a degree of contact with the Revisionists and have everyone proclaim: 'You're a Revisionist.' Then not only does it become necessary to defend the Revisionists against charges of being fascist, but also to convince others that you have no connection with them even though they are good people." [57]

A major issue appearing more in retrospect—in delegation members' interviews, memoirs, and so forth—than during the 1940s was their complex relationship with Jabotinsky and the American Revisionist-Zionist movement. In their memoirs delegation members emphasized that the tension between the two organizations during Jabotinsky's lifetime largely inhered in Jabotinsky's perception, rather than in the actual nature of the Irgun members' activity. This is particularly true of Hillel Kook, who basically stepped into Jabotinsky's shoes as a leadership figure: "The scope of our work may be compared to a tempest in a teacup," Kook claimed. "It's true that we were four or five young men, but we had no funds and people were actually starving. If the truth be told, at the time of my arrival we were unable to put together the two or three hundred dollars necessary for office operating expenses. Our boys faced the constant danger that they would be forced to close our small two-room office." [58]

Not only were the Irgun members engaged in a daily struggle to make ends meet, they were also engaged in a psychological battle of image versus reality, in this case dealing with the NZO's image of their activist success. Jabotinsky's death only exacerbated NZO fears that the young men from Palestine were going to co-opt the few Revisionist supporters remaining in the United States. Delegation members devoted an inordinate amount of time to this subject during their interviews and memoirs, testimony, perhaps, to the extent to which Jabotinsky's death was a watershed event in the delegation's history. The practical outcome followed apace. "After August 1940 . . . the final idyll dissipated," Samuel Merlin recalled.

"The Revisionists, like the Zionists, fought us, waylaid us, and voiced all sorts of rationalizations as to why they had to fight us and to oppose us."[59] Hillel Kook's recollections present a somewhat more complex picture, one that takes the panic that ensued in Revisionist ranks after Jabotinsky's sudden death into account. Kook claims that he was then approached by Eliahu Ben-Horin, who argued that failure to close ranks would destroy the Revisionist movement and also harm the delegation's chances for survival. Kook found this argument convincing and agreed to become a member of the NZO world presidium. He stressed, however, that this by no means meant an Irgun merger with the Revisionist party. The experiment failed. "I think I lasted less than a month," he recalled. "After several meetings I saw what I had known all along even more clearly, that a chasm existed between the ideas and the activity patterns of these people; between what they attempted, and we were uncertain as to what to do, and between our very approaches."[60]

Despite the fact that soon after Jabotinsky's death the delegation struck out from their Revisionist-Zionist colleagues and on to an independent existence, for years after the event Kook, Merlin, Ben-Ami, and to a lesser degree Rafaeli continued to agonize over and justify their failure to work together with the Revisionist movement in the United States. Did this obsession stem from a sense of dissonance between their self-proclaimed "military obedience to orders," as Rafaeli insisted, and their treatment of Jabotinsky? Or did it just emphasize the chasm between Revisionists and Irgun members that characterized the relationship between the two movements in both Palestine and the United States during this period, ultimately ending in the disappearance of the Revisionists within the Irgun's political creation—the Herut party—in 1948? Following Jabotinsky's death all sides agree that the relationship between the two organizations in the United States became tense, but there were also surprises. Two right-wing Zionist activists now drew closer to the Irgun Delegation and even acted within its framework for a time. The initial approach came from Meir Grossman, leader of the secessionist Hebrew State Party that had left the NZO in 1933. Grossman's overtures to the Irgun Delegation, initiated after Jabotinsky's death, were based on his perception that it was the sole entity possibly willing to forward his aims, which did not accept Revisionist hegemony. He maintained contacts with the delegation's members over an extended period of time, and even took an active role in the delegation's 1941–42 campaign for a Jewish army. The second approach came from Ben-Zion Netanyahu, father of the man who would later become prime minister of Israel, Benjamin Netanyahu, a leading NZO activist who was a member of Jabotinsky's spring 1940 delegation to the United States to lobby for a Jewish army. In response to the prevailing pessimistic and defeatist attitude among Revisionist circles, Netanyahu resigned from his NZO post just one week after Jabotinsky's death. Shortly thereafter Netanyahu made his first tentative overtures to Hillel Kook with an eye to joining the delegation, and in fall 1940 he became a member of the delegation executive. Netanyahu was instrumental in building relationships with several figures who later filled key roles in furthering delegation goals, including the well-known writer Pierre van Paassen, head of several delegation offshoots during the 1940s. But the delegation's partnership with Netanyahu lasted a mere six months. Each side maintained its own interpretation of the split, with Netanyahu concentrating upon practical differences while delegation members dwelled on psychological differences of attitude. Little appears in the correspondence of the period regarding the relationship with Netanyahu. "In any case I respected him," Rafaeli remarked, "but he was a revisionist and that was his mentality. He was a capable man, a professor, but we didn't feel he had the military spirit and military response to those situations which often demanded an immediate response."[61]

The most intriguing overtures then made to the delegation, which ultimately bore no fruit, came from an individual then thought to be the most extreme representative of the Zionist right wing: Abraham "Yair" Stern, founder of the IZL in Israel (later, LHI). With the outbreak of European hostilities, Stern opposed David Raziel's stand calling for a unilateral cessation of hostilities with Britain for the war's duration. During the time that the Irgun high command, including Raziel, was imprisoned by the British, this rift widened as Stern and his supporters seized the opportunity to assume command of the Irgun and to draft others to their side. Raziel's attempt to be reinstated after his release from prison met with opposition and a smear campaign by Stern, leading Raziel to tender his resignation. Although eventually persuaded to withdraw his resignation, Raziel was unable to close party ranks. On 26 June 1940 Stern's headquarters issued "order no. 112," which, for LHI supporters, marks the inception of their movement. This announcement's political orientation, which centered on founding of the "kingdom of Israel" in its historical boundaries by use of force, differed sharply from Raziel's. Irgun member Eliyahu Lankin recalled Stern making three principal demands that spelled out his essential differences with the majority group: he called for Irgun members to cease cooperating with British intelligence, insisted upon breaking off contacts with Revisionist movement leaders, and demanded the immediate resumption of anti-British acts. When the Irgun high command emphatically refused to accede to these demands, the split in Irgun ranks became a reality.[62]

News of this split swiftly came to the attention of both the American Revisionists and the Irgun Delegation. Despite an appeal by NZO leaders to Zeev Jabotinsky in mid-July to confirm Raziel's reinstatement and to call Stern to order—and instructions to that effect did circulate among Irgun members in the Yishuv—the split was already irrevocable. In a letter sent to Hillel Kook shortly before Jabotinsky's death, Raziel graphically depicted the atmosphere of mutual mudslinging within the Irgun: "There is no advice and no cure. If you lie on your right side, you are a traitor; if you lie on your left side, you are despicable; if you lie on your stomach, you have sold your birthright for a mess of pottage; if you lie on your back, you have sold your soul to the devil."[63]

During the fall months Stern made overtures to his colleagues in the United States, in what turned out to be an unsuccessful bid to draft them to his cause. In December Samuel Merlin wrote to Stern that despite their close emotional ties he could only reach a favorable decision if factually and ideologically convinced that Stern's course was the correct one, which was not the case. In his negative reply, Eri Jabotinsky argued that further factionalization of the movement wasted energy on the internal front and interfered with outer-directed activity. Jabotinsky Junior's reply also contained a personal note, in which he vented his anger at the insults Stern had leveled at his late father: "You promised me that you would respect the leader of Betar. You disobeyed his orders, but in this you were preceded by others. That is not the crux of the matter. The crux of the matter is the smear campaign against him. 'The old "Petain," he is old and even his son knows this and is with us.' That was not what we contracted for. And it was foolish."[64]

The Irgun Delegation's members' rejection of Yair's efforts to bring them into his fold and their continued loyalty to Raziel carried with it important financial consequences for Stern's group. As the Yishuv was unable to provide monetary support for the implementation of practical plans at that time, groups like the Irgun looked to their overseas branches for funding. The delegation's negative response to Stern's overtures meant that his new organization began its activity without financial support from one of the pillars of funding for Irgun activity in Palestine and in Europe.[65]

One final phase remained before the Irgun Delegation attained absolute autonomy, in theory and in practice. It was now time to begin severing its ties to Irgun headquarters in the Yishuv. This final step occurred in May 1941 in the wake of Irgun commander Raziel's death on a secret British mission in Iraq. Three years would pass until the Irgun would once again have a strong, centralized leadership, something that would only occur after Menachem Begin assumed command in 1944. Despite the dissolution of their link to the mother organization in Palestine, Irgun Delegation members continued to cooperate with Irgun-oriented factors still active in unconquered Europe, such as the London branch of the Jewish Army Committee (to be discussed in the next chapter) and Irgun representative and activist Reuven Hecht in Switzerland. This sense of being set adrift even subsequently prompted them to dispatch Arieh Ben-Eliezer to Palestine in 1943 in an attempt to close Irgun ranks. To conclude, Raziel's death marked a major stepping-stone on the Irgun Delegation's path to autonomy, essentially enabling it to develop into one of the most dynamic right-wing Zionist entities active during the Second World War.

A seminal feature of the relationship between subgroups and the mother organizations within whose framework they function is the ongoing interplay between cooperation and competition.[66] Reference to this oft-cited observation, drawn from studies of small-group functioning, is helpful in defining the coordinates of interaction between the delegation and the various branches of the Zionist right: the American NZO, "Stern's" faction, and, as we shall see, the Irgun high command in Palestine during the 1940s. Shifts toward one or the other extreme of the cooperation-competition spectrum occurred throughout. Hillel Kook's willingness to serve on the NZO presidium in the wake of Jabotinsky's death, notwithstanding his awareness of the two entities' distinctly different approaches, represents a swing toward the cooperative end of the spectrum. The delegation's attitude toward Stern's group, a faction from within a group that itself emerged through a process of factionalization, was also no little influenced by the cooperation-competition dynamic. Although the Irgun Delegation consistently moved toward practical and ideological autonomy during its formative years, it apparently did not reach unilateral decisions without at least first paying lip service to cooperation. Its blatant disregard of Jabotinsky's leadership in May 1940 and its refusal to subject delegation activity to his authority or to funnel all correspondence through him were exceptions in this respect. Discussing this episode in his biography of Zeev Jabotinsky, Irgun activist Shmuel Katz arrives at no conclusive explanation regarding what motivated the delegation members' actions. He does note, however, the unfounded nature of Jabotinsky's fear that they would back Stern.[67]

For a partial explanation of the delegation's behavior vis-à-vis Jabotinsky we must venture beyond the question of what comprised an authoritative chain of command for the delegation to the realm bounded by the poles of cooperation and competition. Alternately, we may evoke the image of a rebellious adolescent engaged in a struggle with parental authority, viewed as superfluous, old-fashioned, and irrelevant. Kook often referred to Jabotinsky as a fading symbol of authority, unable to understand that his former charges were now becoming his equals. Merlin spoke of him with a combination of respect and pity, stressing that "the old man" died at the right time. Eri Jabotinsky's love-hate relationship with his father transcended that of delegation politics; Ben-Ami's nostalgic reminiscences did not manage to mask his tone of "outgrowing" Jabotinsky's authority. Of all delegation members Alex Rafaeli tried the hardest to find an explanation for the complex interactive dynamics that developed between Jabotinsky and the group of which he should have been the proudest: "Jabotinsky treated me like a father, or like an uncle at the very least," Rafaeli remarked on more than one occasion when describing his relationship with the leader of the Revisionist movement. Fifty years later Rafaeli broached an explanation for Jabotinsky's attempt to bend the delegation to his hegemony. He surmised that the process was not initiated by Jabotinsky himself, but rather by another individual, in this case, Eliahu Ben-Horin, who viewed the delegation as a threat to NZO standing in the United States. Rafaeli's reflection seems to represent the obverse of this adolescent rebellion, part of a mature attempt to preserve a more objective image of the founding father and to smooth over the disagreements that characterized Jabotinsky's relationship with the delegation just before his untimely death.[68]

The Irgun Delegation and the American Zionist Establishment

The Jabotinsky-Irgun Delegation controversy and the delegation's subsequent split with Stern mark the final chapters in successive attempts by various Zionist right-wing elements to mold the Revisionist movement in their image or, alternately, to act autonomously within the Revisionist framework without bowing to its founder's authority. But these were internal disagreements. Concurrent with this internal movement friction, the delegation faced what appeared a more palpable danger, one their NZO colleagues shared: the American Zionist establishment's hostility, not simply to their activity but to their very existence.

At the time that the American Friends of a Jewish Palestine was formed and during the years that followed, a number of Zionist bodies were active on the American Jewish scene. Apart from organizations such as the American Jewish Congress and the Zionist Organization of America (with its affiliate organizations) discussed in the previous chapter, several additional bodies became active following the outbreak of war. One of the most important of these organizations, which would play a role in the history of the delegation, was the American Emergency Committee for Zionist Affairs (AECZA), later metamorphosing into the American Zionist Emergency Council (AZEC). This organization had been established in late 1939 and included twenty-four members representing all the major American Zionist organizations. Although Rabbi Stephen Wise chaired the organization, its day-to-day work was directed by Emmanuel Neumann, former director of the Jewish National Fund in America, who, after moving to Palestine, had become the head of the Department of Commerce and Industry of the Jewish Agency. Neumann returned to the United States for family reasons in 1940 and assumed the helm of the new organization in order to "transform America into a second front for militant Zionist action."[69] As we shall see in the next chapter, the AECZA attempted to build public support in the United States for the establishment of a Jewish fighting force and the revocation of the British White Paper of 1939 limiting Jewish immigration to Palestine. During the early 1940s there were even tentative attempts at cooperation with delegation members on these matters, the results of which will be discussed later on.

Another Zionist body active in the American arena was the New York office of the Jewish Agency for Palestine. Opened during the war, the office was directed by journalist and Zionist leader Meyer Weisgal, Dr. Chaim Weizmann's personal representative in the United States. During the war years both Neumann and Weisgal would attempt to feature a Department of Public Relations to further the Zionist cause in the United States. Hampered by problems of inter-Zionist coordination and internal Zionist fears, both would fail to reach the propaganda heights that Bergson and company would scale during the war years.[70]

How did American Zionist organizations react to the formation and activity of the American Friends of a Jewish Palestine? Initially, the Zionist establishment made no distinction between the NZO and the Irgun Delegation, viewing the delegation, as they did the NZO, as a separatist faction with dangerous fascist tendencies. However, in reports of organizations such as the AZEC or the American Jewish Congress, the AFJP received special mention not only because of its ideological leanings but because of a more practical factor. It appears that what the Jewish establishment— Zionist and non-Zionist alike—most feared was that the new entity would encroach upon its hegemony and attract followers from among its traditional supporters. In an internal memorandum the American Jewish Congress leaders summarized their view of the AFJP's true purpose: organizational competition. "Though ostensibly organized for the implementation of Jewish rights to Palestine, [the AFJP] seemed to have only one aim in view, namely, to establish a front against the authority of the Jewish agency."[71] This was not simply an ideological issue, but a practical one touching the core of the Jewish establishment's power base and the barometer of its success: its fund-raising apparatus. Time and again American Zionist organizations such as the American Jewish Congress and the American Zionist Emergency Council devoted meetings to what they saw as the financial unscrupulousness of AFJP activists. An undated AZEC memo summarized the general consensus of the Zionist administration regarding the AFJP: "These boys are stuntists, they have thrived on publicity tricks and money-jerking stunts. Like a little stage army, they come on in various forms and guises . . . but there is always one common feature, a persistent request for contributions. No serious or responsible Jewish organization can compete with them."[72]

As early as September 1939 the United Israel Appeal publicly disavowed any link between Jewish Agency and existing Zionist fund-raising apparatuses and the American Friends of a Jewish Palestine. Also directed against AFJP propaganda for aliyah and aliyah bet, the announcement stressed that only two entities—Keren HaYesod (Palestine Foundation Fund) and Keren HaKayemet (Jewish National Fund)—bore fiscal responsibility for aliyah to Palestine.[73] A similar stance was espoused in a private letter from assistant UJA director Henry Montor to Rabbi Baruch Rabinowitz, a Revisionist backer who sought clarification of the UJA's attitude toward illegal aliyah in general and the lack of establishment support for the *Sakarya* Expedition in particular. Although Montor's reply ostensibly focused on the good of the illegal immigrants and the needs of the Yishuv, its main thrust was the defamation of the American Friends of a Jewish Palestine. To his praise of "selective aliyah," Montor counterposed the claim that Revisionist policy had led to the deaths of those immigrants who were not "young men and women who are trained in Europe for productive purposes" and had received no physical or emotional preparation for the trip. "It is tragically true that scores of some of the unregistered immigrants who have been undernourished and underclothed on the unseaworthy boats that cross the Mediterranean died in the hulks of those ships," he wrote. Near the conclusion of this five-page letter Montor went so far as to state: "I think it is fair to you and to the interests with which you are concerned to point out that many of those who have been brought into Palestine by the Revisionists, on this purely money basis, have been prostitutes and criminals—certainly an element which cannot contribute to the upbuilding of a Jewish National Home in which Jews everywhere might take pride. The increased incidence of crime in Palestine in the past year is the most tragic reflection of the haphazard and irresponsible guidance of unregistered immigration by certain groups."[74]

Montor's stinging comments reflect the prevailing Zionist establishment attitude toward the Revisionist movement in general and the American Friends of a Jewish Palestine in particular. Both bodies were portrayed as groups with fascist leanings, interested primarily in supplanting the long established American Jewish and Zionist institutions in the eyes of the American Jewish public, interested only in financial gain. In particular, the Zionist organizations zeroed in on the topic of illegal immigration, attempting to convince the American Jewish public that even the AFJP's rescue attempts from Europe had a more sinister side. One example may be found in a brief pamphlet issued by the Emergency Committee for Zionist Affairs in 1940 titled "Revisionism—a Destructive Force." Published under the imprimateur of the American Zionist establishment, this pamphlet reiterated Montor's claims: "The conditions on their boats are revolting. . . . They resemble concentration camps in that passengers were hung to the mast and were refused food in retaliation for criticism or complaints. . . . The Revisionists . . . demand more money than necessary, using the surplus for their own party purposes."[75] It concluded with an appeal to prevent the entré of what it dubbed "Revisionist-Fascist" elements to the United States.

In their fight against what they saw as Jewish fascism, American Zionist organizations pulled no punches. In the spring of 1940 the American Jewish establishment attempted to sabotage a mass NZO rally by utilizing behind-the-scenes diplomacy. To recall, in March 1940 Zeev Jabotinsky came to the United States in order to lobby for a Jewish army and made his first public appearance at a mass rally held in New York in mid-March. A number of non-Jewish public figures had been drafted to express public support for the idea at a second rally planned for June, including Lord Lothian, a long-time acquaintance of Jabotinsky from Jewish battalion days who favored the creation of a Jewish army. Lothian even promised to send the British consul general in New York to the rally as an expression of his support for the Revisionist aspiration. But several days before the rally the consul canceled his appearance without explanation. AFJP inquiries disclosed that Rabbi Stephen Wise was the moving force behind the cancellation; in his personal appeal to Lothian he had made it plain that no responsible establishment American Zionist body supported Jabotinsky's ideas.[76]

Not surprisingly, the Revisionists chose not to remain passive in face of this onslaught and did battle in turn. Unable at this stage to publicly denigrate the American Zionist establishment to any great extent, they instead targeted the establishment's tendency to portray Revisionist-sponsored accomplishments as their own in their various fund-raising campaigns. Witness Yitzhak Ben-Ami's ironic comment on their use of pictures of the illegal aliyah boat *Parita* unloading its passengers on the shores of Tel Aviv in an August 1940 letter to the UJA. He wrote: "Of course we do not object to the publicity given to the 'Parita' but we feel it will not be asking too much if, in the future, whenever the picture of the

'Parita' appears in your publications, a foot-note should be added to the effect that the 'Parita's' voyage with her 800 passengers was enabled through the means raised in the United States by the American Friends of a Jewish Palestine."[77]

∗ ∗ ∗

What motivated the American Zionist establishment's campaign against the American Friends of a Jewish Palestine? Was it simply an additional facet of their anti-Revisionist policy, or was there another dynamic at work here, unique to the Zionist establishment-Irgun Delegation relationship? Testimony by delegation activists and from contemporary publications suggests that many American Jewish leaders had difficulty distinguishing between the Irgun Delegation and other Revisionist activists in the United States. This supposition is supported by the statements of various American Zionist establishment activists regarding the AFJP and later delegation groups. A typical example is found in a memo from Zionist activist Meyer Weisgal, Chaim Weizmann's personal representative in the United States. In this memo Weisgal speaks of the NZO and the delegation as one body, even claiming that the NZO had co-opted Kook and his cohorts ("they are under their control"), something that was far from the truth.[78] However, even clarification of its autonomous status, distinct ideology, and different activist stance did not put an end to the sharp antidelegation establishment policy.

One reason for this opposition was traditional-existential: the instinctive hostility on the part of established organizations to any newcomer. Simply the entry of such an entity to the organizational arena automatically elicits a defensive response from existing organizations, pending clarification of the new entity's nature.

Furthermore, there is also the ideological factor. The American Zionist establishment adhered to firmly entrenched Zionist Federation policy, in effect from the 1930s when the Revisionist movement seceded and founded the NZO: strong opposition to all right-wing bodies on the Zionist spectrum. Establishment Zionist propaganda undiscriminatingly termed all right-wing organizations "fascist" and treated them accordingly. At a joint meeting of Zionist establishment representatives and those of the Revisionist movement, Zionist activist Meyer Weisgal, surprised at the number of participants, stated jokingly: "I thought I would only have to annihilate Natanyahu [*sic*]" (head of the NZO in the United States).[79] This perception sheds light on the willingness of some Zionist establishment elements to cooperate with the FBI against Irgun Delegation members, a decade-long trend that had its inception in 1940. An August 1940 memorandum from FBI Chief J. Edgar Hoover to his New York office noted that an informer had brought to his attention articles from the Yiddish press advocating the formation of secret armed Zionist units for the purpose of carrying out anti-Arab raids in Palestine. The memo concluded that these articles "appear to emanate from the office at 285 Madison Avenue. This Office appears to be occupied by one Y. Ben-Ami." When viewed in the context of the 1940s, in the eyes of much of the American Zionist establishment, the delegation's "fascist" leanings legitimated using even these methods in order to remove what they considered a mortal danger to the Zionist movement.[80]

A third factor is linked to what the sociologist Samuel Halperin has termed "the barometer of the power and influence of the Zionist movement within the American Jewish community,"[81] that is, the issue of fundraising. Halperin attributes a major role in the increasing power of the American Jewish community to the philanthropic network. Consequently, any entity that threatened the existing hegemony automatically suffered one of two fates. If a "friendly" organization, with a program not in ideological opposition to the current dominant institutional policy line, efforts would be made to incorporate it in an existing framework as a means of preventing reallocation of finite resources to a larger number of groups. If, however, defined as "hostile," as the American Friends of a Jewish Palestine was perceived as being, efforts would be made to isolate the group and to cast it in a negative light in order to drive a wedge between it and potential donors. Not only were the American Friends of a Jewish Palestine "foreigners" possessed of a "hostile ideology"—characteristics they shared with the American Zionist right wing—they also demonstrated striking ability in an area at which their Revisionist colleagues had been largely unsuccessful: fund-raising. Their rapid penetration of the American Jewish philanthropic network quickly placed the AFJP in the category of "hostile" factors that must be fought at all costs. The establishment ban on the American Friends of a Jewish Palestine was sweeping and unequivocal. Synagogue doors, the main venue for Jewish fund-raising, were barred to them; defamatory flyers were disseminated by the Zionist and

United Jewish Appeals; and behind-the-scenes diplomacy aimed at denying the group legitimacy was exercised, consequently affecting its economic survival.

Despite these consistent establishment efforts to isolate the Irgun Delegation and its members, the American Friends of a Jewish Palestine and later delegation offshoots began to break through the organized American Jewish community's philanthropic monopoly. This success was a result of the delegation's unique perception of potential financial sources in the United States. From the outset, delegation members, under Hillel Kook's leadership, were guided by the understanding that although they could not hope to penetrate the existing philanthropic monopoly, they could bypass it by appealing to elements, Jewish and American, that did not normally support Jewish causes. By this means alone were delegation members able to assure themselves of economic viability and thus to place their causes on the public agenda. Most important were the methods they began to employ in order to reach their public: propaganda techniques that were far removed from what that public was accustomed to. These included loud, colorful public campaigns, intensive activist diplomacy, the creation of an outsider's pact with Jewish organizations that were either not part of or on establishment fringes, and the drafting of support from non-Jewish entities. All provide the key to understanding the dynamic that enabled delegation members to remain in the public eye and the public pocket for almost a decade. These public relations tactics, enlarged and expanded upon by the delegation's later organizational creations, will be analyzed in the following chapters.

The operative buildup of the Irgun Delegation took place by phases. Studies of group dynamics isolate five stages in the development and functioning of groups devoted to promoting a specific cause. The first stage, "forming," is characterized by caution and even acrimony as those involved essay to create a network of internal relationships and operative patterns that will both further group aims and foster successful cooperation. In the second stage, termed "storming," the activists respond to situational needs, test the boundaries of external authority, and gain confidence in their task-filling ability. For the third stage, called "norming," exemplary order in group activity, with group members internalizing the behavioral and activity norms that guarantee their success, is characteristic. The fourth phase is "performing," during which the activists concentrate on necessary tasks now that problems of friendship, orientation, leadership, and functioning are no longer on the agenda. The final stage, "adjourning," is characterized by the realization of the group's declared aims and its disbandment or transmutation.[82]

With regard to the Irgun Delegation, the years from 1939 to 1940 incorporate two concurrent stories. On the one hand, these were the years when the American Friends of a Jewish Palestine, a group that never officially disbanded, was active. Thus these years may be treated as an independent unit that exemplifies all of the five above-mentioned organizational phases. Concurrently, however, these years also represent the formative stage of delegation activity in the United States, during which its members learned how to transfer their successful cooperation from the European and Yishuv fronts to a new and unknown venue: the American arena. The ever-increasing tension with their colleagues in the Revisionist movement, and even more so with their rivals in the American Zionist establishment, catalyzed group crystallization and influenced its decision to seek new avenues of support outside this establishment's immediate Jewish and Zionist environment. Although the cessation of Revisionist illegal aliyah in late 1940 could have spelled the death knell for Irgun Delegation activity in the United States, in actuality it marked the shift from the stage of "forming" to "storming." Instead of "closing up shop," delegation activists responded to the newly defined needs and aims of the hour by adopting an old-new cause, long espoused by the elder Jabotinsky: the establishment of a Jewish army. The shift to activity on behalf of founding a Jewish army in 1941 therefore marks but another stage in the maturation of the Irgun Delegation, a critical step in its transformation into a permanent and colorful addition to the activist entities on the American Jewish organizational scene during the 1940s.

A Time to Fight

The Committee for a Jewish Army
of Palestinian and Stateless Jews, 1941–1942

Stage One: Establishing the Committee for a Jewish Army

Spring 1941. The undefeated German army was on the offensive in an effort to convert the Mediterranean into an Axis mare nostrum. In March Bulgaria joined the Axis powers as the Germans beefed up their military presence in the Balkans. Several weeks later, after a massive German onslaught, Greece and Yugoslavia became the latest victims of the Third Reich, bringing the Balkan region under German control and cutting off access to the Danube—the sole remaining escape route for the Jews of Eastern Europe. Yugoslavia would soon serve as a testing ground for the "Final Solution" to the Jewish problem, and thousands would be systematically murdered in the course of this experimentation to find an expeditious means of making Europe *judenrein*.

German forces were advancing on the African front as well. In April troops under General Rommel's command landed in North Africa, opening a campaign that potentially threatened all residents of the British Middle Eastern sphere of influence. In response the British drafted all available manpower, including Yishuv volunteers. These volunteers, organized as a local militia under British command, both stood guard and carried out special missions, including an ill-fated May 1941 attempt to sabotage Tripoli's refineries during which its twenty-three participants disappeared en route. But all this activity was simply a prelude to the main engagement of the war. On 22 June Germany breached the Ribbentrop-Molotov pact and invaded Russia with an eye to eliminating the "Bolshevik danger." The curtain now rose on what may be termed the dawning of the end: the implementation of the first stage of what came to be known as the Final Solution to the Jewish question in Europe.

The Idea of a Jewish Army

Spring 1941 found the Irgun Delegation at an organizational and ideological crossroads. In his memoir Yitzhak Ben-Ami reevoked the pessimistic atmosphere surrounding their efforts from late 1940 on: "By the end of 1940, our mass rescue work was nearing its end. Our mission in the United States was a financial failure. Our east-central European organization was in ruins. There was not much we could do. The only regret we had was that we had not had the money and support to break more 'laws' during the critical years 1937 to 1940." [1]

In reality, this was an oversimplification. By late 1940 all the basic mechanisms for continued organizational life were already in place. From summer 1940 on, Alex Rafaeli had been involved in laying the groundwork for drawing new sectors into delegation efforts by extending delegation activity to Chicago, the Midwest, and the West Coast. There, California MGM executive Bernie Feinman, the brother of delegation supporter Frances Gunther, assisted Rafaeli to approach Hollywood movie industry personalities. "I had come from the somber world of European war and was now in the midst of Hollywood's bubbling creativity," Rafaeli recalled. "Many of the writers were knowledgeable and well-informed about the situation in the Middle East. Politically, this group leaned to the left and quite a few of them were Communists, either card-carrying or armchair ones, but I refrained from ideological discussions." [2]

Rafaeli rapidly succeeded in organizing a committee drawn from a broad spectrum of Hollywood activists prepared to work toward implementing the delegation's goals as then formulated. He was assisted in these efforts by Miriam Heyman, an Irgun activist who had come from Palestine and subsequently married Bernie Feinman. Consequently, Los Angeles became one of three centers of delegation activity, along with Chicago and New York. However, the changing situation in Europe in late 1940, causing the aliyah bet centers to close down and cutting off access to the Danube, spelled the end of delegation fund-raising for Revisionist-sponsored illegal aliyah. Would the group now find ways to direct the support it had amassed to new aims? And if so, what goal was compatible with the group's ideological credo, wartime exigencies, and its supporters' psychological needs?

Alex Rafaeli recalled his version of how the group underwent its first organizational metamorphosis: finding themselves at a crossroads in early 1941, the "boys" were unsure how to proceed. "On the one hand, we were already on the 'map,' with two successful campaigns to our credit," having raised considerable funds for Revisionist illegal immigration and built a nationwide support network. "We had also become entirely autonomous after Razi's [David Raziel] death, and our links to the American NZO were increasingly tenuous." On the other hand, the group faced a dilemma, unable to amass support for Revisionist aliyah bet because by 1941 there was no more illegal immigration. Nor could the group raise funds directly for the Irgun in the Yishuv, something that would have endangered its members' status in the United States. "We were left with two options: either to change direction or to close up shop. And then the idea which Jabotinsky had come to the United States to promote a year earlier resurfaced and we directed our efforts toward founding a Jewish army." [3]

Hillel Kook reiterated Rafaeli's version of events, recalling the group's response as aliyah bet was dropped from the delegation's agenda: "Our initial direction was to continue thinking and searching." However, as Jabotinsky had come to America to promote the idea of a Jewish army, the group then decided to take the idea under its wing, regardless of the fact that it had once been part of the Revisionist party's platform. "It was the right idea, a fitting one for members of the Irgun Zeva'i Leumi, and we now decided to work toward the formation of a separate Jewish army." [4]

Kook's comments evoke a composite portrait of a period characterized by perplexity, exploration, and compromise, ultimately concluding with the choice of a new and carefully considered goal. This complexity, however, receives scant expression in Revisionist historiography such as David Niv's *Battle for Freedom: The Irgun Zvai Leumi* (1976). Niv depicts the delegation's switch in goals as a self-evident step, presenting Rafaeli's and Ben-Ami's induction into the American army as being integrally linked to the delegation's broader campaign. This portrayal is far more simplistic than Kook's and Rafaeli's aforementioned descriptions, which focus on the group's prolonged search for a new and appropriate direction. Furthermore, an examination of delegation wartime correspondence and memoirs points to a variety of factors that provoked Rafaeli's and Ben-Ami's enlistment in the American army. None of them supports Niv's theory connecting this step to any metamorphosis in the group's goals.[5] Here again one can see the importance of examining the delegation members' self-image using both their recollections and wartime correspondence in order to balance the picture presented by the existing literature emanating from both within and without the Zionist movement.

Yet another dichotomy between wartime documentation and Niv's later reconstruction focuses upon the issues of communication and ideological overseas coordination: to what extent were delegation members aware of the debate raging among right-wing Yishuv circles—the NZO, Betar, and the Irgun—regarding enlistment in the British army? Niv claims that when the delegation adopted the idea of a Jewish army its members were unaware of this controversy. However, he ignores the fact that Eri Jabotinsky had left Palestine to join the delegation just as this debate was at its height in NZO and Irgun circles. In both instances it appears that, in the interest of presenting a united front, "official" Revisionist historiography chose to deliberately play down contemporary internal divisions within the Zionist right wing. By its very two-dimensionality this portrait obscures both the complex interaction between the main factions of the Zionist right and the Revisionist interaction with the Zionist movement in toto.

One example of this tendency is the fact that official Revisionist historiography attributes sole authorship of the idea of a Jewish army to Zeev Jabotinsky, ignoring the role of other Zionist leaders in furthering the idea of a Jewish fighting force. Although Jabotinsky had formulated the establishment of a Jewish army on all Allied fronts in 1939 as one of his main goals for the Jewish people as a whole, in reality the topic of a Jewish army had been on the Zionist agenda even before the outbreak of World War II and remained the central political issue on this agenda for almost two years.[6] Not only was it based on the desire to wreak vengeance on the Nazi foe, it was also seen as protecting the Yishuv from invasion and Arab uprisings, providing greater weight to the Zionist movement's diplomatic struggle and enhancing the Jewish bargaining position vis-à-vis the British at the war's end. Finally, it was hoped that creating such an army would constitute another step in the Yishuv's increased military empowerment.

As early as 1938 Yishuv representatives had approached British military personnel regarding this possibility. In an official letter to the British prime minister, sent two days after the outbreak of the Second World War, Chaim Weizmann proposed the services of the Jewish people in the anti-Nazi campaign. This proposal, and the vague noncommittal nature of the British reply, marked the beginning of a struggle involving forces from the entire Zionist spectrum, one that eventually culminated in the formation of the Jewish Brigade in 1944.[7]

During 1939 both Chaim Weizmann and Zeev Jabotinsky opened parallel channels of communication with the Chamberlain government concerning formation of a Jewish army, envisioned as a sort of legion that would renew the historic Zionist-British alliance of the First World War. Contacts between the Zionist leadership and the British government recommenced after May 1940 following the Nazi invasion of Western Europe and the formation of the Churchill government. However, attempts by NZO representatives to meet with Churchill were rejected out of hand.[8] Jabotinsky was then already in the United States, having decided to continue lobbying indirectly for a Jewish army, utilizing American pressure to force the issue. In a telegram sent to Churchill from the United States he projected "130,000 inductees in the eastern hemisphere alone, together with a worldwide network of centers which will project a new attitude to the allies among those of all beliefs."[9]

Jabotinsky then decided that the time had come to activate a massive diplomatic effort to further his goal. In an attempt to open a direct diplomatic channel to Whitehall, Jabotinsky's representatives in the United States contacted the British ambassador, Lord Lothian, who, in his conversations with these American NZO representatives, made no secret of his admiration for the Revisionist leader. Lothian agreed to employ the diplomatic means at his disposal to promote the campaign and even promised to send an official representative to a rally that the Revisionists were organizing. At this point the American Jewish establishment entered the picture. Well aware of Jabotinsky's efforts in Britain to further the idea of a Jewish fighting force, the Zionist establishment had adopted a "wait-and-see" policy regarding the Revisionist leader's efforts. Now that he had approached the British ambassador, representatives of the anti-Revisionist camp, spearheaded by Rabbi Stephen S. Wise, made the American Zionist establishment's compelling opposition to Jabotinsky's program unequivocally clear. Unwilling to become a pawn in what appeared to be internecine warfare, Lothian withdrew his support for the scheme and reneged upon his promise to appear at the public rally. For Jabotinsky, whose unstinting British orientation was undergoing a metamorphosis, this was a mortal blow.[10]

Jabotinsky's untimely death in the summer of 1940 appeared to have suspended NZO involvement in efforts to promote the idea of a Jewish fighting force. Meanwhile, it seemed that Weizmann's efforts on this front were about to bear fruit. However, beginning in early January 1941, British support for the planned Jewish army underwent constant regression, culminating in a decision taken by the newly appointed minister of colonial affairs, Lord Moyne, in February 1941 to retract his support for the program. Palestinian Jews wishing to take part in the armed anti-Nazi struggle now had but one option at their disposal: enlistment in the British army, a much-debated step within the Zionist movement as a whole. As for "stateless Jews," they had neither means nor opportunity to participate in the military campaign against Nazi Germany.

Not only does the 1939–40 campaign for a Jewish army reveal an ever-widening rift between Revisionists and the Zionist leadership, it also sheds light on a serious internal breach within the Zionist leadership. The frequent dissension between Weizmann and Ben-Gurion that characterized this campaign, grounded in the different tactics each employed in negotiating with the British, also reflects their bitter internecine struggle for hegemony of the Zionist movement. In his study of volunteering, Yoav Gelber submits that, given the circumstances prevailing in 1940–41, the idea of founding a Jewish army was not overly ambitious, that a combined Weizmann/Ben-Gurion approach might have assisted in bridging the modest gap between the formal October 1940 British decision to found a Jewish fighting force and its realization. On the other hand, Revisionist activity on this speculative front of potential cooperation was conspicuously absent until the autumn of 1940, a further indication of the paralysis in NZO ranks after Jabotinsky's death and of the fact that the Irgun Delegation had not yet definitively fixed its new organizational aim.[11]

The Jewish Army Committee

The delegation's decision to promote a campaign for a Jewish army was the outcome of a six-month-long ideological and practical debate that began in early 1941. In his recollections Hillel Kook noted how the sense of being cut loose fostered creation of an ideological hothouse in which the idea of a Jewish army slowly came to fruition in its uniquely delegation form. "We searched and searched [for an idea]—we the Irgun members in the Diaspora who remained 'cut off' in America. . . . It took us a long time to reorganize as we were a small, weak, impoverished entity."[12] Kook's emphasis on the group's metamorphosis was echoed by the few letters left from this period appearing in private collections and the Jabotinsky Archives. Samuel Merlin in particular noted the sense of limbo in his wartime correspondence with Ben-Ami and Rafaeli.[13] This sense of being cut off to which Kook referred was engendered by several factors: the Irgun's disintegration in the Yishuv, irregular mail service between the United States and the Middle East caused by wartime developments, and draconian British censorship of outgoing mail from Palestine. Concurrently, this very same feeling of limbo that had temporarily drawn the Irgun Delegation closer to its American NZO colleagues now caused its members to think twice before adopting an idea so closely identified with the Revisionist movement. The decision to nevertheless adopt the Jewish army issue signified a stage in the delegation's maturation and was a significant gauge of its increasing dissociation from the American Revisionist movement.[14]

Six months before the Jewish Army Committee was officially inaugurated, delegation members took a first practical step toward amassing support for the founding of a Jewish fighting force. On 25 June 1941 the American Friends of a Jewish Palestine organized a huge rally in New York in order to stimulate public awareness of the acute need for a Jewish army. Its organizers—Irgun Delegation members and NZO activists—saw it both as a means of drafting support and also as a trial balloon for determining possible future directions.[15] Germany's invasion of the Soviet Union a few days earlier strengthened Kook's resolve to adopt the idea of a Jewish army as the delegation's theme, but although its direction was now clear, the delegation's initial steps were hesitant. By what means could the organization-in-the-making best obtain maximum public exposure and broad-based public support? Putting their hard-won knowledge of the rules for molding American public opinion to use, Kook and delegation members eventually thrashed out a game plan: first convince a qualitative minority of the justice of your cause and the masses will follow suit. During this tentative phase they sent a circular to one hundred public figures whose names appeared in *Who's Who in America*, arguing the imperative need for a Jewish army and asking addressees to lend their name to the committee now being formed. If they agreed (and a notable proportion did), their names would then appear in the new circular sent to an additional hundred people, a process repeated until thousands had agreed to join the committee. Hundreds of people "starred" in the petitions, advertisements, and leaflets distributed throughout the delegation's campaign for a Jewish army.

"The secret was simple," Eri Jabotinsky wrote in 1943. "The Committee for a Jewish Army was a non-sectarian, non-partisan, American organisation. It was not a Jewish organisation. The principle was that we, a group of anonymous Palestinians, approached the American public with a request to help us in our enterprise. We didn't pose as the representatives of any movement or any party. We were just representing an idea and asking those who were in accord with our arguments to give us the support of their name." [16]

In this wartime letter Eri Jabotinsky highlights one of the main "selling points" of several delegation-based organizations: the fact that the American public in general, and with it parts of the American Jewish public, were unaware of the delegation members' political affiliation. Furthermore, as internal memoranda of organizations such as the American Zionist Emergency Council, calling them "stuntists, thriving on publicity tricks and money-jerking stunts," had not yet been made public, they hoped their anonymity would assist their cause.[17] Consequently, Kook, Merlin, Rafaeli, Ben-Ami, Ben-Eliezer, and Eri Jabotinsky saw themselves as having a good chance of creating an organizational apparatus that would attempt to raise the issue of a Jewish army by creatively manipulating American and American Jewish public opinion.

And succeed they did. During 1941, with Irma Helpern's assistance, the delegation managed to draft hundreds of staunch supporters to its cause, some of whom maintained their association with the group throughout some or all of its metamorphoses. Certain individuals such as Senators Guy M. Gillette, Will Rogers, Jr., and Andrew L. Somers were active in the political arena; others, like the writer Pierre van Paassen and the publisher William Randolph Hearst, assisted in advertising and also filled important official roles on the committee. Of these varied supporters, the most flamboyant, and the one who also became the Jewish Army Committee's moving spirit, was the Jewish writer Ben Hecht.[18]

Hecht (1893–1964) was the prototype of the proud Jew to whom the delegation hoped to appeal: an assimilated intellectual Jew divorced from his Jewishness until sparked to greater consciousness of his roots by circumstances, and not by invoking pathos or Jewish suffering. The New York-born writer, playwright, and journalist was raised in Wisconsin, the heart of American Protestantism, and until 1939 his tenuous connection with Judaism consisted mainly of efforts to convince his employers that he was an Orthodox Jew in order to receive five extra days of annual leave. While stationed in Berlin as a journalist from 1919 to 1920 Hecht developed a profound hatred for the German people, something that later played a central role in his ideological and personal volte-face after Hitler's rise to power.

Hecht recalled how he rediscovered his Jewishness in 1939, in the wake of the war's outbreak. "In that year I became a Jew and looked on the world with Jewish eyes," he wrote.[19] Initially drawn to organizations seeking to increase American involvement in the war, he then published several emotional essays proclaiming his self-image as both a proud Jew and a proud American. One of these essays, appearing in the popular magazine *PM* in 1941, came to Kook's attention, and he immediately scheduled a meeting with the individual slated to become the delegation's number one public relations wizard. In their initial encounter with Hecht in April 1941, Kook and Irma Helpern billed themselves not as Irgun members, and not even as Jews from Palestine, but as "admirers of the journalist." Their conversation opened with a topic close to Hecht's heart, criticism of American Jewish neutrality, and Hecht experienced an almost immediate sense of rapport with his visitors. In his memoir Hecht recalled his first meeting with the men who were to change his life and political orientation. Ordering a third round of drinks for his guests, the playwright was unaware that neither had eaten that day. "They kept their eyes firmly averted from the platters of fine food moving to and fro under their noses—for they were Hebrew heroes trained in self-discipline." Facing Hecht, Kook began by admiring his host's point of view rather extravagantly and then began to regale him with tales of Zeev Jabotinsky, of whom Hecht had never heard. "Being allied with the creator of a Jewish renaissance made me nervous, for I had no such dreams in me. But Bergson spoke the name Jabotinsky with such pride that I asked to meet him and learned that he had died recently in New York."[20]

It was only at their second meeting that Kook articulated a concrete proposal to Hecht to become American leader of their cause, even if the nature of this cause remained somewhat vague. "I had not quite understood what this cause was, beyond that it had to do with Jews and raising millions of dollars to improve their status in Palestine," Hecht recalled in his memoir.[21] But it was already clear to Hecht that his destiny was linked to that of these individuals—his "soul mates," as Kook put it. Thus Hecht became one of what the Zionist establishment termed the Bergsonites, a group for whom Hillel Kook was undisputed oracle, guide, ideologist, and archetypal new Zionist man, the future pride of the entire Jewish world.

While Kook and Merlin were busy wooing Hecht in New York, on the West Coast Alex Rafaeli continued his efforts to draft supporters from among Hollywood writers and its intellectual elite. He described their response: "The usual questions emerged: 'Why do Zionists disapprove of the *Irgun?* Why don't you wait with your problems until after the war? Why do you bother the British when they are fighting a war which is also yours?' But even they changed their minds when we succeeded in showing that, unless we acted, the German murderers may not leave any Jews alive in Europe." This backing by Hollywood personalities was crucial to delegation success, as film world items were featured prominently in the American media. Alex Rafaeli attributed even broader significance to these connections when he claimed that "our later success on Capitol Hill was probably due, at least to some extent, to these early contacts with the film community."[22]

How accurate was this supposition? Did Rafaeli's comment mirror reality or was it an expression of a delegation member's having fallen into his own public relations trap? What did he mean by "success" on Capitol Hill? The answers to these questions depend upon who is being asked. Delegation members, both in wartime correspondence and in their memoirs, reiterate how connections with public figures in the arts and other fields were instrumental in opening doors for them in "high places," in other words, in Washington. The American Jewish establishment scorned this supposition, stating that "show" was just that and little more. However even if they received the red carpet treatment in certain Washington circles, albeit very few, did this access ensure success in attempting to further their various causes, in this case that of the Jewish army? There is little proof for this claim and, as we will see in the latter part of this chapter, there is also little proof of their success in terms of creating a Jewish army. However, for the rest of their lives, delegation members were certain that their political connections, which, in their minds were the route to organizational success, had been furthered by what Rafaeli had once called the "three M's": media, Mafia, and movie moguls.[23]

Fall 1941 saw final preparations for the founding of a group to promote the cause of a Jewish army. Task division among delegation members, initially cultivated in response to circumstances, now became institutionalized. As "first among equals," it was Hillel Kook who initiated contacts with other national liberation movements (such as the Irish, Yugoslav, Czech, Polish, Korean, Chinese, and Free French) in order to foster cooperation on matters of a technical nature and to jointly mold public opinion. Eri Jabotinsky served as a sort of roving delegate. Merlin, the group ideologist whose sphere of responsibility lay in disseminating propaganda material, was the sole group member to remain in New York full-time, whereas Ben-Ami, Ben-Eliezer, and Rafaeli were assigned to different geographical areas as regional heads of the proposed entity. From time to time the trio returned to New York for weekend meetings and to reevaluate their tactics in light of changing conditions. Irma Helpern looked to England, and a decision was reached to send him overseas to promote the cause of a Jewish army as soon as the American committee had gathered momentum.[24]

The delegation's organizational division of labor, ostensibly a way of ensuring their success by utilizing each member's field of expertise, was also a means of limiting personal and political friction. Although post-delegation correspondence and members' memoirs attempt to portray the harmonious relationships that developed within the group, the truth was more complicated. In reality, it was the large geographical distance that existed between many of the members that allowed them to work in peace with each other, and, as we shall see, even that ostensibly seamless working relationship made it an optimal decision for four of the six members to return to Palestine or to depart for the European scene, either as delegation emissaries or as active participants in the fight against Nazism.

Obstacles hindered the delegation's quest for Jewish grassroots support. Under the influence of the American Jewish establishment, synagogue and Jewish community centers barred their doors to delegation members, who continued nonetheless to promote the Jewish army cause in informal settings and in private homes. In his memoir, Arieh Ben-Eliezer blasted the "establishment," as he termed it, which used any and all means to prevent public appearances by the Irgun activists. In late summer 1941, Jewish establishment interference prevented delegation activists from holding fund-raising bingo games at a resort hotel in Atlantic City. Left as a result with no alternate source of funds, the delegation was forced to cancel its entire calendar of scheduled events for that summer.[25]

Fear of Jewish establishment antagonism dogged the delegation's steps throughout, a muted but dangerous undercurrent. Hillel Kook used to argue that the vigor with which the Zionists pursued their antidelegation campaign was directly correlated to delegation success. "Year by year we became larger, stronger, and more successful and the war [against us] grew yearly." Consequently, preparatory fieldwork for the founding of the Jewish Army Committee proceeded clandestinely. "We refrained from informing individuals with ties to the Revisionists or any other Zionist movement branch [of our plans] so that they would not be able to fight us before we had achieved a level of strength."[26]

How accurate were Kook's recollections? Did the entire American Jewish and American Zionist establishment adhere to the policy of thwarting the delegation at every opportunity? Examination of AZEC correspondence shows that although many, if not most, establishment leaders did see the delegation as a threat and attempted to influence others against joining the various organizations that its members founded, until mid-1942 their war on the delegation had not yet become an all-out battle.[27] Even after that date, American Jewish leaders such as Bnai Brith chairman Henry Monsky were often hesitant to use all the weapons at their disposal in their battle against delegation activities, particularly in view of the fact that they were aware of the growing public support for what appeared as an activist, anti-Nazi, humanitarian entity.[28]

News of developments on the European front, which slowly but consistently began reaching the free world, also catalyzed the committee's establishment. Following the German advance on the eastern front, *Einsatzgruppen* began to implement their primary objective: ridding the conquered Soviet territories of political commissars and Jews. In September 1941 German forces conquered Kiev, murdering 34,000 Kiev Jews at Babi Yar a few days later. October saw the creation of a "model ghetto" at Terezin with transports of Reich Jews simultaneously being sent to the

Lodz, Minsk, Riga, and Kovno ghettos. Concurrently, thousands of Jews were murdered in Belgrade and Odessa. In November the infamous Auschwitz II, or Birkenau camp, was founded, another step marking the widening implementation of the Final Solution from the Russian to the Polish arena. This camp, the last earthly station for over a million European Jews, would ultimately come to symbolize the Final Solution.

Domestic developments on the American scene also contributed to the committee founders' sense of urgency. Beginning with the Soviet entry into the war, American isolationists gave public vent to their anti-Semitic sentiments; one such example is the speech in which the famed flyer Charles Lindbergh argued that the British, the Jews, and the Roosevelt administration were pushing the United States into the war, going on to name the "Jewish danger" embodied in Jewish influence on the movie industry, the radio, and journalistic media. An official study of anti-Semitism in the United States from 1941 noted the existence of more than 120 American associations thought to be anti-Semitic to varying degrees, and concluded that under certain circumstances, such as war, economic depression, or massive Jewish immigration, the phenomenon of anti-Semitism was liable to achieve wider currency.[29]

In late 1941 Kook and his coterie announced the founding of an organization to promote the cause of a Jewish army. The timing of this step was motivated by a number of factors: their awareness of the European military situation, fear of Jewish capitulation to rising anti-Semitism in the United States, and desire to keep up the momentum of delegation activity. Unlike other Jewish organizational proclamations that traditionally echoed from New York, Kook issued his announcement in Washington, D.C., a first step in transferring all delegation diplomatic activity to the American capital, something that he saw as imperative if the delegation were to exercise political influence. Moreover, this geographical relocation also symbolized a conscious decision to act concurrently in two arenas: public and diplomatic. Their strategy called for placing nationwide public activity under the aegis of local delegation offices and for pursuing diplomatic activity in Congress and the American administration under the aegis of a permanent delegation on Capitol Hill. Thus, the move to Washington not only marks a new stage in delegation activity but also reveals a new twist to its modus operandi.

The Jewish Army Committee was officially inaugurated on Thursday,

4 December 1941, at the height of a convention held at a centrally located Washington hotel. Its founding session was chaired by Dr. Samuel Harden Church of the Carnegie Foundation, and the writer Pierre van Paassen assumed presidency of the committee. Alfred Strelsin and Meir Grossman were appointed vice presidents. Of the delegation's members, Hillel Kook alone filled an official capacity on the committee as its "national director." By its very makeup the Jewish Army Committee divulges Kook's tactical slant, one he employed repeatedly in all delegation offshoots. By drafting non-Jewish figures to key positions, he enabled the organizations to adopt a nonsectarian label, and, in order to widen his support base and neutralize potential sabotage by the Zionist right wing, he endeavored to bring additional right-wing Zionist elements into the organizations. Both of these tactics had a common aim: the effort to play down the delegation's role in each new offshoot.[30]

In essence, the new organization's game plan, as set forth in a memorandum, combined ideology and tactics: "The purpose of the committee was to bring about, legally and according to American foreign policy, the establishment of a Jewish army which would fight for the survival of the Jewish people and the preservation of democracy. This army, consisting primarily of Palestinian Jews, refugees, stateless Jews and volunteers from free countries, would fight in every battlefield to which it would be sent, side by side with the American, British and other Allied Armies."[31] It further proposed that the American administration lend public support to the idea of a Jewish army, that a presidential appointee assist in its organization, that refugees and stateless Jews be drafted to this army, that its members wear a special insignia to indicate its uniqueness, and above all that the American administration pressure the British to support the establishment of such an army.

Semantic choices often shed light not only on the practical dynamic that the speaker wishes to set in motion, but also on the underlying psychological mechanism for his remarks. The weight assigned to "legally and according to American foreign policy" and to "the preservation of democracy" demonstrates how keenly Kook apprehended the essential nature of his playing field for this contest: urbanized Judaism, committed Christianity, and the American Congress. This new direction is also apparent in the means Kook employed to promote his campaign: full-page newspaper ads, propaganda leaflets, radio broadcasts, fund-raising dinners, and petitions.

Even Pierre van Paassen's speech at the founding convention reflects a comparable approach and understanding: "This Committee feels that humanity, *Christianity*, the very ideals for which we are said to be fighting this war, are embodied in the demand for a Jewish army" (emphasis mine—J.T.B.).[32]

Kook and his associates' conception of a Jewish army was by no means a carbon copy of the Jabotinsky version, but rather an original conception consistent with local sensitivities. It was Ben Hecht who insightfully clarified for Kook the weak points of the American outlook: "We'll have to be very careful about two things. . . . We must make it plain that this Jewish army is not for American Jews. . . . Secondly, we mustn't let any of your hot-headed Palestinian notionalism [*sic*] creep into our propaganda."[33] Although Hecht's first observation appears somewhat off the mark given the general call for volunteers from free nations, the American entry into the war, only three days after the committee's inauguration, enabled it to clarify that the only place for Americans wishing to take part in the armed struggle against Hitler was the American army. This was one essential respect where the delegation's plan differed from Jabotinsky's, which had envisioned a substantial number of American soldiers in this Jewish army.[34]

Fearing an official American reaction, preparations for the committee's founding had remained shrouded in secrecy for months. Kook and his associates were well aware that the United States still maintained diplomatic relations with Germany and that the Germans continued to man a permanent mission to Washington. But the surprise Japanese attack on Pearl Harbor on 7 December 1941 acted as a turning point in all calculations. Kook recalled how the delegation was not only forced to update its plan but also to consider how to best present their case to fit the new situation. The attack on Pearl Harbor also engendered an ideological shift: "Up to that point we had regarded American Jewry much as we had regarded Polish or German Jews, as stupid and unaware of reality, of what was to befall them. . . . Unexpectedly . . . everything blew up in our faces. . . . We were suddenly forced to face the question: What is a Jew? Who are we? In whose name do we speak?"[35] Based on their understanding of the new circumstances, a policy change regarding the place of American Jews in the envisioned army was now put into effect: not soldiers but sympathizers. As sympathizers, their role was clear: to lobby the British government to allow the formation of an independent Jewish army or at the very least a separate Jewish division within the framework of the British army. This policy change was naturally reflected by a name change. Now calling itself the Committee for a Jewish Army of Stateless and Palestinian Jews, a title Ben Hecht termed propaganda suicide, this name nonetheless purposefully proclaimed its founders' fundamental political-national aims.

Hecht's second warning, against employing Palestinian nationalism in committee propaganda, also became an integral aspect of delegation public relations tactics, at least for the duration of the war. For some time Kook's sharply honed instincts had clued him that intermingling any type of Zionist ideology with the committee's declared aim of founding a Jewish army to fight Hitler would spell a fatal blow to the committee's chances for success. This fear of driving away potential supporters prepared to further a humanitarian idea but not to identify politically with the Palestine problem generally guided Kook's policy and actions from 1941 to 1944. Consequently, no overt connection was ever drawn—either in propaganda or in practice—between the idea of a Jewish army (and afterward the idea of rescue promoted by the Emergency Committee to Save the Jews of Europe) and the delegation's original ideological doctrine, between its campaigns for specifically defined aims and its intention to found a Jewish state in line with Irgun principles. Kook's adamant stand on this matter, as opposed to that of the NZO leaders, who tended to project their right-wing Zionist ideology into the crux of any issue they were espousing, ultimately led to a parting of ways. Indeed, according to delegation members' wartime correspondence, this was a major factor in Ben-Zion Netanyahu and Meir Grossman's withdrawal from joint activity.[36]

A different picture emerges when examining Rafaeli and Merlin's postwar memoirs. Citing Netanyahu's lack of military background as the reason for the split, Rafaeli's later writings and interviews make no mention of the ideological differences regarding the issue of Zionist versus immediate goal-oriented propaganda within the Jewish Army Committee. And although he himself was not an Irgun member originally, Merlin also mentioned this issue in his postwar correspondence with Rafaeli.[37] The dichotomy between wartime and postwar opinion on this matter may stem from the delegation's later history, when Kook broke his own taboo, creating an organization in which he overtly identified his own political standing and that of other delegation members. This organization—the Hebrew Committee of National Liberation—will be discussed further on.

Thus it later became more politic to discuss issues such as military bearing and Irgun discipline, rather than ideological-tactical divergence, as an explanation for the schism.

It was now time for action. During the first few months of the committee's existence, its founders approached a long list of individuals, including congressional activists such as Senator Harry S. Truman, the president of the American Federation of Labor, and even American enlisted men, in an effort to interest them in the cause of a Jewish army. From the responses received it became clear to the committee's founders that some confusion still existed regarding the place of American citizens in the new army, something that prompted a decision to elucidate this issue in the committee's forthcoming propaganda campaign.[38]

Although the committee's public support came from a broad variety of circles, most of its core members were Americans not belonging to the delegation but drawn from a handful of Jewish activists of European origin. Some, such as Meir Grossman and Ben-Zion Netanyahu, belonged to the American Zionist right wing, whereas others, including Chaim (Herman) Lieberman of the Yiddish paper *Forverts* and the young artist Arthur Szyk, had no Revisionist ties. Another Jewish core group member was Rabbi Charles Kahane, an enthusiastic delegation supporter whose young son Meir often accompanied him to activist meetings where he absorbed the group's atmosphere. Meir Kahane participated in right-wing Zionist activity throughout his youth, first as an auxiliary to his father in delegation offshoots and later on his own, as a Betar activist.[39]

This core nucleus was augmented by a large group of assimilated Jews. From twenty-five to forty-five years old, these second—and third-generation descendants of European immigrants, primarily affiliated with liberal and radical circles, had not been previously associated with any Jewish organization. Suddenly aware that, regardless of their organizational affiliation or political beliefs, they too were in Hitler's sights, they propelled their Jewishness from a marginal to a central feature of their biographies. Although Ben Hecht represents the prototypical member of this group, he was joined by others, including advertising tycoon Alfred Strelsin, journalist Max Lerner, and actor Eddie Cantor. All were attracted to this cause because of its activist *demand* orientation, so different from the passive *request* orientation characteristic of the contemporary Jewish organizations with which they were familiar.[40]

A third group of committee activists, one that lent legitimacy to the committee's nonsectarian label, was composed of committed Christians. Their presence afforded Kook license to couch the issue of a Jewish army in humanitarian rather than particularistic Jewish terms, thereby enabling him to draft support among Christians with humanitarian leanings. Yitzhak Ben-Ami described the nature of their initial contacts with this group: "We spoke a language that was better understood by gentiles than by Jews. After spending five minutes with them they became friends. They stuck to you. They traveled and lectured, they were willing to accept criticism from their Jewish friends and just shrugged their shoulders and said 'we understand.' The Irish used to say 'we also had informers in Ireland, so what!' For them Stephen Wise was almost on the same level as the informers in the Irish Rebellion."[41]

Ben-Ami's recollections in this matter are similar to those of other Jewish wartime activists in the United States, particularly in the field of rescue. Unlike the delegation members, who saw themselves as participants on the American scene and yet as outsiders, American Jewish rescue activists felt themselves wholly part of the American ethos. Nevertheless, they too preferred to present their case as being humanitarian and not Jewish, and therefore sought to create alliances with Christian groups who would lend their organization the nonsectarian title they craved.[42]

Two ethnic groups that granted full backing to delegation activity were the Chicago Czechs and the New York Irish. The Irish connection in particular, which intensified over the years, is noteworthy. Given Ireland's wartime neutrality, at first glance Irish support for a Jewish army almost seems surprising; nevertheless, the Irish revolutionaries could immediately identify with the Irgun Delegation's anti-British orientation and their perception that by forming a Jewish army they would boost opposition to British colonialism in the Middle East. Asked about his enthusiasm for the group, the ardent delegation supporter Congressman Andrew L. Somers cited his Irish origins and pointed out the parallels between British policy on the Palestine question and British policy on Ireland before independence. "Of course we were allies, but simultaneously we wanted the British to put an end to their appeasement policy towards the Arabs," Somers concluded.[43]

Above and beyond these ideological and practical considerations, there was an additional underlying civic-psychological aspect to the sup-

7. Andrew Somers, a U.S. congressman from New York, strongly supported the work of the Irgun Delegation. Courtesy of Acme Photo.

port these ethnic groups lent to the Jewish army concept. The committee's declared affinity to other movements of national liberation endowed it with political legitimacy in the eyes of a broad sector of the American public. Hillel Kook explained how committee members couched their aim in terms of American interests. "We very often used the Irish Freedom Fighters as an example. It did not occur to others [other Jewish organizations] to do so as they were not freedom fighters. We were a movement of national liberation and we naturally assumed that America would support our liberation movement. . . . That was how we reached peak success in penetrating public opinion and in implementing the machinery of mass support throughout the United States."[44] In addition, the fact that some of these national groups had received permission to found separate "armies" under Allied command buoyed up Kook's hopes for their committee's chances of success. Delegation activity during the 1940s is best understood in relation to its affinity with other national liberation movements in the United States. This affinity will later be examined in depth.

Jewish Army Committee Tactics

The fast-breaking military and political events of the days following the Jewish Army Committee's inaugural session dashed any hope for orderly planning of its future activity. Kook addressed the task of reorienting the committee's platform to fit the fluid situation; however, within weeks the delegation found itself up against the need to formulate practical plans. How should they proceed? With diplomatic activity first? With fund-raising? A broad-based public relations campaign? After brief consideration, the latter possibility—amassing wide public support for the concept—was chosen as holding the key to all future steps. This decision was based on Kook's belief that only public pressure could effectively activate the diplomatic machinery to coerce Britain into allowing the formation of a Jewish army. Kook grounded his hopes on the fact that he had managed to snare military and public figures to top the committee's list of supporters. These included four former American military officers, thirteen senators, thirty-eight members of the House of Representatives, five governors, one assistant governor, six church functionaries, and thirteen intellectuals and American labor movement leaders. Hoping that this largely non-Jewish support would assist in disseminating the concept of a Jewish army to broad sectors of the American public, Kook also paid heed to military considerations. Now that America had entered the war its citizens faced a general draft to fight Hitler's forces. It was to this public that Kook now offered a potential fighting force of 100,000 additional soldiers, hoping that such assistance, involving no American sacrifice, would be welcome. These premises became the guiding principles for the committee's campaign as devised and implemented by Kook over the next fifteen months.[45]

The committee's campaign for a Jewish army was launched during the first week of January 1942 with a full-page ad in the *New York Times*. Under the banner head "Jews Fight for the Right to Fight" the committee set forth its demand for the formation of a 135,000-strong Jewish army, whose enlistees were envisioned as coming mainly from Palestine and South America, but also included volunteers from other countries. This policy was reiterated in the committee's second ad, placed in the *New York Herald Tribune* on 20 February ("Suez Must Not Be Another Singapore"), which explicitly forswore any possibility that the Jewish army would incorporate American citizens: their place was in the American army. Public approval for these, and for hundreds of future delegation-sponsored advertisements that filled the American press throughout the 1940s, came from the scores of names appearing in the margins: actors, writers, journalists, historians, and congressmen. Each advertisement bore an attached donation slip to be filled out and returned to the committee to finance continued activity. This tactic, an appeal to the public via full-spread, bombastic ads whose illustrations, drawn by Arthur Szyk, often verged on caricature—a favorite motif portrayed frightened Jews seeking refuge behind a stalwart Hebrew soldier—became a lasting delegation trademark.[46]

A central question on Kook and his supporters' agenda was how to fund these ads. Their financial messiah was Alfred Strelsin, an advertising tycoon brought to the committee by Ben Hecht, who not only became an enthusiastic supporter of the Jewish army concept but donated $5,000 to cover expenses, "an astronomical sum in those days," as Merlin put it. Donations sent in the wake of an initial ad's appearance were used to cover the cost of future ones. "Jews Fight for the Right to Fight" was not simply the opening shot of the committee's public relations campaign; it became the prototype for this entire campaign in form, content, and concept. The ad conveyed an unequivocal message: no more futile talk of the legitimate right of Palestinian Jews to fight, but a concentrated effort to set all the relevant moral, political, and military arguments for the founding of a Jewish army before the public. This first ad established a recurrent pattern: a provocative headline that drew the reader's eye, focusing his attention on the body of the ad, which employed current marketing techniques. "We bought a page in the New York Times and advertised the Committee for a Jewish Army just as you would advertise Chevrolet motor cars or Players cigarettes," Eri Jabotinsky observed. Hillel Kook's intrusive invasion of the *New York Times* violated a twofold taboo in Jewish circles: their antipathy toward drawing public attention to Jewish-centered issues, and their gentlemen's agreement not to highlight the war's "Jewish aspect." Another committee decision called for its local offices to finance their own public relations campaigns, a step that both enhanced their autonomy and simultaneously reduced friction among their delegation member directors.[47]

Ads from early 1942 mirror the difficulties then facing the Allied forces. In mid-February the Japanese conquered Singapore, taking 64,000 Allied soldiers prisoner. Australia faced the danger of a Japanese invasion, and in North Africa the Germans were advancing toward Tobruk, which fell on 21 June. The opening sentence of an ad published by the committee's Philadelphia office in April 1942 played up the terrors facing the free world: "Spring is *our* time of horror. . . . because it is Hitler's time to strike! And *this* Spring above all others, Hitler will strike his *hardest*. . . . fighting with mad desperation to drive through the Middle East hoping to join his forces with the Japs."[48] This threatening opening was followed by a pointed inquiry: why did Britain steadfastly refuse to allow the formation of a 200,000-strong fighting force of Palestinian and stateless Jews? Committee members took great pains to avoid directly accusing the British government of possessing a negative attitude toward a Jewish army, but rather indicted a small ultraconservative group in the British Colonial Office whose attitude on Palestine and the Middle Eastern question was grounded in past, not present, reality. Even in the course of Winston Churchill's American tour in June 1942, committee ads continued to adhere to this basic tactic. This cautious attitude toward all things British, particularly given British-American cooperation, also conditioned Kook's public pronouncements on this issue and followed the Revisionist-Zionist line since Jabotinsky's days: "Personally I am a great admirer of the British people, and believe the World will always remain indebted to them, for it was their courage and genius that saved us all in the gruesome fall of 1940," Kook announced at a September 1942 press conference, when the threat of a German invasion shadowed the Yishuv. His admiration was, however, tempered by sobriety. He noted: "But we will not win this war by sentimental appreciation," following up this observation with a demand: "I suggest that under the command and guidance of the American forces in the Middle East, a Jewish Army should be created."[49]

Balls and dinners were an additional means used to draft public opinion and financing for their cause. One example was a festive dinner held at the committee's May 1942 national convention. The eight hundred supporters of the committee's aims who attended this testimonial to Pierre van Paassen made substantial donations to the cause. Similar dinners, subsequently sponsored by all the committee's local offices, had a carefully chosen guest list from a broad spectrum of ethnic groups, paying particular attention to those engaged in a struggle for national liberation.[50]

Kook and his associates deliberately chose the intrinsically American charitable institution of testimonial dinners as the crowning jewel of their conventions. These public events combining wining, dining, and speeches played an essential role in Kook's scheme for creating a unique public image—one that portrayed the committee not just as another outdated ineffectual Jewish entity purveying the image of the persecuted Jew, the embodiment of human misery that enlightened humanity felt conscience-bound to assist, but rather as a proud new creation whose activist line boldly declared its intent to contribute, not just to receive. The committee's *demand* orientation—which was consistent with its activist line and became one of its identifying features—contrasted sharply with the passive *request* orientation then current among other contemporary Jewish organizations. Even the media name bestowed on its campaign, "Crusade for Jewish Army," reflects these inherently activist connotations along with the decidedly positive associations they aroused in the American public.[51]

Dinners were by no means the committee's sole method of fundraising. They also held meetings, such as one organized by Hecht in Hollywood for bohemians and movie industry people, for this purpose. Like committee ads, this and subsequent gatherings followed a fixed pattern. First Hecht drafted support from key Jewish figures such as producer David Selznick; he then arranged for senators and committee activists, Colonel John Patterson, for example, who enjoyed the status of a British war hero, to address the gathering. At this first evening's end, the organizers had raised a promised sum of $130,000, of which only $9,000 was realized after two weeks of intensive fieldwork. "Thus our first Jewish propaganda meeting was a fine success," Hecht wrote, tongue in cheek, "if you care to overlook its failure." Now at least the committee had seed money to open an office, print its letterhead, and buy a copying machine. Another means used to draft support for their campaign was radio broadcasts made by committee activists throughout 1942. At a certain point, someone in Hollywood even raised the idea of producing a film on the Jewish Legion, but this plan was never implemented.[52]

Dinners, radio programs, and other media events were supplemented by dissemination of written material regarding committee aims. Starting in 1942 the committee produced scores of publications—memoranda, pamphlets, and letters—addressing the need for a Jewish army. Of these, perhaps the best known is a long letter titled "The Ten Reasons Why a

Jewish Army," which sought to link democratic American ideals with the legitimate Jewish right to found its own fighting force. Other publications were intended for internal distribution. Although a leaflet providing an update of chapter activities appeared regularly in New York, it did not always reach local branches, often causing activists outside the New York area to react bitterly in fear of being cut off from the center of committee events. In June 1942 Arieh Ben-Eliezer complained to Eri Jabotinsky that he felt cut off from what was happening in the New York national office, underscoring his lack of surprise that it took a month for him to learn of their new goal to promote a Jewish army. "You are all certainly doing a good job," he commented ironically. "If I would not receive personal letters from personal friends of mine in New York, I really would not know that the National office is still in existence. I hope it is—or is it?"[53]

Committee-sponsored activity also took the form of a time-honored Revisionist tactic: the petition, in this case a petition addressed to the American president and to Congress backing the formation of a Jewish army. Newspaper ads calling for the formation of a Jewish army bore a slip to be signed, detached, and forwarded to the president. Thousands actually sent these slips to the White House, at the same time taking the opportunity to forward donations, some significant but mostly a dollar or two, to the committee's national office.[54]

This multipronged campaign with its ads, dinners, radio broadcasts, and written propaganda served a dual purpose. First and foremost, it aimed to bring the formation of the committee and its activity to the attention of the American public. But these devices were also intended as a fund-raising mechanism to finance continued activity—publishing additional ads and organizing dinners nationwide. If anything, this publicity campaign may be best envisioned as an ever increasing spiral with a twofold purpose: to mold public opinion and to bring in donations, these to be utilized in turn to finance another advertising campaign to draw public attention to the issue and elicit still further contributions. What prevented this process from becoming a farcical closed circle were parallel efforts taking place in the diplomatic arena: overtures made to Congress for the formation of a Jewish army that were themselves enhanced by the broad-based publicity campaign and ever-widening public support for this cause.

Diplomatic Action

Efforts on the congressional front to promote the cause of a Jewish army began in July 1941, approximately six months before the committee was officially established. Among the cause's most enthusiastic supporters in the House were Congressmen John M. Dingell of Michigan and Andrew L. Somers of Brooklyn, an Irish American who identified with the group's anti-British struggle and placed his congressional office at Kook and his associates' disposal. The Senate struggle for a Jewish army was headed by Edwin C. Johnson, who later replaced Pierre van Paassen as committee chairman.[55]

Internal delegation task division assigned primary responsibility for the Washington diplomatic mission to Hillel Kook. Indeed, Kook's youthful energies found their natural outlet on Capitol Hill and, thanks to his persuasive powers, nearly four hundred congressmen voiced their support for the idea of a Jewish army. Most only lent their names, but several also devoted time and effort to promoting the concept, giving speeches at dinners and trying to draft additional supporters to the cause in the House and Senate. In only a minority of instances can we attribute this support to a desire to attract the Jewish vote; rather, in a majority of cases, these supporters were individuals who had become convinced of the desirability and necessity of employing all and any means to uproot the Nazi danger. As Senator James E. Murray of New York stated, "We in this country find it difficult to understand why the British government is not giving heartfelt support to the Jewish army programme. If this were an issue which was to be decided by the American people I know what they would decide. . . . The Jewish army would be created immediately."[56] Over the course of 1942, the topic of a Jewish army was raised twenty-four times in Congress, mainly by Jewish Army Committee activists.

This congressional activity reached its peak with Congressman Andrew Somers's proposed bill mandating that the president lobby the British administration to allow the formation of armed Jewish units in Palestine, essentially a compromise formula aimed at mustering support from an additional two hundred congressmen allied to the Zionist establishment. Despite Kook and his associates' efforts to bring the bill to the House floor, it remained stalled in the House Foreign Affairs committee, evidently because of the obstructionist tactics of the committee chairman,

Sol Bloom of New York. In their correspondence of the period delegation members state unequivocally that Bloom's antagonism to the bill was grounded in his consistent loyalty to State Department policy on Jewish matters and, as the founding of a Jewish army was then perceived as not being in American interests, Bloom—"the State Department's Jew," as historian Henry Feingold has dubbed him—attempted to block discussion of this issue. This opinion appears to be backed up by historical studies of the period, such as those of Henry Feingold and David Wyman.[57] Another view of this matter was taken by Ben Hecht, who claimed that it was Rabbi Stephen Wise who convinced Bloom to sabotage the bill, but there is no supporting evidence for this claim. This claim, however, appears to fit in with Wise's general attitude toward any efforts proposed by the Jewish Army Committee, which I will later discuss in depth. In addition, these efforts on the congressional front were also impeded by the fact that the bill's strongest opponent, Bloom, was himself a Jew.[58] A composite picture of all the evidence at hand points to the fact that responsibility for the bill's failure to reach the congressional floor ultimately rested with a number of factors and not just a single individual: Chairman Sol Bloom of the House Foreign Affairs Committee. These factors included congressional timing, the fact that there appeared to be little widespread support for the bill, and the general war situation.

Bloom's opposition to the bill was not created in a vacuum, however. Throughout this period the British and American administrations worked in concert regarding British Middle Eastern policy, with State Department officials directing particular effort to blocking American Jewish opposition to British Palestine policy. For this reason they maintained open channels of communication with the American Zionist leadership and particularly with its unofficial leader, Rabbi Stephen Wise. It was more difficult for them to monitor activity by entities outside the Jewish or Zionist establishment, such as the Irgun Delegation, and internal State Department Office correspondence reflects government concern with these entities. Consequently, State Department officials let it be known on Capitol Hill that any attempts by unmonitored groups should be discouraged or even blocked when necessary.[59]

By mid-1941 the battle lines had been drawn between the various groups dealing with the Jewish army issue. Few were actively opposed to the idea, and various Zionist groups attempted to promote the concept of a Jewish fighting force, each in its own way. However, while most "establishment" Zionists still adhered to the policy of quiet diplomacy, the Bergsonites combined overt congressional efforts with a massive public relations campaign geared to encourage public support for this issue. This public support was meant to encourage the congressional campaign, which, in turn, was supposed to pressure the American administration to instigate the creation of a Jewish fighting force. The entire cycle was dependent, however, upon a concert of interests that developed between the Jewish Army Committee and a number of persons: first, newspaper reporters and publishers who saw the group as newsworthy, "front-page material," and were willing to grant them the publicity they needed; second, grassroots supporters who saw the group as promoting either a Jewish or a humanitarian issue, depending on their own leanings; third, congressional figures such as Andrew Somers who acted as a lynchpin for their Washington-based campaign. In both their wartime correspondence and postwar memoirs delegation members naïvely state that Somers, a Brooklyn congressman, was highly influenced by his Irish ancestry and therefore supported the Jewish Army Committee's anti-British struggle.[60] It appears likely that he was equally influenced by his own political ambitions, which required the support of his Brooklyn constituency, composed primarily of traditional Jewish immigrants who were among the delegation's most stalwart adherents. Regardless of his motives, Somers was one of the key figures in attempting to promote the idea of a Jewish army and appeared to take the bill's failure to progress as an almost personal affront. However, there was little practical follow-up to his impassioned declarations, leaving the question of motives and actions open to much speculation.

Establishing the London Branch of the Jewish Army Committee

While Hillel Kook and his associates were engaged in expanding their efforts in the American arena, at least one individual was hoping to undertake a similar initiative on the other side of the Atlantic. This was Irma Helpern, who, although he had worked alongside Kook from the time of his arrival in the States, was not considered an official delegation member. Now, in early 1942, Helpern suggested that his arena of operations be transferred to Britain, in order to open a branch of the Committee for a

Jewish Army there. Kook, worried that the American operation would need outside support, agreed to the idea with alacrity. In February 1942 Helpern sailed for England as an officer on a Norwegian ship, then the fastest way to make the transatlantic crossing, which nevertheless lasted for over two months. In a circular letter dispatched to divisional directors in May 1942, Eri Jabotinsky described Helpern's fears that he would not reach his destination. Referring tongue in cheek to Irgun interrelationships, Jabotinsky noted that an Irgun activist in Britain, Mordecai Katz, had already prepared a very touching speech to be delivered at a Sunday meeting "commemorating the late Captain Helpern when the latter suddenly landed in London on Friday. Captain Helpern says that this is the one thing Mr. Katz will never forgive him for." [61]

Several days after his arrival Helpern opened a small London office, which became the British base for activity on behalf of a Jewish army. His choice of tactics, however, was somewhat low-key compared with those employed by the committee's Washington office. On the diplomatic front Helpern disseminated circulars among members of Parliament, fostering ties with key personalities able to assist him in his diplomatic efforts, such as the longtime Zionist supporter Lord Strabolgi, who assumed the presidency of the London branch. Helpern's British media campaign diverged greatly from Kook's American one. Aware of the limitations of the British sociocultural milieu, he decided against publishing huge ads with bombastic headlines and touching illustrations in the general press, and concentrated instead on submitting letters and essays to the Jewish newspapers, mainly the *Jewish Standard* and the *Jewish Chronicle*. In more reserved British society, only a minority were capable of identifying with the unconstrained openness projected by advertisements of the Hillel Kook type, and given this cultural atmosphere, it seems likely that such bombastic headlines would have repelled rather than attracted potential donors to the cause. Furthermore, in the wartime atmosphere of unity, any criticism of British governmental policy by the committee would have been unwelcome. Finally, both Britain's geographical proximity to the front and the direct hits on the British population obviously placed the military issue in a different context than in the United States. It was therefore necessary for the London committee to adapt its propaganda to this distinct situation and milieu in both wording and form.[62]

How therefore could Helpern reach the British public? Instead of investing energy in a newspaper campaign, Helpern chose to publish propaganda leaflets as the most efficacious means for disseminating the concept of a Jewish army. During its three-year duration of activity, the committee's London branch produced a series of moderately priced pocket books aimed at making the public at large aware of plans to form a Jewish army under Allied supervision. Nor did Helpern neglect the social arena. In line with the American model Helpern sponsored a long series of events—dinners, parlor meetings, and public rallies—with an eye to activating British high society on behalf of the Jewish army cause.[63]

Tactical policy notwithstanding, Helpern's committee stressed the same image as its American counterpart. The Jewish Army Committee was not simply *another* Jewish or Zionist organization, but rather a nonsectarian body working toward a humanitarian aim. This tactic drew public attention to the committee, even motivating the British government to devote several sessions to a discussion of the activities surrounding the Jewish army issue in general and Irgun-based activity toward this end in particular. A secret British War Office memorandum from December 1942 surveying the history of the Jewish Army Committee in both the United States and England noted a plethora of factors that motivated non-Jews to support its aims: natural sympathy for the underdog, a humanitarian outlook, the desire not to appear anti-Semitic, opposition to British imperialism in Palestine, belief that British aliyah policy was unjust (particularly after the *Struma* disaster), as well as the fundamentalist Christian belief that the battle of Armageddon would be fought on Palestinian soil. Although not unduly concerned about these groups, the British government nevertheless was aware that under a special set of circumstances they could evoke both public and parliamentary reaction and that it would therefore be politic to keep an eye on the committee's support base.[64]

Why did Kook agree to form a branch of the Jewish Army Committee in Britain? After all, in early 1942 there was considerable American public support for the Jewish army cause and it appeared that Congress would agree to discuss a bill on that issue. At first glance, the idea of a British branch of the committee seems superfluous, a drain on the delegation's resources, which were always short of both manpower and funds. One explanation is connected to the traditional Revisionist-Irgun attitude toward Great Britain. Knowing that the Jewish army was supposed to be formed under British auspices, Kook felt that it would be more appropriate for a

British entity to present proposals to His Majesty's government regarding the formation of a Jewish army under *British* command. Following Kook's lead, the London committee stressed this matter by promoting British parliamentary activity on behalf of a Jewish army. In early June 1942 two members of the House of Lords, Wedgewood and Strabolgi, initiated a discussion of the issue in the House. There was little follow-up and the matter appeared to have died. However, when MP Ian Hannah introduced a query on this topic in the House of Commons two months later, he received an almost immediate response from British War Minister Sir James Grigg, leading to what appeared to be a shift in British policy regarding the idea of a Jewish fighting force. In order to shift public pressure from Whitehall to the Jewish arena, and in view of the manpower difficulties during the summer of 1942, Grigg announced the formation of separate Jewish and Arab units within the framework of the British army without implementing the operative "parity" principle—the demand for an equal number of conscripts from each of the populations—then in effect. At the time 14,000 Palestinian Jewish soldiers were already serving in the British army, mostly in the Middle East, and this step was supposed to pave the way for additional thousands to join the fight against the Nazis, who were presently progressing along the North African route toward Palestine. The British capitulation regarding the parity issue is one of the three factors historians quote in explaining the dearth of interest in the Jewish army issue after the summer of 1942 by both the Irgun Delegation in the United States and by other Zionist entities. The other two were America's entry into the war, which took the pressure off American Jews who wished to fight the Nazis, and the problems of Middle East defense facing the Allied armies during the summer and autumn of that year.[65]

Unlike the American delegation, which began to drop the Jewish army issue during the latter half of 1942, Helpern appeared unaffected by the ostensible softening of the British hard-line position, and he continued his efforts for two additional years. Why did the London branch of the Jewish Army Committee remain true to its goals long after the American delegation had progressed to other issues? Several factors fueled Helpern's continued campaign for a separate Jewish army: a sense that the majority of soldiers drawn from the Yishuv were not participating in the vital military missions of the war, recognition that separate Jewish units were far from being a Jewish army, and his awareness that stateless Jews were barred from serving in these units. Although the British tried to deter Jewish enlistment in these units by publicizing that they would not be sent to the front, they frequently utilized their formation as a propaganda tactic, citing them as proof of Britain's willingness to involve Jews in the country's military efforts against Nazism.[66] Furthermore, Helpern and his associates were physically closer to the seat of power at Whitehall that would make the decision about a Jewish fighting force, something that gave them more determination to pursue their cause. Finally, there was the organizational factor of Irgun military discipline: Kook had appointed Helpern and the London branch responsible for promoting the concept of a Jewish army and, as he received no orders to the contrary, Helpern continued to adhere to this original plan. In any event, from summer 1943 on, activity on behalf of a Jewish army was centered solely in the British group. We will consider the degree to which this activity influenced the British decision to found a Jewish brigade in this chapter's closing section.

Kook's final involvement in the Jewish army campaign came during the fall of 1942 when he and Helpern initiated a reciprocal exchange of delegations in order to form a joint American-British entity that would meet with British War Office representatives. After repeated applications by Kook on this matter, the American undersecretary of state recommended to the British ambassador in Washington that the group be granted British passports and visas. The ball then passed into the British court, which debated what to do about this recommendation. On the one hand, the British were certainly cognizant of the need to take their American partners' stance into account. On the other, several senior British officials, particularly Colonial Affairs Minister Cranborne and War Minister Moyne, feared that such a step would upset the delicate balance recently attained with the Jewish Agency, a consideration overtly mentioned in the secret British government correspondence of that period. Despite the foreign minister's willingness to allow this delegation to enter the country, the colonial affairs ministry argued that Britain should avoid granting the group official recognition. Stating that the Jewish Army Committee was in fact a Revisionist body, "and the revisionists, whose Zionist aims are more extreme than the Jewish Agency, always try to wear the mantle of the Jewish Agency," the letter went on to claim that the British had an important role to play in keeping the Zionist peace, which would, of course, benefit His Majesty's government. "If we grant them recognition, this will embarrass the Jewish Agency, which is not acting up at the moment and whose relations with us are friendly, and will cause it to radicalize its position," he concluded.[67]

From late 1942 until summer 1944, most activity on behalf of a Jewish army in the British arena originated in initiatives that had their inception overseas. However, during the spring and summer of 1944 independent British activity began once again, this time in the parliamentary arena and with the active and vocal support of the Irgun-sponsored Jewish Army Committee. In September 1944, when the British government announced to the Jewish Agency its intention of forming a Jewish brigade, Helpern and Kook portrayed this announcement as a personal success and backed the welcome initiative. Although it had ostensibly succeeded in its stated goal, the London branch of the Jewish Army Committee continued to function for another nine months, disbanding only in late June 1945, some two months after the European war ended. Over two years earlier their American counterparts had already abandoned the scheme of a Jewish army, concentrating instead on a campaign to rescue European Jewry that will be examined in the next chapter.[68]

Stage Two: The Events of Autumn-Winter 1942

In late fall 1942 a new phase of committee activity began in the United States, affected by events in the military theater, Kook's failed attempt to found a Jewish brigade in the framework of the American armed forces, and reports reaching the free world concerning the fate of European Jewry. Although developments on the North African front during October and November 1942 marked the beginning of the war's military turnaround, the Allied victory at el-Alamein, by removing the threat to the Yishuv and the entire Middle East, significantly reduced public enthusiasm for the concept of a Jewish army.

In a last-ditch attempt to focus upon an American initiative, Kook had even proposed to establish a Jewish regiment within the framework of the American army. His hopes in this direction had been fostered by the American secretary of war's November 1942 announcement that an infantry battalion made up of Austrian residents of the United States was in formation, by the fact that Norwegian and Filipino regiments were already functioning within the American army, and by the formation of a Greek

battalion a month later. Consequently, Kook approached the War Department with a proposal for the similar formation of a Jewish battalion. During the war the delegation was certain that this overture was rejected as a
result of pressure applied by a Jewish colonel named Greenbaum, who had
been appointed to oversee the entire project. Some even suggested that
Congressman Sol Bloom, a personal friend of Secretary of War Stimson,
sabotaged this proposal just as earlier he had prevented a bill on this matter from reaching the House floor, probably for similar reasons. Neither
supposition has support from any other source, and it is likely that the
Bergsonites were eager to view Bloom in particular as their personal bogeyman, preventing any of their efforts from reaching fruition.[69]

A major factor that diverted the Jewish Army Committee from its
original goal was reports of the extermination of European Jewry reaching
them from fall 1942 onward. At a special meeting held in early October,
delegation core members tried to set their future plans to fit the changing
situation. Because of the somewhat clouded nature of initial reports from
Europe, opinion was divided as to both their reliability and the appropriate response. Yitzhak Ben-Ami recounted his debate with Merlin and
Kook, their refusal to believe that such a thing was possible in the twentieth century. While Ben-Eliezer took his side, the others just stood by
silently. "They didn't negotiate with the Gestapo as I did on and off for six
months in Vienna," Ben-Ami concluded.[70] Despite Kook's skepticism all
present voted for a change in committee policy. From now on they would
take direct action on what was happening in Europe, and not concentrate
solely on the restricted military issue.

The committee opened this new phase of its campaign on 7 December
1942, the anniversary of the Japanese bombing of Pearl Harbor, by issuing "A Proclamation on the Moral Rights of the Stateless and Palestinian
Jews" to the *New York Times* and other American papers across the country.[71] In ten succinct paragraphs hundreds of a total of more than 1,500
signatories—military men, congressmen, mayors, governors, judges, and
public officials—expressed their support for democracy and for the Jewish
right to an army of their own to fight the Nazis under Allied command.
Although the Final Solution was not referred to specifically in this ad, it
explicitly noted the heavy price being paid by Jews in areas under Nazi occupation for each Allied initiative and their role as scapegoats for each
Nazi failure, whether diplomatic or military. The accompanying illustra-

tion introduced the Jewish army issue, linking it to the element of rescue. Drawn by Arthur Szyk, it portrayed a handful of thin, haunted-looking Jews handcuffed together; behind them lay an elderly Jew holding a Torah scroll with a swastika-bearing dagger sticking out of his bleeding back; and in the background stood a proud Jewish soldier supporting the dying elderly Jew in his left hand, waving a rifle in his right, and emitting a battle cry. Through its effectively crude symbolism this drawing conferred a concrete emotional-associative aspect on what was essentially an abstract idea. These illustrations would be the delegation's trademark, building on the concept that the visual often has a longer lasting impact than the verbal.

Another phase in the transition from Jewish army to Jewish rescue took place in early 1943 following the publication of an exposé that conjectured that the Nazis had already exterminated an estimated two million European Jews, and that death awaited millions more. As days passed with no succor for Europe's Jews, the possibility of millions more deaths galvanized Ben Hecht into an intense search for new ways of rousing American public opinion. Finally, Hecht came up with a bold, innovative way of bringing both the cataclysmic news of the Nazi exterminations and the concept of a Jewish army to the American public: a dramatic historical extravaganza that would appeal graphically and emotionally to its audience.

Hecht, Billy Rose, Kurt Weill, and Arthur Szyk plunged into intense, month-long preparations for mounting the pageant, titled *We Shall Never Die*. Hopes for overall cooperation on the part of New York Jewish organizations were dashed after an exploratory meeting at which Hecht introduced the play's essential conception and read selected passages. "Other voices arose. English and Yiddish outcries filled the room. Within five minutes a free-for-all, bitter as a Kentucky feud, was in full swing. The thirty-two Jewish organizations were denouncing each other as Socialists, as Fascists, as Christians, as undesirables of every stripe."[72] That dissension spelled the death knell to any attempt at cooperation, and in the final analysis the pageant was sponsored by a single organization: the Committee for a Jewish Army.

Nevertheless, many people rallied to support the pageant. Jerry Lewis, Stella Adler, Dean Martin, Frank Sinatra, and Leonard Bernstein were among the famous actors who took part in the production. The cast also included one hundred yeshiva students from Brooklyn, fifty cantors

8. Scene from the pageant *We Will Never Die*. Courtesy of Acme Photo.

("each able to sing louder and higher than Caruso," as Hecht put it), and fifty Orthodox rabbis who were supposed to recite a prayer on stage.

This cooperation with fifty rabbis also had its comic moments. During the pageant's Washington tour, Hecht was only able to find accommodations for the rabbis in a small hotel owned by an avid Irish patriot. The committee representative, himself an Irishman, took the owner aside and under the cover of secrecy revealed to him that this was a delegation from Ireland seeking a loan from the American administration. In response, the owner spontaneously offered to put the delegation up for free, but he nevertheless finally agreed to accept advance payment for his fifty guests. Thus it was that fifty bearded rabbis in skullcaps and flattened black hats filed up to the reception desk and blindly following orders signed in as "O'Toole, O'Hamilton, Gilhooley, Clancy, O'Casey, Sweeney, Murphy and forty-three other sons of Erin," in Hecht's account.[73]

Although the Bergsonites had already made their mark in the world of public relations, the idea of holding a pageant of this scope was new to the

9. Alex Rafaeli (left), actress Stella Adler, who
performed in *We Will Never Die*, and labor leader
Dean Alfange. Courtesy of Judith Tydor Baumel.

Zionist or American Jewish world. Viewing this endeavor as a tactical escalation, and fearing a positive public response to what they considered a cheap publicity trick, the American Zionist establishment responded with a concerted effort to keep the curtain from rising. Even while in rehearsals, Rabbi Stephen Wise made consistent attempts to block this pageant's production, going so far as to demand that the governor of New York cancel his decision to declare opening night, 9 March 1943, a day of mourning for the two million murdered European Jews. Despite this opposition, the curtain rose twice on opening night, each time before an audience of twenty thousand, while a similar number waited outside. During its full run, *We Will Never Die* played before a total audience of some 120,000 people nationwide.

The pageant opened with a historical prologue, went on to portray Jewish cultural, scientific, and artistic heroes, and then surveyed the Jew-

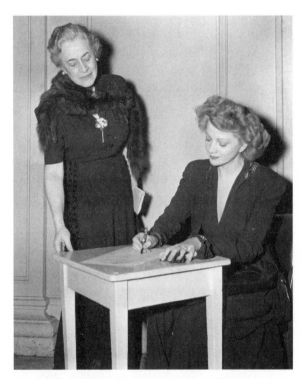

10. Actress Stella Adler, seated, with colleague.
Courtesy of Judith Tydor Baumel.

ish contribution to the war effort, focusing on the absence of an independent Jewish army. "And what flag is missing over the Jews' head?" one
of the soldiers asked, the obvious response being that it was their own flag,
the Jewish one. At this cue three Palestinian Jewish soldiers burst onstage,
emerging from between the tablets of the Ten Commandments that
served as a backdrop. "When people arrive there will no longer be any
Jews left in Europe," the narrator declaimed over voices crying in the
background "Remember us!" The play ended with an explanation of the
Kaddish prayer and the curtain fell on a joint recitation of the Kaddish by
cast and audience.[74]

Hecht's stage attempt to bring the murder of European Jewry to the
American public received mixed reviews. Although the general press reacted favorably, concentrating upon the strongly delivered message, the
pageant received only negligible coverage in the Jewish newspapers and
was sharply criticized in the Yiddish press. Much of the criticism centered

11. Actress Stella Adler. Courtesy of Judith Tydor
Baumel.

upon what reviewers called the play's "unbridled emotionalism" and referred derogatorily to the use of "shapely chorus girls," alluding to the ac-
tresses in white sheets who represented the dead.[75]

Unlike the Jewish press, which was content to simply express a critical
stance, the American Jewish establishment actively attempted to shut
down the production. Using their influence in local Jewish communities,
the American Jewish Congress and other Jewish organizations applied
pressure on various entities not to support the staging of the production,
closing off theaters to the group and preventing tickets from being sold.
These efforts soon bore fruit and led to the cancellation of performances
scheduled for a series of smaller towns nationwide. Despite its initial success on the New York stage, the delegation was now forced to rethink its
public relations strategy in view of its inability to fight the concerted efforts of the American Jewish and Zionist establishment. Thus ended the
Jewish Army Committee's initial endeavor to use stagecraft in order to
bring its message to the American people.

12. Mass recitation of the Kaddish, the Jewish memorial prayer for the dead, from the pageant *We Will Never Die*. Courtesy of Acme Photo.

*Relations with the Zionist Movement
and the American Zionist Establishment*

The decision to end the pageant's run after its initial New York performances was a harsh reminder to delegation members that they were not working in a vacuum. Indeed, of all of the delegation suborganizations, it was the Jewish Army Committee that brought the Bergsonites closest to the American Jewish establishment. Soon after the establishment of the Jewish Army Committee, activists with no previous affinity to the Irgun, such as congressmen and other public figures in contact with Zionist activists by virtue of their jobs, began to pressure Kook about attempting to cooperate with the existing Jewish organizations that had also expressed support for the idea of a Jewish fighting force.

As early as the spring of 1941 delegation members had put out feelers

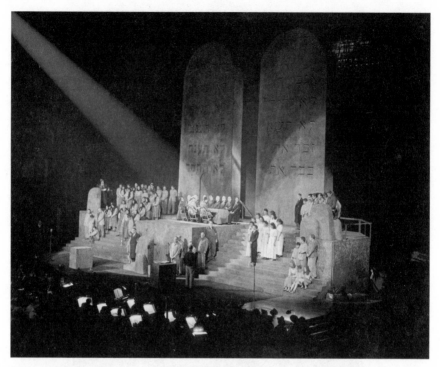

13. Scene from the pageant *We Will Never Die.* Courtesy of Acme Photo.

to Zionist establishment circles regarding the possibility of a cooperative venture. Soon after, Hillel Kook and Abba Hillel Silver even exchanged what appeared to be friendly letters on the imperative need for a Jewish army. Simultaneously, Kook approached Stephen Wise, head of the AZEC, in a bid to reach a cease-fire, but based on Kook's refusal to bow to the authority of the Zionist establishment, Wise rejected this overture, reiterating his view that any subgroup of the Irgun Delegation was not a legitimate representative group in Jewish life. This would remain Wise's attitude until the delegation's dissolution in 1948.[76] Naturally, hegemony was the first issue to raise its head. Viewing the delegation's independence and its bombastic public relations campaign as a threat to the American Zionist establishment, which had finally begun to cooperate within the framework of the AZEC, Wise demanded that the delegation "toe the line" and accept his authority and that of the Zionist establishment. For the independent, Irgun-oriented Kook, the thought was anathema. He later recalled, rather dramatically, his meeting with Wise on this matter: "I

14. Scene from the pageant *We Will Never Die.*
Courtesy of Acme Photo.

remember Wise asking me this very question in his radiophonic voice and his Shakespearean English, in his deep bass he said to me: 'In whose name do you dare to speak and whom do you represent?' " [77] Wise's query was an accurate reflection of the prevailing state of affairs between the Zionist right wing and the Zionist Federation from 1933 onward, when the Revisionist movement seceded, during which any reconciliatory attempts were foiled by right-wing refusal to yield to majority rule. He had little hope that Kook would be willing to compromise where other, less independent Revisionist-Zionist leaders in the United States had not. Indeed, throughout the delegation's history the American Jewish establishment continued to issue communiqués in which they described the various delegation-sponsored organizations as "fronts," created "for the professed purpose of solving the vast problems confronting the Jewish people as a result of Nazi persecution and war." Stressing that "the leaders of these groups have constantly assumed to speak for the Jewish people in this country without having in fact, or endeavoring to secure, a mandate from any constituency," these communiqués lambasted Kook and his cohorts for their independent, factionalizing activity. "Instead of cooperating with established and recognized national Jewish agencies, they have entered into competition and sought to undermine them." Attacking the group's public relations tactics, these public statements claimed that "they have conjured up the illusion of activity by press agentry, financed by the appeals for contributions invariably accompanying their advertisements." Seeking to create the impression that they are the only bodies capable of achieving "action" and results, the Bergson-sponsored organizations were always accused of causing discord resulting in a disservice to the very cause they assumed to represent. Finally, the delegation's activities were usually placed within a larger context of uncooperative Irgun activity in Palestine, stressing how that organization had been unwilling to observe the discipline that would keep the Yishuv intact.[78]

The financial issue also complicated matters. Already in 1941 Wise and the Zionist establishment were forced to acknowledge the delegation's abilities in the field of fund-raising. Calling them "opportunists" and noting that their advertisements would raise money only in New York, Bnai Brith president Henry Monsky declared that nevertheless the American Jewish establishment would have to take concrete steps to stop the Bergsonites before they received more publicity and attracted financial support away from other American Jewish and Zionist causes.[79] Indeed, financial matters relating to the delegation's various organizational manifestations appear to have deeply concerned the American Jewish establishment, which spent many meetings discussing this matter throughout the 1940s.

Yet a third issue complicating matters was of a more personal nature. Within a short period after his arrival in the United States, Hillel Kook appears to have become Stephen Wise's personal bogeyman. Having taken a dislike to what others were calling the "young, dynamic Jewish leader," Wise often stressed how Kook continuously expressed his contempt for the political strategy of the world Zionist leadership and of Jewish leadership in general. Thus he emphasized that his negative attitude toward the delegation's leader was of a more general and not a personal nature. In an AZEC memo summarizing a meeting that Wise chaired, the indefatigable

Kook was described as a rabble-rouser and a troublemaker, confusing "propaganda for performance and advertisement for achievement." [80]

Public relations was another issue that divided the Bergson-sponsored group from the American Zionist establishment. In 1940, the American Friends of a Jewish Palestine had been the first Zionist-oriented group that attempted to harness American public opinion through the concerted use of every means at hand. Although there were a number of Zionist leaders who had emphasized the necessity for similar activity, until that time no mainstream Zionist or even American Jewish organization had adopted similar, albeit less bombastic, tactics. Indeed the committee's unique and often jarring methods disturbed both the American Jewish and Zionist establishments to no end. In a conversation, labor Zionist activist Hayim Greenberg conveyed to Eri Jabotinsky that for the Zionist establishment what was most disturbing was the clandestine nature of the committee's formation and the absence of any hint as to its intentions, "so that it could burst forth like thunder and lightning in the clear skies above the meadow where the Zionist leaders grazed." On the whole, this factor created an exceptionally hostile atmosphere to attempts to cooperate with Kook and his coterie, even leaving its mark on contact with the American Zionist establishment's more moderate wing, which was also sabotaged time after time. [81]

At the beginning of 1941, in what appeared as a step toward achieving a more politically oriented stance, the AZEC finally implemented an earlier decision to establish a Department of Public Relations and Political Action. Headed by Zionist activist Emmanuel Neumann, who had returned from an eight-year stint in Palestine, this department planned to break through the parochialism that had limited Zionist propagandizing to Jewish audiences. Neumann's plans were reminiscent of Bergson's: publishing a monthly newsletter, reviving the Christian pro-Palestine committee (as opposed to the Bergsonites' nonpartisan organizations), publishing pamphlets, coordinating conferences of Zionist publication editors, and organizing nonpartisan support in Congress. Like Bergson, Neumann felt that Washington was the true seat of power; however, it was impossible to move the Zionist base of operations from New York to the capital and he found himself constantly commuting between the two cities. Neumann's foresight in seeing the same operative vistas as the Bergsonites could ostensibly have aided him in supplanting the delegation in the field of public relations. In practice, he was hampered by a factor from which the independent Kook had been freed: the necessity to accept the authority of a larger organization that wished to manage his efforts. Unlike Kook, who had unfettered himself from official Irgun authority in Palestine early in the game (hence delegation members' constant emphasis on being a "cut-off battalion"), Neumann was forced to bow to the dictates of Stephen Wise and the AZEC administration, who feared that the new public relations department would overwhelm their organization. Controlled by inter-Zionist power struggles, hampered by an office committee that attempted to restrict his activities, and plagued by an ever-present lack of funds, Neumann's committee became the story of missed opportunities while Bergson conquered the public arena. Unable even to mobilize Zionist reaction to the tragedy of European Jewry, such as the sinking of the *Struma* refugee boat in a Turkish harbor, Neumann would have to wait for Wise to be supplanted by the activist-oriented Rabbi Abba Hillel Silver, supportive of his directions in the field of public relations, before being able to compete with the delegation on its own battleground.[82]

Finally, there was the issue of interorganizational Zionist establishment rivalry. Throughout 1941 and part of 1942, rank-and-file Zionists were finding it hard to comprehend the issues that were keeping Bergson's Jewish Army Committee and the AZEC apart regarding both groups' support for a Jewish fighting force. In fact, several branches of the ZOA even passed resolutions calling for the formation of a Jewish army. Consequently, Emmanuel Neumann and his specialist in public relations, Meyer Weisgal, Chaim Weizmann's personal assistant in the United States, felt that some type of cooperation would be necessary in order to avoid clashes between ZOA and delegation supporters. Consequently, in late 1941, negotiations began between Weisgal and Kook regarding the possibility of an agreement between the AZEC and the Jewish Army Committee. Fearing to negotiate on his own, Weisgal involved a personal friend of his, Joseph Brainin, who acted as the Jewish Army Committee's go-between with Weizmann.

Bergson was gratified at the idea of such an agreement. Not only would it benefit the creation of a Jewish army, but, in his words, "it would also help clear the atmosphere of Jewish public life in a direction of national concentration for a supreme effort to put an end to the gruesome tragedy confronting the Jewish people."[83] What he did not state, however, was that such an agreement would provide him with the legitimacy he claimed to abhor but actually craved, a recognized entity that the Zionist establishment would deal with as an equal.

Negotiations continued throughout 1942, leading to the draft of an agreement between the two organizations staunchly supported by Neumann, Silver, Weisgal, and others.[84] However, here too, just as in the case of Neumann's public relations committee, inter-Zionist rivalries destroyed the possibility of cooperation and progress. In this case, the rivalry in question was the deep-set competition between the camp of Chaim Weizmann, president of the World Zionist Organization, and that of David Ben-Gurion, head of the Jewish Agency Executive. Indeed, the Ben-Gurion/Weizmann dispute over the Jewish Army Committee was but a sideshow in the raging power struggle between the two for leadership of the Zionist movement. Viewing the issue of a Jewish fighting force in a more global perspective, Weizmann was in favor of the agreement and even initialed the final draft along with Pierre van Paassen on behalf of the Jewish Army Committee, whereas Ben-Gurion, who exercised influence over AZEC chairman Stephen Wise, adamantly refused to have any dealings with the committee because of its Irgun affiliation. In fact, Ben-Gurion's strong antipathy for the Zionist right wing and for the Irgun in particular appears to have played a focal role in shaping his attitude toward delegation offshoots in the United States. Committee tactics, which divorced Irgun Zionist political aims from its immediate military goal, in no way affected this identification. Indeed, in January 1943 the British ambassador to the United States wrote to the British foreign minister regarding Kook's attempt to "hide" his Irgun origins: "This committee, as you are aware, consists of a nucleus of extreme revisionist Zionists, largely concealed from view by the outer rim of misguided humanitarians of every stripe and colour who form the bulk of the membership of the movement."[85]

Weizmann's only stipulation regarding Bergson's group was one of authority, that they would accept the principle that the Jewish Agency must be the only body to negotiate with any governmental authority regarding the establishment of a Jewish fighting force and that there would be no propaganda to recruit enlistment from the United States.[86] However, even when Bergson appeared to agree to this clause, Ben-Gurion, with the encouragement of Wise and Hadassah president Rose Halperin, took steps to nullify the agreement before it was brought to the AZEC for final approval. This action was part and parcel of his distrust for the American Zionist leadership, implicit in his negative attitude toward Emmanuel Neumann and explicit in his vetoing of the agreement with the Bergson group.

Ben-Gurion's inherently antagonistic attitude toward the Bergsonites, which the American Zionist establishment shared, was expressed in a series of publications describing the committee's program as overly utopian, part of an effort to convince the American Zionist public that the Zionist establishment was doing everything in its power to promote the idea of a Jewish army and to discredit the committee as an extreme, fascist, right-wing organization with Irgun leanings.[87] During 1942, American Zionist leaders emphatically stressed the absence of any link between Jewish Army Committee efforts and establishment efforts on behalf of the formation of a "Jewish fighting force," the term that they consistently employed as a substitute for "Jewish army" used in right-wing circles. The greater the Jewish Army Committee success in fund-raising and building broad-based support, the more flagrantly Wise and the Zionist establishment gave vent to their anticommittee sentiments.

A last-ditch effort to reach an agreement with the Zionist establishment, mediated by William Ziff, also failed, leaving mutual accusations for sabotaging the agreement hanging in the air. By the spring of 1943, there appeared to be little chance for any form of cooperation between the delegation and the American Zionist establishment.[88] Weizmann, for his part, continued to support the idea of a Jewish fighting force and even attempted to meet independently with American secretary of the treasury Henry Morgenthau in an attempt to enlist him in the Jewish army debate; however, he achieved little success in this sphere.[89]

Spring 1943: The Jewish Army Committee
Changes Its Tactics

Zionist and Jewish establishment refusal to cooperate with right-wing circles persisted into 1943, even after reports detailing the nature of Hitler's Final Solution had finally begun to penetrate public consciousness. In January of that year thirty-four American Jewish organizations met in Pittsburgh to formulate a united American Jewish plan for the postwar reconstruction of European Jewry. Participants in this conference decided to organize an American Jewish Assembly where representatives of the entire Jewish community could debate the critical issues involving the Jewish world. The result would be the creation of the American Jewish Conference, over half of whose delegates were affiliated with established Zionist organizations, and to which delegation offshoots were not invited. This conference, which will be discussed in the next chapter, was a transitional stage in American Zionist affairs and made a lasting impact on the delegation.

In preparation for this assembly, American Jewish organizations had founded the Emergency Committee for European Jewish Affairs but refused to admit members of the Jewish Army Committee to their ranks. Moreover, they made attempts to block coverage or committee ads from appearing in local newspapers. Having taken note of Kook's success in the public relations sphere, Jewish establishment organizations now sought to take action on this front, and in March 1943 American Jewish organizations sponsored a series of rallies aimed at bringing the destruction of European Jewry to public attention. The largest of these rallies, which drew an estimated crowd of twenty thousand, was deliberately scheduled to compete with a Jewish Army Committee pageant to be held the following week at the very same venue, Madison Square Garden. Concurrently, the Emergency Committee for European Jewish Affairs unveiled a comprehensive rescue program calling for sanctuaries for refugees, a change in the administration of American immigration laws to enable maximum utilization of quotas, agreements with Britain and Latin America to accept refugees, the opening of the gates of Palestine, transfer of food to Jews in Nazi-occupied territory under United Nations auspices, formation of a UN-sponsored entity to implement this plan, and the founding of a war crimes commission to gather information for postwar trials.[90]

Delegation members were adamant in stating that this program had undoubtedly been influenced by another rescue plan that was taking form at the same time: the Jewish Army Committee initiative for the rescue of Romanian Jewry. On 13 February 1943 the *New York Times* carried a report from London of a Romanian government offer to transfer seventy thousand Jews from Transnistria to some place of refuge. The Romanian proposal called for transporting these refugees to Palestine via Romanian ships, and requested payment of 20,000 Romanian *lei* (approximately $50) for each refugee who exited its borders.[91]

This first large-scale ransom offer relating to Jews in occupied Europe made to the free world since the war's inception was treated skeptically by official American and British circles. Both administrations quickly concluded that this was a specious offer. In contrast, delegation members treated it seriously and decided to capitalize on its conditions. Three days after the Romanian offer's initial publication, the Jewish Army Committee placed a full-page advertisement in the *New York Times*. Its derisive headline read: "For Sale to Humanity 70,000 Jews: Guaranteed Human Beings at $50 a Piece," and details of the proposed deal followed. Readers were asked to appeal to their congressmen and to send donations to underwrite the costs of additional ads. This ad evoked an immediate response and as large and small donations began to flow in, Jewish establishment leaders and the Jewish press accused the committee of misleading the public by suggesting that each $50 contribution would save a Romanian Jewish life. The committee steadfastly adhered to its campaign, particularly after Kook received what appeared to him as confirmation for the deal from Irgun contacts in Bucharest. In the final analysis however, this Transnistrian plan was never implemented, but the debate between those who believe it was realistic and those who aver it was fraudulent continues to the present.[92]

From here on Kook's and his associates' efforts proceeded on two parallel planes, one of which concentrated on the formation of a Jewish army and the other on the establishment of an international rescue organization, a call resembling the one issued by the Emergency Committee for European Jewish Affairs. Not to be outdone, the American NZO as well published ads calling for the formation of a million-dollar fund to rescue European Jewry. Jewish Army Committee members now clearly saw the need for a change in direction: it was time to leave behind the topic of a Jewish army of which the public had wearied and to move on to a new, more burning issue raised by reports of Hitler's Final Solution to the Jewish question beginning in fall 1942. This decision to adopt rescue as their theme gave birth to another delegation offshoot, the Emergency Committee to Save the Jews of Europe, founded in summer 1943, which will be the next chapter's focus.

What happened to the Jewish Army Committee? Although its activity in the United States wound down during the course of 1943, the committee was not officially disbanded until the war's end, perhaps because disbanding would have signified withdrawal from the demand for a Jewish army and ultimately from the struggle for Jewish sovereignty over Palestine. Practically speaking, however, the sole entity that continued the campaign for a Jewish army after summer 1943 was the committee's London branch headed by Irma Helpern, which continued its efforts until the formation of the Jewish Brigade in fall 1944 and for several months thereafter.

Evaluating the Jewish Army Committee

In organizational life there is more often than not a specific moment that can be defined as the point when a change occurred. In some instances, it is an actual moment in time; in others, an organizational phase lasting for days, weeks, or even months. Such was the period of Jewish Army Committee activity in the life of the Irgun Delegation, a phase that began in winter 1941–42 and ended in spring 1943 with the switch to rescue activity on behalf of European Jewry. These months represent the organizational stage of storming as outlined in chapter 2 in my description of a model for group development. To recall, storming refers to the stage during which group activists respond to situational needs, test the boundaries of external authority, and grow comfortable with the roles they fulfill to achieve their common aim, processes we have traced as they unfolded in delegation activity to a lesser or greater degree. These processes were accompanied by delegating tasks and creating a unique atmosphere, often swinging from the tragic to the comic. There is, for example, the story of Karni's bath. Karni, Eri Jabotinsky's eldest daughter, was born in New York during this period, and impelled by a sense of mission ("How is it possible that members of the Irgun Zevai Leumi do not know how to bathe a baby?" he asked), the proud father decided to prepare the Irgun members, all bachelors except for himself, for "real life." He lined them up on the porch of his small apartment so that each could bathe the baby in turn and, over the baby's mother's loud protests, the Irgun members lined up and fulfilled Jabotinsky's orders to the letter, as if carrying out a military campaign. These lighter moments also contributed to a deepened friendship among delegation members, delineated by the sociologist Nathan Glazer as an essential stage in the formation of ethnic protest groups.[93]

This solidarity was doubly important given the fact that the delegation was now functioning, for the first time, as a totally autonomous entity, with regard to both its parent movement in Palestine and its former American partners such as the NZO (which had participated in the first delegation offshoot). This independence enabled the delegation to formulate an ethnic orientation, an Irish orientation in particular, which found expression in the forging of profound links with Irish American activists such as Andrew Somers. Some delegation activity patterns were derived from the Irish national struggle in the United States, including the demand for a boycott on British goods first raised in 1942 but implemented only five years later. Indeed, as explicated in this book's final chapter, examination of the Irish national struggle in the United States elicits many points of similarity with delegation activity during the 1940s.[94]

During this period the delegation's campaign shifted from a Jewish to an American context. "Until that time Jewish matters appeared on the next to the last page of the newspaper," Hillel Kook recalled. "We placed them on the American public agenda, providing the momentum for their movement from the dead pages to the news section and even to the front pages. For the first time in the history of the American public, Jewish affairs took up an entire page of the *New York Times*." The struggle for a Jewish army marked the initiation of an American-style publicity campaign, albeit directed to a Jewish topic. Yitzhak Ben-Ami recalled, "Our immediate goal in 1942 was to take the campaign out of the synagogues and the Yiddish press, out of the back pages of the daily press, out of the hands of the traditional Jewish leadership, and to make it universal." Herein lies the key to Kook's outstanding public relations success: his awareness of the influence of the media on American society and his willingness to devote time and resources to this realm, an approach antithetical to the then accepted activity patterns of American Jewish organizations, particularly of the American Zionist establishment. "[We have] virtually no propaganda department," the president of the ZOA noted in 1939. "We have not until this day developed a steady flow of publications on Palestine. . . . We have made only the most occasional and fragmentary use of the radio. We have no Palestinian films to speak of."[95] Emmanuel Neumann had realized the folly of this policy and had tried to implement changes; however, as we have seen, he was blocked incessantly by the Zionist establishment whom he ostensibly represented.

This was not the case regarding the Irgun Delegation. During the years in question, Kook implemented, without organizational impediment, what he had apprehended but a short time earlier: that the way to the American public's heart in general and to American Jewry's in particular was via newspapers, leaflets, theater, and radio. The more bombastic the headline and the more tearjerking the accompanying illustration, the greater chance the ad had of catching the public's eye. In essence, Kook had quickly grasped and implemented a cardinal principle of marketing: the name of the game was to create public awareness for your product. All means were kosher, but it was better if they were innovative, colorful, unique, or, in the professional jargon, "gimmicky." Concurrently, Kook and his associates built a broad-based economically and socially self-supporting network. Their activist orientation, which differentiated between the immediate problem—the need for a Jewish army—and the delegation's long-range Zionist aims, appealed to many Jews who had never before been affiliated with any Jewish organization. Kook's propaganda success was also enhanced by his presentation of the struggle for a Jewish army as being in American, and not simply Jewish, interests, a tactic cited by Glazer as another means enabling ethnic interest/protest groups to attract followers from the public at large.[96] The committee's nonsectarian orientation also contributed to its success in attracting activists from a broad spectrum of sectors. But neither can we ignore the fact that its hard core of activists was mainly Jews—immigrants and first-generation Americans—who were drawn both to the group's activism and its goals and who later played a role in the delegation offshoot founded in summer 1943. Their number included some individuals slated to become militant Jewish right-wing activists in the United States two decades later.

Nor can we overlook the separate issue of the delegation members' relationship to other Zionist bodies during this period, whether to the right or the left. As noted, the Committee for a Jewish Army was the delegation's first attempt to act autonomously from the American NZO, a fact not always viewed favorably by rank-and-file Revisionists, who in early 1942 even attempted to break up committee meetings in Philadelphia and Brooklyn. These disturbances ceased only after countless appeals to American NZO headquarters.[97]

For its part, the Zionist establishment also tried to deal with this new phenomenon in the form of the Jewish Army Committee, swiftly perceived as posing a greater threat than Revisionist activity of the thirties with which it was already familiar. The "push-pull" reaction that characterized the entire Zionist movement spectrum—attempts to negotiate with the committee nearly always ended in mutual ostracism—is more indicative of divisions within the Zionist establishment than of an inherent examination of either the committee or the delegation. Essentially, it appears that it was the committee's public campaign that most aroused establishment ire, as it pointed up Emergency Committee for Zionist Affairs failure to amass support for the concept of a Jewish fighting force in spring 1942.

During its eighteen-month period of activity, the Jewish Army Committee raised more than a quarter of a million dollars and attracted fifty thousand supporters.[98] In the public relations sphere it was unique on the American scene: militant, but espousing a patriotic aim that was difficult to oppose; loud and bombastic, but incorporating these qualities into the American ethos of freedom and minority rights in a way that answered the human, and particularly American, need for sensationalism. Consequently, the committee did succeed in lifting the Jewish issue from the back to the front pages of the newspapers, as Samuel Merlin noted, and by so doing overturned the decades-old principle of "quiet diplomacy" espoused by the American Jewish establishment.

But can we speak of practical success? In his study of the Zionist right wing from 1925 to 1948, historian Ya'akov Shavit noted, "As a political movement Revisionism failed to achieve most of its objectives."[99] Is this evaluation also applicable to the Irgun Delegation's first autonomous offshoot, the Committee for a Jewish Army? The answer to this question lies in consideration of the degree of delegation influence on two British decisions relating to the enlistment of Yishuv Jews to the war effort: the 1942 decision to establish separate Jewish units without reference to the hitherto sacred parity principle, and the fall 1944 decision to found the Jewish Brigade. In neither of these cases does it appear that the Jewish Army Committee had any considerable impact on the decisions of the British government. Twin factors appear to have influenced the parity issue: the military situation and American pressure. The deteriorating situation of the Allied forces in summer 1942 led to a general call-up of all potential soldiers in order to further the war effort. Simultaneously, however, delegation members are adamant about claiming that American lobbying played a decisive role in the British decision to draft Palestinian Jews. This American pressure, they emphasize, was no little influenced by Jewish

Army Committee activity, which moved the issue from the back room caucuses where quiet Zionist diplomacy took place to the headlines and the halls of Congress.[100] It is understandable that delegation members wished to emphasize their contribution to the initial British decision in summer 1942 to allow the formation of separate Jewish units without requiring parity to the number of Arab enlistees. However, their connection with the British government's moves in this direction are circumstantial, to say the least.

It is even more difficult to determine any degree of committee involvement in the fall 1944 British decision to found the Jewish Brigade. Both during the war and after that time, committee adherents in Britain and the United States largely attributed the British about-face to the parliamentary debate in which the London committee member Lord Strabolgi played a decisive role. Concurrently, they claimed that the founding of the brigade was an outcome of unceasing pressure by Irma Helpern and his associates in England from the spring of 1942 onward. Documentation from the period tells a slightly different story. True, during the summer of 1944 Lord Strabolgi introduced a bill into Parliament to created a world Jewish fighting force unconnected to Palestine.[101] This bill was sponsored by the Jewish Army Committee in Britain and its wording had been worked out with Helpern and Kook. However, at the same time, Chaim Weizmann and the Jewish Agency had been secretly lobbying for a Jewish fighting force and had met with the British prime minister, who appeared to be favorably disposed to the idea of a Jewish brigade. In truth, it appears that this favorable disposition was to no little extent influenced by the news then reaching the West regarding the annihilation of Hungarian Jewry. Unable or unwilling to involve itself in diverting military resources to rescue Hungarian Jewry, the War Office's announcement of 20 September 1944 regarding the establishment of a Jewish Brigade was meant as a meager compensatory step in view of the events of that period. As for Zionist establishment claims, the British government's decision was indeed announced as a response to the Jewish Agency, something that aided them in claiming that it was not the overt Revisionist-Strabolgi efforts in Parliament that had turned the tide but Weizmann's covert diplomatic efforts, and particularly his meetings with Churchill.[102]

As usual, Zionist establishment and delegation documentation from the period present the historian with a *"rashomon."* Sharett and Weizmann's constant appeals to His Majesty's government were undoubtedly the deciding factor that set the political and military ball rolling, eventually leading to the formation of the Jewish Brigade. In order to negate these claims, Revisionist-Zionist publications of the period attempted to stress that the Jewish Agency had abandoned the idea of a Jewish army sometime in 1943, adding that only their efforts had kept the issue alive. As Jewish Agency efforts from that period onward had all been clandestine, there was little public proof to negate the Revisionist narrative.[103] Nevertheless, British government documentation made almost no mention of Strabolgi's bill, and thus it appears highly unlikely that the Revisionist parliamentary efforts were the decisive factor in creating the Jewish Brigade. Then there was the matter of public opinion. It is impossible to gauge what, if any, effect public opinion had on the British government's decision to establish a Jewish Brigade. There is no reference to any positive influence of this sort in the War, Colonial, or Foreign Office memoranda from that period and only the Jewish Army Committee correspondence and circulars refer to this topic incessantly. However, bearing in mind the subliminal influence of public opinion upon decision-makers, it is impossible to measure what impact the Jewish Army Committee in Britain may have had upon those in power. All of these factors figure in the documentational mosaic that emerges. Revisionist circles appear to have taken advantage of the fact that Jewish Agency agitation regarding the brigade had been carried out covertly; thus they could take full credit for a decision over which they had little influence. When faced with this accusation, delegation members retreated into the realm of publicity and public opinion, putting forth the statement that had it been up to the Zionist establishment, so lacking in any public relations apparatus, no one would have heard either of the Jewish army issue or of the Palestine problem. Thus, they claim, their constant agitation prepared the fertile ground for Jewish Agency members to sow in their meetings with Churchill. Long after the end of the Second World War the two groups remained at a standstill regarding this point.[104]

This distinction also enables us to achieve an understanding of the committee's American success from 1941 to 1943. In his *From Philanthropy to Activism*, David H. Shpiro argues that the committee's successful penetration of American public and Jewish consciousness was a direct consequence of the lack of public activity during those years on the part of established Jewish organizations. Hillel Kook's group filled the vacuum between the distressing reports from Europe and what was seen as contemporary American Jewish organizational impotence. Accordingly, Kook's group enjoyed a positive public image: it at least had plans, proposals, and noisy protests in comparison to the low-key protest whispered by the Jewish establishment until 1943.[105] What happened to this image of the Bergsonites in 1943, when American Jewish organizations began to raise their voices in protest against the extermination of European Jewry? The answer to this question lies at the heart of the next chapter, which treats yet another delegation offshoot, founded in 1943: the Emergency Committee to Save the Jews of Europe.

A Time to Save

*The Emergency Committee to Save
the Jews of Europe, 1943–1944*

Establishing the Emergency Committee
to Save the Jews of Europe

Spring 1943: a time of despair. During the first months of the year over a
half-million Jews from all over Europe were exterminated, brutally murdered in one of six death camps working around the clock in occupied
Poland. In February a major *aktion* took place in the Bialystok ghetto: one
thousand Jews were murdered on the spot and ten thousand transported
to their deaths in Treblinka. During the same month a ghetto was established in the Greek port of Salonika, and three weeks later the first group
of Greek Jews were transported to their deaths in Auschwitz. During the
same period the Krakow ghetto was liquidated and its inhabitants transferred to the nearby Plaszów work camp. In April the final liquidation of
the Warsaw ghetto began, and in May the first groups of Dutch Jews were
sent to their death in the east.

Spring 1943: a time of hope. In February German forces surrendered
at Stalingrad, a city that came to symbolize Soviet determination during
the Second World War. In March the German army met defeat at the
Mareth Line in Tunisia, and in May German and Italian forces in Tunisia
surrendered and the Russians began an all-out attack on German forces in
the Kharkov area. It was clear to all that a turning point had been reached,
and that the German defeat was now only a matter of time. But there was
then no way of knowing that victory would be achieved only after an addi-

tional one hundred weeks of battle and at a cost of more than twelve million victims, soldiers and civilians alike.[1]

Spring 1943: months of activity. During the spring the delusive image of an impregnable German army evaporated, and the beginnings of armed Jewish resistance emerged throughout Europe. In February an armed uprising took place in the Bialystok ghetto, in March the United Partisan Organization was formed in the Vilna ghetto and a first armed group departed from yet another ghetto for the Lithuanian forest, and in April the Warsaw ghetto uprising began, creating a mythical symbol of Jewish heroism during the Holocaust. Armed Jewish resistance was not restricted to Eastern Europe, however; on the very day the Warsaw ghetto uprising began a group of Belgian Jewish partisans stopped an Auschwitz-bound train, allowing its passengers to escape and thereby to evade death in the gas chambers.

Spring 1943: months of debate. The winter months saw increased public pressure in the United States and Britain—particularly among British MPs (Members of Parliament) and clerics—to take some meaningful step in light of mushrooming reports of European Jewry's extermination. In an attempt to divert pressure from itself, Whitehall once again utilized a tried-and-true recipe: transferring the issue from the British to the American arena. Early that year Whitehall approached the U.S. State Department with a proposal to hold a joint conference devoted to the twin issues of refugees and rescue. The American response, worded by Undersecretary of State Breckinridge Long, reached the other side of the Atlantic weeks later and negated the necessity for a new framework to deal with this problem. Instead, it suggested resuscitating an existing framework—the Intergovernmental Committee on Refugees founded in summer 1938 in the wake of the Evian Conference—and proposed a joint Anglo-American exploration of the most efficient means to reactivate this committee. In one vital respect the British and the Americans were in total agreement: both viewed the refugee problem as a universal one and not as a peculiarly Jewish problem. The British found the prospect of being flooded by thousands of European Jewish refugees daunting; for their part, the Americans feared that concentration on the refugee problem's Jewish aspect would enhance administration vulnerability to indigenous anti-Semitic forces.

The Bermuda Conference

In early March 1943 the Joint Emergency Committee on European Jewish Affairs and the Committee for a Jewish Army sponsored demonstrations in New York, each of which was meant to prod the Roosevelt administration into action. Hoping to alleviate public pressure, the Roosevelt administration announced a joint conference with the British on the refugee problem. Nevertheless, its planners encountered difficulties from the start, having to contend with allegations that the conference was simply a ploy to cover up Allied failure to rescue Jews. Indeed, Jewish organizations soon accused the administration of choosing Bermuda as the venue for the conference in order to keep their representatives out while at the same time distancing the media. Furthermore, the conference's organizers met with difficulties when they attempted to find someone to chair the conference, and their choice ultimately fell on the president of Princeton University, Harold W. Dodds, an individual with no diplomatic training. Other conference participants included Senator Scott Lucas of Illinois and Representative Sol Bloom of New York, chairman of the House Foreign Affairs Committee, the only member of the group with any sort of expertise in dealing with the rescue issue.

The two-week-long Bermuda Conference opened on 19 April 1943, just hours after the outbreak of the Warsaw ghetto uprising. Held in almost complete isolation, in a small hotel located between blossoming fields, only five media representatives were admitted to its sessions and its participants maintained a partial blackout in their press releases. The conference's results—which can be summed up in three main points—were a far cry from Jewish expectations for a breakthrough on the refugee question: they comprised an American announcement to the effect that the refugee problem was best resolved by a speedy Allied victory, a decision to establish refugee camps in North Africa, and a resolution to reactivate the Intergovernmental Committee on Refugees.[2]

Organized American Jewry's reactions to the Bermuda Conference ranged from disappointment and rage to despair. Zionist organizations now debated how best to proceed: should they intensify the struggle to rescue European Jewry, or should they continue to back the May 1942 Biltmore resolution, which demanded a Jewish commonwealth in Palestine? At one end of the Zionist spectrum, establishment Zionist forces reached a principled decision to subordinate the struggle for refugees to the Zionist cause, over Weizmann's objections. At the other end of the spectrum were the members of the Jewish Army Committee, who as early as 1942 had already consciously differentiated between the Irgun Zionist program and the committee's declared aims, a stance now implemented in its actions during the Bermuda Conference. On the second day of the conference a giant committee-sponsored ad addressed "To the Gentlemen at Bermuda" greeted conference participants from the pages of the *Washington Post.* It proposed a two-stage plan: evacuation of all Jews from the Nazi sphere of influence to Palestine or any temporary refuge and formation of a Jewish army to fight the Nazis. As Yitzhak Ben-Ami later stated, when it became understood that "the Bermuda Conference had only been a flimsy curtain behind which Washington and London hid their inaction, and even tried to hide the facts of the extermination," committee members published yet another ad, this one in the *New York Times:* "To 5,000,000 Jews in the Nazi Death-Trap Bermuda Was a 'Cruel Mockery.' " [3]

In timing and content this second ad sparked a fierce controversy, not only because it utilized signatures from a previous proclamation backing the moral rights of Palestinian Jews and stateless Jews without first receiving permission, but also because it appeared before the official release of the Bermuda Conference resolutions. Results were not long in coming. Led by Senator Lucas, a noisy protest ensued in Congress, and several of his colleagues, including Edwin Johnson and Harry Truman, now announced their withdrawal from the Jewish Army Committee because it had used their names without their knowledge or permission. Kook's profound apologies to Truman received only a brief rude reply. Links with certain congressional supporters were now severed, teaching Kook an important lesson: "the early bird catches the worm" is not necessarily an effective operational principle in diplomatic and parliamentary circles. [4]

The period surrounding the Bermuda Conference was a time of transformation for the Jewish Army Committee, a second metamorphosis for the delegation, which was about to found yet another organization. Hillel Kook described how sometime in spring 1943, while he was reading the *Washington Post,* a small article located on page ten caught his eye. Its two-column headline read "Two Million Jews Dead," and it went on to report that the extermination continued. That was the moment Hillel Kook identifies in retrospect as when the full import of the Final Solution hit him. "I couldn't understand why this report was not on page one with an eight-column-spread headline. . . . how the death of two million people received a report the size of one about two people killed in an accident." Kook requested a meeting with an acquaintance in the State Department to ask what was being done about the news. "I asked him, 'So what are you doing?'. . . . And he started to talk about Stephen Wise and I again asked him, 'What's all this about Stephen Wise, what are *you* doing?' Then he looked at me as if this had nothing to do with them but was a Jewish matter." The meeting galvanized Hillel Kook into action. Leaving in even deeper shock than before, because he had hoped that the headline was a typographical error, Kook telephoned New York and requested an emergency meeting of the executive board of the Committee for a Jewish Army that very evening. "I rushed there greatly alarmed. . . . And then I told them that I could no longer even think about a Jewish army, that I could no longer devote energy to any other topic, that each and every one of us had to get up in the morning and go to sleep at night with but a single thought: what action can we take to save those who are still alive, what can we do to stop this murder?" [5]

In his memoir of this period, Alex Rafaeli continued Kook's train of thought and explored what motivated delegation members to now set a new course: "We wanted to challenge the 'Let's win the war first' notion as well as the impotence of the Jewish establishment, busily involved in a 'love affair' with the American president. . . . We again managed to attract public attention by placing full page ads in the *New York Times* and other leading newspapers." [6] More important, from 1942 onward the delegation had begun to work within a declared nonsectarian framework, representing what they thought would appear as a cross-section of the American people. This framework would become extremely important in view of one important lesson learned from the Bermuda Conference and its aftermath: the futility of relying on the American and British administrations to rescue European Jewry. Only via independent activation of public opinion and Congress through just such a cross-section of Americans could the group hope to force these governments into taking practical steps regarding rescue.

Following the abortive Bermuda Conference, committee members took steps to implement their new focus on rescue, founding an independent press—the Answer Publishing Company—as a means of flooding the American public with an unceasing stream of publications treating current issues from the delegation perspective. Its first issue of its maiden publication, the *Answer*, a bimonthly journal aimed at bringing the work of the Jewish Army Committee to the public at large, boldly declared: "The *Answer* may anger you but it will never bore you." The journal, whose circulation numbered about 1,000 copies per issue during 1943 and 1944, appeared at two—to three-week intervals and had a threefold purpose: it advocated the formation of a Jewish army, presented Palestine as European Jewry's ancient homeland, and promoted the rescue of European Jewry. In June 1943 Samuel Merlin assumed the post of editor-in-chief and decided to tone down the initially aggressive attacks on the established Zionist leadership. Simultaneously, he entered the expressions *Hebrew people* and *Hebrew nation*—synonyms for European Jewry and Palestinian Jewry—into the *Answer*'s public mind, heralding the appearance of a new ideological concept that would play a decisive role in post-1944 delegation history.[7]

The Emergency Committee to Save the Jews of Europe

In addition to venturing into publishing, the group now took a second step, deciding to form a separate entity to spearhead efforts to rescue European Jewry. In his recollections of the circumstances surrounding this decision, Alex Rafaeli gave vivid expression to the overpowering sense of helplessness experienced by the American Jewish community, which, its sorrow and rage notwithstanding, found itself incapacitated. " 'What can we do?' " they argued. " 'Jews are a powerless, marginal group. How can anyone be forced to do anything to help the victims? We must wait until Germany is crushed!' " This attitude contrasted with Kook and Merlin's determination to take decisive action, initiating plans for a huge convention to be held under the rubric of "The Emergency Conference to Save the Jewish People."[8] As in the past Kook decided to utilize the delegation's proven formula for engaging American public opinion: publishing full-page ads in major newspapers; drafting religious and secular organizations, union leaders, artists, and academics to the cause; putting on theatrical pageants; lobbying Capitol Hill—essentially, any and all means of effectively placing the Jewish problem on the public agenda.

Successful activity group functioning often calls for the ability to make cognitive or practical shifts. In his analysis of activity groups, Tom Douglas identifies two succeeding stages in such a shift, each of which constitutes a separate challenge. In the first stage concerted group problem-solving catalyzes a needed change, while the second stage defines the essential nature of this change. In the case of the delegation, this process's initial stage seems to have commenced sometime in late 1942 when reports of the extermination of European Jewry first reached its members and delegation members immediately sought ways to integrate the new challenge into their existing efforts on behalf of a Jewish army. The second stage took place six months later, in May-June 1943, when the Bergsonites took concrete steps to found a new entity in order to deal with this fresh challenge. Douglas's paradigm also notes several enabling factors that facilitate such complex organizational shifts, including task delegation among the group members as a whole and encouragement of a risk-taking cultural norm in which each individual member equates risk with positive challenge. Without a doubt the Irgun Delegation, with its clearly defined task delegation, audacious daring, and risk-taking on the personal and organizational levels, more than fulfilled these conditions.[9]

It was this combination of daring, audacity, and unconventional thinking that spurred Hillel Kook to announce the Emergency Conference to Save the Jewish People of Europe. This was a carefully planned event: in June 1943, about a month before the conference opened, Eri Jabotinsky and a number of Jewish Army Committee activists met in order to set the conference agenda and to explore ways to link the Jewish army issue with rescue. Ultimately, the group decided to concentrate on three main thrusts: to evaluate the potential contribution of a Jewish army to the rescue of European Jewry, assess the potential impact of retaliatory action by the United Nations or a Jewish army on the Final Solution, and, finally, to examine the feasibility of forming Jewish units within the framework of the American army, to serve mostly in North Africa and the Middle East. But by its very nature, this preliminary discussion also indicates the existence of some discomfort on the part of delegation members for having abandoned the Jewish army issue in favor of rescuing European Jewry. Criticism along these lines was voiced by the delegation's London branch, where Irma Helpern, whose organizational temper was not in tune with that of his colleagues overseas, continued his unceasing efforts on behalf of a Jewish army.[10]

Nevertheless, delegation members attempted to give the planned Emergency Conference a military dimension in order to integrate the Jewish army issue into the agenda. Eri Jabotinsky recalled how frustrated the delegation members were, feeling that "each and every practical suggestion brought before different branches of the American administration received the response that it might endanger 'the war effort.' "[11] Consequently, the group decided to include on the conference agenda a plan to stop the extermination of European Jewry, conceived as part of the overall American war plan and prepared by military and diplomatic experts.

Kook and his associates made another seminal decision at that time—to draw a sharp distinction between efforts to rescue European Jewry and the Palestine question—that was a much disputed step, then and in the future. In describing the philanthropic structure of American Jewry sociologist, Samuel Halperin has shown how many leading members of the Jewish economic oligarchy viewed support for the Zionist movement as having the potential to lower their status in non-Jewish eyes. Consequently they granted only token support to any Palestine-related causes and gravitated instead to what Halperin terms "non-ideological and non-political" entities such as the Joint Distribution Committee as recipients for funding. Kook and his friends were aware of this sensitivity among both wealthy Jews and the American public at large, who could identify with a humanitarian challenge while finding it difficult to support the Zionist cause, not to speak of the political program of the Irgun. Following the advice of his non-Jewish entourage and particularly his congressional supporters, Kook therefore decided to completely divorce the rescue issue from the Irgun's political aspirations as previously promoted by various delegation members.[12]

It was Eri Jabotinsky who noted how this goal differentiation played an instrumental role in bringing the Emergency Conference many of its most important backers, who ran the gamut from declared liberals favoring assimilation to oil magnates with pro-Arab leanings on the one hand, and also how it sparked incessant conflict with the American Zionist establishment. Inevitably, this emphasis on primarily amassing non-Jewish support led delegation members to utilize their public relations budget differently from other American Jewish organizations; it was also natural that invitations to the conference be first extended to those individuals who had supported earlier delegation offshoots. An accompanying cover letter from the organizing committee outlined the conference's essential goal: a call to create a United Nations-sponsored entity to implement plans to rescue the millions of Jews still remaining in Europe.[13]

The response to this appeal far outweighed the organizers' expectations. There were also some surprises in store for the conference organizers, particularly with regard to their supporters' political affiliation. Eri Jabotinsky's contemporary report from July 1943 noted what was for him a startling anomaly: it was the Republicans (whom the Jews considered to be reactionaries) who expressed their desire to participate and help, primarily because the administration refused to budge from its policy of doing nothing to stop the European massacre or to recognize the Jewish people as a cobelligerent. "Therefore, when we approach an honest man, if he is a Republican, he will accept our offer and join us. If he is a New Dealer, however, he will be sympathetic but as for joining us and lending us his support, he will first ask 'somebody in Washington,' with the result that we will receive from him a beautiful letter expressing his sentiments and his regrets at not being able to participate because of a sudden trip to the West Coast." This partisan split provides additional evidence for a lesson well learned by Kook, the wisdom of creating nonsectarian entities. The delegation's Washington office even sent out directives calling for all official correspondence by local branches to stress their nonsectarian character.[14]

Preconference preparations included efforts by its organizers to solicit expressions of support from key American administration figures who they then expected to speak at the opening. Expressions of support poured in from such figures as former American president Herbert Hoover and newspaper tycoon William Randolph Hearst, and sympathetic telegrams arrived from American Secretary of State Cordell Hull, Treasury Secretary Henry Morgenthau, and First Lady Eleanor Roosevelt. "No one in this country will withhold any help that can be extended and I send every good wish to your Committee which is trying to save the Jewish people of Europe," Mrs. Roosevelt wrote. "It is hard to say what can be done at the present time but if you are able to formulate a program of action, I am sure that the people of this country, who have been shocked and horrified by the attitude of the Axis Powers toward the Jewish people, will be more than glad to do all that they can to alleviate the sufferings of these people in Europe and to help them reestablish themselves in other parts of the world if it is possible to evacuate them."[15]

Eleanor Roosevelt's openly supportive statements provide little inkling of the complex, almost unfathomable relationship between her, the president, and delegation leader Hillel Kook. Witness Kook's acid observation regarding the presidential couple: "Eleanor Roosevelt was a woman who was half anti-Semitic and half saintly, whereas her husband was more than half anti-Semitic and not saintly at all." [16] Although Kook's efforts to arrange a meeting with President Roosevelt met with no success, Mrs. Roosevelt received him at the White House on several occasions during this period and, as we shall see later, even agreed to prepare a short radio broadcast devoted to rescue on the Emergency Committee's behalf. There is no way of uncloaking the Roosevelts' true intent, of determining whether this was a sort of planned "good cop/bad cop" routine agreed upon by the Roosevelts with FDR playing the bad guy, thereby enabling the first lady to assume the role of the supportive good guy who essentially assumes no responsibility. Nonetheless, Eleanor Roosevelt consistently supported humanitarian gestures throughout the entire war, including the spring 1939 Wagner-Rogers bill aimed at rescuing child refugees from Germany.[17]

How did the Zionist establishment react to the news of this planned conference? No telegrams of support poured in; rather we can trace behind-the-scenes attempts to mitigate the future effects of the conference by various establishment leaders. For example, after learning about the proposed conference, in late June 1943 Rabbi Jonah B. Wise of the American Jewish Joint Distribution Committee urgently contacted one of the delegation's congressional adherents, Senator Edwin C. Johnson, informing him of another conference that had long been planned by mainstream Jewish organizations. This conference would be the result of a meeting of eighty Jewish leaders, representing all the major groups, who had met in Pittsburgh in late January 1943, issuing a declaration that called for the convening of an "American Jewish Assembly." The assembly's purpose would be to consider and recommend action on problems relating to the rights and status of Jews in the postwar world, including Palestine. Ultimately, this action would metamorphose into the American Jewish Conference, whose proposal was then drawing fire from mainstream American Zionist organizations such as the Mizrachi because it did not deal directly with the rescue issue.[18] Doubting the advisability of holding two conferences, he suggested that "your people be advised of the fact that the Emergency Conference . . . seems to be a rival organization. This situation will

probably create more difficulty for the Jews of Europe than any conference (no matter how well attended) may be able to alleviate." Jonah Wise
suggested that the committee hold their conference only after the American Jewish Conference had convened their meeting and ended his missive
with an assurance that "your deep interest in the sufferings of the Jews will
lead you to concern yourself with this advice. It comes from one who has
been involved in the problem for many years and who would clutch at any
straw to save this desperately persecuted people." [19] Needless to say, Johnson and the Emergency Conference organizers were singularly unim-
pressed by this piece of advice.

The idea to hold an Emergency Conference came at a difficult organizational crossroads for the American Jewish establishment. News of the
proposed Emergency Conference and of the planned participation of a
number of important American figures, which came to their ears in June
1943, reawakened Jewish establishment fears regarding the danger a
bombastic Revisionist-style campaign posed to their quiet diplomatic efforts of the previous months. But this was not their sole concern; apparently Wise also feared the Zionist establishment would lose its primacy,
both practical and psychological, in presenting the Jewish question to the
American public, leading to a partially successful series of appeals in early
July to administration figures and church leaders not to support the
planned conference.

Preparations for the Emergency Conference to Save the Jewish People
now went into high gear, and 1,500 participants, including 166 well-
known public figures, attended its 20 July gala opening at New York's
Commodore Hotel. On the agenda were rescue plans, transport problems, diplomatic negotiations, military issues, publicity, and even the role
of the church. At the evening sessions, which were open to the public,
prominent figures such as New York City mayor Fiorello LaGuardia, Dean
Alfange of the American Labor Party, author Dorothy Parker, and former
president Herbert Hoover addressed the assembly—in Hoover's case via
radio broadcast.[20]

In the final analysis, three major resolutions emerged from this conference: first, that it was imperative to break the "conspiracy of silence"
surrounding the extermination of European Jewry and to separate rescuing European Jews from the general refugee problem; second, that it was
feasible to rescue most of the four million surviving Jews in Europe with-

15. Prof. Max Lerner, Senator E. Langer, Eri Jabotinsky (son of Zeev Jabotinsky), Will Rogers, Jr., Arieh Ben-Eliezer, and Alex Rafaeli were among the members of the Emergency Committee to Save the Jewish People of Europe, formed in 1943. Courtesy of Judith Tydor Baumel.

out detriment to the war effort; and finally, calling for the creation of a governmental agency devoted to this specific purpose. The detailed rescue program, which later formed the policy cornerstone for the new entity created at the conference's closing session, called for a variety of steps: founding a rescue agency, convincing Axis satellite governments to treat Jews humanely and persuading Axis countries to allow Jewish emigration, providing Jewish refugees with temporary asylum in nonbelligerent countries and at the same time pushing for their admission to Palestine, and also calling for all available means of transportation (such as boats) to be channeled to rescue. Their resolutions also called for warnings to be issued of impending postwar punitive measures against perpetrators of atrocities and for a public campaign to inform Americans of the extermination of European Jewry. The conference's closing resolution was an announcement to the effect that, in order to further its stated aims, it was now transforming itself into the Emergency Committee to Save the Jewish People of Europe.[21]

Consistent with Kook's formula that whatever had no press coverage did not exist, delegation members made certain to invite widespread media coverage for the Emergency Conference. Reports on the conference participants, speeches, decisions, and newly founded entity appeared nationwide, but it was the New York papers whose editorial pages featured the rescue issue. One editorial by Max Lerner of *PM*, provocatively titled "What About the Jews, FDR?" challenged the American president to promote rescue efforts: "You, Mr. President, must take the lead. . . . The methods are clear. Neither conscience nor policy can afford to leave them unused. And the time is now."[22] Another media-related individual with a central role in Emergency Committee activity was newspaper tycoon William Randolph Hearst, who, in August 1943, directed the thirty-four newspapers in his chain to publish editorials in support of Emergency Committee activity, calling for nationwide backing for its program. This enthusiasm for the committee was also shared by the *New York Post*. Hearst's support was a major factor in bringing word of the Emergency Committee to the public, although his motives were not necessarily solely humanitarian but can be considered equally economically pragmatic. The sensationalist Emergency Committee founders made good copy, and apart from other considerations, this was a central factor in deciding which issues would receive coverage and which ones would be buried on the back pages. Although the historian David S. Wyman attributes Hearst's support for the committee largely to his strong anti-British bias and his desire to strike at the British even indirectly, Hearst's support typified the encouragement delegation members received from both intellectuals and public figures, who perceived the rescue issue as a humanitarian, rather than a Jewish, problem. Kook's strategy of totally divorcing the rescue issue from the Palestine question was crucial to this attraction.

No sooner had the Emergency Committee program been made public than the Jewish establishment began to voice its criticism. Led by the American Jewish Congress, several American Jewish organizations argued that Bergson's plan was nothing more than a rehashing of a program they themselves had presented at a 1 March 1943 rally held at Madison Square. Garden. This program, which called for negotiations with the Germans to allow Jewish emigration; opening of refugee shelters in neutral countries;

lifting of restrictions on immigration to Britain, the United States, and Latin America; opening the gates of Palestine; providing economic aid to neutral countries giving refuge to displaced persons; sending food packages to Jews in Nazi-controlled territories; forming an intergovernmental entity to handle the rescue issue; and the founding of a commission to prosecute Nazi war crimes indeed shared many features with the Emergency Conference resolutions and may well have served as a basis for them. These accusations of redundancy reached their height in an acrimonious anonymous report disseminated shortly before the delegation disbanded.[24]

Indeed, the two plans bear striking similarities. Both identify the same main problems and suggest comparable solutions, albeit differing slightly in detail. Only one essential difference, Kook's call for active reprisals and punitive measures to be taken against war criminals, divided the Emergency Conference resolutions from the Jewish establishment plan; this demand, which can also be viewed as part and parcel of Allied psychological warfare, was not only consistent with delegation militarism, it tallied with the centrality Kook and his associates assigned to public opinion in both their internal deliberations and practical activity. Nevertheless, the point had already appeared in the American Jewish Congress's ten-point program, formulated in June 1943, which they hoped would be adopted by the proposed American Jewish Conference soon to be convened. It appears, therefore, that the Emergency Committee was innovative primarily in its timing, being established just a few weeks before the American Jewish Conference was convened. Few, if any, of its suggestions were new; however, even if its contents were well known, its packaging was what drew adherents who would normally not have paid attention to the issues it represented.[25]

Having already examined how Kook and the delegation operated, it should not surprise us to learn that the two main areas in which the Emergency Conference could be considered innovative and even successful were the realms of publicity and organizational development. Conference media coverage brought the cruel fate of European Jewry to public attention and, in contrast to U.S. State Department claims, showed the feasibility of evacuating Jews from Nazi-occupied territories to safe refuges via sea or land. Organizationally speaking, the conference did not confine itself to issuing abstract resolutions but went on to found a permanent entity devoted to rescue: the Emergency Committee to Save the Jewish People of Europe. Nonetheless, we can identify a focal weakness in the conference rescue plan: its dependence for implementation on external agencies and institutions, some of which had not yet come into existence and/or were outside its scope of influence. The Emergency Committee was not meant to act directly in order to rescue European Jews through ransom efforts or even through fund-raising to pay such ransoms. All of its activity was indirect in nature: to make recommendations to the American president and activate congressional and American public opinion to work toward realizing its objectives.

The establishment of the Emergency Committee marks a decisive organizational transition from delegation activity on behalf of a Jewish army to efforts to rescue European Jewry. Although the Jewish army issue did receive mention in the section of the conference resolutions dealing with reprisals, for the delegation's American branch this was apparently its swan song. From here on delegation efforts zeroed in on rescue, and the American Committee for a Jewish Army finally disbanded in late fall 1943 without having achieved its aim.

Committee Activities During Summer and Autumn 1943

A recurrent theme in our story has been the phenomenon of group dynamics, as it relates to both the delegation core group and its offshoots. Despite the fact that every activity group is composed of individuals with their own unique patterns of interaction, scholars make reference to three key elements that reveal each group's inherent nature—activity, interaction, and sentiment—also taking the contribution of other elements, such as member status and internal task division, into account.[26] Closer examination of Emergency Committee activity provides a clear indication of both this group's nature and its orientation. By integrating internal activity (which would enhance solidarity among central activists and foster their adherence to the cause) with externally directed activity (meant to arouse American public opinion and to foster congressional activity on behalf of a governmental agency for rescue), the Emergency Committee created a unique model unlike any existing American Jewish organization. This modus operandi sheds light on the delegation's singularity: its recognition of the fact that only a group of fanatical devotees could implement a plan on an international scale; its willingness to accept the psychological makeup of its American audience, which demanded just the right dollop of sensationalism, and its awareness of the need to concentrate on humanitarian goals that did not ruffle the feathers of decades-long American isolationism.

As structured, the Emergency Committee was certainly an effective tool for implementing its goals. Unlike the American Jewish establishment, which founded parallel Christian organizations to gain outside support for what was conceived as a particularistic Jewish problem, delegation offshoots used their nonsectarian character as a springboard to obtain support from non-Jewish sources, including American church leaders. As Alex Rafaeli noted, "The presence of non-Jews was a central difference between the Committee and other contemporary rescue organizations for European Jewry. They endowed us with the degree of respectability and Americanism needed to draw mass support for our activity in Congress." [27] Once again, we must distinguish here between declarations and reality. In actuality, the majority of the committee's central activists were Jews: four of its six chairman, three of its thirteen vice-chairmen, and eighteen of its twenty-six board members, as well as most of its local activists. Nonetheless, the committee deliberately chose to project a nonsectarian image, based on the principle that particularism must be avoided at all costs if the broad-based footing necessary for organizational success were to be created.

It is to the committee's local branches to which we must look for the key to this broad-based footing. Exercising almost complete autonomy in the spheres of public relations, organization, and fund-raising, they had at their disposal a variety of means to enhance their activists' "sense of belonging": circulars disseminated by the Washington branch and participation in events in which delegation members took part, such as public rallies, festive dinners, and board meetings. All these means enabled local activists to keep up their emotional and practical ties to the committee's leaders and to its main branch, ties local branch autonomy might otherwise have attenuated. In addition, six Emergency Committee-sponsored conferences during 1944 and eighteen rescue-issue-related rallies during 1943 and 1944 also played a role in closing ranks. [28]

If we have characterized the Emergency Committee's internal activity as having a psychological-organizational orientation, its outreach activity was mainly directed at creating unceasing public pressure on the American administration and Congress to implement the July 1943 conference resolutions. In line with the conception established during earlier delegation-inspired campaigns, from late July to early August 1944 the Emergency Committee bombarded the public with nearly two hundred ads, utilizing the tried-and-true formula of bombastic headlines accompanied by tear-jerking illustrations, but with an even more pronounced "demand" orientation than that found in Jewish Army Committee ads from 1942. Two ads in particular are noteworthy for the unusually intense response they evoked: the "Ballad of the Doomed Jews of Europe," a Hecht-authored/Szyk-illustrated coproduction, and "My Uncle Abraham Reports," a satirical piece written by Hecht in late fall 1943. The ballad, whose opening read "Four million Jews waiting for death. / Oh hang and burn but—quiet, Jews! / Don't be bothersome; save your breath— / The world is busy with other news," hammered home the message that, for the Allies, rescuing Jews was not a priority.[29]

The second ad, "My Uncle Abraham Reports," was Hecht's reaction to the fall 1943 Moscow Declaration: the Allied announcement that the Germans would be punished for war crimes after the war. It expressed Hecht's personal disappointment with FDR, the final shattering of his illusions. "It is difficult to get rid of illusions, for they are the product of our deepest hopes," Hecht wrote at the time. "They need no fact to feed on. Worse, fact can rarely destroy them." Like a considerable number of American Jews Hecht had believed in Roosevelt's personal and intellectual integrity, seeing him "not on the side of the Jews, but . . . on the side of the angels."[30] For Hecht, the Moscow Declaration's failure to name the Jews among its sixty-two categories of Nazi victims was devastating, and "Uncle Abraham" was his response.

If, as Hillel Kook later observed, "an ad is an attention-getting device," Hecht's "Uncle Abraham" successfully penetrated contemporary public consciousness, drawing fire from the Jewish and general public alike. The ad, whose opening read "I have an Uncle who is a Ghost," unfolded the tale of Hecht's purported Uncle Abraham, who attended a convention of Jewish ghosts, all Nazi victims, and of his report to this convention: "In the Kremlin in Moscow, in the White House in Washington, in the Downing Street Building in London where I have sat on the window sills, I have never heard our name. The people who live in those buildings—Stalin, Roosevelt and Churchill—do not speak of us. Why I don't know. . ." Following lengthy deliberation, the ghosts resolved to send Uncle Abraham to Washington as a one-ghost delegation to determine how this silence came about. From that time forth, although he sits on the windowsill of the White House, a mere two meters away from Roosevelt's desk, his pencil and pad at the ready, the pages of his notebook remain blank. He already knows that he will hear nothing worth mentioning about Jews, dead or alive.[31]

"As was usual after a full-page ad in the newspaper, this short story," Kook further observed, "was followed by pragmatic suggestions: the Germans are exterminating Jews, take action, write to Congress." But "Uncle Abraham" succeeded where no previous ad had: it drew the attention of Roosevelt himself. It was Eleanor Roosevelt who, in a conversation, conveyed to Kook her husband's acute displeasure, the message that he viewed this ad as a blow below the belt, as a personal affront. Kook exploded. He recounted the course of their conversation: "I said to her: 'You know, Madam, I sometimes wonder where I find the strength to sit here with you and to talk reasonably about these matters. If I were now to take two pistols and shoot you and anyone else who stood in my way and burst into the president's office and shoot him, it would not be overreacting. I sometimes wonder from whence I derive the strength not to lose my mind and do such things. How . . . can the president say that in a situation where five thousand people are being murdered daily . . . and we are simply trying to shout "Help us" . . . that we are doing too much, how is it even possible to do too much?!' She looked at me and said, 'I can't argue with that.' "[32] After sitting with Kook a while longer, she then excused herself, saying she had to attend a family celebration. It subsequently turned out that she deemed her meeting with Kook important enough to be late for her wedding anniversary celebration, but was either not willing or not able to change the president's mind on the rescue issue.

Eleanor Roosevelt's attitude toward Emergency Committee rescue programs typified the prevailing attitude of a sector of the sitting Congress and of the American administration, which, despite its recognition of European Jewry's very real distress, its humanitarian empathy for Emergency Committee members, and its willingness to take supportive measures, particularly in the rhetorical sphere, ultimately failed to take a definitive stand backing committee recommendations calling for formation of a rescue agency. A case in point is Eleanor Roosevelt's featuring of the committee in her "My Day" column and her brief radio broadcast conveying American horror at German atrocities and expressing the hope that Europe's Jews would "try to fight in any way you can for your existence." This broadcast concluded not by setting forth detailed plans for rescue but by reiterating the theme so pleasing to American administration ears, that the most effective means of rescue was a speedy Allied victory.[33]

Emergency Committee efforts on behalf of rescue employed more than one means to convey their message, using both the written medium—exemplified by Washington branch press releases and a political manifesto reporting approaches made to the administration and to the American Congress, personal appeals, the Answer Publishing Company publications, and the spoken medium—via a committee-sponsored "speakers service" for Jewish and general events, at which committee activists spoke or took part in public debates. At a later date, Alex Rafaeli summed up their to him almost surprising accomplishments in this sphere; it was hard to believe that all of the delegation members knew only basic English, and that learned as they went along. Faith and enthusiasm were somehow enough. "We were invited to participate in debates with important speakers, on the radio, in newspapers, at town-hall meetings and in the universities. The achievements of our group were mainly educational and political. We succeeded in our attempts to broaden understanding of the plight of European Jewry, and shared with the American public the tragic results of the silence and isolation which had surrounded it."[34]

Delegation success in radio broadcasting now bred a new initiative: an attempt to found an independent radio station with the ability to broadcast to European Jewry directly. It was Alex Rafaeli who took the initiative here, even gaining the support of the OSS (Office of Strategic Services), a branch of the American Secret Service, for this project. Here too the Gunthers played an essential role as their intervention expedited licensing and funding for the project. It was Frances Gunther who introduced Rafaeli to the project's potential financial backer, Samuel Zammuray, the "Banana King," who had immigrated to the States from the Ukraine as a child. But these plans came to naught when FDR vetoed this project outright, arguing that turning the war into a "Jewish war" might encourage anti-Semitism. Appeals to Mrs. Roosevelt to overturn her husband's veto were in vain.

To this day Roosevelt's motives for vetoing this request remain obscure. Whereas the historian Joanna M. Saidel suggests a link to interdepartmental rivalry between the OSS and the War Information Office for control of propaganda and psychological warfare, we must also consider another possible factor: Roosevelt's desire to avoid legitimating any Irgun Delegation-associated activity, given its contentious relationship with the American Jewish establishment. In any event, the presidential veto blocked the possibility of any unmediated Emergency Committee activity aimed toward the Jews of occupied Europe, if only on the propaganda level.[35]

Although stymied in this attempt to venture into overseas broadcasting, the Emergency Committee continued to pursue its efforts on behalf of rescuing European Jewry via additional avenues, including direct approaches to governmental agencies. Six separate delegations highlighted specific crises, such as the plight of Hungarian Jewry, or presented petitions to the American administration or national agencies. One such delegation, which met with American Secretary of State Cordell Hull in August 1943, urged the founding of a governmental rescue agency and the opening of refugee camps in neutral countries, an idea that other refugee organizations had already broached in the past. Notwithstanding the chilly reception afforded this delegation, Hull did express some willingness to dispatch Emergency Committee delegations to Palestine, Turkey, and Spain. But execution of this understanding was slow in coming because Undersecretary Breckinridge Long stonewalled its implementation for several months.[36]

Unlike other American Jewish and American Zionist organizations that were publicly grappling with several issues at once—rescue, Zionist goals, postwar Jewish rights, as seen from the deliberations of the American Jewish Conference—the Emergency Committee appeared to the public to be a single-minded organization, yet another coup in terms of public relations. Indeed, using their indomitable method of concentrating on one issue at a time, delegation members had long decided that a main Emergency Committee goal was to keep the rescue issue—and only that issue—in the public eye. It was with this end in mind that the committee now took a different tack and organized a march on Washington in conjunction with a new partner, the American Union of Orthodox Rabbis. This march, scheduled for 6 October 1943, several days before Yom Kippur, the height of the penitential season, was the projected apex of a three-pronged campaign whose other facets included collecting a million signatures for a petition to be presented to the president and to Congress requesting the formation of a rescue agency and a plea that church leaders make Sunday, 10 October, a "Day of Intercession" for the Jews of Europe. Ignoring any long-range connotations of cooperation with the Orthodox-Jewish organizations, in the delegation members' eyes the march was conceived of primarily as a media tactic to draw attention to the rescue issue. It was on this basis that Kook made overtures to the two American organizations of Orthodox rabbis to join him in a public march and in presenting the petition—a typical Revisionist tactic—to the American president. Kook specifically sought out the rabbis, although he himself was not especially enamored of ultra-Orthodox circles, because he saw them as a representative political-influence group that did not fear showy gestures. As a scion of a distinguished rabbinic family, Kook was acutely aware of the immense visual and emotional impact of the sight of hundreds of black-coated rabbis marching on the White House while engaged in reciting a prayer on behalf of European Jewry and its rescue. In addition to what he hoped to accomplish in the public relations sphere, Kook found he shared a common language with leading members of Agudath Israel—who also headed the Union of Orthodox Rabbis—regarding the need to use all and any means to bring the rescue issue to discussion at the highest administrative levels. For the same reason, members of the American Zionist establishment were unable to dissuade the rabbis from participating in the march, which proceeded as planned. This joint project marks the first step in Irgun Delegation/Union of Orthodox Rabbis cooperation on rescue-related issues, a link that, as we shall see, assumed various guises in both Europe and the United States and lasted throughout the war.

Few sights could have more visual impact than four hundred black-clad rabbis praying aloud and chanting from the book of Psalms as they formed a stately procession to Capitol Hill, where twenty congressmen and Vice President Henry Wallace greeted them, accepting their call for a rescue agency. *Time Magazine* preserved a description of how the vice president "shifted uneasily as he gave a short diplomatic answer" to the hundreds of heavenward-staring rabbis captured in the photos of this event.[37]

The march continued, reaching the Lincoln Memorial at twilight, where the rabbis now offered a prayer for the safety of American soldiers, for a speedy Allied victory, and for the survivors. They then set forth for the White House, to be received by White House secretary Marvin McIntyre as President Roosevelt was out of town. What made Roosevelt deliberately evade this delegation? David Wyman submits both a bureaucratic and an ideological basis for this evasion: bureaucratic because of a decision then reached to refer all requests from Jewish elements to the State Department and not the president; ideological because of the principled and prolonged Jewish establishment antagonism toward the Irgun Delegation and its activities.[38] We have already seen that some establishment Jewish leaders even took steps to stop the march, and although these efforts failed, their request that the president ignore the march did meet with success.

The year 1943 came to a close with "A Salute to Sweden and Denmark," the final Emergency Committee public relations campaign for the year. On 31 October 1943 an overflow crowd of thousands gathered at Carnegie Hall to pay tribute to the residents of Denmark and Sweden for saving Denmark's seven thousand Jews from the Nazis several weeks earlier in a massive rescue effort that encompassed most of the nation. But the evening did not simply devote itself to homage; it climaxed by challenging the United Nations, the American president, and the British prime minister to explain their failure when a daring campaign by two small nations—Sweden and Denmark—had succeeded in rescuing nearly all of Danish Jewry.[39]

Critics of the delegation and the Emergency Committee—both those of that time and contemporary historians—often point to the fact that apart from the sphere of media and interorganizational cooperation, the group had little success. Yet it was in these two spheres that the delegation left its ultimate legacy. Several factors account for the widespread media coverage given Emergency Committee activity. One was the intrinsic drama of the rescue issue; another, the unconventional means used to drive its message home; yet a third, the backing provided by prominent journalists, publishers, and radio personalities who at the same time also endowed the committee with a cloak of respectability. Delegation members did not think twice about making deliberate use of public figures, movie stars, and media personalities whose each and every move received wide journalistic coverage. There were also the economic considerations:

as an important and frequent advertiser in the daily press, the committee was a persona grata with regard to press coverage. And most newspapers worked along the lines that stated that any person or entity that provides a newspaper with tens of thousands of dollars in ads is entitled to have at least some of its activity featured in the news section of that paper gratis.

Interorganizational cooperation was yet another arena where the Emergency Committee made its short—and long-term impact. In his study of American Zionism, Samuel Halperin claims that "the influence of an interest group varies with the number and quality of alliances it can construct with other groups [and] alliances are a means of enlarging a public and of facilitating propaganda."[40] This influence may be seen by the actions of the Emergency Committee, which succeeded in creating partnerships with a large number of ethnic interest groups, first and foremost with Agudath Israel representatives in the United States. On what basis were ultra-Orthodox elements prepared to cooperate with the Emergency Committee? How did it come about that prominent non-Zionist rabbis like Eliezer Silver and Abraham Kalmanowitz or even anti-Zionist religious elements were willing to take part in a public relations gimmick spearheaded by a Zionist organization?

It appears that two factors played a central role in fostering a strong bond—albeit an ad hoc one—between the Emergency Committee and Agudath Israel: their shared criticism of the Jewish and Zionist establishments' failure to engage in rescue efforts and their common "outsiders" status among American Jewish organizations. Even before they were approached by Kook, ultra-Orthodox rabbis had experienced deep frustration in their contacts with the American Jewish establishment and its organizational offshoots such as the American Jewish Committee. This frustration held true as well for their relationship with the Zionist organizations, based on their feeling that they had been shortchanged by both establishments with regard to representation in joint organizational initiatives. Against this background both Agudath Israel and the Union of Orthodox Rabbis seceded from the American Jewish Conference of 1943, held only a short while after the Emergency Committee was established. It was the same conference that also barred the delegation from its ranks.[41] Angered by the failure of American Jewish Conference organizers to assign top priority to rescue, the rabbis were also aware that the Emergency Committee was the sole entity on the American scene totally immersed in promoting rescue efforts and directing all its available resources to this purpose.

These strange bedfellows also shared tactical harmony. As Palestinian Jewish nationals in a foreign land, Emergency Committee promoters did not feel themselves bound by the social, diplomatic, and emotional constraints governing patterns of interaction between local Jewish organizations and the American administration; consequently, they had no inhibitions about employing any and all means, even those seen as being exhibitionist, in order to forward what was for them a burning issue. A similar stance governed the approach of Orthodox and ultra-Orthodox Jews, for whom the principle of saving an endangered life overrode conformity to accepted social norms. They too were prepared to employ all means, legal and illegal alike, to save Jewish lives.[42]

A brief look at the task division in this partnership shows that it had clearly defined parameters. The Emergency Committee oversaw the spheres of preparation, funding, logistics, and press releases for the march; the rabbis' area of responsibility centered on the recitation of psalms and prayers, and speechmaking. The petition presented to the White House was a joint effort. This partnership had the benefit of assisting each side in its stated goals without, however, affecting its unique identity. Rabbinic participation in the march in no way legitimated the Irgun Delegation's political-military goals, which, as we have seen, received no overt expression in Emergency Committee activity. For its part, Irgun cooperation with the rabbis in no way meant identification with Agudah fundamentalism. In both its nature and its activity patterns, the partnership between the Irgun Delegation and the Union of Orthodox Rabbis represents ad hoc localized cooperation between two marginal groups par excellence.[43]

Financing the Emergency Committee

A key determinant of the success of a particular campaign or in continued organizational life is finances, and the most frequently asked question is usually "where will the money come from?" In the case of the Emergency Committee, not only was the financial issue an accompanying undercurrent throughout its history and an essential condition for its continued existence, in addition it was a weapon in the arsenal of the American Jewish establishment, used to blast Hillel Kook and coterie.

As reported in its financial statement, during its initial year of existence the Emergency Committee succeeded in drafting $146,000 to its cause, mainly through mail solicitation, ads, radio broadcasts, dinners, and personal appeals. Two Jewish groups formed the mainstays of committee financial stability: the rabbinic unions and the *landsmanshaften*. The latter organizations, which were founded in the late nineteenth and early twentieth century as associations of Jews from the same areas in Europe and which functioned as substitute families and microcommunities, were particularly important to Kook and his associates as they provided them with access to lower—and middle-class American Jews.[44]

Who were the donors? In his study of the Emergency Committee, Yonah Ferman argues that the majority of its funding derived from Jewish sources, basing his conclusions on the delegation's mainly Jewish-directed fund-raising appeals and the fact that the bulk of the money came from the New York area. He also notes a socioethnic factor that played a role in financing the Emergency Committee: a natural tendency on the part of Jews to assist their brethren in times of distress. Nevertheless, there were numerous donations made by non-Jews on humanitarian grounds. Alex Rafaeli noted how some of the donations came from Christians who sought thereby to express their identification with Jewish fate and to assist what they viewed as an activist humanitarian organization. "Some were even impressed by the fact that we were different and much noisier than the others, and that we presented the Jewish problem as a humanitarian one. Support by church leaders also gave us access to publics that would never have considered supporting anything remotely connected with a Jewish cause."[45]

Jewish support for the Emergency Committee came mainly from appeals directed to the non-Zionist Jewish philanthropic oligarchy and to the lower—and middle-class Jews mentioned earlier, until then the bastion of Zionist organizations. In his analysis of the economic power structure of the Jewish philanthropic network, Halperin argues that this philanthropic oligarchy traditionally shied away from Zionist causes and, at certain stages, even took a hostile stand toward Zionism. Not only did Kook's success in penetrating this group's pocketbook by divorcing the Zionist issue from rescue further widen the rift between him and the American Zionist establishment, its antipathy for delegation activity was further fueled by Kook's incursion into what this establishment viewed as its turf: the Eastern European immigrant communities. The alarm of the Zionist establishment is more understandable if we compare its fund-raising efforts with those of the Emergency Committee: during its first six months of existence the Emergency Committee succeeded in raising a sum equal to two-thirds of that raised by the ZOA, the largest American Zionist organization, during the same six-month period.[46]

The American Jewish establishment soon took up the gauntlet of the perceived challenge from its ostensible rival, and in October 1944 the Jewish-owned *Washington Post* published a series of four front-page articles attacking the Emergency Committee from different angles, including the financial one. Its writers, however, displayed less interest in where the money had originated than in where it was headed. The committee had raised hundreds of thousands of dollars, the article claimed, but for what purpose? How could it be that the committee was not required to make its financial sources and the causes to which funds were directed a matter of public record? These questions, later reiterated in an anonymous report published shortly before the delegation disbanded, served as heavy-gauge ammunition for anti-delegation forces.[47]

Although subsequently forced to retract some of the allegations found in these articles, which were replete with inaccuracies, nonetheless their very appearance on the front pages of the *Post* provides an inkling of the true extent of American Jewish establishment animosity toward the delegation, and of its underlying fears regarding the central role this entity was beginning to assume in the public eye. This establishment effort to cast aspersions on the Emergency Committee may be viewed as yet another stage in its campaign against its new "competitors," who, they believed, had the potential to harm its efforts on behalf of European, American, and Palestinian Jewry alike.

As early as December 1943, American Jewish organizations had held lengthy meetings in order to determine how to treat the Emergency Committee. At an interim committee meeting of the American Jewish Conference held in late 1943, suggestions ranging from libel suits to public statements were aired. Calling the Emergency Committee founders "anarchists" and "bodies which do not accept discipline from a superior body," Rabbi Abba Hillel Silver spoke of "liquidating them on the American Jewish scene" by a concerted effort of American Zionist organizations. Ultimately the participants spoke of adopting a strategy of "struggle, of fight, of battle," and of releasing a public statement stating what the Emergency Committee's true agenda was: dynamic fund-raising and power politics without the ability to carry out any of its plans. Noting the necessity of informing "the goyim whom they [the Bergsonites] manipulate" about the group's true nature, Stephen Wise proposed drafting a scathing exposé of the Bergson Committee, acknowledging Hadassah president Rose Halperin's warning of "horrible repercussions" that she expected from Kook and company.[48] However, the draft of the statement was so scathing that it was rejected by several of the meeting's participants, and in particular Henry Monsky of Bnai Brith, who spoke of not taking on the task of "publicly disciplining Jewish organizations."[49]

The statement issued by the American Jewish Conference had little effect upon either the prominent Jews or the Gentiles who had cast their lot in with the Emergency Committee. Responding to the statement, Secretary of the Interior Harold Ickes wrote Stephen Wise that he would not permit himself "to become engaged in another of those finger-pointing disputes that only weaken the great purpose for which many are making the supreme sacrifice." Should the time come when Ickes found it necessary to withdraw his name from the committee, he would do so. However, as long as he was of the opinion that the committee was organized "to save lives and prevent suffering, as explained to me by men in whose word and honesty I have entire confidence, I expect to let my sponsorship stand."[50]

Yet another attempt was made to discredit the Emergency Committee in May 1944, after Pierre Van Paassen resigned from the committee, making public his reasons for disassociating himself from the group. These attempts included public statements issued by the American Jewish Conference regarding what they termed "false rescue claims" put forth by the committee. Quoting a telegram by Moshe Shertok, head of the political department of the Jewish Agency, who declared financial support for the committee "a criminal waste," conference representatives attempted to sway public opinion against the Emergency Committee but to little avail.[51]

Congressional Activities until the Establishment of the War Refugee Board

A single goal lay at the heart of Emergency Committee fund-raising and public relations activities: promotion of congressional activity on behalf of the committee's resolutions. With this end in mind, the delegation's Washington office initiated contacts with various congressional representatives. Sometimes using an Emergency Committee associate as a middleman, they would persuade them to forward the committee's aims, consistently placing emphasis on its nonsectarian nature and humanitarian goals. Alex Rafaeli recalled how their explanations also consistently stressed the compatibility of their proposed plans with the American ethos. Devastating reports of extermination from Europe, coupled with their sense that neither the White House nor the State Department were on their side, were another factor convincing Emergency Committee members to direct their efforts to the congressional arena. Yitzhak Ben-Ami recalled their despair during that period: Delegation members were not ready to give up rescue work, yet "we knew we did not have reliable friends in the White House and the State Department, and that we had to try to work through Congress." [52]

Emergency Committee members made varied approaches to individual representatives: soliciting them to become Emergency Committee members and to lend their names to its official letterhead and publications; attempting to persuade them to send letters to the White House on Emergency Committee matters or to approach the State Department directly; suggesting that they bring the committee's proposals to the knowledge of their congressional colleagues; requesting that they mention committee proposals in their speeches or have them entered in the *Congressional Record*, that they sign petitions or introduce bills, and finally, that they lecture on the committee's proposals before various audiences. Those congressmen who responded favorably not only received prepared printed material from the committee's propaganda bureau, but oral and written praise from its members. This willingness to participate in Emergency Committee activity may be attributed to several factors, primarily to the issue's humanitarian aspect and to these representatives' affinity to the rescue issue. Nor can we discount the role of desire for publicity as a factor attracting these congressmen, given the fact that Emergency Committee activity almost always enjoyed widespread media coverage.

Meanwhile the war continued. As delegation members concentrated their efforts on the American Congress, Allied forces were advancing slowly on all European fronts. In the Baltic region the Royal Air Force was carrying out nonstop bombing of Strettin and completing preparations to cross the English channel; in the east the Red Army had defeated the Germans at Kiev and had entered Poland; in Italy, although winter rains and difficult conditions slowed the Allies' northward advance, January saw the beginning of the main thrust that in June 1944 brought them to Rome. The Allies also made positive inroads in the air. With the conquest of the Foggia airfield in 1943, targets in central Europe and the Balkans were now accessible to Allied attack, including the train tracks leading to Auschwitz.

But this slow but steady Allied progress only intensified the question of the tragic fate of the Jews remaining in Nazi-occupied Europe, and Washington Emergency Committee members now decided to direct their congressional efforts to one pivotal issue: pushing a bill to form a governmental rescue agency through Congress. On 9 November 1943, the fifth anniversary of Kristallnacht, three Emergency Committee members—Senator Guy Gillette and Representatives Joseph C. Baldwin and Will Rogers, Jr.,—introduced a resolution with bipartisan support to Congress calling upon the president to create an agency that would act immediately to save the remaining European Jews. A special Washington branch of the Emergency Committee, specifically set up to lobby for passage of this Rescue Resolution, now issued appeals to Jewish organizations, labor unions, churches, rabbinical unions, newspapers, and the American Jewish Conference to support the bill. In addition, over twenty thousand postcards sent to committee supporters urged them to write to their congressmen, singling out House Foreign Affairs Committee chairman Sol Bloom in particular.

It did not take long for the Emergency Committee to discover that the Rescue Resolution's main opponents were the Jewish establishment and the State Department, specifically State Department official Breckinridge Long. This official, who oversaw the issuing of American visas, opposed the bill because he viewed it as an obstacle to the planned renewal of the intergovernmental committee on refugees decided upon at Bermuda. Foreign Affairs Committee hearings held in mid-November 1943 drew clearly defined battle lines. Testifying in favor of the Rescue Resolution were Dean Alfange, Frances Gunther, Hillel Kook, and New York mayor Fiorello LaGuardia. Their basic argument: deliberate State Department sabotage of each and every positive step the American administration has attempted to take on behalf of the refugees.

Pressing against the resolution was the State Department, which pre-

16. Labor leader Dean Alfange presented this photograph
of himself to Alex Rafaeli. Courtesy of Judith Tydor
Baumel.

sented its case later in the month. Long himself testified on 26 November,
immediately going on the defensive. After surveying his visa-granting activity from the war's beginning at length, Long argued that a significant
number of refugees had gained entry to the United States over the past
decade. "We have taken into this country since the beginning of the Hitler
regime and the persecution of the Jews, until today, approximately
580,000 refugees. The whole thing has been under the quota, during the
period of ten years—all under the quota—except the generous gesture we
made with visitors' and transit visas during an awful period [after Kristall-
nacht]," he testified.[53] A public outcry now erupted as this statistic seemed
significantly higher than the actual number of refugees admitted. Subsequent clarification elicited that Long's numbers referred to the maximum
number of visas he could have issued during that period, and not to the actual number of Jews who found refuge in the United States. Long also objected to the bill on administrative grounds, submitting that any new

entity would necessarily duplicate the work of the intergovernmental committee he now sought to resuscitate.

Surprisingly strong opposition to the Rescue Resolution also came from within the Jewish establishment, from none other than Rabbi Stephen Wise. His three-pronged opposition campaign first targeted committee ads for requesting donations whose final disbursement was unknown. Before singling out the proposed bill itself he put forth the claim that the Emergency Committee represented but a handful of Jews and Christians. To the Rescue Resolution itself he assigned a "failing" grade, both because it presented no specific plan of action and because it did not demand free immigration to Palestine.

Wise's testimony before the Foreign Affairs Committee nearly buried the proposed resolution. Eri Jabotinsky recalled the reaction of enraged Orthodox Jewish circles, who summoned Wise to appear before a rabbinic court. Others, including congressmen, found Wise's vocal opposition confusing, surprised to find a Jewish leader publicly opposing a bill to rescue Jews, as one Senate Foreign Relations Committee member commented: "I wish these damned Jews would make up their minds what they want. I could not get inside the committee room without being buttonholed out here in the corridor by representatives who said that the Jewish people of America did not want the passage of this resolution." Nor did committee chairman Sol Bloom—who has already been characterized as "being a *shabbos goy* for the State Department and performing certain duties which the administration itself finds distasteful"—look upon the Rescue Resolution favorably. Bloom's problematic and ambivalent attitude surfaced while Hillel Kook was testifying in the guise of a series of questions about the Emergency Committee—Kook's legal status in the United States, his biography, and his salary—which had no bearing on the Rescue Resolution itself.[54]

Neither State Department nor Jewish establishment opposition prevented the Rescue Resolution from passing the Senate during the third week of January 1944, as its opponents had not yet penetrated Senate deliberations. Congress then recessed for three weeks, leaving the fate of the resolution unclear. During this three-week hiatus, a new element entered the fray: Treasury Secretary Henry Morgenthau, Jr. Himself a Jew, Morgenthau, Jr., came from a home where political involvement was integrally woven into the fabric of family life, starting with the example set by his father, the American ambassador to Turkey during the First World War who took on the State Department in an effort to halt the Armenian genocide. From 1943 on Morgenthau, Jr., followed in his father's footsteps, becoming ever more involved in the intricacies of the refugee problem. Kook's first overture to Morgenthau to assist rescue plans in August 1943 received a hesitant but supportive reply. "I need not reiterate to you my interest in any intelligent plan which offers any reasonable hope of success for saving the Jewish population of Europe, which is rapidly being annihilated," Morgenthau wrote. "You may rest assured that I am already doing everything in my power, consistent with my position in the Government, to facilitate the rescue of these oppressed people." Over the next few months Morgenthau was made aware of numerous State Department efforts to sabotage any attempt to rescue European Jewry, peaking with a report submitted by his assistants on 13 January 1944—"Report to the Secretary of the Acquiescence of This Government in the Murder of the Jews"—that detailed the delays, unwillingness, and deliberate refusal to implement plans to rescue Europe's Jews.[55]

Fearing for the fate of the Rescue Resolution if it again came up for debate in Congress and the confrontation with the president if the resolution passed, Morgenthau and his assistants decided to sidestep Congress and to approach Roosevelt directly with their data, bringing with them a copy of a proposed presidential order mandating the immediate formation of a rescue committee. After brief consideration Roosevelt acceded to their proposal with but minor changes. This immediate approval was evidently inspired by FDR's awareness that, given public criticism of Long's testimony before the Foreign Affairs Committee, he would find it difficult to resist congressional pressure. The result was "Executive Order 9417 Establishing a War Refugee Board," issued on 22 January 1944. Having achieved the Rescue Resolution's main goal, Gillette now took it off the Senate agenda.[56]

What transpired while the Rescue Resolution was under discussion raises three vital questions. The first concerns the Jewish scene: in what light should American Jewish and especially American Zionist opposition to Gillette's resolution be viewed? The second question relates to Morgenthau's timely intervention: what factors now prompted this Jew to act on behalf of rescuing European Jewry? The third and final question relates to the Emergency Committee: what role did the committee ultimately play in the establishment of the War Refugee Board?

American Zionist opposition to the proposed resolution must be viewed within the larger context of the ongoing internal debate concerning the role of Palestine in any rescue scheme. Stephen Wise, along with other American Zionist leaders, sincerely believed that the next, most appropriate, step in the rescue of European Jewry was to open the gates of Palestine to Jewish immigration. Consequently, all Zionist proposals in this sphere zeroed in on the demand for unrestricted immigration to Palestine, leading to the summary dismissal of any plans that failed to incorporate this essential condition. Of necessity this policy led them on a collision course with the Emergency Committee, which, in order to amass broader-based support than that normally afforded any particularistic Zionist cause, deliberately divorced the Palestine question from rescue.

Up to that point, the conflict between the delegation and the American Zionist establishment revolved about three main areas of friction: namely, who had the right to air the Jewish question before the American public; competition for potential backers, both financial and emotional, among American Jewry and interested non-Jews; and the ideological interpretation afforded the other's political aspirations. For Stephen Wise, the delegation members were no more than hooligans, as Robert Silverberg observed: "They were little more than hoodlums in his eyes, and the fact that they were dedicated hoodlums, pledged to the same sacred cause he served, did not matter." Now the Palestine issue emerged as a new sphere of friction in the fray between the delegation and the American Jewish, and especially Zionist, establishment. We have already seen how an official December 1943 American Jewish Conference press release grounded its opposition to the Rescue Resolution in its having been proposed "in complete disregard" of rescue programs being promoted by authorized Jewish groups in Washington. In response, Emergency Committee members would state that the American Jewish Conference, which had been convened in August of that year to treat the questions of what would happen to Palestine after the war and the reconstruction of European Jewish communities, had only added rescue to its agenda as an afterthought. Furthermore, although intended to act as a representative body for all American Jewish organizations, it excluded both the ultra-Orthodox, who backed out in protest against rescue's marginal role, and the Irgun Delegation, whose overtures were rejected out of hand.[57]

Jewish establishment opposition to the Emergency Committee-sponsored Rescue Resolution did not restrict itself to noisy vocal protest, but even extended to attempts to physically remove Irgun Delegation members from the political playing field. As early as 1942 Stephen Wise saw fit to remind government officials that the delegation's members were young healthy males whose status in the United States in no way exempted them from military service. This reminder led to an exchange of letters between Hillel Kook and Assistant Secretary of State Adolf Berle regarding conscription of delegation members. It also appears that following the Bermuda Conference an angry Senator Scott Lucas requested an FBI investigation of Hillel Kook's fitness to serve in the armed forces; nevertheless, aside from their nuisance value, these efforts had little actual effect.[58]

The pressure on delegation members to enlist was not directed solely at Hillel Kook, however. In early 1942 the Chicago draft board contacted Alex Rafaeli, who was more than prepared to join the armed forces. "I asked the *Irgun* command permission to enlist. The political activity was becoming repetitive and I felt personally drained," he wrote in his memoir. But the Irgun command refused to release him on grounds that there was no one to replace him, and Rafaeli informed the draft board that he was unable to serve at present. Rafaeli was also the sole delegation member not actually subject to the draft as he carried a Latvian passport. "In those days [fall 1943] I was informed that Stephen Wise was behind the efforts to have us drafted," Rafaeli recounted. "When we also began to embarrass the Washington administration he was the one who sent out reminders that this was a good way to get rid of us. At last the die was cast: Yitzhak Ben-Ami was the sole Delegation member who was physically fit and liable to the draft. All the others were released on medical grounds: one had back problems, another ulcers, and the like. I couldn't allow him to go on his own, and the truth was that I very much wanted to take part in the war and to be sent to the front as soon as possible in order to do something for my family."[59]

Rafaeli's retrospective brings us back to the internal situation within the delegation in late 1943. After three years of intense activity, it appears that its members had lost some of their initial enthusiasm and had even developed some distaste for the established routine. Although their firmly entrenched task division continued to forestall intermember friction, at the same time tensions arose over a sense of being cut off from the hub of activity in the central office. In addition, the question of internal hierarchy

17. Alex Rafaeli at the podium. Courtesy of Judith Tydor
Baumel.

now reared its head. Normally, the internal hierarchy within a group, the
ranking of its members, and the divvying up of authority are a function of
power, authority, or persuasion. In the delegation's case it seems that all
three factors were losing ground, allowing the inevitable, ordinarily subliminal tensions to surface. Setting aside their personal, familial, and patriotic motivation, Ben-Ami and Rafaeli's induction into the American army
provided a simple solution to a potentially explosive long-standing situation. As early as July 1943 Eri Jabotinsky had written to Revisionist activist
Aryeh Altman in Jerusalem concerning the need to expand the delegation
for both political and personnel reasons, noting that he himself regarded
enlistment in the army as an easy out of a difficult situation. "I for one
would not feel so very unhappy about becoming a soldier over here. It

would mean, any way, getting away from the responsibility and the disappointments of the work that we are doing," he wrote. "We are working under very different conditions from those we had in Palestine. There is no glamor and no excitement attached to it—only plodding, lobbying and shnorring." [60]

Emergency Committee publications featured Ben-Ami's and Rafaeli's enlistment in the American army, touting it as an indication of its members' personal commitment to and participation in the anti-Nazi war effort. Organizationally speaking, however, their departure left a gap in both the delegation and the Emergency Committee, further widened when Eri Jabotinsky and Arieh Ben-Eliezer next left on assignment overseas. [61]

But the Zionist establishment's attempt to hurt the Emergency Committee by physically scattering its members by no means constituted the sole feature of its anti-committee campaign. Apparently the Zionist establishment was also behind reports appearing in the American press regarding financial improprieties in the framework of committee activity. Emergency Committee opponents also implied, both orally and in writing, that several key figures, such as Pierre van Paassen, had resigned from its chairmanship because of their dissatisfaction with the handling of personnel and financial matters. As many of these allegations could not be substantiated, the *Washington Post* was forced to publish a retraction several days later. [62]

The main protagonist of the anti-Emergency Committee struggle was the American Jewish Conference. Its condemnatory press release of 29 December 1943, which put forth the claim that the Emergency Committee had no mandate to speak for American Jewry, is instructive. Not content with simply censuring the Emergency Committee for its unwillingness to "play ball," it went on to accuse the committee of sabotaging the efforts of existing Jewish organizations, also arguing that Emergency Committee allegations of organized American Jewry's silence in face of the refugee problem and its inability to respond to current needs were aimed at blackening organized American Jewry's reputation.

For its part, the Emergency Committee could not leave this challenge unanswered. It responded that it required no mandate to speak in the name of American Jewry, as it did not claim to do so, taking special care to note the committee's nonsectarian, and not particularistic-Jewish, nature. With regard to accusations of their failure to cooperate, the committee pointed to delegation willingness to collaborate with existing Jewish organizations, noting that it was those very same organizations that had turned down its request to participate in the American Jewish Conference. Finally, even though an article in the first issue of the *Answer* had explicitly blamed the Jewish establishment for taking a do-nothing stance, they denied ever having made this allegation.[63]

Yonah Ferman submits that in many respects the polemic between the American Jewish and particularly Zionist establishment and the Irgun Delegation did not differ much from the conflicts that characterized the relationship between rival American labor organizations such as the American Federation of Labor and the Congress of Industrial Organizations before their merger, or between various special interest groups lobbying for changes in American foreign policy. Each of these conflicts had a twofold basis: competition for the loyalty of a particular public and a struggle for primacy in representing its interests to the administration. Both elements are clearly identifiable in the complex relationship between the American Zionist establishment and the Irgun Delegation throughout the latter's entire existence. But against the background of the rescue issue and Emergency Committee operations, this conflict now widened from one based on disparate ideological, operative, and instrumental approaches within the Zionist sector to an all-out battle between the delegation and all sectors of the Jewish establishment involved in broaching rescue plans. As we have seen, there were differences of opinion within the establishment regarding how to thwart the Emergency Committee in its thrust for public support. However, almost all leaders were in agreement: the existence of a "renegade" organization, one that refused to bow to the authority of the Zionist establishment, could not be tolerated. This stance was not just a matter of pride or an organizational power struggle. Bearing in mind the tenuous position of American Jewry during the years in question, leaders of Bnai Brith, the Joint Distribution Committee, Hadassah, the American Jewish Congress, and the American Jewish Committee truly believed that any serious division in the ranks of American Jewish organizations would act as an opening for anti-Semitic bureaucrats to thwart their efforts for world Jewry.[64]

Having summed up Jewish and Zionist establishment opposition to the Rescue Resolution, let us now return to the second question raised earlier regarding Henry Morgenthau, Jr.,'s support for the Rescue Resolution and his involvement in the founding of the War Refugee Board (WRB). What induced this Jew, along with other treasury officials, to take action on rescue in fall 1943? In both documentation from the period and later interviews, Hillel Kook takes some credit for this step, pointing to the fact that before the convening of the July 1943 Emergency Conference organized by Kook, Morgenthau's diaries reflect no interest or involvement in rescue.[65] Kook claims that his propaganda efforts also exercised some influence over Morgenthau's two assistants, Josiah DuBois and John Pehle, with whom he claims Emergency Committee members were in constant contact. This point, however, has not been corroborated by other sources. However it was Pehle, with his principled objections to American State Department policy, who persuaded Morgenthau that a direct appeal to Roosevelt was the only possible way to effect a policy change.

Yet another influence on Morgenthau appears in ultra-Orthodox sources, which claim that Morgenthau's personal secretary was a woman from an ultra-Orthodox background whose family had ties to the Union of Orthodox Rabbis, which, as we have seen, cooperated with the delegation. It was she, they submit, who saw to it that newspaper clippings detailing the situation of European Jews in occupied Europe were placed on her boss's desk daily. Again, however, this claim is not corroborated by any outside source, nor is any mention made of it in the Morgenthau diaries.[66] It therefore appears that the connection between Kook and the Emergency Committee on the one hand, and Morgenthau and his associates on the other hand, can be considered tenuous, if existing at all. However, it is apparent that the secretary's two male assistants played a major role in bringing the refugee issue to mind. This role, along with the rivalry between the State Department and the Treasury, and Breckinridge Long's damning testimony in front of the congressional committee, which raised Morgenthau's ire, were definitely among the impetuses that drove him to further examine the rescue issue. Having found financial irregularities in the State Department regarding the rescue issue, Morgenthau then proceeded to the president, who, in turn, was forced to issue the proclamation creating the War Refugee Board in order to avoid having a scandal exposed. Most historians claim that FDR considered this the lesser of evils, particularly in view of the fact that the Rescue Resolution was close to passing, something that would have forced him to face the issue in any event. By proclaiming the establishment of the War Refugee Board without congressional legal prodding, FDR would come out the hero in a battle that could have no winners, something extremely important in view of the fact that 1944 was an election year.

This proclamation leads us to our third question, which I deal with here only in brief, as I will return to it toward the end of this chapter: the role played by the Emergency Committee and the Irgun Delegation in the establishment of the War Refugee Board. As we have seen, it is difficult to make a direct connection between Morgenthau's pressure on the president to issue a rescue statement and the efforts of the delegation to meet with Morgenthau and his assistants. However, as the Rescue Resolution in Congress was delegation-sponsored, and the existence of this resolution played a somewhat psychological role in forcing FDR's hand in a specific direction, there is some basis to claims that the delegation played a partial role in the creation of the War Refugee Board. The gap between this statement and the delegation members' claims forms the basis for the historiographical debate over their role in the establishment of the rescue agency.[67]

The Irgun Delegation from Winter 1943 Onward

Ben-Eliezer's Mission to Palestine

With the approach of winter 1943 the Irgun Delegation again found itself at a crossroads. For three years the delegation—self-dubbed "the political arm of the Irgun"—had operated as an autonomous entity, a state of affairs enhanced de facto by the crisis in Yishuv Irgun ranks until Menachem Begin assumed command of the organization during the war and by its relationship with the American Zionist right wing—the New Zionist Organization and Betar—who were overshadowed by the ever-growing success of delegation offshoots. To get some sense of the balance of power between these entities, it is instructive to compare NZO membership, which then numbered about 10,000, and Betar membership, then about 4,500, with the 125,000 supporters of the Emergency Committee. Although there was no ongoing interaction between the delegation and the NZO at that point, the delegation did develop a warm relationship with Betar youth, seen as the Revisionist movement's future reserves. "Of course they influenced us," Moshe Arens, then chief officer of Betar's New England district, recalled. "Delegation members used to visit Betar summer camps and we learned from their methods. All in all, they were objects of admiration." Contemporary American Betar activity reports from the 1940s onward reflect this admiration and influence. Subsequent repercussions of this link will be examined below.[68]

Concern for the state of the Irgun in Palestine was one factor that prompted a delegation initiative to dispatch Arieh Ben-Eliezer overseas in fall 1943. Officially bound for Turkey, he was slated to meet with the American ambassador and to set up transit camps, and, at the same time, to convey an Allied promise to the Turkish government that no refugees would remain in Turkey after the war. However, Ben-Eliezer's primary task was to renew communication between the delegation and the Irgun in the Yishuv, to meet with Irgun leaders in an attempt to shore up the crumbling organization and to "get it back on track," as David Niv put it. One bit of evidence even submits that Ben-Eliezer transferred a small sum of money to the Irgun's Yishuv branch to fund its continued activity.[69]

While in Palestine Ben-Eliezer met not only with Irgun activists but also with a number of public figures from competing organizations, including Haganah member Eliyahu Golomb. Yitzhak Ben-Ami's retrospective summation made no secret of the organizational disintegration of the Irgun's Yishuv branch, noting, "When Ben-Eliezer talked to the young *Irgun* members in Palestine, he found that though their spirits were temporarily low, their dreams were still alive."[70] In the course of his conversations with Golomb, Ben-Eliezer proposed Irgun-Haganah cooperation on two fronts: on the local front, in fostering civil and military disobedience in Palestine, and on the European front, as a means of laying the groundwork for broad-based public support of activities for Jewish national liberation in the postwar period. Although at first seemingly receptive to these ideas, Golomb took a hard-line position at their second meeting and the joint program was dropped from the agenda. Renewed contacts with the underground Lohamei Herut Yisrael (LHI) movement also brought no concrete results as LHI leader Nathan Friedman-Yellin (Yellin-Mor) nixed all suggestions for a merger.

Two burning organizational issues were then on the Yishuv Irgun agenda: the need to find a strong commander to rehabilitate the organization and the desire to promote a new activist mode among the underground movements in answer to current needs. As for appointing a new commander, it was clear that Yaakov Meridor—who had nursed the organizational flame after Raziel's death—was endowed with neither the charisma nor the authority necessary to head the Irgun, and following consultations a decision was reached to make Menachem Begin commander in chief. But because the former leader of Polish Betar, then serving in the Polish army-in-exile, refused to assume this position unless formally released from the Polish army, it was Ben-Eliezer who now stepped into the breach and set this process in motion. Six weeks of intensive negotiations brought about Polish agreement to release Begin and another four Jewish soldiers, ostensibly as a means of promoting evacuation of Polish Jews who had found refuge in Russia. In exchange Ben-Eliezer promised that delegation members in the United States would use their political contacts to win support for the London-based Polish government-in-exile. As later summed up by Ben-Ami, the outcome was "a good, sound political deal for all concerned."[71]

Begin went underground immediately after his release, remaining in close contact with Ben-Eliezer over the following months during which Ben-Eliezer still functioned outwardly as a representative of the American Emergency Committee. In the course of this collaboration they discovered a number of shared premises: both agreed on the necessity of an armed struggle and of laying the foundation for a provisional Hebrew government; of approaching the Arabs with a request to prevent civil strife; and of intensifying propaganda efforts in Turkey, the Balkans, and the United States to open the gates of Palestine to Jewish immigration. A first operative step saw the formation of a new Irgun high command headed by Begin and manned by Ben-Eliezer, Shlomo Levi, Yaakov Meridor, and Eliyahu Lankin.

Having instituted a new high command, Irgun members were now free to turn to their second goal: activating the underground movements to work together for a common cause. But, based on Golomb's refusal to cooperate and the fact that the LHI was in the midst of a search for an ideological orientation at that point, the Irgun concluded that it must go its own way in implementing a third goal: using activist means to answer current needs. On 1 February 1944 Menachem Begin announced the initiation of a Hebrew revolt in Palestine. "Four years after the cease-fire declared on September 1, 1939, by Jabotinsky and Raziel, the *Irgun* went into battle," Ben-Ami wrote in his memoir. "It mustered four hundred men and women against the British Empire. Our weapons were several dozen handguns, some machine guns and a half a ton of explosives. The treasury contained approximately three thousand dollars. For communications we had a small transmitter and a paper called *Herut* which appeared intermittently. Training courses were going on in about a dozen towns and villages, and a few individual soldiers were scattered around the country."[72]

These developments not only changed Ben-Eliezer's plans, they also led to the formulation of new operative delegation goals for the Palestine region. Expected to be brief, the aims of Ben-Eliezer's visit to Palestine were originally conceived of as to renew contact, reorganize the Irgun command, and jointly establish new Irgun policy and military action. Following accomplishment of this mission, Ben-Eliezer was expected to continue on to Turkey in order to set rescue programs into motion. And once having completed his work in the British sphere of influence, he was slated to begin a continent-hopping campaign between the United States and Europe in conjunction with Eri Jabotinsky, also slated to work in the Turkish arena.

"Our plans did not work out the way we hoped they would," Ben-Ami later wrote. "Ben-Eliezer was afraid that it would seriously endanger our work if he disappeared underground; Kook and Merlin, by association, would become more vulnerable in the United States. He decided to stay above ground. By not going underground, he acted to shield his comrades."[73] As it turned out, these fears were by no means unfounded. On 17 April 1944 British Criminal Investigation Division arrested Ben-Eliezer, detaining him in the British Military Intelligence Center in Cairo for several months before deporting him, along with another three hundred Jews, to internment camps in East Africa. From that point on until his escape to France and return to Palestine in 1948, Ben-Eliezer was cut off from his colleagues in the Irgun Delegation.

Eri Jabotinsky Goes to Turkey

The second delegation overseas "ambassador" was Eri Jabotinsky. As early as September 1943 the groundwork for his trip had already been set in place, but it was not until the formation of the War Refugee Board in January 1944 that the State Department granted him a visa. Even within the

WRB Jabotinsky's mission to Turkey was unwelcome. Ira Hirschmann, a talented Bloomingdale's executive and a former Emergency Committee member who resigned when dispatched to Turkey by the WRB, stated his objections to War Refugee Board chairman Pehle in no uncertain terms: "My only reservation . . . is connected with his ability," Hirschmann wrote. "If he is a 'genius', he might be able to overcome the natural obstacles. Otherwise he will cause great embarrassment and difficulties to your representative in Ankara, be what will may." Despite State Department stonewalling and WRB objections, Jabotinsky eventually managed to reach Turkey via Palestine in May 1944, taking care to convey the impression that he was acting on behalf of the WRB and not as an Emergency Committee representative during his brief stay there. Thus he added further fuel to the American Zionist leadership's objections to the young Revisionist's presence and status in Turkey, objections they swiftly conveyed to the heads of the War Refugee Board.[74]

Turkey's choice as an operational theater by the delegation and the WRB was not fortuitous. As a neutral country close to the European front, Turkey not only became a center for international intrigue, its proximity to Palestine also made it a natural center for rescue operations and a Rescue Committee dispatched by the Jewish Agency was already operating there when Jabotinsky arrived. Some of its members, particularly Revisionist representative Joseph Klarman, even gave Jabotinsky partial cooperation.[75]

Jabotinksy's first reports to the Emergency Committee and the WRB on the situation in Istanbul were dispatched in June 1944. One memo, which bestowed effusive praise on Klarman and his rescue efforts, also mentioned another personality later destined to fulfill an important role in joint activity with the Emergency Committee: Jacob Griffel, the Agudath Israel representative to the Relief Committee, described by Jabotinsky as an honest, decent person. Jabotinsky's report also noted that in their role as representatives of the American-Orthodox-based rescue committee [the "Va'ad Hahatzala"] Griffel and Klarman were already working together with a Czech businessman by the name of Ludwig Kastner, going on to suggest that the Emergency Committee reach a cooperative agreement with the threesome on rescue. "Rabbi Eliezer Silver heads a rescue committee which is represented here by a Mr. Griffel. . . . they seem to be generally active. I want an amalgamation of their committee with the Emergency Committee," he wrote.[76]

Brief negotiations soon brought this hoped-for amalgamation into being, whose main goal was envisioned by its partners as promotion of aliyah via a joint Agudah-Revisionist initiative with American Va'ad Ha-hatzala funding. Their cooperative activity reached its acme in the summer 1944 attempt to purchase a large cargo ship to transport Romanian Jews to Palestine, portrayed by the Griffel-Klarman-Kastner trio as a final despairing step in efforts to find a safer alternative for the small aliyah bet boats. Given the fact this campaign was undertaken shortly after the German sinking of the small aliyah bet boat *Mefkura* not far from Istanbul, this claim appeared to be not entirely without justification. Eri Jabotinsky backed this endeavor, suggesting that Va'ad Hahatzala funds be directed toward the purchase of a Turkish ship. But, despite ongoing efforts on this front, for a variety of financial, diplomatic, and security reasons this initiative never got off the ground, partially as a result of strong disagreements between Jabotinsky and Hirschmann, who believed that negotiations—both on rescue and on temporary shelters for refugees—should only be carried out through official American channels in Turkey and not via an Emergency Committee representative. Others claim that the venture was never taken seriously in view of the bureaucratic difficulties involved and the inability of the persons at hand to take on such a mission.[77]

The Jabotinsky-Klarman-Griffel cooperation in Istanbul, that is between representatives of the Irgun, the NZO, and Agudath Israel, brings to mind the October 1943 "Rabbis' March" in Washington, as it too constitutes a model of localized cooperation in the sphere of rescue, a partnership bolstered by psychological and practical considerations alike. An "outsiders fellowship" between Agudath Israel and NZO representatives was a natural result of their feelings of exclusion from Zionist-run Relief Committee activity in Istanbul. But beyond the psychological reasons that drew them together, this partnership had a concrete basis: each side brought to the partnership a feature the other lacked. The Revisionists, and young Irgun activist Eri Jabotinsky in particular, provided Agudath Israel with initiative-grabbing activists prepared to use unconventional means to pursue their common goal of rescue; Agudath Israel not only provided the Revisionists with contacts in Europe (via Switzerland and the Polish government-in-exile) but also with sources of funding, through the American Union of Orthodox Rabbis in particular. It seems then that this trifold partnership provided mutual benefits to all parties.[78]

Despite its cooperative spirit, in the final analysis this partnership, which lasted until fall 1944, was a failure on the practical level. The sought-after Turkish vessel was never purchased, nor was the Mossad le-Aliyah Bet monopoly on rescue breached, and Eri Jabotinsky was unable to convince the American-Orthodox-based Va'ad Hahatzala to fund an additional planned campaign. Like Arieh Ben-Eliezer's mission to Palestine, British intervention cut short Jabotinsky's mission to Turkey. In early 1945 His Majesty's government deported Jabotinsky to Palestine, where he was jailed, ostensibly in connection with the murder of Lord Moyne. In reality, this step was evidently a British response to delegation activity in the States. When banished from Turkey, Jabotinsky was in the midst of negotiations for bringing 2,500 Jews monthly from the Balkans en route to Palestine. Although released from jail shortly thereafter, his repeated requests for an American visa were denied; consequently, from mid-1944 onward only two of the six original delegation members remained in the States: Samuel Merlin and Hillel Kook.[79]

It was not simply by chance that this specific pair remained in the United States and not any other twosome. Despite the delegation's overall cooperative nature, which we have already noted, we cannot ignore the development of subgroups within the context of the larger six-member group. Studies of successful group functioning show how the presence of flexible coalitions and subgroups within the larger group facilitates adaptation to changing conditions. However they simultaneously note that while these coalitions provide evidence of operational flexibility, over a period of time the composition of these subgroups tends to repeat itself, which suggests their members possess a large degree of shared characteristics.[80] To be more specific, in the case of the delegation, Kook and Merlin paired off as the delegation "ideologues" while Rafaeli, Ben-Ami, and Ben-Eliezer functioned as field workers. Being a Betar commander (and not an Irgun activist) and because he was last to arrive in America, Eri Jabotinsky was initially an outsider. It was only natural that Kook and Merlin constituted a subgroup within the larger context even before external circumstances—their ill-health, which prevented them from being drafted—forced them to remain together in the States. This partnership culminated in the mutual cross-fertilization that gave birth to the delegation's greatest ideological innovation, the idea of "Hebrews" vs. "Jews" treated in the next chapter.

Activities of the War Refugee Board

Eri Jabotinsky's activities in Turkey reflect but one aspect of WRB activity, which also extended to construction of shelters for refugees and development of rescue and help programs for those suffering from Nazi persecution everywhere. Although slated to receive funding from the American State and War Departments as well, in actuality the WRB was dependent on the good will of a single American agency: the Treasury Department headed by Henry Morgenthau, Jr., who, as we have seen, was already favorably disposed toward rescue operations. Although an American agency formed to implement programs formulated in Washington, its staff did not consist solely of Americans. At times the WRB used American personnel; in other cases it utilized the services of local or foreign agents for its activity in Turkey, Switzerland, Sweden, North Africa, Italy, and Portugal. In addition, the WRB worked alongside existing rescue agencies, such as the Va'ad Hahatzala or its European representatives. Finding funding for its activity was a constant concern plaguing the WRB, whose limited administrative budget came largely from Roosevelt's emergency fund, with an additional million-dollar grant for food packages for concentration camp inmates. But for any activities beyond the above, the WRB's dynamic young chairman, former treasury official John Pehle, turned to Jewish organizations, including the Joint Distribution Committee (which donated $15,000,000 to rescue operations), the Va'ad Hahatzala of the Union of Orthodox Rabbis ($1,000,000), and the World Jewish Congress ($300,000).[81]

Studies of the American attitude to the Holocaust, including those by Henry Feingold and David Wyman, devote close attention to WRB activity. These studies credit the WRB with founding temporary shelters for refugees, seeing to the transfer of some 7,000 Jewish refugees from the Balkans to Turkey and then to Palestine, and the rescue of the 48,000 remaining Transnistrian Jews by exerting pressure on the Romanian government to allow them to enter its borders.[82] Although the American ambassador to Spain refused to cooperate with WRB representatives, Portugal agreed to absorb any European refugee arriving via Spain, and Italy gave refuge to tens of thousands of Yugoslavian, mainly non-Jewish, refugees, of whom 28,000 were transferred to shelters in Egypt until able to return to their homeland. WRB representatives even approached the pope with a request to appeal to the Germans to stop the transport of Jews from northern Italy, receiving a negative reply.

From Sweden, WRB representatives inserted teams into Estonia, Latvia, and Lithuania, but succeeded in rescuing only 1,200 individuals, none of them Jewish. In Switzerland WRB representatives assisted welfare activity in Nazi-occupied territory, and also prepared false papers as part of the smuggling and rescue operations they organized in partial cooperation with the Va'ad Hahatzala and Irgun member Reuven Hecht. The final arena of WRB operations was its attempt to rescue Hungarian Jewry from the Nazi pincers that closed around them in March 1944, some eight weeks after the WRB came into existence. Overall, Wyman credits the WRB with saving approximately 200,000 Jews: 15,000 brought out of Axis territories, 10,000 European Jews who received protection from the underground and were granted Latin American passports, and more than 48,000 Transnistrian Jews transferred to Romania. WRB pressure also put a stop to transports from Hungary. Finally, some 120,000 Budapest Jews were saved, thanks to either direct or indirect pressure from the WRB, its representatives, and partners, including Swedish diplomat Raoul Wallenberg. Having briefly summed up its accomplishments, I will concentrate here on three spheres of WRB activity, in addition to the Turkish arena covered above, in which Irgun Delegation members in the United States or their European representatives took part: temporary shelters, efforts to save Hungarian Jewry, and Swiss-based rescue operations.

A significant sphere of WRB activity concerned the establishment of temporary shelters for refugees who succeeded in escaping from occupied Europe. A suggestion along these lines had been raised at the Emergency Conference held in July 1943, echoed by other organizations throughout the year. Now the Emergency Committee lent public support to the establishment of temporary shelters worldwide, publishing a huge ad in the American press—"25 Square Miles or 2 Million Lives, Which Shall it Be?"—that called for setting up temporary shelters in Palestine, Turkey, and North Africa in abandoned American training camps and in the British-controlled territories. As this plan had Henry Morgenthau, Jr.'s backing—and the president's blessing—it achieved immediate results, and in June 1944 a temporary shelter to house some one thousand, mostly Jewish, refugees opened at Fort Oswego in upstate New York. With Emergency Committee encouragement, Congressmen Andrew Somers and John Smertenko now introduced a bill calling for similar camps to be set up in Palestine, a bill that aroused strong American Zionist establishment opposition. As opposed to the Emergency Committee, which, as we have seen, made a clear distinction between the refugee question and the Palestine question, the Zionist establishment saw any call for granting even *temporary* asylum in Palestine as conflicting with its demand for free immigration and ultimately sabotaging its long-term efforts, particularly in view of what they considered a total inability to free Jewish refugees from occupied European territory. And indeed, the persons who ultimately found refuge in the U.S. refugee territory were those who had already been liberated from occupied Europe.[83]

Somers and Smertenko's call for setting up temporary shelters in Palestine was paralleled by a WRB decision to open such camps for refugees in North Africa. Although ostensibly a straightforward matter, agreement was by no means simple to achieve, and a June 1944 telegram from the American secretary of state to the American consulate in London reported failed efforts to reach an agreement with the British regarding the setting up of such camps in Tripolitania and Cyrenaica. Others suggested transferring some Yugoslavian refugees who had reached Italy to Sicily, but in the final analysis the North African option was given preference.[84] As these efforts by and large aided non-Jewish refugees, in the summer of 1944 Emergency Committee members again turned the spotlight on the problem's Jewish aspect, issuing a call for temporary shelters to house Jewish refugees, in this case Hungarian Jews.

The German invasion of Hungary, home to the last large remaining Jewish concentration in Europe, sparked intense Emergency Committee activity. In addition to placing giant ads in the American press demanding that the gates of Palestine be opened, the committee organized meetings between a delegation of Hungarian Jews and congressmen and WRB leaders. The committee also forwarded a telegram to Stalin offering to exchange 50,000 Ukrainian Jewish refugees for Hungarian prisoners being held by the Soviets.

Emergency Committee activity on behalf of Hungarian Jewry changed direction in July 1944 with the announcement by Hungarian head of state Miklós Horthy that he would allow all children under the age of ten with foreign visas and Jews of any age with Palestine certificates to emigrate. The ball was now in the Allied court, galvanizing Kook into a campaign to rouse American public opinion; his first step employed the tried-and-true tactic of publishing eye-catching ads demanding the setting up of temporary shelters for these refugees in Palestine. Following Kook's usual two-pronged conception, this campaign's second stage addressed the congressional front, presenting Congress with an Emergency Committee petition with a half-million signatures and proposing that it back the founding of temporary shelters in Palestine for Hungarian refugees. These steps, like previous ones, again drew fire from Zionist establishment leaders who, as we have already noted, opposed detaching the refugee question from the broad issue of Palestine's political future. In a public statement the American Jewish Conference denounced "sensationally displayed advertisements . . . asserting that there are great possibilities at present for the rescue of thousands upon thousands of Jews from Nazi territory" and negated the claim that the Emergency Committee had instrumentality in Turkey for the actual rescue of Jews from occupied Europe. Insisting that the committee's claims had no foundation, it warned the public not to support any of the committee's endeavors, financially or otherwise.[85] In the final analysis, as the British absolutely refused to open the gates of Palestine—even temporarily—to European Jewish refugees, this campaign failed to achieve its goal. Without British approval the hands of the Allies were tied, and although negotiations on this matter continued into late summer 1944, by that time it was far too late to rescue most of Hungarian Jewry.[86]

Rescue efforts carried out via Switzerland constitute another arena of WRB activity where we find Irgun member involvement. This was where Reuven Hecht, a NZO representative and Irgun member, a long-time friend and fellow student of Alex Rafaeli from their Heidelberg days, came into the picture. Hecht maintained constant contact with the Irgun Delegation in the United States throughout the war years and was the Emergency Committee representative in Europe. The turning point in this activity occurred when Hecht linked up with industrialist Isaac Sternbuch and his wife, Recha, Swiss rescue activists closely affiliated to Agudath Israel circles. Hecht found the young ultra-Orthodox Jew with his "Agudah beard" charming. For his part, Sternbuch was much taken with the energetic Irgun activist and shortly thereafter proposed that Hecht join the European board of the American Va'ad Hahatzala of the Union of Orthodox Rabbis. Taken by surprise, Hecht's response was "I am neither Orthodox, nor a rabbi, nor an American," but in the final analysis, pragmatic considerations, sparked by personal chemistry, overrode formal criteria. Following a brief consultation with Kook, Hecht accepted Sternbuch's proposal and from that point on the twosome teamed up on matters of assistance and rescue, playing a role in organizing the so-called Musy train in cooperation with the WRB, and in late-war efforts to rescue Jews from Bergen-Belsen and from Buchenwald. During this entire period Hecht switched hats, alternating among his roles as representative of three different organizations—the NZO, the Irgun, and the American Va'ad Hahatzala—and thereby averting a conflict of interest.[87]

This relationship appears to repeat a pattern similar to the one created in the context of the "Rabbis' March" and in joint activity between the delegation and the Agudath Israel representative in Turkey. An essential component driving the Sternbuch-Hecht partnership was the elements each lacked: Hecht for his part obtained organizational machinery and funding from the Agudah representatives, providing them in turn with a Swiss front possessed of useful local political and economic connections. A shared essential goal, to rescue as many Jews as possible as quickly as possible, and a similar modus operandi, a willingness to employ unconventional means to achieve their goal, further lubricated the wheels of this partnership. Questions of politics and religion never surfaced openly. "With the Agudah one didn't speak ideology," Hecht recalled. "One spoke 'tachlis' [bottom line]. There was no time for long ideological debates as in the labor movement." And, as we have seen, there was no shortage of tasks demanding immediate attention. It seems then that this tripartite partnership between an Irgun representative in Switzerland, the Va'ad Hahatzala of the American Union of Orthodox Rabbis, and the WRB representative gave rise to what may be assessed as one of the more colorful rescue collectives of the entire wartime period.[88]

The Delegation During Spring 1944

The delegation activity in Europe outlined above was paralleled by efforts on the part of its two remaining representatives in the States—Hillel Kook and Samuel Merlin—to further its aims in the United States. Although we might have expected the loss of two-thirds of its members to slow delegation momentum in general and Emergency Committee momentum in particular, this was, however, not the case. The well-oiled local Emergency Committee organizational machinery continued to function, as did activity in the two realms so vital to forwarding Emergency Committee aims: public relations (provocative ads and the Answer Publishing House publications) and congressional activity. Certainly the fact that the remaining delegation members in the States were its leader and its ideologue respectively was not detrimental to this state of affairs.

An additional explanation for continued Emergency Committee momentum lies in its nondelegation committee activists such as Ben Hecht, Guy Gillette, William Ziff, and Professor Johan Smertenko. I refer here to group analyst Rodney W. Napier and Matti K. Gershenfeld's observation: "Generally, a successful group has clear objectives . . . and members of a group have personal objectives that are compatible with the group's objectives." Beyond their personal and moral involvement in the specific issue of rescue, these individuals associated with the Emergency Committee also met the conditions essential to continued operational functioning even after personnel changes at the top: that is, a strong desire to continue working together toward their common aim; a stress on shared features like commonly held moral values, not member differences; a strong degree of group cohesion; and finally, recognition that any deviation from group behavioral norms would lead to sanctions, if only moral ones.[89]

A prime motivation for Emergency Committee members was the sense of mission—humanitarian and Jewish—that fired their resolute dedication to the cause, reinforced by what they saw as the first fruits of their efforts: the founding of the War Refugee Board. Kook and Merlin now saw fit to revive their much-beloved tactic of appealing to the public via fireworks and celebrities, organizing an extravaganza titled *Show of Shows,* which opened on 18 March 1944 to celebrate the founding of the WRB and, naturally, to raise funds for Emergency Committee activity. According to one source, this pageant netted more than $100,000 in donations.[90]

Another topic on the agenda of committee activists, mainly in late 1944 and early 1945, was war crimes and bringing war criminals to justice in the postwar era. Although mentioned by other organizations—and the U.S. government—as early as 1943, the delegation later attempted to promote itself as having been the initiator of the idea. In anticipation of postwar tribunals, delegation members now lobbied the American and British administrations to declare the murder of European Jewry a war crime. Eri Jabotinsky recalled how the committee sought to disseminate reports throughout Europe that the Allies had determined to put a stop to the extermination, no matter what. "We thought that one of the reasons for the extermination was that Jewish lives were considered cheap and would not be avenged. . . . We thought that if it were known throughout Europe, particularly in the small satellite nations under German influence who already feared for their future, that America favored this, they would put a stop to the extermination."[91] Notwithstanding their active airing of this issue, delegation members were denied representation on the Allied War Crimes Commission.

Nazi criminals in Europe by no means constituted the delegation's sole source for concern, as enemies at home endangered its goals as well. By late 1943 Zionist elements in the United States, including Irgun members, had become fully aware of plans afoot by a group of State Department officials who opposed Zionist aspirations to tip the Palestine question in favor of the Arabs even before the war's end. Alarmed by the loss of Arab importance as a strategic barrier to the Germans after the Allied victory in North Africa, these officials now sought to force a political decision on Palestine. Even those State Department officials interested not in forcing but in freezing the debate on the Palestine issue until after the war were a cause for alarm to delegation members and the Zionist establishment alike. Witness, for example, the panic created by State Department official Harold Hoskins's 1943 memo, in which he suggested that a joint Anglo-American declaration be issued to the effect that no solution would be sought to the Palestine question until after the war, and that any such arrangement would have to win full Arab agreement. Beirutborn Hoskins, son of American missionaries, predicted full-scale rebellion by the Arabs in the event that such an arrangement was not reached. Hoskins also noted the divisive struggle between the Zionist establishment and the Revisionists, singling out the Irgun Delegation for mention. Backed by other officials known for their unfavorable disposition toward the Jews, heavy pressure was now placed on the American Zionist establishment to agree to the Hoskins memo. At this point, several figures closely associated with the Emergency Committee, including Senator Edwin Johnson and Henry Morgenthau, Jr., and Zionist establishment leaders including Stephen Wise, stepped into the breach. In the final analysis Hoskins's proposal was shot down, not because of Zionist opposition, but mainly thanks to opposition by Secretary of War Stimson.[92]

Although the Hoskins's memo no longer posed an imminent threat, the anti-Jewish bias in the State Department flashed a warning signal to delegation members concerning the need to commence Zionist activity alongside their nonpartisan rescue efforts. For some time now Kook had been contemplating the formation of yet another delegation offshoot specifically geared to Zionist activity. In the final analysis, two offshoots emerged: the Hebrew Committee of National Liberation and the League for a Free Palestine. Although founded during 1944 these entities initiated their coast-to-coast campaign only in January 1945, when Emergency Committee activity was clearly drawing to a close.

By May 1945 it was obvious that the Emergency Committee was folding up shop. A circular letter distributed to thousands of activists nationwide announced the committee's profound regret at its failure to achieve more victories in the war against murderers, that during its three-year existence millions who could have been saved died in gas chambers, by firing squad, in crematoria, and of starvation, and went on to declare that it was in no way its intent to cover for anyone, to pat itself on the back, or to grant forgiveness. These were in the hands of God and history. The letter ended on a note of continuity—the Hebrew Committee of National Liberation would now act on behalf of the survivors—concluding with an appeal for contributions to defray the costs of a special summary issue of the *Answer* devoted to Emergency Committee activity for distribution both to the American public and to survivors.[93]

As this letter evoked only a minimal response, Merlin's planned special issue was pared down to a four-page booklet titled "A Final Message from the Emergency Committee to Save the Jewish People of Europe to its Co-fighters for a Decent Humanity."[94] Summing up committee activity and ranking various political entities with regard to their responsibility for the extermination of European Jewry, the booklet ended with an appeal for donations and for readers to send in the names and addresses of their surviving relatives. But the pamphlet's essential message was not one of closure but of continuity. It was now time to focus the spotlight on the delegation's original goal, to work both to draft support for evacuating the Jews from Europe and toward realization of the Irgun's central political goal: an independent Jewish state. This booklet marked the delegation's final transition from an entity that had divorced itself from Irgun political aims in order to rescue European Jewry, into an entity that readopted these aims publicly in order to establish a homeland for those European Jews who had survived.

Evaluating the Emergency Committee

The period of Emergency Committee activity is without a doubt the most researched piece of delegation history in the United States. As early as the sixties various scholars devoted attention to this phase, and Kook's activity received mention in some half-dozen books that appeared in the United States during the 1970s and 1980s.[95] This timing fit the burning question then on the American and the American Jewish agenda: the attitude of the American administration and of American Jewry to the Holocaust, an attitude that emerged full force when government war year archives were opened. Moreover, it was during the phase of Emergency Committee activity that the delegation reached what is often viewed as the apex of its achievements: the founding of the War Refugee Board.

As defined in the organizational model for group activity proposed earlier, the years 1943 and 1944 represent the period of "norming" in the history of the Irgun Delegation in the United States, a stage characterized by orderly organized activity and internalization of accepted group norms that in turn guarantee success. During this phase, more than any other in delegation history, delegation members worked in concert, putting the patterns established during the days of the Jewish Army Committee to good use. The dissolution of the nuclear group following Ben-Eliezer and Jabotinsky's departure on overseas missions and Rafaeli and Ben-Ami's induction into the American army also enabled the group to maintain the illusion of "togetherness" without having to engage in potentially divisive introspective examination.[96]

Nineteen forty-four marks a halfway point for the delegation, a point at which it had already crystallized in form and content. Consideration of this phase raises the two related issues of classification and orientation. Classification—that is, locating the delegation within the Zionist spectrum, and the degree to which it fit the right-wing Zionist stereotype in terms of composition, ideology, and activity patterns—will be broadly discussed in the final chapter. This leaves us to narrowly consider delegation activity under the Emergency Committee to Save the Jews of Europe rubric.

As for classification of activists, at first glance it is difficult to elicit any similarities between Emergency Committee activists—with the exception of the delegation's hard core—and the stereotype of the Zionist right-winger for the simple reason that the Emergency Committee was not a

Zionist but a nonsectarian entity with many non-Jewish members. As for orientation, having already briefly considered who manned the committee, we turn to its goal: distilled rescue without any reference to the original core group's national-political objectives. This distinction, which guided the delegation throughout Emergency Committee activity, infuriated the American Zionist establishment, then pressing for the notion of a Zionist commonwealth. This policy only added fuel to the Zionist establishment's arguments vis-à-vis the delegation and any of its organizational creations and, as we have seen, led to a boycott of any Emergency Committee-sponsored rescue programs. In the final analysis, the issues of Zionist political orientation, acceptance—or lack thereof—of organizational authority, and a sincere desire on behalf of all groups—delegation and establishment—to do the utmost in order to care for Jews worldwide, according to their definition, did not unite the parties involved, but divided them irrevocably. In this battle there were no winners, only losers.

This "distilled rescue" orientation characteristic of the 1943 to 1944 years brings to the fore another question regarding Hillel Kook's chosen path. At first glance it appears that, at the height of the Holocaust, delegation members temporarily abandoned the Palestine issue. However, careful chronological consideration of delegation offshoots reveals not a purely sequential but an overlapping picture. The early period of Emergency Committee activity took place in tandem with Jewish Army Committee activity, whose aspirations were connected, even if only indirectly, to the Palestine question. And only a few days separated the official disbandment of the Jewish Army Committee in fall 1943 and the founding of the League for a Free Palestine in late November of that year. Although not unveiled to the public until spring 1944, by its very existence the new league and its fellow offshoot, the Hebrew Committee of National Liberation, provide evidence of Kook's steadfast devotion to promoting Revisionist ideology within a purely Zionist context. Thus it would be a distortion to reduce delegation activity from 1943 to 1944 solely to Emergency Committee activity and its concentration on rescue.

Another important area to be considered concerns the delegation's intergroup relationships. As Samuel Halperin has observed, "The influence of an interest group varies with the number and quality of alliances it can construct with other groups."[97] Not only did the delegation forge ties with non-Jewish ethnic groups, the Irish in particular, but 1943 saw the initiation of a fruitful partnership with ultra-Orthodox Jewish elements, including Agudath Israel. This partnership was realized in three venues: the United States, Turkey, and Switzerland.

How should we view this wartime partnership between Irgun members and representatives of the ultra-Orthodox Agudath Israel movement? Reminiscent of the type sociologists term "strange bedfellows"—cooperation between groups that at first glance seem to possess no shared characteristics—for a time the delegation's relationship with the "ultras" seemed to flourish. Put more precisely, this type of relationship does not simply refer to groups with a mutually neutral standpoint, or to those that find themselves in conflict from time to time, but also encompasses hostile groups actively espousing antithetical positions. In such a partnership both sides transcend barriers of political ideology, economic policy, social approach, or religious stance to create a pragmatic alliance in the interest of a common goal. Although these alliances often dissolve once the specific goal has been achieved, in some cases, based on the need to maintain the status quo once the original goal has been attained, they can be long lasting.[98]

This description certainly applies to the "strange bedfellows" partnership between the delegation and Agudath Israel during the 1940s, of which an absence of religious confrontations and a sense of outcasts' brotherhood were essential components, facilitated by Irgun structure during the war and especially by the lack of contact among its different centers. The two groups also had a shared operational language: as outsiders in establishment circles they neither felt constrained by accepted norms, nor did they fear a reckless misstep would destroy their fragile, carefully built relations with the non-Jewish establishment. Also, their shared sense that the Zionist establishment was essentially looking out for its own interests intensified delegation and Agudath Israel devotion to the rescue issue. Finally, unlike the Jewish establishment, as members of the opposition both the delegation and Agudath Israel enjoyed the luxury of being able to concentrate on a single issue, not having to divide their energies over a number of fronts linked to present Jewish existence and preparation of a future home for survivors.[99]

From orientation and partnerships we now move on to an attempt to evaluate overall achievement. Certainly, as the largest of the delegation offshoots with its more than 125,000 members, the Emergency Committee was a mid—to large-sized organizational player on the American Jewish scene. By way of comparison, Hadassah membership then numbered 140,000 and the ZOA had 136,000 dues-paying members.[100] Organizationally and financially, the Emergency Committee conformed to the patterns established earlier by the Jewish Army Committee: it promoted fund-raising campaigns aimed at creating a public relations network capable of lobbying Congress, in this case, to mandate a government-sponsored rescue agency. Both numerically and financially, it appears that the Emergency Committee was a force to be reckoned with on the American Jewish scene. This influence explains the plethora of debates within American Jewish establishment organizations—the American Jewish Conference, Bnai Brith, Hadassah, the American Jewish Committee, and the AZEC—regarding the Emergency Committee: how to deal with it and how to counteract its impact on both the American Gentile and Jewish public.

As for what is often viewed as the delegation's crowning achievement in the sphere of rescue, the War Refugee Board, the Emergency Committee's role in its founding has been the subject of debate since the 1970s. As would be expected, Revisionist historiography awards sole credit for the founding of the WRB to the Irgun Delegation. Other scholars, including David Wyman, also allocate a significant role to the Bergsonites in the founding of the WRB, assigning them full credit for their successful congressional campaign and for creating public interest in the rescue issue: "The Bergsonite Emergency Committee tried to fill the gap in the rescue campaign. Its work was vital in finally bringing the War Refugee Board into existence," Wyman wrote. Although in Wyman's estimation the WRB came far too late and accomplished far too little, he nonetheless views it as an important step in the rescue field, estimating it "played a crucial role in saving approximately 200,000 Jews." [101]

At the other end of the academic spectrum we find American Jewish historian Monty Penkower, who deals not only with issues of rescue but with a broad overview of American Zionist activity during the period in question. Although he notes a by no means exclusive delegation role in the founding of the WRB, albeit mentioning the delegation's prowess in the public relations sphere, generally speaking he assesses their success as "meager" at best, ultimately assigning greater weight to Morgenthau's role in persuading the president to establish the WRB. Penkower's harsher judgment of the delegation's role may stem from his Palestinocentric bias, leading him rightfully to stress delegation failure to change Anglo-American policy on the Middle East or to promote its concept of Hebrews versus Jews. Indeed, Penkower deals more with the bottom line of policy making and agency establishment and less with organizational follow-up. Nowhere does he note the WRB's success in various fields or the number of people its representatives rescued; rather he emphasizes the delegation's inability to act independently, and its reliance on British and American goodwill, directly attributing its failure to its members' overly strong belief in the American democratic ethos, a belief that failed to empower them to shift administration policy.[102]

For a third position in this debate we turn to Henry Feingold, who takes the unequivocal stance that "the Emergency Committee could do little more than label the public display of strife within the Jewish community 'a tragic error'. . . . When the breakthrough was made, it was by neither the Zionists nor the Emergency Committee." Like Penkower, according to Feingold it was Henry Morgenthau, Jr., and not the Emergency Committee who convinced Roosevelt to change his policy, ultimately leading to the establishment of the WRB.[103]

Essentially, this historiographical debate revolves around the weight assigned to each of the various factors in Roosevelt's decision to found the WRB. Closer examination of how events unfolded shows the "Kook vs. Morgenthau" controversy to be at the center of the debate regarding the delegation; however, in truth the two factors appear more complementary than contradictory. Even if one accepts that Morgenthau's intense involvement in rescue efforts from summer 1943 had no connection to any approaches made by Emergency Committee members, but was influenced by his assistants' role in charting the hostile State Department attitude toward rescuing refugees, one can not ignore the impact of the delegation-sponsored Rescue Resolution then being debated in Congress. While it may be debated that either factor alone might have been enough to force the president's hand to establish the WRB, in practice the two worked in tandem to convince FDR to establish a rescue agency at that particular time. And one can not ignore good timing: the fact that it was an election year, something that made FDR more amenable to creating the WRB; the Allied progress on the war front; the fact that definitive word had been received regarding the fate of much of European Jewry; and finally, the desire to make a gesture that would not require too much American government effort but would, to a great deal, rely on the support of outside bodies.

Historians share greater agreement regarding the degree of delegation success in arousing public awareness and in drafting public opinion to the rescue issue. If, as Samuel Halperin argues, "propaganda is effective in arousing and mobilizing public opinion only where there is an already existent predisposition in that direction," then the delegation members' sharply honed instincts indeed directed them to receptive publics with humanitarian leanings. Their clear differentiation between their Zionist ideology and rescue also enabled them to address individuals who would never even have considered supporting the Irgun's national aspirations, thereby affording them a double advantage. On the one hand, the Emergency Committee was able to make the rescue of European Jewry a matter of public record; on the other, Jewish organizations in general—including Zionist ones—benefited from the growing American public awareness of a wartime and postwar Jewish problem.[104]

The public debate surrounding Emergency Committee activity scaled new heights in the 1980s with the creation of the "Goldberg Commission," formed to investigate the American Jewish response to the Holocaust. This commission, headed by Chief Justice Arthur Goldberg, for whom it was named, approached a number of scholars, asking them to assess the American Jewish response to the Holocaust in cooperation with a City University of New York research team headed by Seymour Maxwell Finger. But this commission's much-debated activity soon mushroomed to polemical proportions, particularly after the *New York Times* published initial findings citing missed opportunities for rescue.[105] These findings, toward which much criticism was directed for their one-sided a priori ideological bias, came not from a trained historian's pen but originated with a personal friend of the research team director: Samuel Merlin.

After reviewing Merlin's tentative report, several historians who had earlier expressed their willingness to serve on the commission now withdrew from the project, having concluded that this was not an investigative commission but rather a body with foregone conclusions. Some, like the American historian Lucy Dawidowicz, absolutely refused to be associated with the commission in any way. Others, such as Yehuda Bauer of the Hebrew University, Jerusalem, agreed to participate only if Merlin were ousted.[106]

Merlin's report, which had in the meantime acquired an academic ve-
neer, arrived on the desks of the Goldberg Commission in spring 1982
and again aroused controversy, even though, as a result of the fierce debate, Merlin himself had earlier resigned from the commission. Consequently, Jack Eisner, a Holocaust survivor who had provided the funding
for the commission's activity, now announced that he too was withdrawing his support, and this Eisner-Merlin-Goldberg dispute made the *New
York Times*. Goldberg subsequently announced that he was prepared to resuscitate the commission and also to find other funding. In the final analysis, the commission's sole scholarly achievement was the publication of a
volume of essays on wartime rescue opportunities, edited by Seymour Finger, that included studies of the American attitude toward the Holocaust
and of opportunities to rescue Romanian, Slovakian, and Hungarian
Jews.[107]

But like the Irgun Delegation, the Goldberg Commission's essential
contribution was not so much in the sphere of research—the above-
mentioned volume of articles—but in the public relations sphere, in focusing the public spotlight on the behavior of the American Jewish
leadership during the Holocaust. We see here a clearly discernible similarity to Irgun Delegation achievements, to its success in moving the Jewish
question from back rooms to the public arena. Merlin's awareness of this
achievement cushioned his personal disappointment at being forced to resign from the commission, as reflected in a letter to his colleague Finger at
that time: "The main goal was to break the taboo surrounding any examination of the policy, responsibility and behavior of the American Jewish
leadership during the Holocaust. . . . This you achieved by actually creating the Commission without any connection to its findings. . . . The
Commission will act as a catalyst for studies on the behavior of the American Jewish leadership . . . and no individual interests, self justification,
ethnic subjectivity or fear about what the 'goyim' will say can stop the
wave. There are no more taboos, no more immunity."[108]

The debate surrounding the Emergency Committee even extended
beyond the scholarly realm to the film community. While the Goldberg
Commission investigation was in progress, producer Laurence Jarvik
screened a documentary titled *Who Shall Live and Who Shall Die?* which
treated the burning questions of American immigration policy, the Roosevelt administration's attitude toward the Holocaust, Zionist wartime organizational activity, and the founding of the War Refugee Board. Seeking

to give a voice to both establishment and antiestablishment forces, the film incorporated interviews with such diverse figures as World Jewish Congress chairman Nahum Goldmann, wartime Swiss World Jewish Congress representative Gerhart Riegner, and delegation members Hillel Kook and Samuel Merlin.

This documentary aroused the ire of several historians, first and foremost that of Lucy Dawidowicz, author of the best-selling *The War Against the Jews, 1933–1945,* one of the major and most popular historical studies of the Holocaust available for many years to the English-speaking public. In her review in *Commentary,* Dawidowicz summed up her grounds for opposition to the Goldberg Commission, Jarvik, and the Irgun Delegation. Ironically, her analysis of the strange political hybrid then characteristic of the political arena linked Kook, Merlin, and Jarvik with the anti-Zionist American Jewish left.

> In its day the Irgun stood on the Right in Jewish political life—in Eastern Europe as in Palestine. Like its ideological progenitor, the Revisionist party, it defended bourgeois capitalism and was the declared enemy of the socialists within the Zionist movement. Yet Irgun veterans like Bergson and Merlin, having cut their ties with Begin and the Herut party, are welcomed by the Left which regards Begin as its primal foe. The [non-Jewish] anti-Semites of the Right, as I have had prior occasion to point out in these pages, deny that there was ever a Holocaust. The [Jewish] anti-Semites of the Left blame it on the Jews.[109]

Her comments highlight the difficulty of classifying the phenomenon of the Zionist right wing in general and the Bergsonites in particular using the traditional distinctions between left and right, with regard both to personnel and program. This inherent difficulty and an attempt nonetheless to situate the Irgun Delegation on the spectrum of the Zionist right will occupy us in the following chapter.

A Time to Build

The Hebrew Committee of National Liberation
and the League for a Free Palestine, 1944–1948

Nyack, late 1943. Hillel Kook and Samuel Merlin were discussing the state of the Jews in Palestine with Ben Hecht. " 'The Jews of Europe are a dead issue,' stated Merlin. 'If we continue to discuss and lament them we will be doing only what Jews have always done—concerning ourselves with a dead past.'

" 'The British must be driven out,' said Bergson, 'and Palestine must become a Hebrew republic. There is no other solution for the Jewish problem. Only if the Jew has his own nation, will the slaughtering of Jews end. As a nation he can speak to other nations, win allies and have a standing in the world. As a Jew he can speak to no one.'

" 'Except God,' said Merlin, grimly."

Feeling a certain discomfort with these statements, Hecht recorded his impatient reply in his autobiography. "If you want to start a country, go find Washington or Bolivar or Garibaldi. And go dig up . . . Joan of Arc," he wrote. "There are no such characters in Nyack. Besides, what's the use of talking about the Jews driving the nasty British out of Palestine when ninety-eight per cent of the world's surviving Jewry, including its Zionists, the Jewish Agency supporters, and the Palestinians themselves, are on their knees to the British? All of them trying to whimper a nation into existence. . . . I'll write no more propaganda babble about Jews. Let the dead ones keep silent, and the living ones keep on whimpering." [1]

Spring 1944. On New Year's day tired citizens greeted each other with the wish that this be the last year of the war. Indeed, victory seemed near. The Allies had already landed at Anzio near Rome, and in Russia the siege of Leningrad had been lifted. During the spring months broad areas of eastern and southern Europe, including Odessa, Sevastopol, Minsk, Vilna, and Rome, were liberated, and Russia began its thrust against the German "central" forces. Progress was seen on the Western European front as well. In early June the Allies landed at Normandy and continued on to liberate Paris and Brussels.

Only on the Hungarian front did the Germans continue to advance. Following the March 1944 German invasion, Hungarian Jewry became yet another Jewish enclave under Nazi oppression. Elsewhere in Europe the Final Solution was being carried out full tilt. As late as February, the Jews remaining in Amsterdam were transported to Auschwitz, to be joined a month later by the Jews of Athens. Toward the end of April the Hungarian ghettos began to be liquidated, and in May the first transports of Hungarian Jews left for Auschwitz. By late June some 380,000 Hungarian Jews had been transferred to Auschwitz, followed by the liquidation of the last remaining Lithuanian ghettos, Kovno and Šiauliai (Shavli). In August the Lodz ghetto was liquidated, eradicating the largest remaining Jewish concentration under Nazi control outside of Hungary. For the hundreds of thousands of Jews who met their deaths in spring and summer 1944 the coming liberation seemed light years away.

"Here our table collapsed under the weight of our goodies . . . / our men fatted steers, our women fatted cows / . . . we did not miss a single festivity. / At night we lawfully hugged our wives / fat layered our necks, our bellies."[2] Using this strong imagery to describe the gap between "here" and "there," the Hebrew poet Uri Zvi Greenberg went on to give rein to the discomfort and guilt many Jews in the free world experienced during the postwar period. Nonetheless, to their credit, there were also thousands prepared to leave the "fatted table" late in the war out of a sense of obligation to their brethren in Europe, actively seeking out ways to assist them. Among those chosen for this mission were a group of over three dozen mainly European-born Yishuv volunteers who parachuted into their former homelands or reached them overland after parachuting into Yugoslavia. Seven of them died during this mission—five men and two women, four of them in Nazi camps.[3]

Nor did the situation in the Yishuv remain static. New political developments affected both official and underground circles alike. On 1 February 1944, Irgun commander Menachem Begin declared a Hebrew revolt against the British mandatory forces, expressing the more militant line that the organization assumed from that time hence. In adopting terror as a legitimate means in the anti-British battle, the Irgun now moved closer to the Lohamei Herut Yisrael (LHI), which had espoused this ideology since its founding; but, despite Begin's desire for cooperation the two organizations did not come to a meeting of the minds.[4] A main cause was the November 1944 murder of Lord Moyne in Cairo by two LHI members, which brought crisis in its wake. The official Yishuv institutions now decided to cooperate with the British authorities and to open a hunting season, known in Hebrew as the *saison,* against the dissidents. Paradoxically, the Haganah avoided confronting the LHI, which was directly responsible for Lord Moyne's murder, but chose instead to make the Irgun its primary target, irrespective of the fact that its leadership had not backed the Cairo operation.

Initial Haganah efforts to push the Irgun Zeva'i Leumi (IZL) out of the Yishuv arena and to force it to go on the defensive later escalated to kidnappings, with Irgun activists even being turned over to the British authorities. Electing not to fan the flames of internecine strife, Irgun commander Menachem Begin did not respond to the kidnappings, to informing, and to turning over of Irgun activists to the British by the Haganah, and concentrated his main efforts upon the anti-British struggle instead.[5] The six-month-long campaign carried out by the Haganah's secret service, Palmach volunteers, and *saison* activists to annihilate the IZL and Betar brought the latter organizations' activity to a virtual halt, with the exception of written propaganda activity. With the wrapping up of World War II and the publication of the full dimensions of the tragic fate of European Jewry, the *saison* came to an end in late May 1945, further motivated by the organized Yishuv institutions' recognition that their bitter struggle against the "dissidents" had in no way improved their relationship with the British mandatory authorities. Less than six months later the Haganah was cooperating with those very same dissidents who had earlier been the objects of persecution—the IZL and the LHI—in declaring and promoting the United Hebrew Resistance Movement.

Establishing New Delegation Offshoots

Spring 1944. Of the delegation nucleus only Hillel Kook and Samuel Merlin remained in the United States, its other members being involved in overseas missions: Alex Rafaeli and Yitzhak Ben-Ami in the American army, Eri Jabotinsky in Turkey, and Arieh Ben-Eliezer in Palestine. It was precisely at that moment, when but a third of its members were on hand in the American arena, that Hillel Kook conceived of a fresh initiative: to found two new committees—the Hebrew Committee of National Liberation (HCNL) and the League for a Free Palestine—in order to complement Begin's February 1944 Hebrew "revolt" by means of efforts on the diplomatic and public relations fronts.

The founding of these two new offshoots represents a divide in delegation history, one that necessitates employing an analytical approach differing somewhat from the one used earlier with regard to the 1939 to 1943 period. First we note the conspicuously changed nature of the delegation's relationship with the Irgun in the Yishuv. No longer a "cut-off battalion," the delegation maintained close and regular contact with the Irgun in the Yishuv from 1944; consequently, the role played by the Yishuv arena is now more significant for understanding delegation history than it was during the early war years. A second noteworthy difference relates to the open espousal of Zionist aims by these final delegation offshoots, in direct contrast to the Emergency Committee. Furthermore, events in Palestine, in particular "Black Saturday" (29 June 1946)—the British roundup of members of the Jewish Agency Executive and the Vaad Leummi in response to the blowing up of all bridges on the borders of Palestine by the Haganah—moved the delegation, along with its offshoots, for the first time to openly declare their identification with the Irgun, a shift that requires separate and intensive consideration. Therefore, our discussion of the Hebrew Committee and the league moves along three axes, encompassing the American, the European, and the Yishuv arenas, the main spheres of activity for the delegation's final offshoots during the 1944 to 1948 era.

The notion to found an offshoot devoted to Zionist activity per se first came up in 1943 while delegation members were intensely engaged in plans to rescue European Jewry. Eri Jabotinsky recalls its genesis as being dated even earlier, to the period of Jewish Army Committee activity, when delegation members called themselves the Free Palestine Committee and sought to pursue an orientation slanted toward Zionism. Reports emanating from this Free Palestine Committee in 1943 elucidate its self-image, its self-definition as sponsor for both the Jewish Army Committee and the

Emergency Committee, this despite the already mentioned efforts to stress the latter's complete dissociation from the Zionist cause.[6] This entity evidently emerged against the background of an August 1943 initiative by Yitzhak Ben-Ami, his response to fears of an increasingly anti-Zionist trend in the U.S. State Department, as outlined in a contemporary letter: "A combination of pro-Arabic, anti-Jewish oil and international business interests (each for its own well-known reasons) has gotten together and formulated a plan to liquidate all political aspirations of Zionism within the coming year or two." His recommendation: to work for the immediate formation of a "League for a Free Palestine."[7] Ben-Ami then went on to draft his proposed plan, which called for this league to define its aims vis-à-vis the founding of a Hebrew state, to set policy on the Arab question, to prepare a massive public relations campaign, and to hold a founding convention in October or November 1943. In closing he noted the current dangers hovering over world Jewry at large: "In conclusion, may I say that if some of the above suggestions sound radical, far reaching and very serious, so does the political situation in Palestine and the future of the Jews of Europe and probably the world over."

Mention of this proposed entity also appeared in an internal memo from September 1943 in which Kook noted the need for a League for a Free Palestine with branches in the United States, Britain, South Africa, and Canada. But internal delegation deliberations as to how best to attract American Jewry to the Zionist idea à la Irgun without unleashing the demon of "double loyalty" delayed this entity's official founding until November 1943. Although there were those who suggested holding a founding convention immediately, a decision was reached not to present the new offshoot to the American public before the Emergency Committee to Save the Jews of Europe showed some palpable achievements. This delay ultimately lasted until 18 May 1944, some four months after the WRB began functioning. It was not until then that the establishment of the Hebrew Committee of National Liberation—the name now bestowed on the Free Palestine Committee—was officially declared.[8] Patterning itself on committees of national liberation founded by occupied nations during the World War II, formed to pursue objectives mainly in the diplomatic sphere, on 7 July the Hebrew Committee officially registered as a "foreign agent"—a status bestowed on public entities seeking to pursue their aims on American soil. Naturally, without an appropriate backdrop Kook could

not pursue his diplomatic aspirations, and in the spring of 1944 the group
purchased the former Iranian embassy building in downtown Washington, dubbing it a "Hebrew embassy" and earmarking it as a center for
diplomatic relations.[9]

At the press conference held to announce the coming into being of
this new entity, Kook opened with a ringing declaration: "For the first
time in 1809 years (the last Hebrew revolt under Bar Kochba was crushed
in 135 AD), a unified group of Hebrews have joined together to redeem
the Hebrew national sovereignty and established, in exile, the Hebrew
Committee of National Liberation." Next he presented its members:
Arieh Ben-Eliezer, Theodore Ben-Nahum, Professor Pierre Delougaz,
Irma Helpern, Eri Jabotinsky, and Samuel Merlin. Missing from this
purely Palestinian Jewish lineup were Alex Rafaeli and Yitzhak Ben-Ami,
then serving in the American army. It was also in the course of this press
conference that Kook first publicly aired the existence of a link between
the delegation's offshoots, stressing their Jewish and Palestinian connection before specifically zeroing in on the Hebrew Committee program: to
achieve UN recognition for the Hebrew nation, to gain representation on
the War Crimes Commission and the UN Relief and Rehabilitation Administration, to found a Jewish army, and to raise funds for a free Palestine.
He concluded this press conference with a statement of his key ideological
premise. Making it clear that the Hebrew Committee did not speak in the
name of American Jewry, which was an integral part of the American nation, he stated that American Jews do not " 'belong' to Palestine and to
the renewed Hebrew Nation . . . but are surely proud of their origins." [10]

This distinction between *Jews* and *Hebrews* formed the cornerstone of
Kook and Merlin's national ideology, conceived as a means of enabling
American Jewry to support the Irgun version of the Zionist cause without
in any way posing a threat to their American identity. In line with this way
of thinking, the name for the new delegation offshoot was carefully and
intentionally chosen to create a clear distinction between religion and nationality. Unlike American Jews, seen in this conception as belonging to
the Jewish religion (and not to the "fictitious" Jewish nation), Palestinian
and stateless Jews, as well as all Jews persecuted anywhere, were part of the
"Hebrew nation." Vital to this conception was the desire of the Jews making up this "Hebrew nation" to attain national sovereignty in the Palestinian territory. The role of American Jews was not only to take pride in their

"Hebrew" coreligionists, but to lend financial and diplomatic support to these aims, albeit without having to profess national belonging.

For the origins of this concept of a Hebrew nation we look not to Kook and Merlin, but rather to Adolf Gurevitch (Ben-Horin), a Revisionist and Betar activist who had worked alongside Merlin in Paris during the 1930s. Gurevitch joined the Revisionist movement's Paris branch as a youth, going on to become a Betar cell commander and, later, essentially chief Betar ideologue in France. Gurevitch's marriage to a relative of Zeev Jabotinsky enhanced his connection to both the founder of the Revisionist movement and to his son Eri, then in Paris. As an outgrowth of his university studies in Semitic languages and the history of religion, Gurevitch evolved a hypothesis concerning ancient Hebrews' philological and cultural origins that formed the basis for his notion of a Hebrew nation. Using his discovery of the cultural-linguistic unity of the Israelites and the surrounding nations as a springboard, Gurevitch developed a historical worldview in which the term *Hebrews* broadly designated the nations residing in Canaan, whereas *Israelites* designated a tribal covenant within a larger national context. Gurevitch's thinking influenced others, including Uriel Halperin (Yonathan Ratosh), founder of the Canaanite movement, and two future members of the Irgun Delegation: Samuel Merlin and Eri Jabotinsky.[11]

It was Merlin, however, who first aired this notion of a Hebrew nation on the American scene, in articles that appeared in the *Answer* during the course of 1943. This was by no means Ratosh's maximilist Canaanite ideology, which called for merging into a pan-Middle Eastern milieu, but a more refined version that related only to the distinction between Hebrews and Jews. Merlin himself described this notion as a unique metamorphosis of a concept born in prewar Europe: "We had already thought of and discussed this idea even in Poland in the late thirties, but it did not then crystallize. It began to congeal in the United States during the forties. . . . For us, it was obvious that there was a Hebrew nation which was being reborn, that it was undergoing a process of formation, and that its nucleus and striking force were in the Yishuv."[12]

Enthused by what appeared to him a handy solution to the American Jewish specter of dual loyalty with regard to Zionism, it was Hillel Kook who gave the American version of this concept its finishing touches, fixing the concept of the Hebrew nation at the center of the newly founded off-

shoot's national, diplomatic, and semantic core. By means of this ideological innovation Kook hoped to achieve the well-nigh impossible: a synthesis between extreme nationalism and extreme assimilation, as represented
by the delegation and American Jewish intellectuals respectively, paying
lip service to the latter's assimilationist stance as a drawing card to foster
their connection to the delegation's Zionist ideology. Although certainly
aware of the problematic implications of this synthesis, nonetheless Kook
chose to go ahead and publicize the conception of Hebrews vs. Jews with
an eye to widening his support base among American Jewry thereby. Even
his minority position among delegation members did not deter Kook
from putting his new semantic labels to use in early 1944.[13]

Indeed, delegation members shared no consensus with regard to the
newly coined division between the "Jewish people" and the "Hebrew nation." Alex Rafaeli recalled his reaction to this Kook—and Merlin-
generated "innovation" upon his return from Europe. "I was not exactly
pleased. I feared that American Jewry would find this notion incomprehensible, but it was impossible to change everything at once."[14] Antidelegation forces also reacted negatively to this Jews vs. Hebrews
distinction and now added it to their arsenal, denouncing it as an essentially anti-Zionist ideological distinction and seizing the opportunity to
put forth the claim that the Hebrew Committee's true aim was to destroy
the Jewish Agency. Even the American Revisionists distanced themselves
from the Hebrew Committee, issuing a statement effectively denying any
practical or ideological links to the newly formed entity.[15] Irgun members
in the Yishuv, including commander-in-chief Begin, also voiced reservations concerning this ideological innovation. As reported by Ben-Ami, in
the course of their lengthy discussions of this issue in Palestine during
1945, Begin stressed that "the distinction between Jews and Hebrews
should be understood in a positive and not an exclusive sense. The Hebrew nation was not going to isolate itself from or exclude the rest of the
Jews in the world. Very much the opposite—the new nation would edu-
cate the Diaspora and make it more aware of its national roots, the ultimate aim always being to expand the nation."[16] Finally, American Jews,
who were supposed to enjoy the status of "Americans of the Mosaic faith,"
by and large experienced difficulty in penetrating Kook's intention, as the
conception he presented was completely foreign to their way of thinking.
It appears then, insofar as it was intended to amass broad-based support

among American Jewry, that the Hebrew Committee's ideological innovation missed its mark.

What underlay the founding of another parallel offshoot—the League for a Free Palestine—that shared the same objectives as the Hebrew Committee? The necessity for two parallel organizations emerged in response to the restriction of Hebrew Committee's membership to so-called Hebrews, that is, to stateless and Palestinian Jews. Kook and Merlin envisioned the league as a means to draft broader support, to enable the American public, Jewish and Gentile, to identify with and to promote the Hebrew Committee's aims. Former Iowa senator Guy Gillette agreed to chair the league for what amounted to symbolic pay, and the league's official unveiling on 24 May 1944 followed the proclaiming of the Hebrew Committee by but a week. Its first official appeal to the public, in the form of an ad titled "The American Answer to a Call for Life and Liberty" published in the *New York Post* one month later, on 26 June, called for mass support to promote the Hebrew national struggle. At the same time, this ad cited the example set by other national struggles for liberation, in particular the Czech and the Irish, who had also appealed to the American public to support their struggle for freedom and sovereignty.[17]

Kook was acutely aware of what this link signified, that by patterning himself on existing national liberation movements he was providing legitimation for his Hebrew Committee. "Our chosen name was deliberately patterned on a similar name used by De Gaulle's or Tito's committee," he explained. "Some five or six committees for those occupied nations which did not have governments-in-exile were then functioning. The Poles had their government-in-exile; the Greeks had a committee of national liberation as did the French and the Yugoslavs. We deliberately chose to use national liberation in our committee name, with an eye to going on to found a provisional government-in-exile."[18] Kook's remarks disclose his focal objective in founding the Hebrew Committee, one that combined a long-standing Revisionist aspiration with innovative national maximalism: the desire to create an alternative to the existing Zionist institutions, the Zionist Federation in particular, combined with a newly formulated ultimate aim: to establish a Hebrew government-in-exile. Whereas Kook's first aspiration was totally devoid of any chance for success, his second formed the nexus of a raging debate in Irgun circles for more than two years, that is, until the founding of the State.

The virtually simultaneous founding of two new offshoots presented the delegation with an administrative challenge: how to juggle tasks so as to avoid duplication. In practice what happened was that the league assumed most of the Emergency Committee's functions, whereas the Hebrew Committee now once again took up the call for a Jewish army. To the league goes credit for its activity on behalf of Hungarian Jewry, promoting temporary shelters for refugees and efforts to bring Nazi war criminals to justice. For its part the Hebrew Committee tried to promote the idea of a Jewish army, even attributing to itself a role in the September 1944 founding of the Jewish Brigade. Officially at least, these entities worked in tandem until the earlier still-functioning delegation offshoots—the Emergency Committee to Save the Jewish People of Europe and the London Jewish Army Committee—disbanded.[19]

The intervening eleven-month period from the founding of the Hebrew Committee to the war's end marks a transitional period in delegation history. At its conclusion delegation members no longer devoted their main energies to localized issues such as illegal immigration, a Jewish army, or rescue, but rather concentrated their efforts to a broad political issue: the question of Palestine's future. This change found expression in the delegation's response to British policy on two fronts: the question of aliyah and Irgun activity in Palestine. Although the group directed venomous attacks at British aliyah policy in the *Answer* editorials, in practice it took a more moderate stance toward mandatory policy in the Yishuv. This stance changed following the assassination of Lord Moyne in early November 1944. In response to the death sentence passed on the two assassins, both LHI members, the Hebrew Committee petitioned the British king and prime minister and the Egyptian government for clemency. A second response utilized the dramatic arts. The protagonist of a new Ben Hecht production, *A Jewish Fairy Tale*, which now played before New York audiences, was a Briton: Lord Moyne. From here on, delegation members took an increasingly militant political stance, one that peaked in the months preceding the declaration of the State of Israel.

Postwar Diplomatic Activity

In view of the significant military, demographic, and political changes that followed the end of World War II, the delegation found itself facing new challenges. Ideologically and practically speaking we can isolate a series of key events that affected delegation policy making: the formation of the United Hebrew Resistance Movement in the Yishuv, the rise of the organized *sheerith hapleta* (Jewish Displaced Persons) in Europe, and the formation of a Labor government in England. Founded in October 1945, the United Hebrew Resistance Movement brought together the Haganah and the two underground movements, the Irgun and the LHI. It represents Ben-Gurion's attempt to achieve what the "hunting season" had not: to block independent activity by the two dissident organizations and to establish Haganah hegemony. Its establishment necessitated a degree of synchronization between the three organizations on strategic and operative matters, in turn influencing Zionist-movement-directed league and Hebrew Committee rhetoric during the months while the Resistance Movement functioned as a united body.

Foreign Minister Ernest Bevin's 13 November 1945 speech in the British House of Commons in which he outlined British policy on the Palestine question represents another significant turning point for the delegation because it destroyed any lingering illusions its members harbored regarding Labor intentions and policy on this question. A sole shred of hope came from Bevin's announcement of Whitehall's readiness to form a joint Anglo-American commission to determine Palestine's future and the possibility of absorbing Holocaust survivors there, and from the results of the commission's tour of Palestine in March 1946 and its subsequent announcement that 100,000 Jewish displaced persons from Europe should be allowed to enter Palestine immediately. On the other hand, the report's failure to note the lack of a homeland or a Jewish state led to intense disappointment among the Zionist and Irgun leadership alike, and His Majesty's government's subsequent rejection of its recommendations both intensified United Hebrew Resistance Movement activity and evoked a sharp delegation reaction.

This cooperative United Hebrew Resistance Movement lasted for nearly nine months, until summer 1946, when two separate but related events destroyed the delicate balance achieved between the Haganah and the two underground movements: "Black Saturday" and the bombing of British headquarters in Jerusalem's King David Hotel. At dawn on Saturday, 29 June 1946, British forces initiated "Operation Agatha," declaring a Yishuv-wide curfew during which British forces raided Jewish settlements in search of weapons, also carrying out a series of arrests. During this Yishuv-wide search, much material of strategic importance fell into British hands, ranging from discovered weapons caches at Kibbutz Yagur to important documents confiscated from the Palmach national headquarters uncovered at Kibbutz Mizra and from the Jewish Agency's Jerusalem offices. Some two thousand Jews were placed under arrest, including the Jewish Agency leadership and other prominent Yishuv figures such as Moshe Shertok, Dov Joseph, Yehuda Leib Maimon, David Hakohen, and Berl Repetor.

The organized Yishuv responded to these events with alacrity. In addition to calls for a self-appointed curfew and a work stoppage as a sign of identification with the hunger-striking detainees, the planned Irgun reprisal, organized in cooperation with its partners in the United Hebrew Resistance Movement, sought to strike at the mandatory government's administrative heart. On 22 July 1946 Irgun members blew up the southern wing of Jerusalem's King David Hotel, which housed the British mandatory secretariat and its central military headquarters. British failure to heed a phoned warning and to evacuate their headquarters led to nearly one hundred deaths. For the Haganah, which withdrew its support for this operation at the twelfth hour, this operation further widened existing rifts within the Resistance Movement, ultimately bringing its demise in summer 1946.

Two additional milestones affected delegation activity at that time: the Morrison-Grady scheme and the August 1946 British decision not to intern illegal immigrants in Palestine but to deport them to special detention camps on Cyprus. This latter decision in no way deterred Haganah emissaries from organizing illegal aliyah, nor did it shake the immigrants' determination to achieve their ultimate goal, in the interim creating a unique Zionist ambiance in the Cyprus camps. Meanwhile, on the diplomatic front, the Morrison-Grady scheme, which called for an overall solution to the Palestine question based on cantonization of Palestine and would allow 100,000 Jews to enter Palestine under those conditions, aroused disappointment and apprehension on the Zionist leadership's part. The airing of this proposed plan, radically different in content from earlier understandings reached with the Palestine Inquiry Commission, prompted the dispatching of Weizmann confidante Nahum Goldmann to Washington by the Zionist leadership in order to renew negotiations regarding the possibility of founding a Jewish state in part of Palestine. Under the mistaken impression that Goldmann's proposals had British support, in October 1946 Truman publicly renounced the Morrison-Grady scheme, accepting the Jewish Agency plan for the "establishment of a Jewish commonwealth" and reiterating his call for the immediate admission of 100,000 Holocaust survivors to Palestine. Both moves were part of a series of political gestures linked to the upcoming November 1946 elections in the United States.

For the British, this American declaration now created a feeling of stalemate. Concerned that the Palestine problem would remain interminably deadlocked, this fear was heightened by the cessation of talks between Britain and the Jewish and Arab sides to the dispute, as no delegation had full authority to represent its cause. In January 1947 talks were renewed in London whose implied agenda was to arrange for the partition of Palestine. But Bevin's plan, which envisioned an end to mandatory rule five years hence, was rejected by Arabs and Jews alike. As a last resort, the British cabinet resolved to bring the Palestine question before the United Nations without making any recommendations, nor did it set guidelines as to when and how this matter should come up for discussion.

From that point on British intentions were clear, albeit with no binding timetable. In April 1947 Britain requested a special session of the UN General Assembly in order to create an entity to propose solutions to the Palestine question. A majority of the members of the UNSCOP Commission (United Nations Commission on Palestine) recommended partition with economic unity, a decision largely influenced by two factors: first, by the Soviet Union's newly changed, now positive attitude toward the founding of a Jewish state, and second, by increased terrorist activity on the part of the underground movements in the Yishuv during spring and summer 1947, which peaked while the Palestine situation was under commission investigation. Concurrently, the Haganah continued to intensify its illegal immigration operations. In April 1947 the first Jewish prisoners in the Yishuv were executed by hanging, and the Irgun was not long in responding. When the number of Jews sitting on death row increased, the Irgun took British hostages, hanging two British sergeants on 29 July 1947 in reprisal for the execution of three of its members. In mid-April the British seized the illegal immigration ship *Exodus* with its more than four thousand passengers, sending it back to Germany. The question of how much the ship's fate played a role in influencing the decision of UNSCOP members on the future of Palestine is still one of historical debate.[20]

The ultimate conclusion of this Via Dolorosa—the 29 November 1947 UN resolution and the announcement of the founding of the State of Israel some five and one-half months later—not only marked the conclusion of a difficult, tension-laden period on the one hand, but also the initiation of a unique period that saw the renewal of Jewish sovereignty in Palestine. The events described herein also shaped the framework for delegation activity in both the diplomatic and the practical realms. Not surprisingly, in many instances this activity did not toe the official Zionist leadership line; by the same token, neither was it always consistent with Revisionist thinking or even with declared Irgun policy in the Yishuv. Delegation history from 1945 to 1948 is framed by the interface between these clashes and delegation attempts to pursue an independent policy.

The Hebrew Committee of National Liberation (1945–1946)

The seemingly crucial question—how does one form a committee when most of its potential activists are overseas—did not appear to trouble either Kook or Merlin. Indeed, the fact that neither Ben-Ami, Ben-Eliezer, Rafaeli, nor Eri Jabotinsky was in the States endowed Kook and Merlin with greater ideological and operative maneuverability than in 1943. But the return of almost all of the original delegation members to the United States within a two-year period again altered this picture. Ben-Ami recalled the optimistic spirit of this reunion in his memoir: "Most of our delegation was back together: Kook and Merlin had more than fulfilled the hopes we placed in them when we scattered in 1943; Eri Jabotinsky was back from the British jail, and Alex Rafaeli was back from the wars. So, despite the odds against us, we felt a spirit of renewal. This time we knew we would succeed both in Palestine and the United States."[21] Only Ben-Eliezer, exiled to a British camp in Eritrea, was missing to round off this idyllic picture.

Plainly, Ben-Ami's brief remarks barely touch upon the full complexity of this reunion. He omits to mention, for example, Alex Rafaeli's refusal to resume his role on the team after his release from the army, because of depression, which Rafaeli described in his memoirs: "I returned to New York sick and depressed. The world seemed a large desert and I shared nothing with those around me. I began drinking and leading a wild life, obsessed with thoughts about my family. Could I have saved Mother and Asya?"[22] With the help of good friends Rafaeli rehabilitated himself, and six months later dove into the business world, founding a company that would serve Irgun needs in the United States. Only in late 1946 did Rafaeli agree to return to intensive activity within the framework of the League for a Free Palestine, taking charge of both its propaganda and fund-raising efforts.

Ben-Ami's own situation was somewhat different. In fall 1945, while still serving in the American army, Ben-Ami had been dispatched to Palestine on delegation business, to hold meetings with the Irgun leadership there and to explore the possibility of jointly planning their moves. "My discussions with Begin were intense," he recalled. "We usually met alone so we could have a free play of our ideas. My job was to help Begin and his associates understand the political scene in Washington, London and the United Nations, so we could best coordinate strategy between our delegation in the United States and the *Irgun* in Palestine."[23] The ideological-semantic debate between the two centered on the need for a provisional government, envisioned as having two bases, one underground in Palestine and the other in the Diaspora. Although Begin agreed in principle on the need for a provisional government, as Ben-Ami tells it, he "was adamant about timing. As he put it, if we were not careful, instead of freeing the country, we would 'find ourselves in a bloody civil war'. . . . The gist was this: we would never give up our principles but we had to await the propitious time. . . . Since our inception [of the Revisionists], they had dubbed us fascists and claimed that our only real goal was to usurp control of the *Yishuv.* We did not want to prove them right," is how Ben-Ami relates Begin's forceful conclusion.[24]

Out of these meetings came a series of strategic and international aims for the delegation, including a plan to found a European headquarters for the Hebrew Committee in Paris from which units would operate in Displaced Person (DP) camps in Germany and Austria and in the Jewish communities in France, Italy, and North Africa. A second role envisioned for this headquarters was to serve as a meeting point between Irgun activists from the Yishuv and delegation members. His close contacts with Yishuv Irgun activists notwithstanding, Ben-Ami found the sharp transformation in the Haganah/Irgun relationship following the cessation of the *saison* and the institution of the United Hebrew Resistance Movement troubling. When Ben-Ami queried Begin regarding the nature of this cooperation, the latter replied that he was well aware that his new partners—the Haganah and the Palmach—could just as easily distance themselves from the Irgun. "Don't worry," Begin assured him, "we will not sell ourselves for a pot of gold." At that point Begin's chief of staff, Haim Landau, pointed at Ben-Ami and commented, "The only pot of gold we're looking for is to come from you fellows." [25]

This anticipated financial support by the delegation for the Irgun treasury rapidly became another bone of contention between the two entities. Delegation refusal to bow to the Yishuv Irgun leadership's expectations that Hebrew Committee activities would be used to fund their operations once again raised the specter of organizational "sovereignty," a more than passing leitmotif throughout delegation history. Although while in Palestine Ben-Ami successfully avoided a confrontation with the Irgun high command over this issue, he feared future salvos between the parties over this issue, fears that we shall see were later borne out.

Several weeks after this visit to Palestine Ben-Ami returned to his army base in Germany via Cairo. His arrival in the United States to take up delegation activity was delayed until March 1946, more or less the time when the Anglo-American Palestine Inquiry Commission was touring Palestine. It was also about this time that Eri Jabotinsky, who had been in Palestine since his release from British jail in 1945, was finally able to rejoin his delegation colleagues in the United States. Despite a series of appeals by his wife, Aviva, to various American diplomats, all his previous requests for an American visa had been denied, and it was only the intervention of WRB activists that at last enabled Jabotinsky to return and take up the work of the Hebrew Committee of National Liberation.

Activities of the Hebrew Committee of National Liberation, 1945–1948

Changes in the political and military arena in late 1944 now shifted Hebrew Committee emphasis from efforts to save Hungarian Jewry to activity on behalf of bringing the *sheerith hapleta* to Palestine. This shift signals an early adjustment to the fluid international situation even before the war's end, one that entailed an attempt to deal with the implications of the

Final Solution on world Jewry and the Zionist movement alike. Much has been written on the metamorphosis in the Zionist attitude toward the survivors and Oriental Jewish communities that resulted from the loss of its greatest "human reservoir"—European Jewry,[26] changes that affected the Irgun Delegation as well, forcing it to reevaluate its program at the war's end and to choose new arenas for its activity. From the time that its efforts to save the Jews of Europe wound down, Hebrew Committee members turned their attention to three main areas: "war addenda" in the international arena, diplomatic activity for the recognition of the Hebrew nation and its right to a state, and activity on behalf of bringing *sheerith hapleta* to Palestine by any and all means. Whereas the first two areas fell mainly under the aegis of the committee's American base, its European base, which became operational in late 1945, was largely responsible for handling the third.

"War addenda" meant primarily the bringing of Nazi war criminals to justice, a focal issue for the Hebrew Committee from its inception. A February 1945 memo from Kook and Merlin addressed to Roosevelt, Stalin, and Churchill, calling for judeocide to be declared a war crime, was penned in reaction to the American representative's resignation from the War Crimes Commission in protest over its refusal to move the trials of murderers of Jews from local to UN jurisdiction. Concurrently, congressional supporters of the Hebrew Committee requested that judeocide be treated no differently from the murder of Poles, Czechs, or Englishmen. The Hebrew Committee lobby in Congress and elsewhere saw the fruits of its efforts in the creation of a new legal category by the committee in charge of convening the Nuremberg tribunals: "crimes against humanity," defined as "murder, annihilation, slavery, deportation and other inhuman actions which were carried out against every civilian population during or before the war."[27]

In addition, the Hebrew Committee targeted the mufti of Jerusalem, Haj Amin al-Husseini, an ardent supporter of Hitler and a partner in the Iraqi pro-German revolt sponsored by Rashid Ali, for war criminal status. Al-Husseini's wartime collaboration with Hitler centered on recruiting Muslim units in Bosnia, Yugoslavia, to work for the Nazi side. With the war's end, al-Husseini renewed his anti-Yishuv campaign and was appointed head of the Arab Higher Committee, a position he assumed following his escape to Egypt. Following the mufti's capture by Allied forces, the Hebrew Committee opened a campaign to include him on the list of war criminals, dispatching a memo detailing his war crimes and Nazi connections to the UN Commission. Kook's meetings with the Yugoslav representative to the War Crimes Commission finally achieved the desired effect: the mufti's name was now added to the list. This addition, however, brought no practical action against the mufti, who continued to operate freely in Arab lands without interference from the former Allies for close to thirty years, until his death in Beirut in 1974.[28]

Another component of the Hebrew Committee's international agenda concentrated on achieving recognition for the Hebrew nation and support for its national aspirations. Even before the war's end, Kook had proposed to Zionist Federation president Weizmann the federation's reorganization as a "Hebrew" agency that would work toward amassing international support for its aims. Having evoked no response from Weizmann to this proposal, Kook decided to go it alone, directing his campaign to what he identified as key foci of international support: Congress and the American administration, Parliament and the British administration, and the larger diplomatic community, including the United Nations.

May 1945 saw the opening shot of this diplomatic campaign. Representative Andrew Somers introduced a bill in Congress calling for European and Palestinian Jews to be recognized as a Hebrew nation with a right to self-definition and granting them UN membership. At the last minute, a similar bill, sponsored by Senator James E. Murray, was withdrawn from the Senate agenda when Murray was made aware that it did not enjoy the broad backing of the American Jewish community. Needless to say, under the circumstances this proposed resolution lost its potential effect.[29]

Kook also set his sights on American president Harry Truman for backing for his national aspirations. We recall that Truman had been a staunch supporter of the Jewish Army Committee in the early 1940s and that he withdrew his support after his name appeared in a delegation ad without his permission. Following Truman's assumption of office, Kook attempted to renew his contacts with the president with an eye to having him exert influence on the British prime minister with regard to the Palestine question. These overtures having evoked no response, Kook now chose to employ a more novel approach. Shortly before Christmas 1946 he sent Truman a case of wine from Palestine, asking him to toast the New

Year with it. The accompanying note conveyed the message that after often having bothered the president on the Palestine question, he was now happy to present him with something "not steeped in troubles." [30] But this present failed to bring about the desired effect.

The formation of the Anglo-American Commission gave Hebrew Committee activity a further impetus. Before their departure for England, Kook made a presentation to the commission's American members, in which he aired the Hebrew Committee's ideological-political vision. The committee also presented the commission with a memo, essentially voicing the same arguments as a manifesto published by the Irgun high command in the Yishuv at the same time, which took a critical stance on British Palestine policy, demanded an end to the mandate and the withdrawal of British troops from Palestine, and called for the granting of Hebrew sovereignty over Palestine with guarantees of equal rights for all its residents. Like the American Zionist establishment, the Hebrew Committee also attempted to lobby the president and the State Department to oppose the Morrison-Grady scheme. [31]

Zionist historian Samuel Halperin has stressed that the number of alliances a pressure group constructs is indicative of its chances for success. We must view Hebrew Committee members' attempts to now reach understandings with anti-imperalist groups and with foreign diplomats as part of a potential anti-British front in light of this observation. It was Alex Rafaeli who stood in the vanguard of these attempts, in addition to serving as Hebrew Committee observer at the UN. Not only did Rafaeli play an instrumental role in presenting a request to the UN to recognize the Hebrew nation as an independent nation and calling for separate assistance for Jewish survivors in Europe, he was later involved in presenting an October 1947 memo to the UN that outlined the ideological underpinnings for the Hebrew nation and the rationale for the founding of a free Hebrew republic.

As a UN observer, Rafaeli made the most of the opportunity to develop contacts with a variety of individuals predisposed to support the Hebrew Committee's aims. These included such varied figures as the Czech foreign minister, Jan Masaryk, and the Chilean, Venezuelan, and Guatemalan ambassadors to the UN. Contacts were also initiated with anti-imperalist forces battling for independence: the head of India's Congress movement Nehru, the founder of the Korean Republic Rhee, and diplomats from Indonesia, Kurdistan, Ireland, the Spanish Basque region, and Serbia, for example. Actual assistance came from a surprising direction, from Maurice Thorez, the leader of the French communist party, who assisted Rafaeli in purchasing French arms for the Irgun's anti-imperialistic struggle in Palestine.[32]

Another project Rafaeli took under his wing was the purchase of "consulates" as a means of overcoming barriers to aliyah by the *sheerith hapleta*. "At this time the authorities in Italy, France, and Greece gave in to British pressure and barred Jewish DPs from entering their countries, which had served as exit ports to Palestine," he recalled. "They now required DPs to have visas for a final destination as a condition for receiving transit visas. But no humanitarian democracy had as yet agreed to take in homeless Jews, so how could we obtain final destination visas?" As a means of acquiring the right to issue those sought-after visas, Rafaeli now initiated contacts with several Latin American countries, seeking to purchase the right to serve as their consul. Rafaeli described the initial hesitation displayed by Honduran officials regarding this scheme. Used to selling consulates to launder money or narcotics, they were "wary of involvement in a plan dealing with thousands of cases." Rafaeli also had to allay fears that Jews might actually come to their country by issuing guarantees they "would only be used by our people to reach European ports that would serve as departure points to Palestine." At last these lengthy negotiations achieved results. The Hondurans agreed to sell Rafaeli two consulates, so that the Irgun representative could "issue fictitious entry visas to Honduras, which Jewish DPs could then use to obtain transit visas to enter the Mediterranean countries from which they could board ships to Palestine." For his part Rafaeli had to guarantee "that no one would actually use these visas to enter Honduras." But this success by no means meant a breakthrough. When Rafaeli was ready to purchase his "consulates," he discovered that they had already been sold. He recounted: "All the Hondurian consulates in the Mediterranean cities where we were active, such as Marseille or Toulon, had already been 'sold' for commercial transactions and we kept looking for suitable venues. I then remembered my school history lessons and suggested Avignon. True, Avignon was not a seaport, but who cared? So Avignon it was." A similar arrangement with the Nicaraguan authorities enabled Hebrew Committee members to proffer assistance to the remaining Holocaust survivors in Europe.[33]

18. Alex Rafaeli and Hillel Kook, known as Peter Bergson, in 1993. Courtesy of Judith Tydor Baumel.

The League for a Free Palestine (1945–1948)

We have already noted the founding of the League for a Free Palestine as a companion organization to the Hebrew Committee, intended for sympathizers to the Hebrew cause who were not themselves "Hebrews." Among league aims were to raise funds for Hebrew Committee activity, to rouse American public opinion against Britain, and to present its stance opposing British Palestine policy to the American administration. Former senator Guy Gillette served as league chairman from August 1945, having forfeited a position in the Truman administration in order to assist the Hebrew nation. "I am aware that many will regard it as unusual that I have chosen to decline the gracious offer of a government position by the President and to dedicate myself to the effort of achieving a solution to the Hebrew problem in Europe and Palestine, particularly since it is a non-Hebrew and a non-Jew who has undertaken this task," Gillette noted in his inaugural speech. He observed further, "I have decided to accept my present task as an American who seeks to live up to the traditions and principles of our nation." [34] Gillette's presence enabled delegation members once again to project a nonsectarian image for this, their newest offshoot, as they had for earlier offshoots, with the exception, of course, of the Hebrew Committee. This nonsectarian label not only attracted American Jewish intellectuals to its ranks, but also a small but vocal non-Jewish contingent that was especially important given the status and composition of American Jewry and American Zionism at that given point.

In their *Roots of Radicalism: Jews, Christians, and the New Left,* Stanley Rothman and S. Robert Lichter note the problematic nature of membership in radical movements for American Jewry during the period of delegation activity in the United States. Until the fifties American Jewish intellectuals—the group Kook uniquely hoped to draft to his cause—formed the hard core of the American left, of the American socialist and, later, the communist movement. In the postwar years, by utilizing outside non-Jewish catalysts like Senators Gillette and Johnson, who endowed their league with respectability and lifted it out of the known rubric of American Zionist organizations, delegation members succeeded in creating an almost impossible synthesis between these left-wing Jews and their right-wing Zionist organization.[35]

Other American Zionist organizations shared the delegation's awareness of the need to broaden their support base in order to elicit wider public backing; at the same time, they also hoped to compete with the delegation's multifaceted public relations and fund-raising apparatus. Halperin argues that, for the period in question, fund-raising for Palestine is a convenient measure of the power and influence the Zionist movement exercised among American Jewry. Similar to the Irgun Delegation, in the postwar era the American Zionist establishment sought to broaden its support base by founding umbrella organizations such as the National Conference for Palestine. In the public relations field the ZOA successfully widened its activity, selling some three to four thousand books and pamphlets on Palestine-related topics monthly. Notwithstanding this increased activity on its part, the American Zionist establishment never attained the public relations success of the Hebrew Committee and the league, particularly as these came to the fore during the 1945 to 1947 period.[36]

During that period, in order to promote its aims and to build a strong support base for the Hebrew Committee, the American League for a Free Palestine operated on five parallel fronts. The first, and perhaps most successful, front was the public relations one. In addition to its regular publi-

cation of the *Answer,* the league also published ads supporting Irgun activity in Palestine and denouncing the British reaction, distributed Irgun
literature in the United States, and organized a November 1946 rally in
New York under the rubric "Salute to Resistance." A key participant in
this rally was Dr. David Wdowinski, a Revisionist activist from the Warsaw
ghetto uprising, who had just arrived in the United States that very month
and had joined the Hebrew Committee. The league even forayed into the
cinematic arts, preparing a movie describing Irgun activity in Palestine, titled *Last Night We Attacked.*[37]

One public relations axiom cites the need to create a feeling of partnership on the part of the target public with the message being imparted.
With this end in mind, the league made a tactical decision to employ the
"1776" motif, frequently and explicitly comparing the two struggles—the
American war of independence and the league and Hebrew Committee
struggle against the British for an independent Jewish state. In his appearance at the "Salute to Resistance" rally, for example, David Wdowinski
used this motif, explicitly equating the two anti-British campaigns: "If you
would help us, tell the world the truth,—that we are patriots fighting to
liberate our soil and our people. And wish us the same success that your
forefathers had in the same struggle against the same oppressor in 1776. It
is 1776 in Palestine today." [38]

This same period also saw the mounting by the league of another Ben
Hecht production: *A Flag Is Born.* A young actor named Marlon Brando,
whose destiny was intertwined with the league from that point on, was
cast in the starring role. The play opened with an encounter between
Brando, in the role of David, a young Holocaust survivor, and two older
survivors, a couple, who decide to join forces in an attempt to reach the
Mediterranean and then Palestine. The play's second act, punctuated by
typical Hechtian sarcasm, depicts a meeting at diplomatic levels to set policy for the illegal immigrants interned on Cyprus and elsewhere. But before David and his friends can even begin to implement their plans the
elderly woman dies on a Friday afternoon, soon followed by her husband.
In deep despair, David considers suicide but is stayed at the last moment
by the sound of music and voices: the strains of *HaTikvah* (the Zionist an-
them) and the voices of approaching soldiers. Three soldiers suddenly appear onstage, representatives of the Haganah, the Irgun, and the LHI
respectively, each of whom attempts to draft David to his ranks while at the

same time stressing the torturously long way to Palestine. The closing scene was an effective combination of pathos and the Irgun's ideological platform. The curtain fell on David converting the old man's prayer shawl into a new Jewish flag by sticking a star of David on it, which he now carried in the direction of the singing and shooting.[39]

According to Hecht, this play brought the Hebrew Committee and the league $1,000,000 dollars in revenues, but evidently from this almost legendary sum only $166,000 remained in delegation hands. This play's success was mirrored in the antagonism it aroused among Hebrew Committee and league opponents. Hebrew University president Judah Magnes dispatched a letter to former first lady Eleanor Roosevelt requesting that she withdraw her support for this production, whose profits, he claimed, were being used to fund terrorist activity. In Britain as well the play's success aroused concern, as seen from an exchange between the British mission to the United States and the British Foreign Office.[40]

Like previous delegation campaigns this league public relations campaign had a dual purpose: to raise funds to finance its activity and to amass support as a means of lobbying the American administration to back the Hebrew state-in-the-making. Delegation uniqueness did not lie in the amassing of support (we have already seen that in the postwar era Zionist organizations as a whole became much more actively involved in propaganda activities and fund-raising), but rather in the sectors from which it drew its support. A new and singular sector infiltrated by league activists, which then showed willingness to support Irgun activity, was the Mob. Attracted by the delegation's militant activism, initial contacts came via Jewish mobster Mickey Cohen, who approached Ben Hecht with a proposal to assist the Jewish fighters, whose renown had reached his and fellow mobsters' ears. Hecht's autobiography contains a lively description of a "party" held to raise funds among these underworld figures. After the "hat" was initially passed, Cohen gave orders to his henchman: "Tell 'em they're a lot o' cheap crumbs and they gotta give double. . . . Man by man the 'underworld' stood up and doubled the ante for the Irgun," reaching a total of $200,000, double the initial amount promised.[41]

Additional links to the underworld were forged by Alex Rafaeli. While in Sicily to find boats to transport weapons from France to Palestine, Rafaeli had an unexpected encounter with the head of the American Mafia, Lucky Luciano, who was primarily interested in Rafaeli's connections to the American administration, to Henry Morgenthau, Jr., in particular. Having received a pardon in 1944 from life imprisonment in the United States in exchange for assisting the Allies to open a second front in Sicily and on condition that he not return to the States, Luciano now hoped to ascertain if Rafaeli's connections could pave the way for his return to America. In return, Luciano promised to provide Rafaeli with twenty boats. Although this "partnership" ultimately failed to achieve the desired results, it does nonetheless shed light on the prestigious standing of delegation members in the eyes of the underworld and on delegation modus operandi: its inclination to collaborate with all and any entities capable of forwarding the Irgun's aims. A similar stance governed the alliances of delegation "disciples," particularly the New York branch of the Jewish Defense League. This topic will be explored in the next chapter.[42]

The fund-raising issue involved additional complexities, raising both the question of where the funds were headed and the long-standing issue of organizational hegemony. Many donors sought to earmark their contributions solely for Irgun activity, and not to underwrite delegation operating costs in the United States. In response to this development, the Hebrew Committee and the league kicked off a July 1946 fund-raising campaign for the purchase of medical supplies, equipment, and services, emphasizing that the majority of the funds raised would go directly to the above-mentioned cause in accord with American law that prohibited sending of weapons or of funds for the purchase of weapons abroad. Additional funds were earmarked to support jailed political prisoners and their families. Jewish Agency and Whitehall opposition to these campaigns, each for its own respective reasons, was ineffectual, and they enjoyed the widespread backing of American Jewish and non-Jewish sources.[43]

League activity also continued on the diplomatic front, with the dispatching of delegations to Europe and to Palestine. The first delegation, although slated to leave for London in September 1945, left for that city only in November. Its purpose was to "expose official and unofficial pubic opinion in Britain to the mistakes of British government policy and to prove that this policy was detrimental to English interests and to Anglo-American friendship."[44] Headed by Senator Guy Gillette and joined by Representative Andrew Somers and Professors Johan Smertenko and Fowler Harper, this delegation met with Foreign Minister Bevin, Labor Party leader Harold Laski, Colonial Affairs Minister Hill, and other British figures. Its aim was to encourage Whitehall to expedite the immigration of 100,000 Jewish DPs to Palestine without waiting for the Anglo-American Commission report, but it returned to the United States without having achieved this objective.

One year later another league-sponsored delegation, initiated by Senator Gillette, left the United States, this time for Palestine. Its aim was to make British mandatory officials aware that the majority of Palestinian and European Jews desired independence. This delegation, manned by Gillette, Harry Louis Selden, and Zipporah Levy, a young Palestinian Jew who had come to the States in the late 1930s and who served as league secretary, left for Palestine in July 1946. But the Irgun bombing of the King David Hotel one day earlier not only interfered with their planned meetings with British officials, it also led to the cancellation of their meetings with Irgun leaders in the Yishuv with whom they had hoped to reach an agreement concerning disbursement of league monies. Once again this delegation met with failure on all fronts. Selden later recounted the strong impression made by his encounter with a British intelligence officer in Cairo on the homeward journey. The latter informed Selden of his intense desire to lay his hands on two terrorists: Menachem Begin, for whom there was a bounty of five thousand pounds sterling, and another fellow of whom he was almost certain Selden had never heard, someone named Bergson.[45]

Although neither of the above-mentioned delegations achieved its primary objective, they did trigger a new initiative: the founding of European branches for league and Hebrew Committee activity. Early in the postwar period it had already become clear that a new arena was opening overseas, and in order to exploit this opportunity, two centers were chosen simultaneously for activity: London and Paris. The London branch had its origins in the delegation sent to Britain in late 1945, at the conclusion of which Professor Smertenko, a close disciple of Jabotinsky and Netziv Betar in the United States, decided to remain in London to found the league's first overseas office. Although his initial overtures to the Communist Party were rejected on the basis of ideological differences, he did receive assistance, however, from Shmuel Katz, a member of the Irgun high command then on Irgun business in Britain. During his year of league activity in Britain, Smertenko encountered ongoing hostility from official British circles, and following a December 1946 press conference during

19. Senator Guy Gillette (left), a member of the Emergency Committee, together with Zipporah Kassel and Harry Selden, who helped organize the ill-fated journey to Israel of the *Altalena* in 1948. Courtesy of Judith Tydor Baumel.

which he voiced approval and encouragement for the underground movements' anti-British campaign in Palestine, found himself deported from England. Smertenko spent some time in Paris before moving on to Italy, where he handled the release of young Irgun members arrested in connection with the bombing of the British embassy in Rome.[46]

A second center for Irgun Delegation overseas activity was Paris, for which Hillel Kook set off in late 1946, in order to put into motion a plan developed by Yitzhak Ben-Ami and Menachem Begin during the course of their conversations in Palestine in 1945: the founding of a European headquarters for the Hebrew Committee of National Liberation. Kook also harbored hopes of laying the foundation for a provisional Hebrew government-in-exile thereby, a much-disputed subject between Kook and the Irgun high command in the Yishuv. His broader aims aside, Kook naturally pursued a program similar to the one successfully utilized in the United States: concentrating on propaganda, fund-raising, and similar activities, symbolically locating his office in the building that had served as

Gestapo headquarters during the German occupation of France. He later placed this office at the disposal of the Irgun representation in Europe, "the Diaspora headquarters." The complex relationship that developed between these two organizations constitutes a story in its own right, to be told below.

Samuel Merlin, who had worked in Paris for a lengthy period before the war, was now appointed head of the Hebrew Committee's European branch. With his arrival he implemented a propaganda policy similar to the one in use in America: utilization of an independent newspaper to disseminate information to the public at large, taking over the weekly *La Riposte* under Albert Stara, with its circulation of ten thousand copies, for this purpose. He also attempted to elicit the support of the intellectual, social, and diplomatic elite: members of Parliament, writers, professors, clerics, and union and industrial leaders. Merlin's new organization also attracted to its ranks veteran Revisionist activists remaining in Europe such as David Wdowinski and longtime Swiss Revisionist activist Reuven Hecht, who cooperated with the members of the French committee, particularly on matters relating to immigration and finance. Hecht related an amusing incident concerning a reception at the Santo Domingan embassy. After dining by candlelight Hecht was introduced to the assembly and all toasted the newly appointed honorary consul of Basel. "I also raised my glass in honour of the new Honorary Consul of Basel," Hecht recalled. "I looked around, but did not locate him. At the end, I began to understand. . . . It was very funny. When I arrived at the ambassador's residence, I had no idea. Hillel Kook had forgotten to advise me that he had arranged with Trujillo for me to become consul, in order to be able to bring gold from Switzerland to Paris and to have the possibility of free travel." [47] It was not Hecht's vibrant personality alone but also his Swiss passport that greatly assisted Hebrew Committee members to move funds within Europe. Thus it was that a network of activists with foci in several European cities came into being, which from 1946 to 1948 implemented delegation goals, particularly in the realms of finance and illegal immigration.

Although a major item on its agenda, the league experienced only one success in the sphere of illegal immigration: the sailing of the SS *Ben Hecht*. The story of the *Ben Hecht* opens in the latter half of 1946, in the wake of the success of the play *A Flag Is Born*. League members funneled revenues from the play to the purchase of the SS *Abril*, which they planned to man with an American crew before the illegals boarded, this to force the British to arrest American citizens, with an eye to then challenging their actions in the courts of Palestine. But the boat's derelict condition raised doubts in Ben-Ami's mind regarding the logic of refurbishing the boat for illegal immigrants. "Did we have the right to deprive the *Irgun* in Palestine of funds now?" he wondered. "Would we do better to leave the breaking of the blockade entirely to the *Haganah* and devote all our meager funds to building the armed strength of the *Irgun?* The answer lay not in the illegal immigration enterprise itself but in the relationship with their rivals in the Zionist camp. He continued: "But on the other hand we had to show them that if they did not act, we surely would, backing up with action our public campaign for free immigration. And also, we were gaining experience in moving people across the continent and running the present blockade for possible future armed landings. We must build a network in Europe capable of moving thousands of *Irgun* soldiers to Palestine when the final battle came." These grandiose aims were ultimately the focal point of disagreements between the Irgun and the Jewish army in Palestine, reaching a breaking point in the *Altalena* affair.[48]

Following a "farewell visit" from the FBI, which searched for weapons and found lifebelts, the ship embarked for Marseilles on 26 December 1946, where it was outfitted with a new crew. On 28 February the *Abril* sailed from Port de Bouc and was renamed the SS *Ben Hecht*. On 8 March two British destroyers intercepted the *Ben Hecht,* transferring its passengers to detention camps on Cyprus and imprisoning its crew in Haifa. This interception sparked the immediate opening of a league-sponsored advertising campaign calling for their release, and league members in Congress introduced the topic on the House floor. Although the storm of protest compelled the British to release the crew, allowing it to return to the United States, the illegal immigrants who had been on board remained in detention on Cyprus until the founding of the State of Israel.

Slated to be the first, and not the sole, league-sponsored illegal immigration ship, shortly after the sailing of the *Ben Hecht* plans were made to purchase another ship, this time from American army surplus. Abraham Stavsky, a key figure in Revisionist illegal immigration during the 1930s and later a protagonist in the Arlosoroff affair, was charged with this task. Although an LST (landing ship tank) was purchased, for a variety of reasons a sailing of illegal immigrants never materialized. With the 29 November 1947 UN vote for partition, the ship's owners were asked to now divert it to transport arms and ammunition for the coming battle in Palestine. The story of this LST, now renamed the SS *Altalena,* will be discussed below.

The passing of the UN resolution did not bring league activity to a halt. In addition to a league-initiated boycott on British goods, started in 1946, the league continued its activity on the diplomatic front as well as its fund-raising for illegal immigration (which was not realized) and its public relations campaigns, including an emergency conference held from 8 to 13 May 1948. Among its resolutions were recognition of the government of the newly formed Jewish state, and a call to lift the embargo and to use American pressure to end the marine siege and restrictions on aliyah. In addition, it resolved to extend financial aid to the Yishuv and to lobby other governments to prevent foreign armies from moving on Palestine. In line with changes then taking place within the delegation and among its supporters, we find the expression *Jewish state,* and not *Hebrew state,* appearing for the first time in league history.

During its final days, the league attempted to draft volunteers to join the fighting in Palestine within the framework of the George Washington Legion. Although thousands answered the call, their numbers fell to hundreds following a State Department announcement that it would not issue visas to those wishing to fight and that volunteers would lose their American citizenship. In the final analysis these volunteers never made their way to Palestine, but they did serve as a bargaining chip in the league's current public relations campaign. At the same time, efforts to raise funds for illegal immigration and for gun-running to Palestine continued, forwarded primarily by a dedicated group of mostly non-Jewish volunteers, like the Catholic lawyer Paul O'Dwyer. These individuals continued to act on behalf of forwarding delegation policy until the *Altalena* affair in summer 1948.

Relations Within the Delegation (1945–1948)

In his study of groups, the sociologist Tom Douglas submits that every group must be regarded as an organism with closely interrelated parts and that it is the essential character of these interrelationships that often holds the key to intergroup differences. Nor does it suffice to analyze outward member behavior, as group pressures often create a conformist system that does not reflect the hidden subterranean forces. Only a panoramic view of member functioning can provide the key to a true understanding of each activity group's essential nature.[49]

These observations are certainly cogent to the Irgun Delegation and its members, even more so to their final period of activity, which extended from the war's end to the founding of the State of Israel. During this three-year period, internal friction, until then largely tacit, came bubbling to the surface and, as opposed to earlier periods of delegation history, during these final years led to alterations in the group's hierarchical structure, almost unthinkable but a short time earlier.

This friction came to the fore in the decision to place the delegation's underlying democratic basis to the test. Alex Rafaeli summed up the heart of the matter in retrospect: "When we returned to the United States we saw what had happened to the Delegation and how Hillel Kook had operated. Over time we came to the realization that we must take action to prevent a double explosion: one over the idea of the 'Hebrews,' which American Jewry found totally incomprehensible, and second, with the Irgun high command in the Yishuv, between whom and Hillel there were ever-increasing disagreements. We had no desire to hurt him, but we also knew things could not continue thus."[50] Things came to head in January 1948, when Hillel Kook was ousted from chairmanship of the Hebrew Committee and of the delegation. Albeit the choice of Samuel Merlin to replace him sweetened the bitter pill, as of all delegation members Merlin was closest to Kook and could best be envisioned, more than any other delegation member, as following in Hillel's footsteps on most of the burning issues of the day.

On most, but not all. The underlying reasons for this step were complex, and touch upon the roots of the ideological struggle between the Irgun high command in Palestine and members of the Irgun Delegation in the United States. One disputed point was Hillel Kook's desire to announce the formation of a provisional Hebrew government in the Diaspora. For his part, Begin demanded that the timing for this step be determined by the "people on the front line," that is, the Irgun high command in the Yishuv, whereas Kook understood that such a government would come into existence only if he contravened the party line and made an independent declaration. Concurrently, Begin stepped up his demands for massive financial support from the Hebrew Committee and the American League for a Free Palestine. This demand was countered in turn by Eri Jabotinsky's demand that the Irgun in the Yishuv back all public statements issued by the Hebrew Committee in the Diaspora, a demand Begin hesitated to accept. We must look beyond the specific issues at stake to the broader question of hegemony, a recurrent theme in the delegation's relationship with other entities throughout its existence.

Another debated issue was the question of the partition plan. Whereas Merlin doubted this plan would ever be implemented, Kook, for his part, disagreed. He recommended that if approved, the plan be accepted as a fait accompli and, that in such a case the delegation abandon its independent activity and effect an organizational merger with the Zionist Federation's institutions. Only thus, he argued, would it be possible to press for a revision of the proposed geographical borders and to "monitor" the Zionist leadership from within. Whereas Ben-Ami and Rafaeli leaned toward Kook's view on this latter matter, they dissented from his attitude toward the Irgun high command in the Yishuv. Kook defined the role of the Irgun high command as a technical one, assigning to delegation members the role of the "political leaders of our national revolution," in his words. A final topic under debate within the delegation was Kook and Merlin's notion of the Hebrew nation, which they had tried to sell to the American public as a solution to the problem of dual loyalty. Although theoretically the raison d'être for the Hebrew Committee, the distinction between "Hebrew" and "Jew" remained completely foreign to American Jews, who digested this newly marketed ideational commodity with difficulty, and a range of opinions existed regarding the degree to which the delegation should adhere to this new concept. Ultimately, taken in conjunction, these disputed areas led to a split in the delegation on ideological and personnel grounds, culminating with Kook's ouster and Merlin's election as chairman in his stead.[51]

Reference to criteria pertaining to small group dynamics helps clarify the changes in delegation structure and hierarchy between 1946 and 1948. Among the outstanding characteristics of small groups, we must note consensus, conformism, identification, internalization, cooperation, and competition, characteristics that find expression to different degrees in each individual member according to his function. It is the leader who usually sets the standards that form the criteria for consensus, conformism, and identification, and the coordinator who elicits cooperation, while the initiator and the energizer often exhibit competitive characteristics. In contrast, the elaborator and the recorder exhibit identification and internalization, as do the information givers and seekers.[52]

Role task division within the delegation may not always have been clear-cut, but until the group's final period of activity Hillel Kook's position as group leader was irrefutable. As the ideational and practical standard setter for the group, identification with his definitions also served as a criterion for accepting Kook's authority. From 1946 on, when delegation members found themselves unable to accept Kook's views on current issues, this inability was eventually translated into a practical step: ousting Kook from chairmanship of the Hebrew Committee and the delegation. It was Merlin, who simultaneously filled the roles of initiator and energizer—both roles that enhance competitiveness—who now assumed the chairmanship. In contrast, Jabotinsky, Rafaeli, and Ben-Ami functioned as elaborators, information seekers, and givers, roles characterized by a significant degree of internalization and identification. Thus it was a natural move for Merlin, as opposed to any of the other members, to step into Kook's shoes while the rest carried on with their behind-the-scenes activity.

Another issue confronting the group was challenges from dissidents who had left its ranks, the most outstanding example being Rabbi Baruch Korf. Originally associated with the league, in 1947 Korf split off to found the Political Action Committee for Palestine, which called for recognition of European and Palestinian Jews as an ethnic-national entity entitled to realize its right to a sovereign state. Unlike delegation members, however, Korf was prepared to give up Transjordan provided the Arabs recognized a Jewish state in the other parts of Palestine. Another area of disagreement between the two groups related to Korf's objections to a loan the American administration intended to make to Britain, an issue on which the delegation maintained neutrality. Finally, Korf denied any difference between Hebrews and Jews, claiming that they were one and the same ethnic group. Throughout this period Kook and his associates maintained a correct relationship with Korf, but never succeeded in eliciting any practical cooperation. After the founding of the State Korf fell into oblivion until he resurfaced in the late 1960s as a rabbinic figure closely associated with President Richard Nixon.[53]

Relations with the British Government

In addition to the above-mentioned relationship networks, delegation members confronted a number of forces—some hostile—within and without the Zionist movement. One such force was the British government, which never deviated from its policy toward the delegation: tracking its activity but taking pains to avoid any direct contact with its members. An exchange of letters dating from 1944 to 1948 between the British mission to Washington and the Foreign and Colonial Offices in London regarding the delegation, correspondence in which Kook is alternately named "the extremist Zionist leader," "the terrorist Bergson," and the "gangster," reflects the heights to which British animosity could climb.[54]

Closer examination of this correspondence sheds further light on the British modus operandi vis-à-vis the delegation. A March 1945 letter from the embassy clerk to the British Foreign Office noted the scores of approaches made by Mr. Bergson and his gang from the founding of the Hebrew Committee and labeled them "gangsters," noting that a decision had been made to have no contact with the group. On another occasion, this embassy official summed up the efforts made to deport Bergson from the United States. As a holder of a British passport, now up for renewal, Bergson enjoyed tourist status in the United States. Embassy officials now approached the mandatory authorities in hopes that the High Commissioner would refuse to renew Bergson's passport, thus opening the way for his deportation from the United States. Notwithstanding these attempts to neutralize Kook and to sabotage Hebrew Committee activity, the letter concluded on a less optimistic note: "We shall take this point up with the Department of Justice, though we rather doubt whether they will feel inclined to deport him in view of (a) transportation difficulties, and (b) the influential friends who seem to be able to protect him."[55]

British authorities pertinaciously tracked delegation activities until the end of the mandate, concentrating on the delegation/Zionist establishment rift, which they sought to utilize for their own ends: to push the small group out of the political arena. A July 1945 memo from the British embassy in Washington summed up the attitude of His Majesty's government toward this vexatious force. "The principal organizer of these organizations is a certain Mr. Peter Bergson, a Palestinian subject, who, with several of the other co-founders, is associated with the Irgun, a terrorist ultra-nationalist Jewish organization in Palestine, responsible for several activities of violence in that country." This memo also outlined official British policy vis-à-vis the Hebrew Committee and the league: a refusal in principle to have any contact with them and a threefold attempt to neutralize their public influence by emphasizing establishment Zionist opposition to them, by highlighting their link to terrorist organizations in Palestine, and by consistently stressing their fascist inclinations. In Britain, the local British administration pursued a similar tack toward Smertenko and the British League for a Free Palestine.[56]

At first glance British administration interest in delegation activity during 1944 to 1948 is seemingly disproportionate. Certainly the British were well aware that the delegation consisted of a mere handful of activists with limited organizational machinery operating outside mainstream Zionism. Although this handful had successfully drafted forty thousand sympathizers to the league, even its members admitted that they had failed to register any diplomatic achievements. Nor had they succeeded in gaining the ear of American administration figures. Yet British correspondence from that period conveys the distinct impression that the British feared delegation activity even more than established Zionist movement activity. The explanation for this fear must lie in Kook and his coterie's field of expertise: public relations. If indeed the British feared the Hebrew Committee and the League for a Free Palestine, their dismay was grounded in and commingled with admiration for the delegation's ability to take a topic and make it the center of public interest, to train the media spotlight on it, arousing public awareness. Evidently, in the uncertainties of the postwar period, British administration officials fully grasped the implications of a media storm surrounding a particular issue. Even without access to diplomatic circles, delegation members still possessed the ability to make things sticky for His Majesty's government. It is this ability to which we must look for an explanation to the sharp British reaction to league ads, particularly ones penned by Ben Hecht. Hecht's May 1947 "Letter to the Terrorists of Palestine" so angered the British as to prompt them to invoke a boycott of his movies.[57]

Relations with the Zionist Establishment

The ad containing Hecht's "Letter to Terrorists of Palestine," with its reference to American popular support for Irgun activity in Palestine and its comparison of the Irgun to the American Revolutionary Army, not only sparked a strong British reaction but also aroused Zionist establishment ire in the United States and in the Yishuv. But this reaction represents but one aspect of the tension between the Zionist establishment and the Hebrew Committee and the league that erupted with their founding in spring 1944. Attacks came from several directions at once. The American Zionist Emergency Council (AZEC) issued an announcement to the effect that this group operated with a mandate from no one but the Irgun in Palestine, "a small insignificant group of gun toting extremists who claim that they stand behind a number of terrorist acts which were recently carried out." The American Jewish Conference chimed in with a declaration that the Hebrew Committee's sole true aim was to destroy the Jewish Agency. Lastly, ZOA president Israel Goldstein announced that the founding of the Hebrew Committee and the league was "a comic farce which is possibly suitable for operas," but not a solution for the difficult situation now prevailing within the Zionist movement.[58] These responses were but the tip of an iceberg that once again surfaced among the delegation's opponents, pointing once again to the inordinate amount of time that these organizations spent dealing with the delegation, something completely disproportionate to the meager results of the delegation's offshoots during the same period. Other examples were the letters penned by Nahum Goldmann, warning the "powers that be" in Washington and various ambassadors from foreign countries against Bergson; the attacks of the Palestine Labor Federation (Histadrut) against the Bergsonites, including a letter from Golda Meir; and letters from forty-six rabbis denouncing the League for a Free Palestine.[59]

The Hebrew Committee's and the league's overt and unequivocal identification with the Irgun in the postwar period—for the first time in the history of any delegation offshoot—catapulted Jewish establishment opposition to these organizations to new heights. From here on, like their counterparts in the Yishuv, delegation activists were labeled "fascists." Now establishment leaders could argue that these groups espoused the same dangerous ideology as the Irgun, which aggrandized political murder, utilizing it as a political tool. At one point Stephen Wise even voiced his fears of a delegation assassination attempt on his life to a WRB representative. Attempts to draft Kook and later to deport him from the United States went into high gear; concurrently, Jewish administration leaders put forth claims of financial irregularities in the administration of delegation offshoots, something they had not succeeded in proving during the delegation's entire existence. Finally, Zionist establishment organizations attacked delegation illegal immigration, arguing that it had not brought even a single immigrant to Palestine, presenting the 1947 sailing of the *Ben Hecht* as little more than a clever public relations trick.[60]

In late 1947 an anonymous report evidently emanating from some establishment Zionist force characterized the *Ben Hecht* as a diversionary ship. Its headings are instructive. They summarize the main lines of Zionist establishment opposition to the Bergsonites: "The Hebrew national: an anti-Zionist concept," "The Group's Confused Terminology," "Why only European Jews?" "Denouncing the Jewish State Idea," "Giving up the Jewish majority Postulate," "The Attitude towards Terror," "No Mandate no Authority," "A 'mute' Hebrew Nation," "The Slogan of Provisional Government," "Misleading Propaganda," "The Financial Mess." Many of these arguments—in particular those not related to the concept of a "Hebrew nation"—had been raised earlier in the decade against the delegation's first offshoots. Nor had the reasons for establishment opposition to the Hebrew Committee and the league altered much; we find embitterment over the loss of their monopoly on presentation of the Zionist-Jewish problem to the American public, over their refusal to accept the authority of the established Zionist movement (which exemplified its relationship with all elements associated with the Revisionist camp), and finally, concern lest the delegation modus operandi act to the detriment of Zionist aims as well as to the status of American Jewry.[61]

Relations with the Zionist-Revisionist Movement

The delegation's ongoing battle with the Zionist establishment was accompanied by attempts to build regular patterns of interaction with bodies within and closely associated with the Zionist-Revisionist movement. We have already seen the negative American NZO reaction to Hillel Kook's announced founding of the Hebrew Committee in 1944, a reaction symptomatic of the rift between the delegation and the NZO during that period. Although many individual Revisionist movement members identified with Jewish Army and Emergency Committee aims, and some, like Ben-Zion Netanyahu, even served as active members of either of these organizations for a time, the post-1944 rift between the delegation and the Revisionist movement was now clearly revealed as unbridgeable.

This gap did not hold true for the American Betar youth movement, however, which maintained an especially close relationship with the young Irgun members from Palestine for the entire period of their stay in America. Moshe Arens, commander of the New England branch of Betar in the mid-1940s, recalled how enthused Betar campers reacted to visits by delegation members and the tales of their most recent campaigns. Despite Betar reservations regarding the ideology of Hebrews vs. Jews, Betar youth, who identified with the Irgun struggle in Palestine and themselves sought to adopt an activist mode, patterned themselves on the delegation's modus operandi. One delegation-inspired operation was the April 1947 invasion of the British embassy by forty Betarites to hold a memorial ceremony for Dov Gruner, who had been executed by the mandatory authorities. Crew members from the *Ben Hecht,* who were closely associated with the delegation, helped organize this protest. Another delegation-inspired activity adopted by Betar members was a boycott on British goods, and Betar newsletters published lists of British commodities currently for sale in the United States. Delegation-inspired modus operandi—now raised to canonical status, turned into symbols, and used as models for imitation—continued to shape Betar campaigns into the 1950s. To this influence we must attribute the decision by the New York Betar drama club to mount a production of *A Flag Is Born* in spring 1950, a production given wide coverage in the movement bulletin by one of its editors, young Betar activist Meir Kahane.[62]

No parallel existed between this close, at times symbiotic, American Betar/delegation relationship and the delegation's relationship with the Irgun mother-organization in Palestine. It is noteworthy that it was precisely the period when the delegation openly identified with the Irgun and gave its policy in the Yishuv unrestrained backing that the issue of hegemony reached its height. The cornerstones of this struggle inhered in the spheres of ideology, diplomacy, and finances. Irgun commander Begin's hesitation to adopt the idea of a "Hebrew nation" as an ideological bombshell and his adamant refusal to immediately declare a Hebrew government-in-exile posed a direct challenge to two central conceptions in Hillel Kook's ideological-political weltanschauung. In the financial realm as well efforts were made to bend Hebrew Committee members to Irgun dictates, but to no avail. The demand of Begin and European Irgun leaders for most Hebrew Committee and league revenues to be turned over to the mother organization in the Yishuv met with absolute refusal on grounds that these funds were earmarked for their independent public relations campaigns and for organizing aliyah bet.

Against the background of their diverging interpretations of the role of the Irgun Delegation in the United States, this Kook/Begin dispute intensified. Whereas Begin viewed it primarily as a public relations tool, for Kook the delegation was the intellectual vanguard for the Irgun as a whole. In 1946, in an attempt to coordinate positions with Irgun leaders in the Yishuv, Ben-Ami returned to Palestine on a mission disguised as a honeymoon. In the course of these contacts Irgun commander Begin openly condemned what he termed mere gestures on the Hebrew Committee's part, no substitute for positive action: the name "Hebrew embassy" used by the press to refer to the Washington Hebrew Committee headquarters, the committee's registration as the agent for Hebrew people, and Kook's releases to the press and to Congress, intended to publicly establish the de facto existence of the Hebrew nation. "Begin had congratulated the HCNL on all of this, but deep inside he and the rest of the *Irgun* leadership in Palestine deemed these activities secondary to the military battle in Palestine, and they resented funds being spent on 'gestures,' " Ben-Ami later formulated the underlying tensions. "They also resented that Peter Bergson (Kook) and others in the HCNL were receiving such a buildup which appeared to smack of personal ambitions for the future, rather than total commitment to the armed struggle." [63]

For his part, Kook did not spare Begin, berating him for his failure to understand the delegation's aims and its successes. Years later he argued that the disputes of that period did not simply emerge against the background of differing ideological interpretations of the delegation's postwar role, but also from a deliberate attempt on Begin's part to reinterpret the original mandate granted to delegation members when they first left for the United States. "Begin was a very talented professional liar," Kook commented caustically in retrospect. "Generally speaking he is a talented person and perhaps lying is one of his outstanding talents, because he manages to conceal it." [64]

But the complex Begin/Kook interaction did not necessarily carry over into the relationship with other Irgun members, who gave the Hebrew Committee a degree of cooperation. Shmuel Katz, an Irgun member who worked in conjunction with Hebrew Committee representatives in Paris, made no secret of his distaste for their ideological pronouncements, but nevertheless deplored what he termed "the unnecessary antagonism it aroused." He went on: "But I was filled with admiration for what the Bergson group had achieved in America and believed that we had a common objective. I thought it would be ridiculous not to co-operate with them." [65]

Cooperation with the Irgun reached its apex in joint activity in Europe, following the founding of the Irgun's European headquarters in Paris. Founded in 1946 with the opening of a "second front" in the anti-British revolt, it was envisioned that Irgun activists would draft young people, mainly Holocaust survivors, to the ranks of the underground. At the same time they would provide these draftees with military training and bring them to Palestine, raise funds, purchase weapons and ammunition, and transport them to Palestine. Another envisioned sphere of activity was a propaganda campaign among European Jews and non-Jews regarding the Irgun struggle to free the Jewish homeland, and the planning of military actions against British targets in Europe. First opened in Rome, at a later date a joint headquarters was created in Paris where Hebrew Committee members had their European headquarters. The aim of this joint headquarters was to coordinate between the European representatives of the Irgun, the NZO, and Betar, three organizations on the Zionist right that ostensibly belonged to the same camp but nevertheless did not coordinate their platforms. Begin's intent was to allow this headquarters free rein in the realms of fund-raising and organizing Revisionist aliyah bet as quid pro quo for operational freedom in Palestine. [66]

In April 1946 Eli Tavin, then chief of the Irgun's Diaspora headquarters, met in Rome with Samuel Merlin in order to work out an agreement between the Hebrew Committee and the Irgun in Europe. Although initialed in principle, this agreement never received operational ratification, and its use of *Hebrew, Jew,* and *Palestinian State* aroused negative reactions among the Yishuv high command. Nonetheless, a measure of cooperation was reached, which deepened in early 1947 with Eliyahu Lankin's appointment as chief of the Irgun's Diaspora headquarters. At that time both Hillel Kook and Eri Jabotinsky were in Paris and expressed their willingness to cooperate with Lankin and the Irgun Diaspora headquarters. In spring 1947 an agreement was worded for founding an Irgun branch in the Diaspora, to be comprised of NZO, Betar, Hebrew Committee, and Irgun representatives and to be chaired by Hillel Kook, who would resign from his chairmanship of the Hebrew Committee. At the same time, this would pave the way for Kook's replacement by Samuel Merlin as delegation leader. But because of lack of authority, lack of clarity of orders emanating from the Yishuv, and tensions between the various parties, this organizational framework never came into being. In October 1947 this joint representation disbanded, to be replaced by the Irgun's Diaspora headquarters, manned solely by members of that organization.[67]

The ideological and practical differences between the Irgun and delegation members reached their height against the backdrop of joint activity in the framework of the Diaspora headquarters. It was Eliyahu Lankin who served as Hebrew Committee advocate to Irgun headquarters, who displayed faith in its members, sharing their pain at the treatment they received at the hands of Irgun headquarters in the Yishuv. Lankin even took exception to Begin's ultimatum to Kook, Merlin, and Ben-Ami demanding that they choose between continuing their activity on the Hebrew Committee or official Irgun business. This ultimatum exemplified attempts by the Irgun high command to incorporate delegation members in joint frameworks with an eye to neutralizing their autonomous tendencies and bending them to the will of the Yishuv Irgun leadership on questions of authority, semantics, and tactics.

Money matters continued to provide an unfailing source for disagreements and harsh disputes between the Irgun and members of the Hebrew Committee. Alex Rafaeli recalled how hundreds of thousands of dollars belonging to the American Irgun were deposited in Swiss banks to which only a few select individuals, including Ben-Ami, Rafaeli, and two Revisionists by the name of Cohen, had access. "A decision was reached not to touch these funds without a direct order from headquarters, that is, from Begin or Ben-Eliezer, to make a withdrawal. And along came Shmuel Katz with two individuals named Cohen whose names were identical with the two Revisionists and managed to withdraw money from the bank. I called headquarters in the Yishuv and they gave the order that the money be returned."[68] In the wake of this incident Shmuel Katz was dispatched to the United States to organize political propaganda activity and to found an independent fund-raising project for the Irgun, but with little success. An additional mission by Katz to the States in spring 1948 further heightened intergroup tensions.

Angered by Irgun headquarters' attempts to neutralize his independent activity, Hillel Kook played a major role in exacerbating this tension. Shortly after his arrival in Paris in 1947 to take over chairmanship of the Diaspora headquarters, IZL activist Yaakov Meridor wrote to Begin concerning the difficult relationship with Hebrew Committee members. "I talked with Hillel. He is full of complaints. He doesn't see his own hump, though he sees that of others well enough." Meridor had come to Kook concerning the possibility of receiving funds from his campaigns in the United States, to which Kook ironically replied that it was certainly possible on condition that Meridor "sell" the Hebrew Committee and its right to raise funds to the Zionists. Meridor's conclusion regarding Hebrew Committee effectiveness was unequivocal: "With the Committee's human material we can create a propaganda arm, primarily a political one. . . . In my argument with Hillel Kook I proved to him that he and the Committee had not made any political moves, as he had failed to ensure the political base necessary to provide real aid to the front. What he had done was nothing more than outstanding propaganda work. Essentially, the 'Kook problem' remains unsolved, although we will have to find some means not to alienate him but also not to unleash a destructive force." [69]

Indeed, as already noted, strong differences between the member groups of the joint representation blocked Kook's appointment as chairman. But this was not the case regarding Samuel Merlin, who succeeded Kook as chairman of the Hebrew Committee and proceeded to commit himself to a series of steps Kook had found distasteful. One such commitment was a promise not to take any diplomatic or propaganda steps in contradiction to the Irgun party line; another was to cease the public debate over the Hebrews/Jews dichotomy. In addition, they also called for an in-house reorganization of the Hebrew Committee and for a promise that committee members and contacts would be placed at the disposal of the Diaspora headquarters if necessary. In turn, Merlin was granted special dispensation to organize fund-raising in the United States as he saw fit, and retained the status of a headquarters officer on special assignment. But disagreements between the Hebrew Committee and Irgun headquarters continued even after Merlin's appointment. Following Katz's mission to the United States, Merlin asked to be released from this assignment in order to travel to Palestine. [70]

This attempt to create a partnership with the Irgun, Betar, and the NZO did not, however, rule out delegation overtures to the LHI. As early as his 1945 visit to Palestine, Yitzhak Ben-Ami had tried to foster contacts with this body, even meeting with Nathan Yellin-Mor in an attempt to draw closer to the LHI. Because of the polarities dividing their outlook at that point, this tentative approach brought with it no practical results. In his *The Stern Gang: Ideology, Politics and Terror, 1940–1949,* Joseph Heller notes the main areas of disagreement between the two organizations that obviated their entering into partnership. First, whereas the LHI viewed itself "as a political liberation movement with broad [ideological] horizons," it viewed the IZL solely as a military movement. Second, LHI saw itself as a "sovereign and independent liberation movement" that could not be part of any other organization. Third, in contrast to the IZL, the LHI's social program called for a "just social system": "a planned economy within the framework of an *étatist* regime" with no room for unlimited private enterprise. Foreign policy orientation also differed. LHI saw foreign dominion over Palestine as an enemy to be fought with no holds barred, the purpose of this struggle being to elicit support from foreign powers recognizing the Palestinian Jews' right to freedom and independence. LHI figures feared that IZL sympathizers did not fully understand these principles. Finally, the LHI accused the IZL of engaging in a personality cult, of hero-worshiping the dead (Jabotinsky and Raziel) and/or the living (Begin), whereas the LHI was based on "a supra-human ideal." Given these differences, it is therefore difficult to imagine a merger between the LHI and any IZL-associated entity like the Hebrew Committee.[71]

The End of the Delegation

If the spring 1940 arrival of the final delegation members in the United States marks the "end of the beginning," then the declaration of the State of Israel eight years later represents the "beginning of the end" in delegation history. It was self-evident that after the founding of the State delegation members would have to adapt to the new political and military developments. But in early May 1948 the direction of these developments was not yet clear. All delegation members in Paris knew was of the Zionist executive's intention to proclaim a Jewish state on 15 May 1948. Alex Rafaeli recounted how everyone obviously wanted to be present on that occasion, but how were they to get there? "In our group were several

Irgun members who had escaped from British camps in African countries and others who had come to Europe after the war to conduct military operations against the British. Some had Palestinian passports and some had no passports at all. No one would rent us a plane to fly to Palestine, which was considered a danger zone."[72]

Rafaeli finally managed to convince the French office of British Airways to fly to Lod, after providing assurances that it was safe to land. The group included Yaakov Meridor, Arieh Ben-Eliezer, Hillel Kook, and Eri Jabotinsky, among others. And then the great adventure began:

Everybody was in very high spirits, though no one actually knew where we were going to land and who controlled Lod airport. After flying over Athens we heard on the radio that Lod had been captured by the Arabs and that a battle was going on in Ramleh. What were the other options? Haifa was still in British hands and that left only Sde Dov, near Tel Aviv, a small airport used mainly for light planes and Pipers. The British pilots refused to land, claiming that the airport was too small for a Dakota and the risks could be fatal. They decided to land in Cyprus. I informed them we could not accept their decision and that our own pilots, who were with me in the cockpit and were armed, would land the plane if they did not want to. The British gave in. We began circling Sde Dov and managed to land by the skin of our teeth.[73]

Their visit to celebrate the founding of the State lasted a mere three days, in the course of which they also met with Irgun commander Begin. During this meeting, Begin informed them of his intention to disband the Irgun as a military organization and to found the Herut party, which would run in the upcoming elections. He proposed that they join his list and received positive answers from Kook, Merlin, Jabotinsky, and Ben-Eliezer. Alex Rafaeli, by his own report, preferred to wait until he learned more of the proposed party's platform, political program, and intended work patterns. On 16 May the Hebrew Committee's New York branch announced that as part of the national land had been liberated there was no longer a need for a Diaspora liberation movement; moreover, the liberation movement in Israel could now come aboveground and operate openly. The next day Kook and Rafaeli held a press conference in Tel Aviv at which they repeated this announcement. A day later the group traveled north to Haifa, still a British enclave, where the British Airways Dakota awaited them to return them to Paris, where they were to wind down their activity before returning to Israel permanently. Only one campaign remained to be completed by the delegation overseas, the sailing of the *Altalena*.

To this day the *Altalena* affair, which had its inception in spring 1947 with the purchase of an American army surplus LST, constitutes the focal point of a historical and historiographical debate regarding each side's true intentions. The story begins with delegation members' plans to prepare another ship to transport illegal immigrants, similar to the *Ben Hecht*. News of the impending end of the British mandate changed this plan, fostering a decision to utilize the ship to transport arms and fighters for the Irgun instead, and during winter 1947 and spring 1948 the boat was refitted for this purpose. Harry Selden recalled how he succeeded in insuring the boat with Lloyds of London, almost an impossibility for ships of unknown origin sailing for undetermined destinations. Despite efforts at secrecy, evidently the French authorities got wind of what was really happening. Years later, a story circulated of a preboarding chat one passenger had with a French policeman. "As he was waiting at the foot of the gangplank to board, a gendarme posted there, to make conversation, asked: 'Where are you going?' Conscious of the visa he carried, he replied: 'Bolivia.' 'Ah Bolivia,' mused the gendarme. 'I know it well, I was stationed in Syria for four years.' "[74]

Much has been written on the sailing of the *Altalena* and its tragic ending—the negotiations with the "dissidents" even before the War of Independence regarding their merger with the Haganah; the early June 1948 agreement to disband the Irgun and the Jerusalem battalion's refusal to accede to this order; Ben-Gurion's fear of independent IZL activity; the attempt to negotiate with Yisrael Galili; Zipporah Kassel's failed attempts to radio the *Altalena* not to approach shore; the disembarkment at Kfar Vitkin; the shelling of the ship by Israel Defense Forces (IDF) opposite Tel Aviv on 22 July; the death of three IDF soldiers and sixteen passengers on the *Altalena,* including Abraham Stavsky, and the wounding of Samuel Merlin—and it is not my intention here either to detail the sequence of events or to enter the historiographical debate that attempts to unravel Ben-Gurion's true intentions on the one hand, or of the Irgun members' intent to found an independent army and stage a coup on the other. Rather, what interests me here is the involvement of delegation members in these events and the pinpointing of the focal issue underlying the *Altalena* affair, the ongoing problem that for years had persistently disturbed the equilibrium of Revisionist movement/Irgun relations and Irgun/delegation relations: the question of authority. Essentially at the root of many of the internal divisions within the Zionist movement over the years, this issue continued to plague the Irgun even after it had "swallowed up" the delegation and the Revisionist movement with the founding of the Herut party.[75]

With the *Altalena* affair's tragic conclusion came the final disbanding of the delegation. In summer 1948, the Hebrew Committee received a loan of approximately $100,000 from the balance of the Irgun's Diaspora headquarters in order to cover its outstanding debts. Naturally, a dispute broke out between the Irgun high command and the delegation as to the date when the loan was due, and the money was repaid in installments. Now it was time to wind down delegation activity in the Diaspora. During the third week of September general headquarters issued an ultimatum to the Irgun's Jerusalem headquarters in Ben-Gurion's name with the demand to cease all independent military activity forthwith and to bow to the dictates of the state law governing the army, conscription, and weapons. Starting on 22 September, Jerusalem Irgun battalion members began their orderly appearance before IDF draft boards, and the very next day a rally was held in downtown Jerusalem at which Menachem Begin announced the founding of a Herut party branch in the capital. This marked the final dissolution of the Irgun Zeva'i Leumi.

On 22 September, the very day that the Irgun's Jerusalem battalion was being disbanded, an official decision was reached in New York to disband the League for a Free Palestine. On that occasion Ben-Ami also announced the official dissolution of the Irgun in Jerusalem, its integration into the IDF, and the founding of the Herut party. It was resolved to close the league by year's end and to collect funds for a new foundation for rehabilitation of Irgun soldiers. At a 28 September 1948 press conference held in Tel Aviv, Hillel Kook announced the dissolution of the Hebrew Committee of National Liberation, and a telegram to that effect was forwarded to its remaining members in Washington.

Several additional matters remained to be settled before the conclusion of almost a decade of activity. First there was the need to help organize Begin's December 1948 trip to the United States in order to amass backing for the Herut party in preparation for the January 1949 elections for the founding assembly. During his American tour Begin received assistance from league backers such as Guy Gillette and even Ben Hecht, who had withdrawn from the Zionist arena in the wake of the *Altalena* affair. It was also necessary to unload Hebrew Committee assets, particularly the "Hebrew embassy" building. Kook's proposal that the building be turned over to the Israeli government for use as a diplomatic embassy was not implemented after government officials announced that they were willing to accept it only for the purposes of sale. In the final analysis, committee representatives sold it to the Pakistani representation in October 1950. Even their public relations campaign drew to a close, and the final edition of the *Answer* appeared on 17 December 1948.

At a press conference held on 15 October in Tel Aviv, Kook, Merlin, Jabotinsky, Ben-Eliezer, and Irma Helpern summed up ten years of delegation activity and announced the current political aims of most of its members: joining the ranks of the Herut party. In the January 1949 elections Herut received 11.3 percent of the total vote and its MPs included Arieh Ben-Eliezer, Hillel Kook, Eri Jabotinsky, and Samuel Merlin, who became four of the fourteen Herut Knesset members. Thus began another fascinating story, one that is not within this book's purview: the role of delegation members in the Herut party.[76]

Evaluating the Hebrew Committee and the League for a Free Palestine

The delegation's final four years of existence may be defined as the stage of "performing," a stage during which the group was able to concentrate exclusively on implementation of the task at hand, having passed through the stages of crystallization, choosing a leader, fixing a direction, and task role division. Now the group could function in the supportive atmosphere created earlier during the stage of "norming," in order to engage in problem solving. From early 1948 the delegation entered the stage of "adjourning," during which we would expect to again see changes in intragroup interaction.[77]

Two characteristics that typified the delegation offshoots of the "performing" stage were the broadening of member cooperation with other ethnic interest groups in the United States, and their prominent role on the spectrum of the Zionist right following their public identification with Irgun policy in the Yishuv. Both features will be discussed in chapter 6.

How did delegation members and sympathizers view themselves during their final period of activity? The first sphere of self-evaluation concerned the ideological realm, in particular the internal debate within the delegation (and between the delegation and Irgun headquarters) regarding the use of the terms *Hebrews* and *Jews*. Samuel Halperin argues that internal ideological conflicts are of secondary importance if the ideology successfully drafts broad support, enhances member activity, or weakens the opposition.[78] In the delegation's case, it appears however that the internal semantic-ideological debate carried greater weight since it contributed to none of the above-mentioned spheres of activity. Kook and Merlin's failure to sell the conception of Hebrews to the American Jewish public testifies to their inability to correctly decipher the American Jewish cultural map. Nor did this conception strengthen the delegation's standing in the international arena, as we saw with regard to the founding of the Hebrew Committee's European branch. Finally, neither did it contribute to the strengthening of the link with the mother organization. For more than three years, Kook's adherence to the Hebrews vs. Jews distinction formed the crux of his debate with Irgun headquarters in the Yishuv.

Kook's failure to read the conceptual map of American Jewry was paralleled by failure in the political sphere: his inability to decode the relationship with the Irgun high command in the Yishuv. In a sweeping retrospective summation, Yitzhak Ben-Ami noted the main point disputed by the delegation and the Irgun high command, which essentially revolved about the weight assigned to the political vs. the military struggle. "We in the diaspora felt that all the heroism on the front line could be in vain without our political campaigns in the United States and later in France. Throughout history, many freedom movements had fallen short despite heroic military resistance, precisely because the political battles had not been fought well. Our incessant campaign in the U.S. had given the struggle international and historic dimensions; its was our publicity, we felt, that had allowed the *Irgun* to withstand the British, Zionist Establishment and State Department campaigns against it and against its precepts. Without us the *Irgun* might have been wiped out, and the State of Israel might not have been born." Other activists, like Harry Selden, shared this resolute opinion, found in correspondence written years later: "I am convinced that had we—Peter—not succeeded in maintaining public interest in the U.S. at the high pitch to which we raised it, there would have been no Aliyah Bet, no War Refugee Board, no Anglo-American Commission, no 1947 UN resolution, no Israel."[79]

A somewhat different picture emerges from "canonical" Irgun historiography. In his books, "official" Irgun historian David Niv gives the Hebrew Committee and the league positive billing, but this from the perspective of an entity that supported the main Irgun struggle, that is, from a Palestinocentric orientation. The reason for these *rashomons* becomes apparent if we recall the role each entity assigned itself in the larger picture during the period under consideration. In his *Days of Fire* Shmuel Katz takes a slightly different tack of each group's self-image and its conception of the other. While Katz assigns the Hebrew Committee high marks in its early years for amassing widespread support in the United States by providing the American public with essential knowledge regarding the Hebrew renaissance in Palestine, in his view, from the war's conclusion this role in drafting public backing was no longer vital as the Zionist struggle now enjoyed widespread media attention. Essentially Katz pinpoints the delegation's problem as a failure to realize they were being overtaken by events, to adapt themselves to the new postwar situation, and to take a complementary but secondary role to Irgun activity in the Yishuv.[80]

Another area relevant to this self-evaluation lies in assessment of the delegation's influence on the Zionist movement as a whole during that period. We have, for example, the comments of Aryeh Altman, who filled many roles in the Revisionist party in the Yishuv and in the United States: "I was in contact with the Delegation members while I was in the United States. Although I valued their efforts, I did not agree with them on every detail, for example, 'Jews and Hebrews,' but the Delegation was a huge springboard in America which also mobilized the Zionists."[81] Altman went on to note that American Zionist leaders had never left the ghetto, and every time a delegation ad appeared on the front page of the newspaper, they reacted with fear and trembling. As for the relationship between Kook and Begin, Altman noted, based on close personal acquaintance with both figures, that each was an egocentric leader, possessed of self-confidence and used to functioning as an organizational leader, one in

Palestine and the other in the United States. Personal encounters between the two were often stormy, as seen from Herut activity in the first Knesset.

Yitzhak Ben-Ami shared the assessment that, like other delegation off-shoots, the Hebrew Committee and the league served primarily as catalysts: "If nothing else, we had at least served as a stimulus, pointing to new approaches, and shaming Jews and non-Jews alike to look up, to take notice, and sometimes to act. Whether or not we succeeded, we had done our best." [82]

Does historiographical evaluation accede to this picture? In his studies of Jewish organizational life during the Holocaust, the American historian Henry L. Feingold treats Hebrew Committee and league activity in the late war years, when they were still involved in attempts to rescue European Jewry. In Feingold's view, internal feuding—including the mutual hostility between delegation offshoots and the Zionist establishment—was the central factor impeding American Jewry's effectiveness in implementing rescue plans. He condemns the entire spectrum of organizational Jewish life, from the Revisionists to the establishment, for fanning the flames of dispute. Nor does he assign any positive role to the delegation as a catalyst in the American organizational arena. [83]

Aaron Berman, a historian dealing with the Zionist movement in the United States, takes a different, less negative view, noting that delegation influence waned in the post-1944 years, when it was no longer able to prove that the American Zionist establishment did not faithfully represent American Jewish interests. But although weakened from its Emergency Committee heyday, nonetheless, in his opinion, "Bergson and his followers remained an annoying, but perhaps healthy, stimulant for American Zionist leaders," who feared that a wrong move on their part would send their supporters straight into the arms of the Hebrew Committee and the league. [84]

An even more positive assessment can be found in Charles Levine's study of the delegation's propaganda techniques. Levine argues that we cannot evaluate delegation success—particularly during the Hebrew Committee and league period—solely by its self-defined goals. He casts these entities as a provocative goad that was responsible, for example, for the inclusion of pro-Zionist clauses in the platforms of the two major American parties. "The Bergsonites felt at home in the role of agent provocateur, inciting the Jewish organizations to simultaneously condemn them and to act positively on the issues raised in order to satisfy their constituents' apprehensions. . . . Like the prophets of Ancient Israel the Bergsonites railed against injustice and shrilly demanded alleviation and rectification. And when the current finally began moving in their direction—sluggishly but surely—they immediately skipped to another dire injustice and began anew!" [85]

Whereas the activism pursued by the Hebrew Committee and league leadership generally receives a positive historiographical assessment, it appears that the anti-authoritarian bent that fueled this activism worked to its detriment. Levine notes the hidden contradiction between these two characteristics and the fact that what propelled its independent innovative activism was ultimately responsible for its failure to arrive at a working relationship with the Irgun high command in the Yishuv, from whence the initiative to dispatch the delegation had originated. A similar sentiment finds even sharper expression in an article by Frank W. Brecher in which he takes issue with David Wyman's positive assessment of the delegation. Brecher objects strongly to Wyman's casting of Hillel Kook and his associates as "heroes" to Roosevelt's "anti-hero" role. The truth is, according to Brecher, that the delegation members' fascist leanings, their support of Irgun terror operations in Palestine, and Kook's anti-authoritarian approach led to their being outcast by the American Jewish establishment and the American administration alike. This was even more true for Hebrew Committee and league activity, which received no response at all from either the president or the administration. [86]

A different approach to the Hebrew Committee and the league than Brecher's negative assessment of them as nuisances rather than catalysts appears in the work of another historian of American Zionism, Monty Penkower, who views their activism, innovativeness, and antiestablishment tendencies in a more positive light. According to Penkower what prevented them from succeeding in the American Jewish arena was the ideological dimension: their abortive effort to sell their notion of Hebrews vs. Jews to the American Jewish public. Here the Bergsonites only succeeded in driving away supporters from among the Zionist, non-Zionist, and anti-Zionist publics. Another problem lay in their inability to implement their plans. When it came to formulating concepts, implementing public relations campaigns, or dramatic presentation of ideas to the American public, the Hebrew Committee and the league were not to be outdone. But when it came time to realize these ideas, "implementation had to be left to other hands. Action lay beyond the Bergsonites' capabilities," Penkower strongly affirmed.[87]

Each of the above-mentioned historiographical evaluations judges Hebrew Committee and league activity from the perspective of a specific context: Revisionist, American Zionist, or American Jewish. The broadest perspective comes from the meeting point between the delegation, the American administration, and His Majesty's government. On the other hand, largely absent from existing studies is discussion of a central issue for the delegation, one that found its sharpest, most focused expression in Hebrew Committee and league activity. I refer here to the anticolonial struggle taking place on a number of fronts worldwide at that time and to nationalistic activity that erupted on various continents in the postwar era. Can we then see the delegation as a vanguard, or at least a typical example, of such phenomena? This topic is treated in the book's final chapter, which examines the delegation in historical perspective against the background of the three framing issues that have been a recurring theme in our story.

A Time to Evaluate

The Irgun Delegation in Historical Perspective

The history of the Irgun Delegation came to an end toward the latter half of 1948. Married to an American who did not see her future in the new State of Israel, Yitzhak Ben-Ami remained in the United States until his death in 1983. Hillel Kook, Samuel Merlin, Eri Jabotinsky, and Arieh Ben-Eliezer joined the Herut party headed by Menachem Begin and served in the first Knesset. Shunning the political scene, Alex Rafaeli made his mark in the business world, ultimately becoming the owner of the Jerusalem Pencil Factory while keeping his hand in a number of additional enterprises.

Those of the Bergson Boys who forayed into Israeli politics experienced little satisfaction. Toward the end of the First Knesset Kook and Merlin found themselves at tactical and ideological loggerheads with Begin, based, in part, on their separatist tradition and memory of independent activity. Consequently, the two left the Herut movement and returned to America, Kook going into business and Merlin into research. During the 1970s Kook returned to Israel and was confined to his home throughout most of the 1990s because of worsening health. In the four decades since he left the Knesset, until his death in 2001, his disgruntled opinion of party politics remained unchanged. The same held true for Merlin, who spent the remainder of his life in New York, directing a research institute for Middle Eastern affairs.

As for the three who stayed in Israel, Ben-Eliezer was the only one who maintained an active political career. Having been elected speaker of the Knesset, he remained in the political arena until his death in 1970. Eri

Jabotinsky resigned from the Knesset and taught mathematics at the Technion until his death in 1971. Refusing to involve himself in internecine political strife, Alex Rafaeli continued to express his commitment to the party via various philanthropic endeavors and was active in business endeavors until his death in 1999.

How did the group members see themselves after disbanding? When asked this question Hillel Kook embarked upon a long political harangue that centered around what he considered the lack of understanding that its members encountered among mainstream Zionists, from Revisionist to Labor adherents. Ben-Ami wrote glowingly of what he considered to be the group's success in promoting the idea of rescue during the Holocaust. Similar sentiments were expressed by Eri Jabotinsky and Arieh Ben-Eliezer in their writings and speeches. Samuel Merlin, in his correspondence with Alex Rafaeli, wrote about the group's ultimate success in molding an American Jewish and American Zionist mode of thought and action, while Rafaeli spoke to me of the difficulties in politically pigeonholing the group. Noting how the Bergsonites had come a long way since they left the United States, he emphasized that they had all remained faithful to the "Nationalist" way of life. "Yes," he added, "I know that today people talk about 'right' and 'left,' but you can't really call us a 'right-wing' group. These are social and economic terms and after all, we dealt primarily with the political and territorial aspects of Zionism. We weren't really Revisionists. We were members of the Irgun, or to be precise, the Delegation was the political arm of the National Movement." My attempts to pin him down to any type of retrospective social or political judgment were met with his characteristic smile and European-style charm, which belied little of his true sentiments vis-à-vis his former comrades' successes and failures.[1]

The Irgun Delegation in Historical Perspective

Historians have long been committed to controversy as a way of life. All historical inquiries, scholarly as they may be, can theoretically metamorphose into "open season"; all persons may ultimately become legitimate targets.[2] The historical treatment of the Bergson Boys is no exception to this rule. Since the group disbanded in 1948, various scholars, primarily political historians, have attempted to analyze its impact upon the Zionist arena. Some have widened their scope to include the American Jewish scene as well. Few, if any—Revisionist-Zionist historians inclusive—have labeled the Bergsonites a success with regard to their stated goals. Among the points of debate are those pertaining to the group's nature, its successes and failures within the American Jewish and Zionist camp, and its short—and long-range influences in the United States and particularly among American Jewry.

The difficulties surrounding the first of these questions, that is, the nature of the group, was alluded to by Rafaeli's categorical refusal to use what he called socioeconomic terminology to categorize a political phenomenon. Was the delegation indeed a "right-wing" body? If so, how did it differ from other European right-wing movements and organizations within the Zionist movement that were also defined as being on the "right"? A second issue centers upon evaluating the delegation in view of its goals on the Zionist and American Jewish scene. Was the group a success or a failure? How did it contribute to the Zionist and Jewish cause? The third and final issue focuses upon the American and American Jewish arena. Did the delegation exert any short—or long-term influence upon non-Jewish American organizations? In what way was it unique on the American Jewish scene and did it have any political "descendants" on the operative, instrumental, or integrative levels? These questions frame our final discussion as we analyze the delegation from a historical perspective and attempt to characterize it as a political and social phenomenon within both an American and an international context.

The Irgun Delegation as a "Right-Wing" or Fascist Movement

Throughout its existence, opponents of the Irgun Delegation—and particularly the leaders of the Zionist left—treated it as if it were the devil incarnate and classified it as a military-fascist arm of the Zionist movement. Was the delegation indeed a right-wing Zionist movement? Can its members be considered fascist, similar to the accusation leveled against the Revisionist-Zionists and the Irgun during the 1930s and 1940s? To answer these questions we must first examine the terms *fascism* and *right wing* as they appear within a European context and only then analyze their meaning within the Zionist spectrum.

"At the end of the twentieth century, *fascism* remains probably the vaguest of the major political terms. This elusiveness may stem from the fact that the word itself contains no explicit political reference, however abstract, as do *democracy, liberalism, socialism,* and *communism.* . . . Moreover, the term has probably been used more by its opponents than by its proponents, the former having been responsible for the generalization of the adjective on an international level, as early as 1923."[3] With these words historian Stanley Payne begins his study of the history of fascism between 1914 and 1945. Following the lead taken by Hans Rogger, Eugene Weber, and Ze'ev Sternhel, Payne claims that fascism was a multifaceted phenomenon that did not concentrate solely upon the economic or political sphere. In his typology of fascism Payne lists several of its characteristics: it desires to create an authoritative national state that is not based on traditional principles; strives to form a national-economic structure that is based within a multiclass society; is willing to use violence and war in order to achieve its goals; negates liberalism and communism; concentrates upon the aesthetic character of rallies, symbols, and political liturgy that emphasize emotional and mystic aspects; accepts male primacy and admires youth. As many of these factors characterized the Revisionist-Zionist movement and its political offshoots (such as the Irgun Delegation), historians traditionally refer to them as the Zionist right wing.

Sternhel in particular emphasizes the cultural aspects of fascism, and claims that it should be viewed as an aspect of the intellectual, scientific, and technological revolution that swept through Europe during the late nineteenth and early twentieth centuries. Fascism should not be viewed solely as an ideology of protest and revolution but as a total alternative concept. Taking this view one step further, in his study of Revisionist-Zionism historian Ya'acov Shavit states that "right wing" is not only an operative ideology or a political system but "a political tradition and weltanschauung which together creates a solid framework of political and cultural tradition." Whether this tradition characterized members of the Irgun Delegation remains to be seen.[4]

Although fascism is usually considered a right-wing phenomenon, all right-wing movements are certainly not fascist. While the right wing has a primarily conservative weltanschauung, fascism sees itself as revolutionary and radical. Right-wing nonfascist groups include those that define themselves as nationalist (but not ultranationalist) or conservative church groups as opposed to those referred to as "clerico-fascist." One must therefore differentiate between fascist and right-wing groups while not overlooking a third category: protofascist groups, which manifest several fascist characteristics while retaining a democratic framework. This typology begins to provide us with insight regarding the unique nature of the Irgun Delegation among right-wing movements.

Right-wing groups are traditionally considered to be conservative and ultranationalist while left-wing parties are labeled "progressive." However, as Rogger and Weber have shown, the lines of demarcation between left and right are often blurred. "There are revolutions on the left and on the right, dictatorships on the left and the right, planned economies on the left and the right and of course, totalitarianism on the left and the right." [5] Another problem is connected to the nature of the radical movements on both ends of the spectrum. While the aims of these movements are totally different, they often tend to use similar terminology and even to adopt identical operative tactics in order to achieve their goals. One example is the attitude of both camps toward the bourgeoisie and their use of this class in their ideology. Whereas the right builds on the bourgeoisie as a support group, both the radical right and the radical left scorn its members. The difference in attitude stems from the type of society that each radical movement wishes to build. The left desires to purvey a universalist social message; the right concentrates upon a particularistic social message.

The relationships between the two groups only add to the terminological confusion. One common phenomenon cited by Rogger and Weber is the love-hate relationship between the new right and the traditional right, and between the radical right and the radical left. It is also imperative to define each right-wing phenomenon within the context of the situation in which it was formed. We must therefore differentiate between the right (including the fascist right) in its East-European form and the same phenomenon as expressed in the West. Among the unique characteristics of the radical right in Eastern Europe are its utilization of nationalism and its ties with religion, its adoption of concrete terms common in the West (such as bourgeoisie) when such phenomena do not exist locally (a tactic also utilized by the East European left), and the employment of Eastern European expatriate activity in order to further internal Eastern European matters. Eastern European fascism is also characterized by radicalism and opposition to the bourgeoisie. The distinction between the Eastern and

Western European right-wing phenomenon is particularly important when examining the Zionist right wing, as so many of its members were influenced by their Eastern European cultural roots.

How do the terms "right wing" and "fascist" translate into a Zionist context? Former delegation member Alex Rafaeli hesitated to use the term *right wing* in the Zionist context because of the traditional reluctance of right-wing Zionist groups to define themselves as such. Ya'acov Shavit explained why these groups rejected the accepted European political terminology. First there is the historical explanation: they claim that the division of European political culture into "right wing" and "left wing" does not apply to the unique historical circumstances affecting both Diaspora and Palestinian Jewry. This claim stems from the fact that the Zionist right wing did not base its ideology on a romantic, ultranationalist, or imperialist framework but on the basis of the historical and national goals of the Jewish people. A second argument is one of principle: we may examine Jewish history only by using "Jewish" and not Western European terms. Then there is the anti-Semitic explanation: the anti-Semitic nature of right-wing European groups forestalls any attempt to draw parallels between them and the Zionist right wing. This explanation brings to mind the story told about Rabbi Dov Ber Meisels, who in 1848 was chosen to represent Krakow in the Austrian parliament. When the speaker of the parliament noted that the rabbi had chosen to sit on the left side of the chamber, which was reserved for the liberals, Meisels responded, "Juden haben keine Recht" (Jews have no right), a play on words that referred both to Jewish political tendencies and to the traditional anti-Semitism of the European right wing. Finally, according to the Zionist right wing, the division into "right" and "left" leads to an antinationalist class struggle that undermines what they consider to be the basis of Zionism.[6]

Despite these objections, most historians have nevertheless adopted the term "right wing" to describe certain Zionist political divisions. Two main attributes characterized the Zionist right wing during the British Mandate period: the demand for Palestinian territorial integrity and the insistence upon establishing a sovereign Jewish state, even at the risk of political or armed struggle. To this Shavit adds several common denominators characterizing Zionist right-wing political culture: the Revisionist credo of "honor" *(hadar),* which was inherited from the European nationalist emphasis on character building *(Bildung);* the use of national messianism as a practical eschatology (something that characterizes what

Shavit calls the "new" Zionist-Revisionism), making overtures to the "ordinary Jew," a bourgeois orientation—all these either partially or fully characterized the Zionist right wing between the two world wars.[7]

An additional difficulty in categorizing the "nationalist camp" in Zionist history is that fact that the Zionist right wing was not the product of a single mold. The division between "old right wing" and "new right wing" (or "right" and "radical right") implies that each group's relationship with the European right and fascist movements must be examined separately. Revisionist-Zionism saw itself as a mass movement that addressed the "ordinary Jew" and offered him salvation; the Irgun considered itself an elitist militant movement that was far more radical than the Revisionists. The distinction between the "conservative right" and the "radical right" (which has been equated with fascism) existed within the Zionist movement during the 1940s and exemplified the difference between Meir Grossman's group (the "State Party"), which ceded from Revisionist-Zionism, and the Irgun. Political characterization becomes even more difficult when one bears in mind that contrary to the common image that the term "conservative" evokes, it was the "conservative right wing" in Palestine that symbolized the struggle for change.

When comparing Revisionist-Zionism with the European right wing, it appears that the Irgun—the breeding grounds for most of the delegation's members—was closer to the East European right-wing movements, and even to the protofascist movements that arose there between the two world wars, than it was to West European fascism. This state of being was partially because of the Polish orientation of the Revisionist New Zionist Organization and the Irgun during the 1930s and the fact that they considered Polish marshall Jozef Pilsudsky to epitomize the concept of a national leader. Another factor was the contacts these groups maintained with right-wing Polish organizations and the radical antibourgeois position of Eastern European fascism, which was echoed within the Irgun. The distance between the Zionist right-wing and Western European fascism becomes apparent upon noting that the former group built their economic program upon contrast and not revolution. Apart from the leaders of the Revisionist-Zionist labor unions, the Zionist right wing had little or no original economic orientation. Finally, the fact that the Irgun lacked any program to build a new society makes it difficult to draw a comparison between them and French or German fascism, both of which contained elements of social radicalism.

Where was the Irgun Delegation situated within this intricate vortex of definitions, characterizations, and parallels? To answer this question we must examine the group's power base and the partnerships that it formed during its ten-year existence. At first glance, the delegation evinced many of the unique characteristics of Eastern European protofascism. In spite of its members' secular lifestyle it made use of the connection between nationalism and religion by forming a partnership with the Union of Orthodox Rabbis in the United States. Simultaneously, it conveyed the same type of radicalism that characterized the radical right in Eastern Europe. This orientation is demonstrated by the partnerships it formed with radical and often irredentist bodies in the United States. Similar to Eastern European protofascist groups, the delegation made use of expatriate activists. Finally, throughout the 1930s, most of the delegation's nucleus were active in Poland together with right-wing Polish groups in organizing illegal immigration to Palestine and giving Polish Jews military training in preparation for their immigration.

Nevertheless, a second look at the situation shows the similarity between the Eastern European radical right and the Irgun Delegation in the United States to be only a partial one. While the first group objected to the bourgeoisie as both an abstract and concrete concept, the delegation was not at all interested in the social and class positions of their partners. They therefore formed partnerships with bourgeois groups that were the lynchpins of their committees during the 1940s. Two additional partnerships into which the delegation entered—one with communist activists and the other with Jews who belonged to left-wing American groups—hint at the differences between them and Revisionist-Zionism and to the difficulty in totally equating them with the East European right wing. Although the delegation exhibited two basic characteristics of the Zionist right wing— the demand for Palestinian territorial integrity and a militant willingness to use power in order to establish a state—the partnerships that it formed may, in fact, hold the true key to understanding its unique and complex political nature.

Evaluating the Delegation's Goals and Achievements

Was the Irgun Delegation a success or a failure? Most historians consider this to be the litmus test of the Bergson Boys' history. Were its members "an active and determined nucleus which administered what became a flourishing mass movement," as Hillel Kook described them, or were they rather "Peter Bergson and his apostles, charlatans and opportunists 'par excellence' who succeeded in only one thing—manipulating the donations which they received," as stated in an anonymous report about the delegation written sometime during the late 1940s?[8]

As we saw at the end of chapter 4, with the exception of Revisionist chroniclers and a small number of Holocaust experts such as David Wyman, most historians tend to side more with the latter evaluation than with the former one. To all intents and purposes it is difficult to credit the Irgun Delegation with many—if any—concrete successes. Its members raised large sums to be used in saving European Jewry and in covering the costs of illegal immigration to Palestine; however, more than half the funds raised were used for organizational expenses and publicity. The group had little to do with creating a Jewish army in 1942 but credited itself with part of the glory surrounding the establishment of the Jewish Brigade two years later. There are those historians who claim that Kook and company played a very minor role in pressuring the American administration to create the War Refugee Board; however, in view of the political constellation of 1943–44, it is likely that the board would have been created even without the delegation's input. It organized and partially financed the illegal immigration and supply ships *Ben Hecht* and *Altalena* before the establishment of the State of Israel, but at least the latter of these two ships was the cause of much inter-Yishuv strife that led to the ultimate surrender of the Irgun's independence for which the Bergsonites had so strived. The group managed to achieve internal equilibrium only after dwindling to the sum total of two for more than eighteen months, and never managed to reach any type of agreement with the Irgun high command in Palestine during the entire period in question. In view of all these outcomes, most historians state that what the delegation claimed as its greatest achievements—fundraising, influencing the Irgun, its part in creating the Jewish Brigade and establishing the War Refugee Board—can hardly be considered its achievements at all. On the other hand, the delegation failed to reach a modus vivendi with the Zionist establishment in the United States, the Revisionist-based New Zionist Organization in America, or the Irgun high command in Palestine, even when it expended a great deal of energy in those directions. All in all, throughout its entire existence the Irgun Delegation remained a problematic and debatable factor within both the Zionist movement and American Jewry.

In view of what appears to be the delegation's consistent failure rate, why do they deserve to be the subject of this book? To answer this question I must return to the book's introduction. It has not been my intention to enter into the historical controversy of whether the Bergson Boys were a failure or a success in their stated goals; neither have I attempted to judge them as a Zionist or even a Revisionist-Zionist entity. Instead I have laid the background for examining their tactical legacy in the sphere of public relations, which I consider their most—and possibly only—significant long-term contribution to the history of Zionism, the Holocaust, and American and particularly American Jewish life. As opposed to other groups and individuals functioning on the American Jewish scene during the late 1930s and early 1940s, the Irgun Delegation's primary triumph was first and foremost the fact that its members understood the power of Madison Avenue and the impact of positive advertisement.

Shortly after reaching the United States, Kook grasped one of the golden rules of American marketing: make the public aware of the product. All methods were fair, but the best ones were innovative, unique, or even "gimmicky." Acknowledging the power of the media in American life, he was willing to invest most of the group's resources in that direction, something that none of the existing Jewish and Zionist organizations had been willing to do. Even when an individual such as Emmanuel Neumann or Abba Hillel Silver had come to the same conclusion, they were thwarted by their organizational bodies, which, for a long time, attempted to control and limit their efforts in that direction. Not so the delegation, which answered to no one, took orders from no other group, and delighted in flouting convention.

Furthermore, the delegation's publicity campaigns were quite different from the low-key ones promoted by the other Jewish organizations: not a solid campaign but a bombastic, noisy, and tantalizing one. Kook turned one of the nightmares of the American Jewish establishment—media exposure—into the keyword of his public relations campaign, drawing fire from all directions except from the curious public, which learned about the Jewish problem via illustrated full-page advertisements and sensationalist guest appearances on the radio.

Kook and his colleagues rapidly internalized the importance of the media because of a combination of factors. As opposed to the American Jewish establishment, all of the delegation members were newcomers, foreigners with no prior commitment to their passive policies of quiet diplomacy. Furthermore, they were ready to use uncommon methods and had the courage to adopt extraordinary techniques, which were always Irgun trademarks. While most Irgun members saw themselves as a Revisionist-Zionist avant-garde, the delegation's members considered themselves part of a populist and not an elitist movement. Consequently, they rapidly adopted marketing techniques that aimed at the man in the street, not the elites. And, as we well know, the interest of the man in the street is best caught by short slogans, illustrated advertisements, and seductive curiosity-whetting gimmicks.

The delegation also understood that in order to make inroads among the American public, they had to portray the Jewish and Zionist problem as an American issue. This had been one of the tactics that Emmanuel Neumann wished to adopt before he was thwarted by his own superiors and colleagues at almost every turn. Noted immigration scholar Oscar Handlin has stated that while various groups in the United States continued to support their old homeland because of connections of birth, culture, or tradition, they did so "according to the standards which acted as a universal coin between the other citizens of the country—spreading democracy . . . self-definition . . . international activities to further peace . . . assisting small nations against big enemies."[9] Thus, Irish Americans profited from the anglophobic atmosphere in the United States at the end of the nineteenth century, while Armenian Americans did not succeed in obtaining an American mandate in Armenia because of Wilson's isolationist approach. Using the same reasoning the Irgun Delegation attempted to catch the interest of the American public by portraying Jewish and Zionist issues as being part and parcel of the basic principles of the American nation.

Kook adopted the relevant marketing theories and turned them into part of the delegation's modus operandi. He failed to receive public acclaim only once, when he tried to market the concept of "Hebrews" versus "Jews." This failure stemmed primarily from his overenthusiasm in presenting American Jewry with an instant equation to solve the problem of dual loyalty once and for all, without his having taken into account the local psychological coordinates. The tenaciousness with which he tried to "sell" this product to the American Jewish public proved that although he had rapidly understood the American mind he was completely unsuccessful in understanding the Jewish one. Kook failed to comprehend that the Jews of New York, Boston, Chicago, Philadelphia, and Los Angeles would not agree to separate themselves—even semantically—from their brethren throughout the world. American Jews could never fully understand the meaning of the term "Hebrew Nation," which would not include them as well.

Kook's innovations in the field of public relations had several results. The first was circumscribed in time and topic. For almost a decade the delegation members managed to keep the Jewish and Zionist issues alive in the public eye. By doing so, all Jewish and Zionist organizations in the United States ultimately benefited from the public awareness of these issues. Furthermore, as we have already seen, the delegation's public relations activities, noted time and again in dismay by other American Jewish and Zionist organizations, were always a topic of discussion and catalyzed certain figures—particularly Rabbi Abba Hillel Silver—to adopt similar techniques. Silver, who succeeded veteran American Jewish Zionist leader Rabbi Stephen S. Wise as public spokesman for American Jewish Zionists, was the antithesis of Wise, who had been an advocate of quiet diplomacy. Using Kook's success as an argument for publicly taking a more active stand on Zionist issues, Silver adopted a tactical position that was reminiscent of the delegation's modus operandi.

Members of the Irgun Delegation knew their limitations. Far away from the spotlights and microphones they admitted that their public relations campaign had been their prime contribution to the Zionist idea. In a 1943 letter to Revisionist leader Dr. Aryeh Altman in Jerusalem, delegation member Eri Jabotinsky described the group's activities and expressed his disappointment over their progress. Toward the end of the letter, Jabotinsky wrote about what he saw as the group's success: Had the group not been here, he stated, the situation would have been much worse. "At least we have managed to place the Jewish problem . . . squarely before the American public. We have not achieved all our goals. However, the newspapers, the public and the American administration are today aware of the fact that such a movement exists. And that is saying a great deal." [10]

Eri Jabotinsky saw the delegation as having achieved public recognition by carrying out a policy that could be summarized in seven words: "If you're aware of me, I exist." What he couldn't know at that time was the long-term impact that the delegation would have upon the American and the American Jewish scene. The first would be its impact as a prototype of a modern ethnic interest/protest group; the latter would be its tactical legacy expressed by a radical American Jewish body led in the 1960s by the son of one of the delegation's active American members: the Jewish Defense League headed by Rabbi Meir Kahane. Both of these legacies will be discussed later on in this chapter.

In view of these broad-ranging formational and tactical legacies, why are so many historians scornful of the delegation as a significant historical phenomenon? Let me propose two answers, one dealing with historical orientation and the other centering upon the influence of public mood. The first answer is based upon the "Palestinocentrism" and "Holocaust-centrism" characterizing so many researchers who deal with Jewish history. When mentioning the Irgun Delegation, most of these historians tend to focus solely upon the group's impact in the Zionist arena, or to discuss the number of Jews it rescued during the Second World War. Simultaneously, however, they completely ignore its legacy in any areas that venture beyond the Nazi axis, American Jewish politics during the 1940s, or the creation of a Jewish state. And as they claim that the group had no long-term Zionist impact, failed to make its mark among American Jewish organizations during the 1940s, and did not manage to rescue any Jews during the Holocaust, the delegation is not a topic worthy of note. At the same time, however, these historians may conveniently overlook the fact that for at least half of its existence the delegation did not function as a Zionist body. Neither do they acknowledge that during the war no American Jewish or American Zionist organization succeeded in rescuing Jews from Hitler. In short, they subscribe to the school of thought that finds it much easier to speak of the delegation in terms of success or failure, rather than looking beyond these coordinates toward a broader context.

A second answer has its roots in the sphere of public political mood. In certain circles, particularly those with a political orientation that customarily denigrated any groups belonging to the right, the delegation's political label ultimately acted as its leper's bell, leading to an almost knee-jerk response to its existence, not to speak of its activities. The response on the other end of the spectrum was equally biased, leading to a situation where Revisionist-Zionist chroniclers such as David Niv and Shmuel Katz would almost automatically praise the group without delving into the issue of whether it did or did not have any long-term historical impact. Anthropologist Jonathan Boyarin has claimed that one of the most striking aspects of liberatory movements within modern Western societies is the attempt to construct and deploy unitary group memories and identities for all those whom the movements claim as their own.[11] This attempt partially accounts for the stereotypical attitude found in both mainstream left-wing labor Zionist and right-wing Revisionist-Zionist historiography to the delegation, explaining the existence of what Hayden White has called "competing narratives" that result from one historian having interpreted "the facts" as a "tragedy" and another as a "farce."[12]

These attempts to laud or blacken the delegation's name—without, of course, attempting to see beyond the obvious, a failure shared by both the group's critics and its defenders alike—have been echoed in turn by a number of academic studies published since the 1970s. Taking its cue from the "Palestinocentric" and "Holocaustcentric" attitudes toward the delegation, until recently historical research has ignored several facets of the group's existence, including gender—such as the roles played by women such as Frances Gunther, Miriam Heyman, and Zipporah Kassel— the group's internal dynamics, or the long-term effects that it had on the American and American Jewish public. The attempt to describe the delegation's activities in primary colors alone has channeled research away from what were considered peripheral subjects. These topics were obviously considered insignificant in comparison with the main issue interesting most researchers: whether Hillel Kook was an angel, a devil, or just a fool; this is but a generational metamorphosis of the dichotomy between "a striking and self-determined nucleus of activists" and "Peter Bergson and his apostles" that has been a point of debate since the 1940s. This study has hopefully broadened the discussion to include several aspects of the delegation's history and aftermath that have received scant attention by other historians.

The Irgun Delegation as a Prototype of an Ethnic Protest Group

Almost all studies that examine the delegation, particularly during the war years, attribute its failures and successes—even those in the realm of public relations—to factors such as timing, ideology, and total dedication to the idea of rescue. Almost all such studies have ignored a major facet of the delegation's organizational existence, which later influenced the entire American political scene: the fact that it functioned as an ethnic interest/protest group and even acted as a prototype for such groups in the United States—both Jewish and non-Jewish—from the 1950s onward.

As early as 1906, sociologist William Graham Sumner coined the terms "ingroup," "outgroup," and "ethnocentrism." However, serious study of intergroup relations, particularly those involving ethnic or racial dominant minorities, began only after World War II on the part of sociologists, historians, demographers, anthropologists, and political scientists. Already in the 1950s, these scholars began to examine and analyze minority-majority relations, ethnic interest and protest groups, and, finally, the social and political dimensions of the civil rights movement. Nathan Glazer's studies were also a milestone in understanding ethnic protest, as they delineated ethnic bodies as social groups that consciously share aspects of a common culture, are defined primarily by descent, and both foster and further ethnic particularism and protest. Such ethnic particularism is ubiquitous, even in First World countries, and is prone to generating crises. These often lead to the formation of interest/protest groups whose members usually belong to a single ethnic group, protesting a common grievance or attempting to further a particular group interest.[13]

At first glance it appears that these factors played a role in the Irgun Delegation. Already in 1965, historian Yonah Ferman conjectured a tie between the Emergency Committee for the Rescue of European Jewry—sponsored in 1943 and 1944 by the Irgun Delegation—and what he termed "foreign policy ethnic-centered" interest groups.[14] However his elaboration of this hypothesis, tying the Emergency Committee to such subsequent groups as the contemporary Cuban National Movement, was exceedingly brief. Moreover, Ferman referred solely to foreign-policy-centered groups, citing in particular the Irish Free State Movement and the ethnic Italian and Greek movements. In fact, it appears that his conjecture holds true for domestically centered ethnopolitical groups as well, such as the early black civil rights and Native American movements of the 1960s. These foreign and domestic movements often differed in tactics, orientation, degree of militancy, and ability to canvass public support. Yet both types display characteristics that had much earlier appeared in the Irgun Delegation.

The delegation was certainly not the first ethnic protest group that formed in the United States. Over a hundred years before the delegation's members reached America, an early ethnic protest group formed on the northeast coast: the movement to liberate southern blacks from slavery and to grant them civil rights in the North. During the late nineteenth and early twentieth century two additional ethnic protest groups took form: the Japanese Association that fought for Japanese-American civil rights and Six Companies, which represented a large number of Chinese immigrants in the United States until 1910.[15] Later ethnic protest groups followed the tactical pattern set by these first groups: they raised the public consciousness of an issue, recruited leaders from among the ethnic public, and attempted to portray the ethnic group in a positive light. Among these groups were Jewish and Zionist organizations, such as the Irgun Delegation, that were active throughout the twentieth century.

In time, three major types of interest/protest groups emerged. The first concentrates upon a minority that was not of specific ethnic origin (blacks, handicapped, senior citizens) and demanded minority rights but, naturally, not a homeland. The second concentrates upon the situation of the ethnic group in its homeland (the Irish, Greek, Yugoslav, and so forth) or attempts to assist it to achieve independence. A third type cares for the ethnic group wherever its members may be, while ultimately assisting them to obtain sovereignty.

During its ten years of existence the Irgun Delegation in the United States formed a new type of ethnic interest/protest group that crossed the lines of demarcation between the three types listed above. Similar to the first type, one of the delegation's long-term goals was to make Jews in the United States proud of their own identity and of Jewish activism. This pride was to act as a lever for creating an American Jewish public that would support the delegation's activities. Similar to protest groups of the second type, one of the delegation's goals, which was expressed by several of their committees, was to further the idea of a Hebrew State. Finally, similar to protest groups of the third type, the delegation attempted to assist European Jewry by creating a division between their rescue activities and their ultimate goal: the establishment of a sovereign Hebrew State.

In his study of the Scottish nationalist movement, Milton J. Esman notes four factors usually necessary for the formation and success of an ethnic interest/protest group: strong collective identity of the activists;

grievances based upon deprivation or crisis; rising expectations resulting from credible prospects of improving the situation, and declining authority of political centers or the rise of alternative political centers.[16] All of these factors evinced themselves in one form or another in each of the bodies sponsored by the Irgun Delegation, especially in their perceived need to establish a Jewish army during the early years of the war, to rescue European Jewry, and to found a Hebrew state in Palestine. They saw their opportunity in the changing social and political climate of the war and in the years preceding it; they attempted to use the American government as leverage against the political center that they were battling—Great Britain.

What characterizes American ethnic interest/protest groups, especially those involved in foreign policy? They strive for public acceptance as a legitimate interest group and seek strategies to involve representatives of other ethnic groups in order to prove that they are authentic spokesmen for the best interests of the American people; they remain nonpartisan; they seek the clergy's support; their lobbying activities are assisted by congressmen representing ethnic-centered constituencies; they encourage ethnic communalism, are publicly active among the ethnic public, and are overwhelmingly financed by it. They also espouse nonviolent resistance. In addition, they face competition within the ethnic community as numerous groups usually emerge in times of crisis.[17]

The Irgun Delegation did all of these things, laying the groundwork for ethnic protest groups that followed them. True, few of these groups mentioned the delegation by name; however, they learned much from the delegation's modus operandi, which was later adopted by other American Zionist organizations, particularly under the leadership of Rabbi Abba Hillel Silver. Delegation committees had attempted to form bipolar and even multiethnic coalitions, a pattern later followed by the black civil rights movement during the late 1950s and 1960s and by the ethnic Italian groups during the 1970s; they claimed supporters from both major parties, just as the Irish National Movement attempted to do in the United States during the 1960s; they actively sought to enlist Jewish and Christian religious leaders in their struggle, a tactic adopted by the civil rights movement, which drew its support from the church and particularly from the Southern Christian Leadership Conference; they elicited aid from congressmen who as a rule sponsored groups representing ethnic constituencies, similar to those assisting the Free Irish Nationals and the

Cuban Nationalist movement a decade later; and they were publicly active among their own ethnic community, particularly making efforts to galvanize uncommitted sectors. A similar pattern could be seen within the Armenian "diaspora redemption" movement and the ethnic Greek national movement. Also, like all new ethnic protest movements, they faced fear and often hostility from rival Zionist groups that competed with the delegation in portraying the Jews and their dilemmas to the surrounding society. These groups feared that by singling out the Jews or by employing new methods, the delegation would harm the entire Jewish community. Finally, there was nonviolence. Up to the late 1960s almost all American-based protest groups, civil rights and irredentist alike, remained nonviolent. Despite the need for "ingroup identity" to combat "outgroup hostility," throughout its ten-year existence the delegation's "frustration-aggression-displacement" process remained relatively peaceful. As we shall see, this peacefulness would no longer characterize an ethnic protest group that was formed in the late 1960s and considered itself a tactical descendant of the delegation: the Jewish Defense League.[18]

As a predecessor to the ethnic protest groups of the 1950s and 1960s, the delegation was among the first to utilize preexisting sentiments within the American public—such as antifascism and anticommunism—in order to further its own ends. Its activists also never emphasized their Revisionist sympathies, which in certain circles was considered the same as having fascist tendencies. Alex Rafaeli recalled how delegation members would particularly stress their anticommunist sentiments at these meetings, playing on the fears that were then plaguing potentially sympathetic participants. It was therefore ironic that the FBI investigated delegation members as having been in contact with communist circles.[19]

One of the most successful ethnic protest groups in the United States during those years, from which the delegation learned much about tactics, was the Irish National Movement. Already during the nineteenth century Irish mutual assistance groups in New York had broadened their activities to include the issue of Irish independence. Simultaneously the Feinian Brotherhood—a military and diplomatic movement—was formed in order to encourage activism in favor of a free Ireland. Apart from raising funds, this body formed militias and even unsuccessfully invaded Canada in order to pressure the British government regarding its Irish policy.[20]

Simultaneously, a number of Irish mutual assistance societies that had formed in the United States tackled the issue of Irish nationalism by using a large array of tactics: they organized conferences, rallies, and demonstrations against British policy in Ireland, formed coalitions with other ethnic groups such as the German National Bund in the United States, and encouraged congressional debates about Irish nationalism. These activities served as a beacon for Hillel Kook when he initiated the Irgun Delegation's modus operandi during the 1940s. Another issue common to both the delegation and Irish nationals was the question of what attitude to adopt toward Great Britain, especially in wartime. During the First World War, and particularly after American entry in 1917, Irish nationalists in the United States were bitterly divided over this issue. However, after the war's end they renewed the struggle to gain American support for Irish independence, and Eamon de Valera, president of the Irish Freedom Fighting organization Sinn Fein, even came to America in order to raise money to support the Irish national struggle. A second issue common to both the delegation and the Irish national groups was the debate about what to do with the funds that were ultimately raised and how they would be divided among the various Irish organizations: the Irish-Americans wanted to keep the economic control in their hands while de Valera demanded that they turn all the funds raised over to Ireland in order to cover the costs of the national struggle. As we have seen, the same problem arose between the Irgun in Palestine and the delegation twenty years later.[21]

Organized American activity for Irish independence continued even after the Free Irish State was founded in 1921, as Northern Ireland had remained part of Great Britain. In seeking to organize ethnic coalitions, Irish nationalists forged a partnership with several Irgun Delegation committees during the 1940s. The combination of Irgun and Irish fervor, challenge, and daring resulted in a unique ethnic coalition, which was tempered by expediency but spiced up by Hillel Kook's avant-garde tactics. In doing so, he built on the experiences of those ethnic interest and protest groups that had preceded him, and he even surpassed them in various fields, such as public relations, thus creating a model for ethnic protest groups that would follow him from the 1950s onward.

"The size and intensity of interest groups seems to affect their success," states organizational historian William Orbach. "Twenty million Irish and six million Jews aroused have political influence; not so 100,000 Armenians and Jews without confidence."[22] Irish nationalist militancy in the United States was echoed by the activities of the Irgun Delegation, which attempted to portray a new Jew to the American public: one who demanded and struggled, not pleaded and begged. Despite the Irgun Delegation's militaristic rhetoric, it never once adopted force in order to further its goals: to create a Jewish army, save European Jewry, and establish a Hebrew State. The delegation can therefore be considered a transition stage between the peaceful ethnic protest groups common before the Second World War and the more militant ones that formed during the 1950s and onward, and particularly at the end of the 1960s.

The Irgun Delegation as One of the Roots of the Militant Jewish Right in the United States

Apart from acting as a prototype for American ethnic interest and protest groups, the delegation left American and American Jewish society one additional significant tactical legacy: the Jewish Defense League (JDL). More than any other factor, this was probably the most concrete long-range influence that the delegation had on American and American Jewish political and organizational history. Founded in the spring of 1968 by Orthodox rabbi Martin David (Meir) Kahane, the organization adopted a series of Jewish causes, escalating its tactics from rhetoric to terror and drawing its legitimacy from what it considered to be its ideological and tactical predecessors: the Zionist right wing, and in particular the LHI ("Stern Gang") and the Irgun Delegation.

Kahane was well aware of Revisionist-Zionist ideology, its Irgun metamorphosis, and the ultimate tactical form that it had taken among the Bergson group. Throughout the Second World War Kahane's family had been deeply involved in delegation activities, and his father, Rabbi Charles (Yechezkel Shraga) Kahane, had played a pivotal role in several of the group's subcommittees, particularly the Committee for a Jewish Army and the Emergency Committee to Save the Jews of Europe. Throughout his childhood young Meir had accompanied his father to delegation meetings until he was familiar with its founders and their tactics. Upon reaching his teens Kahane became an active member of Betar, coming into direct contact with Kook and Merlin, who were hero-worshipped by more than one Betarist.[23] The destruction of European Jewry deeply affected young Meir, who early on adopted the delegation's activism as his own personal credo. In 1947 he was arrested for the first time when he led an attack on British Foreign Minister Ernest Bevin during the latter's visit to New York. When the elder Kahane came to post bail for his son and rebuked him for his tactics, Meir countered by stating, "it's your fault, that's what I learned from you and your friends." [24]

In the words of one of his close friends, a combination of "fantasy and megalomania" turned Meir Kahane into an ambitious, frustrated, charismatic leader without an audience, other than the young people in the synagogues where he intermittently served as rabbi. At a certain time he was even the sports correspondent for the *Jewish Press.* The turning point in his public career came in the late 1960s when he voiced the idea of creating a Jewish defense organization to protect members of his Jewish community. His initial public appeal was made according to the best traditions of the Irgun Delegation. During the spring of 1968 Kahane published an advertisement in the *Jewish Press* to announce the establishment of the Jewish Defense League (JDL); the advertisement included a coupon to be returned to Kahane along with membership fees and donations. This was the first step in the JDL's public relations campaign, which was soon to become an integral part of the organization's existence. Just as Kook and Merlin had done with the *Answer,* Kahane turned the *Jewish Press* into a JDL mouthpiece and, until the controversial rabbi's murder, it offered its readers a wide selection of his militant articles on subjects of Jewish interest. Kahane did not stop at exposure in the Jewish periodicals, and like the Irgun Delegation he published advertisements in the *New York Times* in which he explained the JDL's rationale. His media gamble ultimately paid off, and consequently the JDL's sensationalist activities received widespread press and media coverage.[25]

In spite of American Jewish liberal tendencies, the fledgling radical organization led by Rabbi Meir Kahane attracted supporters from all walks of Jewish life. A growing radicalism on college campuses, the race riots of 1968, and finally the changes that had taken place within American Jewry following the Six-Day War all created a suitable atmosphere in which a group offering an instant power solution to an acute Jewish problem could flourish. The issue: racial tensions in Jewish neighborhoods that had changed their ethnic composition. The JDL solution: Jewish self-defense, and a rejection of passive policies that had been adopted until then. Throughout its entire existence the Jewish Defense League remained a controversial body for much of American Jewry. To some, it was a source of pride, to others, an embarrassment; for a third group, it endangered all that they had achieved over a period of twenty years.[26]

The group that had begun as a Jewish self-defense body formed to protect elderly Jewish residents of ethnically changing neighborhoods soon changed its cause. Within a short time Kahane adopted the racially based issue of the New York teachers' strike, which began as a conflict over educational policy based on affirmative action for blacks. In late 1969 the JDL, whose militant rhetoric had alienated it from the American Jewish establishment, adopted the issue of Soviet Jewry, demanding that the Soviet government allow free Jewish immigration to Israel.[27] Unlike the liberal protest organizations of that time, the JDL adopted a particularistic, exclusionist Jewish stance, drawing heavily on Revisionist-Zionist symbolism and rhetoric.[28] Indeed, the JDL was initially known more for its "rhetorical" terror than its practical one. However, by 1970, less than two years after founding the JDL, Kahane's militant rhetoric and original emphasis on verbal terror and visual potential had escalated into physical violence and urban terror.[29] Beginning with harassment of Soviet officials and culminating with the bombing of Manhattan-based offices connected with Soviet enterprises (leading to the accidental death of a secretary in one of the offices), Kahane appeared to have adopted a terrorist credo. "Hit-and-run violence" was the way several former JDL members described their new tactics.[30]

As the issue of Soviet Jewry began to take a different course during the early 1970s, Kahane once again changed his orientation. Focusing upon assimilation, intermarriage, and the ultimate destruction of the Jewish people outside of Israel, he began by espousing mass aliyah (immigration to Israel) as the only solution to what he saw as an upcoming Holocaust in the United States.[31] Simultaneously, he once again changed his activist orientation and considered fighting Arab terror his main goal. In late 1971 he began planning the assassination of a notorious PLO terrorist who was then incarcerated in a British prison. A week after the members who were supposed to carry out the mission were arrested, the JDL exploded a bomb outside the PLO's midtown Manhattan office.[32] Following a series of setbacks in 1972 the JDL began to dissolve while Kahane moved to Israel. From here on the JDL founder divided his time between Israel and the United States. Although a number of right-wing Israeli political parties had approached Kahane, he ultimately decided to found his own political party—Kach (Thus)—and to run for Knesset on an independent list. However, in 1975 he was forced to return to the United States in order to serve out a one-year prison sentence for inciting to violence. Following his release Kahane once again threw himself into Israeli politics and was ultimately elected to Knesset in 1984. Fearing that Kahane's party would take away votes from the right, before the 1988 elections Kach was declared illegal because of its racist ideology and was barred from the Knesset. In late 1990 Meir Kahane was assassinated in New York following a fund-raising meeting for his political movement in Israel, thus ending his colorful and turbulent career.

Can the Irgun Delegation be considered the Jewish Defense League's progenitor? Was there actually an ideological and tactical affinity between the two groups, or did Kahane use this argument in order to ensure his own legitimacy in view of JDL radicalism? Is it possible to show how both the delegation and the JDL took advantage of the structure of political opportunities—particularly those presented by the uniquely American system of mass media—to form a progressive pattern based upon what appears to be a single developing model? In order to answer these questions we must distinguish between the issues of ideological affinity and tactical legacy.

At first glance it appears that the ideology of both the Bergson Boys and the JDL was heavily based on the right-wing core tenets of Revisionist-Zionism. Like Jabotinsky's concept of Revisionism, both were exclusionary movements not looking for absolute or universal social justice but proposing solutions for a particular ethnic group; both allotted military leadership and militarism—verbal and actual—a central place in their weltanschauung and spoke of the need to create a "new fighting Jew." Leaders of both groups made extensive use of the Revisionist concepts of *hadar* (honor) and *barzel* (iron) in their ideological writings; both adopted a deterministic credo; both appealed to the past in order to strengthen their legitimacy in the eyes of their adherents. Finally, both groups were to a certain extent youth oriented, like Jabotinsky's original reliance on Betar as the future of the Revisionist movement.

A closer look at the ideologies of the Bergsonites and the JDL shows that despite their use of Revisionist terminology, their ideological content—as opposed to tactical patterns—often differed significantly. One example was the concept of militarism and militantism. The term that the Irgun and its delegation used to indicate military steadfastness was *barzel* (iron), an unyielding strength that one had to use in confronting one's enemies.[33] In practice, the delegation translated this term to mean organizational discipline that expressed itself in an outward show of absolute military leadership and the creation of organizational cells to execute the tasks at hand. Kahane, on the other hand, took the concepts of "militarism" and "barzel" to their greatest extreme. Military discipline, or rather pseudo-military discipline, was a central facet of his attempt to portray the JDL as the reinterpretation of the Irgun and its delegation, organizations that themselves had tried to mimic formal military organizations.[34] Connecting abstract militarism to the concrete dangers facing the Jewish people, Kahane called for the development of a protomilitary unit in the Diaspora that would act as the vehicle for the physical and spiritual salvation of the "new Jew."[35]

The political and militant ideology of the JDL necessitated the creation of cells to bring theory into praxis. In practice, not only did a cult of violence develop among many of the JDL's members, but, instead of condemning this trend, Kahane institutionalized it by creating the organized cell necessary to carry out his absolute military discipline. These were the *chaya* (literally, "wild animal" in Hebrew) squads, complementing the "scholars" who formulated movement ideology, who were given the elite position of translating militaristic ideology into violent practice. By selecting this volatile term Kahane wished to emphasize the metamorphosis of the JDL's "new Jew" who took the concept of vigilante self-defense to new heights. Drawing upon Revisionist teachings, Irgun activism, and biblical injunctions about obligatory wars for his historical legitimacy, Kahane adopted the slogan "every Jew a .22," impressing upon his readers and listeners that this was the only formula that could ensure Jewish survival.[36] Rejecting the passive tradition of spiritual leaders from other faiths, Kahane attempted to posit a belief based on what he proposed as the Jewish spiritual interpretation of what he wished to see as normative Jewish behavior. In truth, this was nothing less than overt militarism given what was to be one of the identifying marks of his movement: the cloak of theological respectability.[37]

The metamorphosis of the Bergson Boys' organizational discipline and subgroups into Meir Kahane's attempts at "mind control" and "ani-

nce was a factor of the American patriotic discourse of the 1940s,
posited the idea that Americans were custodians of an ultimate
liberal capitalism. Affected by the ethnic pluralism of the late 1960s,
ie's original desire to make the JDL member into a "pluperfect
can" and to "save the American dream," as he wrote in an early
esto, rapidly metamorphosed into ethnic particularism and, at a later
even a rejection of liberal Western values. Reaching maturity after
cond World War, Kahane exemplified the distance traveled between
cial, political, and cultural contexts of the 1940s and those of the

second factor was theological: the tension between liberal secular-
d religious fundamentalism. Combining a secular ethos with a pro-
a of secular humanism, the Bergson Boys were imminently capable
iding into the American liberal culture and did so out of a combina-
f prudence and opportunism. Consequently, they were able to gain
ents in both their particular ethnic constituency and among the gen-
nerican public. Coming of age during the postwar growth of Jewish
doxy, despite his American birth and upbringing, Kahane appears to
een more influenced by the impact of Orthodoxy than by liberal
can cultural factors.

third factor was cultural: the growing cultural radicalization in the
d States after the Second World War, which reached its zenith in the
960s. While the Bergson Boys' interpretation of Revisionist ideolog-
iets was often more radical than that of Jabotinsky, Kahane took this
to new heights. Not only were his interpretations of Revisionist ide-
more radical than the original, but in many cases he adopted only
evisionist form or terminology, imbuing it with Orthodox-
alist content. Kahane's "Jewish Pride" lay in the concept of "Hear
el, the Lord is our God, the Lord is One" and in the fact that "God
is from mediocrity and proclaimed for us a difficult but magnificent
And thou shalt be for me a special people, a kingdom of priests and a
ation.' " Nevertheless, a closer look at Kahane's weltanschauung
to a tacit reliance on American liberalism as the tolerating factor
ould ensure the JDL's survival and ensure its free speech. Unlike his
cal predecessors on the nationalist Jewish right, Kahane allowed
f a tremendous amount of leeway in action, testing the limits of
can liberalism and tolerance. Bordering on the extreme, both his

mal squad" vigilantism is but one example of ho
logical concepts underwent radical interpretation
ing a good deal of space in his books to Irgun sa
self-defense, in practice he distilled these concept
nant was the JDL's cult of violence. Army dignity
raderie were long gone. The *mishmaat yisrael-*
unity—that Kahane espoused was a far cry from
pline practiced by the Bergson Boys.[38]

The development of the Revisionist concept
another example of how the use of similar termin
dicative of similar ideological content. Accepted
blocks of Betar, the *hadar* concept was integrate
schauung, becoming an integral part of the Berg
makeup. "Our members were schooled in the wa
was part of every Betari's culture," stated Bergsor
legacy to us," added Alex Rafaeli, "a sense of
member brought to the Irgun and beyond."[39]

In its JDL appearance, *hadar* received an en
bereft of European dignity and imbued instead w
eschatological overtones. "Hadar means dignity,
his *Story of the Jewish Defense League.* However,
tion core concept into a rabbinical sermon: "H
feel in our Jewishness, in our history . . . we tak
was the Jew who gave the world the concept of O
G-d, and of One G-d who created man to reach t
Continuing in this vein, Kahane states that holin
by keeping the commandments of the Torah, th
and laws of family purity, a far cry from the delega
use of the term.[40] As opposed to the Irgun Delega
ideology, Kahane's weltanschauung was theolog
little more than lip service to their self-designated

The problematic of creating an ideologica
Bergson Boys and the JDL is apparent when ex
tinction between the two groups. The first diffe
Although both the Bergson Boys and the JDL w
States, the American liberal tradition and ethos di
mer group's ideology to a much greater extent th

influ
whic
value
Kaha
Ame
mani
stage
the S
the s
1960

ism
jecti
of bl
tion
adhe
eral A
Orth
have
Ame

Unit
late I
ical t
trend
ology
the
natio
O Isr
lifted
task:
holy
point
that
histo
hims
Ame

rhetoric and his actions were based on the knowledge that America functioned along the lines of "I may disagree with what you have to say, but will fight to the death for your right to say it." In this he was a true product of American culture, much more so than Bergson and his Palestinian cohorts.[41]

On the tactical level, however, it is possible to draw direct links between the Bergsonites and the JDL. Like the Irgun Delegation's modus operandi, Kahane's gimmicks were aimed at creating an image of a "new strong Jew" and at providing him with large-scale media coverage. From spray-painting Soviet airplanes with the slogan "Let My People Go" and holding protest rallies across from the Soviet embassy, the JDL turned to violent demonstrations and even to planting bombs in the offices of Soviet organizations such as Intourist (the government tourist office) and Aeroflot (the Soviet national airline). As JDL ideology placed special emphasis upon the use of weapons (a traditional characteristic of American right-wing organizations), young JDL members received quasi-military training at Camp JeDeL, run by a number of former Irgun members. During the early 1970s a sizeable number of young Betar members in New York joined the JDL; for them, Kahane was a direct heir of Jabotinsky and the Irgun.[42]

The American Jewish establishment's relationship with the JDL was also reminiscent of their interaction with the Irgun Delegation. In its early stages, the JDL drew supporters from among prominent Orthodox American rabbis such as Emmanuel Rackman, who even provided Kahane with a forum during the early years of his activist career. However, the establishment leaders rapidly retreated from what appeared to them as an antithesis to the accepted norms of American Jewish activity. Kahane adopted a racist, anti-black ideology, used militant rhetoric, and surrounded himself with a group of young Jewish militants who did not fit the accepted pattern of "nice Jewish boys." After the JDL joined the struggle for Soviet Jewry the group's militant rhetoric began to be expressed in more concrete terms. On the ideological level, this transition was similar to the one that the Irgun Delegation had made in 1943 when Kook decided to abandon the struggle for a Jewish army in order to totally dedicate himself to the rescue of European Jewry.

Throughout the 1940s the American Jewish establishment and the American press had called the Irgun Delegation members "hooligans" and "gangsters"; in the early 1970s the JDL was being labeled the same way. Kahane remained undeterred by the comparisons made between the JDL and the Black Panthers; instead he spent many hours learning the manipulative media tactics of the black militants. "The Talmud says, 'Who is wise? He who learns from all people,' " Kahane boasted. "We are happy when people call us Panthers, because we know a Panther doesn't mess with a Panther."[43]

Like all ethnic protest groups, the JDL's make-or-break issue was support: social, political, financial, and tactical. Most of the Irgun Delegation's Jewish support had come from its ethnic constituency: Jewish immigrants, traditional/religious Jews, and, later, unidentified Jews. Kahane was similarly supported by ethnic and marginal Jewish groups of the 1960s and early 1970s: the orthodox, the newly observant, and the lower middle class. Surprisingly, JDL economic backing came from several unexpected sources such as philanthropist Joseph Gruss, who said that if his own grandchildren wouldn't be Jewish, at least he would be causing others to have Jewish grandchildren. Political support came from right-wing Israeli politicians such as Geula Cohen and Yitzhak Shamir, who encouraged him to take up the struggle to free Soviet Jewry and gave him tactical advice. Similar to the ad hoc partnerships that Kook formed with the Orthodox rabbinical associations during the early 1940s in the struggle to save European Jewry, Kahane reached an agreement (but not full cooperation) with another group that was working to free Soviet Jewry during the 1970s: the National Council for Soviet Jewry, headed by Malcolm Honelein. Despite these temporary coalitions, the JDL's modus operandi appeared so frightening to parts of the American Jewish establishment that the Anti-Defamation League of Bnai Brith infiltrated the militant organization and sent the FBI periodic reports about its activities.[44]

Why did Kahane raise the ire of the American Jewish establishment? For reasons similar to the causes of their attitude toward the Irgun Delegation. First and foremost because he tried to portray the problems facing the Jewish world in what they considered to be a different—and potentially dangerous—manner. These organizations did not only reject Kahane's militant tactics and dangerous rhetoric; like the American Jewish establishment's response to the Irgun Delegation, they feared that the JDL would damage the public image of American Jewry that they had worked hard to create, one of enlightened patriotism and liberalism. Another reason was Kahane's direct attacks on the American Jewish establishment for having done little to save European Jewry during the Holocaust. One example was the JDL advertisement that appeared in the *New York Times* in May 1970:

> Shame on American Jews! . . . In 1942 when we learned about Auschwitz—we did nothing. Our leaders went to President Roosevelt and asked him to bomb the rail lines carrying the cars packed with Jews to the gas chambers. He refused. We did nothing. When the lives of hundreds of thousands of Jews were at stake we did nothing more than hold rallies and mimeograph sheets of protest. . . . In 1970, when we know of the national and spiritual destruction of Soviet Jewry . . . Where is the unceasing effort? Where are the huge crowds? Where are the huge protests? Where are the demonstrators who bleed for every people, every cause, every group—except the Jew? . . . Some day, your children or grandchildren will ask you: "What did you do for Soviet Jews?" What will you say?[45]

Similar to the Irgun Delegation's tactics, the JDL chose to create coalitions with other ethnic protest groups, and particularly with the Italians. During the 1940s Rafaeli and Kook had made contact with the Italian Mafia by using Jewish underworld figure Mickey Cohen, and even reached an agreement with former Mafia chief Lucky Luciano. In May 1971 Kahane announced a partnership with a right-wing organization called the Italian-American Civil Rights League, founded by New York Mafia chief Joseph Colombo Sr. Colombo had first heard about Meir Kahane from his lawyer, who was representing Kahane at his arraignment on bomb-making charges. Colombo was intrigued by the story of a tough Jew and appeared in court the next day to post the rabbi's $25,000 bail. The two ultimately formed a coalition, based on mutual interests and a shared hatred of blacks and Hispanics. While JDL members participated in demonstrations for the rights of Italian-Americans, the Mafia took part in activities to release Soviet Jewry. The coalition had an economic aspect as well: Kahane hoped to enjoy a steady cash flow through Colombo's good offices while the Mafia leader used JDL couriers to launder money in the South. The partnership disbanded after Colombo was shot in the head during the summer of 1971; shortly afterward Kahane decided to move to Israel and commenced a new stage in his political career.[46]

In many ways the JDL's history is reminiscent of that of the Irgun Delegation. Both groups tried to foster the image of a strong, militant, new Jew. True, the JDL developed this militancy to a point that delegation members never dreamed of, but this difference may be the result of a generational gap between the two organizations rather than a tactical or ideological one. Both groups were aware of the importance of a media campaign, manipulated by using shock tactics and other gimmicks. Both organizations tried to form coalitions with splinter groups within their own ethnic constituency and with other ethnic bodies such as the Irish and the Italians and particularly the Italian Mafia. Both groups stood at the right of the Zionist political spectrum, believed in territorial maximalism, and condoned the use of violence when necessary to achieve their goals. True, there were many points they did not have in common: the JDL leader's religious leanings as opposed to the delegation members' secularism, the JDL's racist ideology that had no parallel within the delegation, and so forth. But at least on the tactical level, it appears that the Irgun Delegation was one of the roots of the American Jewish militant right wing in the United States.[47]

Even in the field of achievements the two organizations seem to have several common denominators. JDL and the Irgun Delegation critics both claim that these bodies were unsuccessful and that their rhetoric only hurt other Jewish organizations' achievements in the same spheres. Simultaneously, the critics negate the importance of the publicity that the two organizations generated. On the other hand, supporters of both groups consider their public relations campaigns to be a success unto themselves, with their long-term effects being an additional noteworthy achievement. For example, JDL supporters claim that in 1969, before Kahane began his struggle to free Soviet Jewry, Soviet authorities permitted fewer than three thousand Jews to leave the USSR annually. During 1972 and 1973, when Kahane's campaign was at its zenith, more than sixty-six thousand Jews were permitted to leave each year. It is ludicrous to claim that the Soviets altered their emigration policies as a direct result of Kahane's actions; more likely it was in response to the new mood of detente. Yet JDL supporters claim that the organization at least indirectly affected the issue by bringing home an awareness of the problem to policymakers such as U.S.

Senator Henry Jackson, who initiated the campaign to refuse the Soviet Union the "Most Favored Nation" status as long as their emigration policies remained in effect. In more than one way history was repeating itself: the same claims had been made almost thirty years earlier vis-à-vis the Irgun Delegation and other congressmen such as Andrew Somers.

◆ ◆ ◆

"This is how we see the world," stated Rene Magritte in a 1938 lecture. "We see it as being outside ourselves even though it is only a mental representation of what we experience on the inside."[48] Historians have long been aware of the fact that the victors write the history of the vanquished, even when speaking of an internal victory of one faction over another. We can therefore understand why the story of the Irgun Delegation in the United States was almost completely forgotten within the general historiography of the Irgun, just as the Irgun incorporated and then overshadowed the history of the Revisionist-Zionist movement. Any attempt to document the group's history, to analyze its activities, and to evaluate is achievements from a historical perspective requires us to examine documentation and memoirs but also to delve into the souls of their political heirs; those from whom the delegation members split shortly after the group disbanded. Only thus can we overcome the dearth of references to the delegation in later Irgun historiography, where it is treated primarily as a contributory force to the Irgun's political successes. For the victors who mold public memory, it is irrelevant that these successes were often light years removed from the delegation's original aims.

Let me close with a personal note. When I first began this book an eminent historian asked me what I was writing. Upon learning that it was a history of the Irgun Delegation in the United States, he expressed doubts about whether the topic was worthy of study. "The issue is so unimportant," he remarked. "After all, Hillel Kook and his friends only talked and never really did anything practical." When our paths crossed several months later he again asked me about my research.

"I'm still writing that 'unimportant' book about the Irgun Delegation," I answered jokingly.

"On second thought, that isn't completely accurate," he countered with a half smile. "It could be a very important and even useful book, particularly if you write bad things about them."

This exchange proved to me once again how, even today, topics pertaining to the Zionist right wing raise mixed and even contradictory feelings and are never viewed with equanimity, even those from half a century ago that the sands of time should have long buried.

The degree to which the line of demarcation between past and present is blurred was brought home to all during the events in Israel taking place between Prime Minister Yitzhak Rabin's murder in November 1995 and the national elections in May 1996 and during the period prior to the disengagement from Gaza during the summer of 2005. Even those who wished to view episodes such as the Irgun Delegation as part of the past realized then how much the division between right and left, with all that it entails, continues to threaten the delicate fabric connecting the various segments of Israeli society to this very day. It is my hope that by exploring the less charted waters of a group that was thought of as belonging to the Zionist right wing, I have shown the complexity underlying the simplistic right/left division and underscored the fact that almost all Jewish and Zionist organizations existing today—whether right, left, or center—were ultimately influenced by the Bergson group's tactical and organizational legacy.

Notes

Glossary

Bibliography

Index

Notes

Preface to the English Edition

1. David H. Shpiro, *From Philanthropy to Activism: The Political Transformation of American Zionism in the Holocaust Years, 1933–1945* (Oxford: Pergamon Press, 1994); Aaron Berman, *Nazism, the Jews, and American Zionism, 1933–1948* (Detroit, Mich.: Wayne State Univ. Press, 1990); Samuel Halperin, *The Political World of American Zionism* (Detroit, Mich.: Wayne State Univ. Press, 1961); Menachem Kaufman, *An Ambiguous Partnership: Non-Zionists and Zionists in America, 1939–1948* (in Hebrew) (Jerusalem: Magner and Wayne State Univ., 1991); Henry L. Feingold, *The Politics of Rescue: The Roosevelt Administration and the Holocaust* (New Brunswick, N.J.: Rutgers Univ. Press, 1970); Rafael Medoff, *The Deafening Silence: American Jewish Leaders and the Holocaust* (New York: Shapolsky, 1987); Saul Friedmann, *No Haven for the Oppressed: United States Policy Toward Jewish Refugees, 1938–1945* (Detroit: Wayne State Univ. Press, 1973); Monty N. Penkower, "In Dramatic Dissent: The Bergson Boys," in *The Holocaust and Israel Reborn: From Catastrophe to Sovereignty* (Urbana: Univ. of Illinois Press, 1994), 61–90; Monty N. Penkower, "Eleanor Roosevelt and the Plight of World Jewry," in *The Holocaust and Israel Reborn: From Catastrophe to Sovereignty* (Urbana: Univ. of Illinois Press, 1994), 271–88; Yehuda Bauer, *American Jewry and the Holocaust: The American Joint Distribution Committee, 1939–1945* (Detroit, Mich.: Wayne State Univ. Press, 1981); David S. Wyman, *The Abandonment of the Jews: America and the Holocaust, 1941–1945* (New York: Pantheon Books, 1984).

2. David Niv, *Battle for Freedom: The Irgun Zvai Leumi* (in Hebrew), 6 vols. (Tel Aviv: Klausner Institute, 1965–81); Eli Tavin, *The Second Front: The Irgun Zevai Leumi in Europe, 1946–1948* (in Hebrew) (Tel Aviv: Ron, 1973); Shmuel Katz, *Days of Fire* (Jerusalem: Steimatzky, 1980).

3. Jack E. Holmes, *The Mood/Interest Theory of American Foreign Policy* (Lexington: Univ. Press of Kentucky, 1985), 2; Allan M. Winkler, *The Politics of Propaganda: The Office of War Information, 1942–1945* (New Haven: Yale Univ. Press, 1978); David E. Everson, *Public Opinion and Interest Groups in American Politics* (New York: Franklin Watts, 1982), 98; Robert S. Erikson and Norman R. Luttbeg, *American Public Opinion: Its Origins, Con-*

tent, and Impact (New York: John Wiley and Sons, 1973), 107; Deborah E. Lipstadt, *Beyond Belief: The American Press and the Coming of the Holocaust, 1933–1945* (New York: The Free Press, 1986).

4. Kaufman, *An Ambiguous Partnership,* 357.

5. Wyman, *The Abandonment of the Jews;* Joanna M. Saidel, "Revisionist Zionism in America: The Campaign to Win American Public Support, 1930–1948" (Ph.D. diss., Univ. of New Hampshire, 1994).

6. "They were not afraid to adopt the innovative tactics introduced by the Irgun Zvai Leumi's American committees, nor did they fear the reaction of the gentile community" (Shpiro, *From Philanthropy to Activism,* 181).

1. What Was the Irgun Delegation?

1. Alexander Rafaeli, interview by Judith Tydor Baumel, Jerusalem, 22 May 1995. The expression "cut-off battalion" appears frequently in interviews of Hillel Kook, Oral History Division, Institute for Contemporary Jewry, Hebrew University, Jerusalem (hereafter OHD), 55(b).

2. Rafaeli-Baumel interview, 22 May 1995.

3. Rodney W. Napier and Matti K. Gershenfeld, *Groups: Theory and Experience* (Boston: Houghton Mifflin, 1985), 149–50.

4. Larry L. Barker et al., eds., *Groups in Process: An Introduction to Small Group Communication,* 2d ed. (Englewood Cliffs, N.J.: Prentice Hall, 1983), 63–64.

5. Rafaeli-Baumel interview, 17 Oct. 1994.

6. Yitzhak Ben-Ami, *Years of Wrath, Days of Glory: Memoirs from the Irgun,* 2d ed. (New York: Shengold, 1983), 141–44, 157–58.

7. Ibid., 159.

8. Ibid., 184.

9. Hillel Kook, telephone interview by Judith Tydor Baumel, 26 July 1990.

10. Haim Lubinsky to Judge, 25 Mar. 1939; Lubinsky to Mrs. Peck, 15 Apr. 1939, both in F25 380, Central Zionist Archives, Jerusalem (hereafter CZA).

11. Kook interview, OHD, (55)b.

12. Rafaeli-Baumel interview, 22 May 1995.

13. Yigal Elam, "The Development of Defensive and Underground Organizations: The Underground and Military Aspects of the Jewish Yishuv under the Mandate" (in Hebrew), in *The History of Eretz Israel,* vol. 9, *The British Mandate and the Jewish National Home* (Jerusalem: Keter, 1990), 216–18.

14. Alexander Rafaeli, *Dream and Action: The Story of My Life* (Jerusalem: Achva Cooperative Press, 1993), 67–68.

15. Ibid., 87.

16. Kook interview, OHD (55)b. On his "annexation" to the presidium, see Jabotinsky to Raziel, 6 July 1939, originally in *Hakad,* file 15, quoted in Isaac Alfasi, ed., *Irgun Zvai Leumi: Collection of Archival Sources* (in Hebrew), vol. 1 (Tel Aviv: Jabotinsky Institute in Israel, 1980), 88.

17. Rafaeli-Baumel interview, 17 Oct. 1994; Samuel Merlin interview, OHD, (67)1; Merlin to Yair, 29 Dec. 1940, originally in *Hakad,* file 15; published in Alfasi, *Irgun Zvai Leumi,* 389–90.

18. Rafaeli-Baumel interview, 17 Oct. 1994; see also Eri Jabotinsky, *My Father, Ze'ev Jabotinsky* (in Hebrew) (Tel Aviv: Hadar, 1981).

19. Mike Robinson, *Groups* (Chichester, UK: Wiley, 1984), 11.

20. Ya'akov Shavit, *Jabotinsky and the Revisionist Movement, 1925–1948* (London: Frank Cass, 1988), 84.

21. Ibid., 85.

22. Ibid., 22–31. See also Joseph B. Schechtman, *The United States and the Jewish State Movement* (New York: Herzl Press, 1966), 33.

23. Ch. Ben Yerucham [Chen-Melech Merchavia], *Sepher Betar. Book of Betar: History and Sources* (in Hebrew), vol. 1, *From the People* (Jerusalem: Publishing Committee of Sepher Betar, 1969), 30.

24. Niv, *Battle for Freedom,* 1:121–22.

25. Ibid., 126–27; Elam, 216–17.

26. Niv, *Battle for Freedom,* 1:12.

27. Marvin E. Shaw, *Group Dynamics: The Psychology of Small Group Behavior* (New York: McGraw Hill, 1971), 11.

28. Ch. Ben Yerucham, *Sepher Bethar,* vol. 1, 648.

29. Niv, *Battle for Freedom,* 8:185–87; Ch. Ben Yerucham, *Sepher Betar* (in Hebrew), vol. 2, *From the People* (Jerusalem: Publishing Committee of Sepher Betar, 1976), 677–79.

30. Shmuel Katz, *Lone Wolf: A Biography of Vladimir (Ze'ev) Jabotinsky,* vol. 2 (New York: Barricade Books, 1996), 1403–4.

31. Niv, *Battle for Freedom,* 8:189.

32. Katz, *Lone Wolf,* 1313–17.

33. Joseph Heller, *The Stern Gang: Ideology, Politics, and Terror, 1940–1949* (London: Frank Cass, 1995), 32–33.

34. Ibid., 34–37. For Ratosh, see Yehoshua Porath, *The Life of Uriel Shelah (Yonathan Ratosh)* (in Hebrew) (Jerusalem: Mahberot Lesifrut, 1989).

35. Katz, *Lone Wolf,* 1626–29; Ch. Ben Yerucham, *Sepher Bethar,* vol. 0:863.

36. Shavit, *Jabotinsky,* 100.

37. Katz, *Lone Wolf,* 1631.

38. Rafaeli-Baumel interview, 17 Oct. 1994; Katz, *Lone Wolf,* 1665.

39. Howard Morley Sachar, *A History of the Jews in America* (New York: A. A. Knopf, 1992).

40. Halperin, *Political World,* 45–49.

41. Menachem Kaufman, *Non-Zionists in America and the Struggle for Jewish Statehood, 1939–1948* (in Hebrew) (Jerusalem: Hassifriya Haziyonit, 1984).

42. Naomi Wiener Cohen, *Not Free to Desist: The American Jewish Committee, 1906–1966* (Philadelphia: JPS, 1972).

43. For the history of the Reform movement, see Michael A. Meyer, *Response to*

Modernity: A History of the Reform Movement in Judaism (Oxford: Oxford Univ. Press, 1988).

44. Regarding these two organizations, see Faith Rogov, *Gone to Another Meeting: The National Council of Jewish Women, 1893–1993* (Tuscaloosa: Univ. of Alabama Press, 1994); Yehuda Bauer, *My Brother's Keeper* (Philadelphia: Jewish Publication Society, 1974); Yehuda Bauer, *American Jewry and the Holocaust;* Alon Gal, *Brandeis of Boston* (Cambridge, Mass: Harvard Univ. Press, 1976); Melvin I. Urofsky, *American Zionism from Herzl to the Holocaust* (New York: Doubleday Anchor, 1975); Evyatar Friesel, *The Zionist Movement in the United States, 1897–1914* (in Hebrew) (Tel Aviv: Tel Aviv Univ. Press, 1970).

45. Urofsky, *American Zionism,* 275.

46. Feingold, *Politics of Rescue,* 203; Berman, *Nazism, the Jews,* 17–19; Joseph B. Schechtman and Yehuda Benari, *History of the Revisionist Movement,* vol. 1 (Tel Aviv: Hadar, 1970), 413–24; Chanoch [Howard] Rosenblum, "The New Zionist Organization's American Campaign, 1936–1939," *Studies in Zionism* 12 (1991): 169–85.

47. Berman, *Nazism, the Jews,* xxvii; Halperin, *Political World,* 189.

48. These joint efforts were made in 1930, 1934, 1935, 1939, and 1940. See Halperin, *Political World,* 202–8.

49. Ibid., 201–9.

50. Shpiro, *From Philanthropy to Activism,* 4–5.

51. Ben-Ami, *Years of Wrath,* 238.

2. A Time to Learn

1. Rafaeli-Baumel interview, 17 Oct. 1994.

2. Rafaeli, *Dream and Action,* 89–90.

3. Ben-Ami, *Years of Wrath,* 215–16.

4. Ibid., 215.

5. Samuel Merlin to Alexander Rafaeli, 29 July 1943, Alexander Rafaeli personal collection, Jerusalem (hereafter Rafaeli Collection).

6. Ben-Ami, *Years of Wrath,* 216.

7. Dean Banks, "Creating an American Dilemma: The Impact of Nazi Racism upon American Intergroup Relations, 1933–1940, with Special Reference of Jewish Americans, German-Americans, and the Free Speech Movement" (Ph.D. diss., Univ. of Texas, 1975), 21; David S. Wyman, *Paper Walls: America and the Refugee Crisis, 1938–1941* (Amherst: Univ. of Massachusetts Press, 1968), 14–17.

8. Daniel Judah Elazar, *Community and Polity: The Organizational Dynamics of American Jewry* (Philadelphia: JPS, 1976).

9. Milton J. Esman, ed. *Ethnic Conflict in the Western World* (Ithaca, N.Y.: Cornell Univ. Press, 1977).

10. Joseph Rothschild, *Ethnopolitics: A Conceptual Framework* (New York: Columbia Univ. Press, 1981), 202–4.

11. Eber M. Carroll, *American Opinion and the Irish Question, 1910–23: A Study in Opinion and Policy* (Dublin, Ireland: Gill and Macmillan and St. Martin's Press, 1978), 28–31.

12. Yitzhak Ben-Ami to P. Bergson, 25 Jan. 1941, Rafaeli Collection.

13. Cecil A. Gibb, "Leadership: Psychological Aspects," in *International Encyclopedia of the Social Sciences,* vol. 9, ed. David L. Sills (New York: Macmillan and the Free Press, 1968), 91.

14. Arnold S. Tannenbaum, "Leadership: Sociological Aspects," in *International Encyclopedia of the Social Sciences,* vol. 9, ed. David L. Sills (New York: Macmillan and the Free Press, 1968), 104; Eric Berne, *The Structure and Dynamics of Organizations and Groups* (New York: Ballantine Books, 1974), 142; Gibb, 98.

15. It is still a matter of debate among sociologists as to whether these characteristics can be isolated. I have chosen to rely here on those who believe that they can. For an alternative viewpoint on group experience, see Napier and Gershenfeld, *Groups,* 230–33.

16. Charles Levine, "Propaganda Techniques of the Bergson Group, 1939–1948" (M.A. thesis, Univ. of Texas at Austin, 1974), 16.

17. Ben-Ami, *Years of Wrath,* 242.

18. Samuel Merlin to Rafaeli, 20 June 1988, Rafaeli Collection.

19. Ben-Ami, *Years of Wrath,* 242.

20. Barker et al., *Groups in Process,* 63–64.

21. Ben-Ami, *Years of Wrath,* 251, 318.

22. Rafaeli-Baumel interview, 17 Oct. 1994.

23. Merlin interview, OHD, (67)1; Kook interview, OHD, (55)b.

24. Ben Hecht, *A Child of the Century* (New York: Ballantine, 1970), 513.

25. *The Bulletin,* 9 Oct. 1939, The American Friends of the League for a Free Palestine, 1, Jabotinsky Archives, Jabotinsky Institute in Israel, Tel Aviv (hereafter JAI).

26. Memo, William Stanton to Peter Bergson, undated, The American Friends of the League for a Free Palestine, 1, JAI.

27. American Friends of a Jewish Palestine, *Aims and Achievements* (New York: American Friends of a Jewish Palestine Press, 1940), The American Friends of the League for a Free Palestine, 1, JAI.

28. Ibid.

29. Rafaeli-Baumel interview, 17 Oct. 1994.

30. Rafaeli, *Dream and Action,* 96.

31. Isaac Zaar, *Rescue and Liberation: America's Part in the Birth of Israel* (New York: Bloch Publishing Co., 1954), 9–11.

32. Merlin interview, OHD, (67)1.

33. Niv, *Battle for Freedom,* 111; Rafaeli-Baumel interview, 17 Oct. 1994.

34. Gloria Lubar and E. F. van der Veen, "Functions of Various Groups Backed by Bergson Explained," *Washington Post,* 8 Oct. 1944, 1. From 1939 to 1940 the Revisionists and their associates brought 15,000 illegal immigrants to Palestine in twenty-five boats, about 40 percent of the total number that reached Palestine by ship during that period. See Shavit, *Jabotinsky,* 376; "A Petition for the Restoration of the World's Oldest Democracy," H/10/18, JAI.

35. Harvey Schwann to the British ambassador in Washington, 13 Sept. 1939, The Committee for a Jewish Army, 3/19, JAI; Ben-Ami, *Years of Wrath,* 238; Zaar, *Rescue and Liberation,* 13–14.

36. Eri Jabotinsky, *My Father,* 168. For a full description of the entire episode, see Eri Jabotinsky, *The Sakarya Expedition* (Johannesburg: Newzo, 1945). See also Dalia Ofer, *Escaping the Holocaust: Illegal Immigration to the Land of Israel* (New York: Oxford Univ. Press, 1990), 80–85.

37. Ben-Ami, *Years of Wrath,* 254.

38. Eri Jabotinsky, *My Father,* 173.

39. Ibid., 174.

40. Ibid., 175. For another description of the journey, see Ben-Ami, *Years of Wrath,* 259–62.

41. William R. Perl, *Operation Action: Rescue from the Holocaust* (New York: F. Ungar, 1983), 284. For Hecht's role in assisting illegal immigration from Romania, see Joseph Kister, *Etzel (I.Z.L.)* (in Hebrew) (Tel Aviv: Ministry of Defence, 1993), 66–67.

42. Ben-Ami, *Years of Wrath,* 263.

43. Perl, *Operation Action,* 333; Yitzhak Ben-Ami to Kook, 20 Jan. 1940, H/10/12, JAI.

44. Eri Jabotinsky, *My Father,* 200–201. Quoted in Ben-Ami, *Years of Wrath,* 265.

45. Perl, *Operation Action,* 293.

46. Ben-Ami, *Years of Wrath,* 266.

47. Ofer, *Escaping the Holocaust,* 85–88.

48. Zaar, *Rescue and Liberation,* 11.

49. Zeev Jabotinsky to the NZO Committee (copy to Anna Jabotinsky), 10 Mar. 1940, Zeev Jabotinsky Collection, 2/30/1, JAI.

50. Rafaeli, *Dream and Action,* 90–91.

51. Zeev Jabotinky to Yitzhak Ben-Ami, 24 May 1940, Zeev Jabotinsky Collection, 2/30/0, JAI.

52. Zeev Jabotinsky to Colonel John Patterson, 11 June 1940, quoted in Alfasi, 113. English translation based on Katz, *Lone Wolf,* 1770.

53. Katz, *Lone Wolf,* 1147–48.

54. Rafaeli interview, 9 Apr. 1970, OHD, (67)4. See also Merlin interview, 26 July 1969, OHD, (67)1.

55. Letter from T. to Y. Y., 8 Aug. 1940, S46–392, CZA.

56. Rafaeli-Baumel interview, 17 Oct. 1994.

57. Kook interview, 7 Nov. 1968, OHD, (55)b.

58. Kook interview, 3 Oct. 1968, OHD, (55)b.

59. Merlin interview, 26 July 1969, OHD, (67)1.

60. Kook interview, 1 Oct. 1968, OHD, (55)b; Kook's resignation from the NZO presidium in the United States, 10 Jan. 1941, The American Friends of the League for a Free Palestine, 12, JAI.

61. Rafaeli-Saidel interview, 15 June 1993, quoted in Saidel, "Revisionist Zionism," 43; Aryeh Altman interview, OHD, (67)5.

62. Niv, *Battle for Freedom,* 47; Heller, *The Stern Gang,* 60–76.

63. David Raziel to Hillel Kook, undated letter, 8/21 Haganah Archives, Tel Aviv. Quoted in Alfasi, 382.

64. Samuel Merlin to Abraham Stern, 29 Dec. 1940, quoted in Alfasi, 389; Eri Jabotinsky to Abraham Stern, Feb. 1940, quoted in Alfasi, 39.

65. The importance of the delegation's financial role at that juncture can be inferred from the closing of an August 1940 letter from Raziel to Kook in which he implored Kook to dispatch funds immediately in order to pay for Irgun activity. Raziel, undated letter to Kook, 8/21 Haganah Archives, Tel Aviv, quoted in Alfasi, 382.

66. Tom Douglas, *Groups: Understanding People Gathered Together* (London: Tavistock, 1983), 49–50.

67. Katz, *Lone Wolf,* 1149; Hillel Kook, letter of resignation sent to S. Klinger, acting president of the NZO presidium in the United States, 10 Jan. 1941, The American Friends of the League for a Free Palestine, 12, JAI.

68. Rafaeli-Baumel interview, 12 Oct. 1995.

69. Shpiro, *From Philanthropy to Activism,* 50.

70. Ibid., 62–63.

71. Interim Committee, undated memo, C7 1378, CZA.

72. American Zionist Emergency Council, undated memo, Z5 395, CZA.

73. *The New Palestine,* 29 Sept. 1939, quoted in Zaar, *Rescue and Liberation,* 10–11.

74. Henry Montor to Rabbi Baruch Rabinowitz, 11 Dec. 1940, The American Friends of the League for a Free Palestine, 11, JAI.

75. Quoted in Ben-Ami, *Years of Wrath,* 321.

76. Schechtman, *Jewish State Movement,* 47.

77. Yitzhak Ben-Ami to the executive director of the UJA, 15 Aug. 1940, The American Friends of the League for a Free Palestine, 11, JAI.

78. Meyer W. Weisgal, memo re: Revisionists, 30 Nov. 1943, Z5 919, CZA.

79. Ibid.

80. Quoted in Ben-Ami, *Years of Wrath,* 322.

81. Halperin, *Political World,* 214.

82. Napier and Gershenfeld, *Groups,* 467.

3. A Time to Fight

1. Ben-Ami, *Years of Wrath,* 269.

2. Rafaeli, *Dream and Action,* 94–95.

3. Rafaeli-Baumel interview, 5 Sept. 1990.

4. Kook interview, OHD, 55(b).

5. Niv, *Battle for Freedom,* 115; Rafaeli, *Dream and Action,* 117–18.

6. Vladimir [Zeev] Jabotinsky, *The Jewish War Front* (London: G. Allen and Unwin, 1940), 237.

7. Yehuda Bauer, *From Diplomacy to Resistance: A History of Jewish Palestine, 1939–1945,* trans. Alton M. Winters (Philadelphia: JPS, 1970), 86–96.

8. V. Jabotinsky to Churchill, 12 May 1940, JAI, quoted in Heller, *The Stern Gang,* 64.

9. Jabotinsky to Churchill, 12 May 1940, WO 32/9502, Public Record Office, London (hereafter PRO); Abrams to Churchill, 13 May 1940, FO 371/24566, PRO; Note on Jewish Offer of Military Assistance, n.d., FO 371/24566, PRO; Katz, *Lone Wolf,* 1748–52; Yoav Gelber, *Jewish Palestinian Volunteering in the British Army During the Second World War,* vol. 1, *Volunteering and Its Role in Zionist Policy, 1939–1942* (in Hebrew) (Jerusalem: Yad Izhak Ben-Avi, 1979), 61–70.

10. Katz, *Lone Wolf,* 1760–61.

11. Gelber, *Volunteering and Its Role,* 134, 138; Bauer, *From Diplomacy,* 92–93.

12. Kook interview, OHD, (55)b.

13. Samuel Merlin to Alex Rafaeli, 12 Dec. 1940, Rafaeli Collection; Samuel Merlin to Yitzhak Ben-Ami, H/11/2/3, JAI.

14. Shpiro, *From Philanthropy to Activism,* 43–44.

15. Douglas, *Groups,* 54. Some 3,500 people attended the rally at Manhattan Center and another several thousand attended similar rallies held throughout spring and summer 1941.

16. Eri Jabotinsky to J. H. Dayag, 4 Sept. 1943, FO 371/40129, PRO.

17. AZEC, undated memo, Z5 395, CZA.

18. On Pierre van Paassen's deep feeling for Zionism, see Pierre van Paassen, *The Forgotten Ally* (New York: Dial Press, 1943). For biographical material on the other figures, consult "Bibliographical Notes," The Emergency Committee to Save the Jews of Europe, 2/3, JAI.

19. Hecht, *A Child,* 484.

20. Ibid., 483–84. See also Ben Hecht, *1001 Afternoons in New York* (New York: Viking Press, 1941), 74, 86, 93.

21. Hecht, *A Child,* 488.

22. Rafaeli, *Dream and Action,* 95.

23. Rafaeli-Baumel interview, 22 May 1995.

24. Merlin-Feinstein interview, Apr. 1971; Ben-Ami-Feinstein interview, Apr. 1971; and Kook-Feinstein interview, Apr. 1971, quoted in Marsha Feinstein, "The Irgun Campaign in the United States for a Jewish Army" (M.A. thesis, City Univ. of New York, 1973), 27–28.

25. Maurice Rifkin to Eri Jabotinsky, 17 June 1943, Hebrew Committee of National Liberation Manuscript, Yale University Library, unnumbered collection, quoted in Feinstein, "The Irgun Campaign," 30.

26. Kook interview, OHD, 55(b).

27. Jesse B. Calmenson to Mr. Henry Monsky, American Jewish Conference, 14 Oct. 1943, C7 1378, CZA.

28. Henry Monsky, telegram to I. L. Kenen, American Jewish Conference, 23 Dec. 1943, disapproving the publication of an antidelegation missive by the conference, C7 1378, CZA.

29. Donald Stuart Strong, *Organized Anti-Semitism in America, 1939–1940* (Washington, D.C.: American Council on Public Affairs, 1941); *United States Memoranda and Economic Notes,* no. 142, 5 Nov. 1942, FO 371/31380, PRO.

30. It was on this basis that Ben-Zion Netanyahu was drafted to the committee until he later elected to resign. Samuel Merlin to Kook, 8 May 1942, The Committee for a Jewish Army, 4/30, JAI.

31. "Committee for a Jewish Army of Palestinian and Stateless Jews," *Memorandum on a Jewish Army of Palestinian and Stateless Jews* (New York, 1942), H/10/1, JAI.

32. Yona Ferman, "Analysis of an Interest Group: The Emergency Committee to Save the Jewish People of Europe, July 1943-August 1944" (Ph.D. diss., Hebrew Univ., 1965), 9–12; Pierre van Paassen, "World Destiny Pivots on Palestine," address delivered at the Inaugural Session of the Committee for a Jewish Army in Washington, D.C., 4 Dec. 1941, The Committee for a Jewish Army, 2/5, JAI.

33. Hecht, *A Child*, 502–3.

34. "Suez Must Not Be Another Singapore!" *New York Herald Tribune*, 20 Feb. 1942.

35. Kook interview, OHD, 55(b).

36. Merlin to Bergson, 8 May 1942, The Committee for a Jewish Army, 4/30, JAI.

37. Merlin to Rafaeli, 21 June 1978, Rafaeli Collection.

38. Colonel Julius Klein to the committee, 12 Jan. 1942; William Green, president of the AFL, to Pierre van Paassen, 13 Jan. 1942, both in The Committee for a Jewish Army, 4/34, JAI; Alfred Strelsin to Moe Feld, 1 July 1942, The Committee for a Jewish Army, 4/46, JAI; Harry S. Truman to Andrew Somers, 28 Jan. 1942, The Committee for a Jewish Army, 3/25, JAI.

39. Kahane, Jr., later joined the Betar youth movement in New York, serving in various capacities during the late forties and early fifties. See, for example, the 1950 issue of *Tel-Hai* published by the Betar commission in the United States, whose assistant editor was Meir Kahane, Betar America Files, unnumbered, JAI.

40. Ferman, *Analysis of an Interest Group*, 28.

41. Ben-Ami-Feinstein interview, quoted in Feinstein, "The Irgun Campaign," 37–38; *New York Herald Tribune*, 20 Feb. 1942, 11; *New York Times*, 5 Jan. 1942, 5; author's correspondence with Harry Selden, 17 Sept. 1991.

42. Judith Tydor Baumel, *Unfulfilled Promise: Rescue and Resettlement of Jewish Refugee Children in the United States, 1934–1945* (Juneau, Alaska: Denali Press, 1990), 47–74.

43. Ben-Ami-Feinstein interview, quoted in Feinstein, "The Irgun Campaign," 39; Andrew L. Somers, statement made at a press conference, n.d. [early 1942], quoted in untitled memorandum, London: Committee for a Jewish Army, 19 May 1942; Memorandum: The History of the Endeavors to Obtain Great Britain's Approval for a Jewish Army, a Jewish Army Force or Jewish Home Guard in Palestine, 1942, both in The London Committee for a Jewish Army, 3/1, JAI.

44. Kook interview, OHD, (55)b.

45. Ibid; Feinstein, "The Irgun Campaign," 101.

46. "Jews Fight for the Right to Fight," *New York Times*, 5 Jan. 1942; "Suez Must Not Be Another Singapore!" *New York Herald Tribune*, 20 Feb. 1942. The first advertisement's title was taken from an article then written by Ben-Zion Netanyahu.

47. Merlin-Feinstein interview, Apr. 1971, quoted in Feinstein, "The Irgun Campaign," 102; Eri Jabotinsky to J. H. Dayag, 4 Sept. 1943, FO 371/40129, PRO.

48. *Philadelphia Evening Bulletin,* 14 Apr. 1942.

49. *New York Times,* 22 June 1942; *Washington Post,* 25 June 1942; *Pittsburgh Post Gazette,* 29 June 1942; full text of remarks of Peter H. Bergson at press reception, Washington, D.C., 29 June 1942, The Committee for a Jewish Army, 2/13, JAI.

50. See, for example, text of remarks of Irving Taitel, Chairman, Midwestern Division, Committee for a Jewish Army of Palestinians and Stateless Jews, at testimonial to Pierre van Paassen, Congress Hotel, Tuesday eve., 2 June 1942, The Committee for a Jewish Army, 2/13, JAI. On the invited guests, see Rhee to Wechsler, 12 Nov. 1942, The Committee for a Jewish Army, 5/56, JAI.

51. "First Shot Fired in Crusade for Jewish Army," *Chicago Sun,* 3 June 1942.

52. Hecht, *A Child of the Century,* 509; broadcast by Dr. D. E. Rabinowitz over Station WJSV, 20 June 1942, The Committee for a Jewish Army, 2/5, JAI; Rafaeli-Baumel interview, 5 Sept. 1990; Hecht to Bergson concerning hosting congressmen on radio broadcasts from Washington, 15 June 1942, The Committee for a Jewish Army, 5/58, JAI; Jaffe to Patterson, 26 June 1942, The Committee for a Jewish Army, 4/44, JAI.

53. Arieh Ben-Eliezer to Eri Jabotinsky, 24 June 1942, The Committee for a Jewish Army, 5/53, JAI.

54. *The Ten Reasons Why a Jewish Army!*; *Test Case for Democracy: American Press and the Jewish Army,* both in The Committee for a Jewish Army, 2/6, JAI. See Merlin to Kook, 14 July 1942, The Committee for a Jewish Army, 4/39, JAI; Petition for the founding of a Jewish army, The Committee for a Jewish Army, 2/11, JAI.

55. Speech by Pierre van Paassen on behalf of a Jewish army entered by Dingell, *Congressional Record,* 1941, A3452-A3454.

56. Speech by Senator James E. Murray, entered by Senator Murray, *Congressional Record* (Washington, D.C.: U.S. Government Printing Office, 1942), A1653; *New York Times,* editorial, 22 Jan. 1942, entered by Senator Radcliffe, *Congressional Record,* 1942, A604.

57. Feingold, *Politics of Rescue,* 198–99; Wyman, *Abandonment,* 194–95.

58. Speech of Senator Edwin C. Johnson, *Congressional Record* (Washington, D.C.: U.S. Government Printing Office, 1942), 3493. See copies of telegrams dispatched to hundreds of congressmen during 1942: telegram file, The Committee for a Jewish Army, 3/25, JAI; Feingold, *Politics of Rescue,* 195; Hecht, *A Child,* 512; Minutes of the Executive Committee of the Committee for a Jewish Army, 25 Apr. 1942, 2, The Committee for a Jewish Army, 2/11, JAI.

59. See, for example, Memorandum by the Undersecretary of State (Sumner Welles) to the Chief of the Division of Near Eastern Affairs (W. Murray), 4 Oct. 1941, Foreign Relations of the United States (hereafter FRUS), U.S. Department of State, Washington, D.C., 1954, 623; Memorandum by the Advisor on Political Relations (Murray) to the Secretary of State, 2 June 1942, *FRUS Diplomatic Papers 1931, III, the British Commonwealth, the Near East and Africa* (Washington, D.C.: U.S. Department of State, 1954), 539–40.

60. Merlin to Rafaeli, 20 June 1942, Rafaeli Collection; Kook interview, OHD, (55)b.

61. Circular Letter to Divisional Directors of the Committee for a Jewish Army, Letter 5, 12 May 1942, The Committee for a Jewish Army, 6, JAI.

62. Lord Winchester, Sir Robert Goare, Count de Warr, and Vernon Bartlett also joined in the effort. See "The Jewish Army Project," *Jewish Chronicle,* 24 Apr. 1942; "Political and Strategic Aspects," *Jewish Chronicle,* 1 May 1942.

63. *Are the Jews Fighting?* (London, n.d.); Committee for a Jewish Army, souvenir booklet (London, n.d.); Repatriated Jewish Soldiers: Jewish Army Committee Welcome Meeting, London 1944, Parliamentary Dinner at the Ritz Hotel, 5 Aug. 1943—all three in Yirmiyahu Helpern Collection, 4/11, JAI; The London Committee for a Jewish Army, 2/1, JAI.

64. Memorandum on the Anglo-American Committee for a Jewish Army, War Office, 10 Dec. 1942, FO 371/31380, PRO.

65. Yoav Gelber, *Jewish Palestinian Volunteering in the British Army During the Second World War,* vol. 2, *The Struggle for a Jewish Army* (in Hebrew) (Jerusalem: Yad Izhak Ben-Zvi, 1981), 371.

66. *Hansard Parliamentary Debates* (Commons), 5th ser., vol. 383 (London, 1942), cols. 1270–72.

67. Boyd to Caccia, British Office for Colonial Affairs, 19 Oct. 1942, FO 371/30319, PRO.

68. "Committee for a Jewish Army: Winding up Activities," *Jewish Chronicle,* 6 July 1945.

69. Richard P. Stevens, *American Zionism and United States Foreign Policy, 1942–1947* (New York: Pageant Press, 1962), 47; Hecht, *A Child,* 511–12; Patterson to Bergson, 17 Jan. 1943, The Committee for a Jewish Army, 2/11, JAI.

70. Ben-Ami-Feinstein interview, quoted in Feinstein, "The Irgun Campaign," 184.

71. "A Proclamation on the Moral Rights of the Stateless and Palestinian Jews," The Committee for a Jewish Army, 2/10, JAI; file of appeals to congressmen to join the committee and their replies, H/3/1/3, JAI.

72. Hecht, *A Child,* 522.

73. Ibid., 527–28.

74. *We Will Never Die,* official souvenir program, Rafaeli Collection.

75. Among the newspapers that did not cover the pageant, we find *Congress Weekly, Jewish Forum, Jewish Frontier, Jewish Outlook, Jewish Veteran, National Jewish Monthly, New Palestine, Opinion.* See Leonard Slater, *The Pledge* (New York: Simon and Schuster, 1971), 86; Thelma Berul Richman, "Political Adventurers," *Congress Weekly,* 9 June 1944, 6.

76. S. J. Jacobs to J. Smertenko, 6 Dec. 1943, Stephen S. Wise Papers, box 96, American Jewish Historical Society, Waltham, Mass.; S. Wise statement in AZEC interim committee minutes, 15 Dec. 1943, C7 1378, CZA.

77. Kook interview, OHD, (55)b.

78. Interim Committee of the American Jewish Conference memo, undated, C7 1378, CZA.

79. Monsky to Wise, meeting of the AZEC interim committee, 15 Dec. 1943, C7 1378, CZA.

80. Undated memo summarizing AZEC meeting (1942?), C7 1378, CZA.

81. Eri Jabotinsky to Hillel Kook, 3 Sept. 1942, The Committee for a Jewish Army, 4/35, JAI.

82. See, for example, memorandum presented by D. Petergorsky to Emergency Committee, 30 Mar. 1943 (Petergorsky file in Neumann files), quoted in Shpiro, *From Philanthropy to Activism*, 64–66.

83. Bergson to Judge Louis Levinthal, president of the ZOA, 7 Dec. 1942, F39 556, CZA.

84. See Memo of Agreement between MWW and JB regarding the Committee for a Jewish Army and AZEC, undated, Z5 1023, CZA.

85. Halifax to Eden, 15 Jan. 1943, FO 371/35031; United States Memoranda and Economic Notes, 2 Nov. 1942, FO 371/31380, PRO.

86. Emmanuel Neumann to Abba Hillel Silver, 19 Dec. 1941, F39 561, CZA.

87. *Jewish Telegraphic Agency News Bulletin*, 26 Mar. 1942.

88. See Kook-Silver correspondence, 12 Feb. 1941 and 3 Mar. 1941, and Kook-Wise correspondence during 1941, all in The Emergency Committee to Save the Jews of Europe, 7/2, JAI; Memorandum from the Committee for a Jewish Army of Stateless and Palestinian Jews, to the Emergency Committee for Zionist Affairs, 3 Dec. 1941, The Committee for a Jewish Army, 3/21, JAI; Shpiro, *From Philanthropy to Activism*, 110, 127–28.

89. Jewish Agency Executive, stenographic report, New York, 3 Aug. 1942, Z5 1201, CZA.

90. L. Levland to Alfred Strelsin, 16 Jan. 1943, The Emergency Committee to Save the Jews of Europe, 7/5, JAI; *New York Times*, 2 Mar. 1943.

91. Hava W. Eshkoli, "The Transnistrian Plan: An Opportunity for Rescue or a Deception," in *American Jewry During the Holocaust: A Report for the American Jewish Commission on the Holocaust*, ed. Seymour Maxwell Finger (New York: Holmes and Meier, 1984), 237–60. On the official American and British reaction to the proposal, see Wyman, *Abandonment*; "For Sale to Humanity 70,000 Jews: Guaranteed Human Beings at $50 a Piece," *New York Times*, 16 Feb. 1943.

92. *New York Herald Tribune*, 22 Feb. 1943; Hecht, *A Child*, 540–42.

93. Rafaeli-Baumel interview, 5 Sept. 1990; Nathan Glazer, *Ethnic Dilemmas, 1964–1982* (Cambridge, Mass: Harvard Univ. Press, 1983), 234; Alec Barbrook and Christine Bolt, *Power and Protest in American Life* (New York: St. Martin's Press, 1980), 105–7.

94. Marjorie R. Fallows, *Irish Americans: Identity and Assimilation* (Englewood Cliffs, N.J.: Prentice Hall, 1979), 54–55.

95. Kook interview, OHD, (55)b; Ben-Ami, *Years of Wrath*, 283; Halperin, *Political World*, 268.

96. Glazer, *Ethnic Dilemmas*, 27.

97. See Samuel Merlin, letter to the national headquarters of the American NZO, 4 Feb. 1942, The Committee for a Jewish Army, 3/22, JAI.

98. Lubar and van den Veen, "Functions of Various Groups," 1. The exact figure was $251,630.86. See Penkower, "In Dramatic Dissent," 82.

99. Shavit, *Jabotinsky*, 377.

100. Rafaeli-Baumel interview, 5 Sept. 1990; Kook interview, OHD, (55)b; Merlin interview, OHD, (67)1; Kook to Merlin, 25 Oct. 1942, Hillel Kook Collection, JAI.

101. *Hansard Parliamentary Debates* (Commons), 5th ser., vol. 383 (London, 4 July 1944), cols. 636–46.

102. Chaim Weizmann to Sir James Grigg, War Office, 28 Mar. 1944, Z5 1023, CZA; Shertok to Silver, 10 Oct., Z5 1208, CZA.

103. Irma Helpern, "The Jewish Brigade" (in Hebrew), *Hamashkif,* 12 Jan. 1945.

104. "The Bergson Group," an anonymous undated report, evidently from late 1947, David Niv Collection, 2/5, JAI. For a complete picture of what preceded the formation of the Jewish Brigade, see Gelber, *The Struggle,* 371–430; Bergson, telegram to Irma Helpern regarding responsibility for founding the brigade, 22 Sept. 1944, FO 371/40132, PRO.

105. Shpiro, *From Philanthropy to Activism,* 127.

4. A Time to Save

1. Eli Tzur, *The Second World War: The War That Changed the World* (in Hebrew) (Jerusalem: Ministry of Education, 1995), 47–57.

2. For a fuller treatment of the Bermuda Conference, see David Wyman, *Abandonment,* 104–23.

3. Minutes of the American Emergency Council for Zionist Affairs Office Committee Meeting, 1 June 1943, Silver Papers, Abba Hillel Silver Memorial Archives, quoted in Berman, *Nazism, the Jews,* 107; "To the Gentlemen at Bermuda . . ." *Washington Post,* 20 Apr. 1943; Ben-Ami, *Years of Wrath,* 289; "To 5,000,000 Jews in the Nazi Death-Trap Bermuda Was a Cruel Mockery," *New York Times,* 4 May 1943.

4. Truman to Bergson, 7 May 1943, and Bergson to Truman, 13 May 1943, The Emergency Committee to Save the Jews of Europe, 10/3, JAI.

5. Kook interview, OHD, (55)b; Kook-Baumel interview, 26 July 1990.

6. Rafaeli, *Dream and Action,* 104–5.

7. Ferman, *Analysis of an Interest Group,* 43.

8. Rafaeli, *Dream and Action,* 114.

9. Douglas, *Groups,* 143.

10. Committee for a Jewish Army of Stateless and Palestinian Jews, 1 July 1943, quoted in Feinstein, "The Irgun Campaign," 209.

11. Eri Jabotinsky, *My Father,* 160.

12. Halperin, *Political World,* 198–99.

13. Eri Jabotinsky, *My Father,* 161; Edwin C. Johnson, letter addressed to all signatories of the Declaration of the Moral Rights of Stateless and Palestinian Jews, 23 June 1943, The Emergency Committee to Save the Jews of Europe, ´, JAI.

14. Eri Jabotinsky to Aryeh Altman, 9 July 1943, The Committee for a Jewish Army, 4/35, JAI; Letter from the head office to Arieh Ben-Eliezer, 13 June 1943, The Emergency Committee to Save the Jews of Europe, 10/1, JAI.

15. Cordell Hull, telegram to participants of the Emergency Conference to Save the

Jewish People, quoted in Zaar, *Rescue and Liberation,* 44–45; Eleanor Roosevelt, telegram to participants of the Emergency Conference to Save the Jewish People, quoted ibid., 46.

16. Kook interview, OHD, (55)b.

17. See Baumel, *Unfulfilled Promise,* 28.

18. See, for example, Medoff, *The Deafening Silence,* 117–24.

19. Jonah B. Wise to Senator Edwin C. Johnson, 25 June 1943, C7 1378, CZA.

20. Ben-Ami, *Years of Wrath,* 578.

21. Ibid., appendix H.

22. Max Lerner, "What About the Jews, FDR?" *PM,* 22 July 1943.

23. Wyman, *Abandonment,* 147–48.

24. "The Bergson Group," *New York Times,* 2 Mar. 1943, David Niv Collection, 2/5, JAI.

25. Jonathan Kaplan, "Rescue Efforts by the Irgun Delegation in the United States During the Holocaust" (in Hebrew), *Yalkut Moreshet* 30 (1980): 122.

26. Shaw, *Group Dynamics,* 16–17.

27. Rafaeli-Baumel interview, 17 Oct. 1994.

28. Press release, 7 Dec. 1943, statement by Mr. George M. Morris, chairman of the Washington Committee to Save the Jewish People of Europe, The Emergency Committee to Save the Jews of Europe, 61, JAI.

29. Hecht, *A Child,* 529; Ben-Ami, *Years of Wrath,* 290.

30. Hecht, *A Child,* 542.

31. "My Uncle Abraham," quoted in Wyman, *Abandonment,* 154–55. See also Hecht, *A Child,* 543.

32. Kook interview, OHD, (55)b.

33. Quoted in Penkower, "Eleanor Roosevelt," 275–76.

34. Babette Deutsch, "Only the Living," Pierre van Paassen, "The Forgotten Ally," Henry Babette, "No Traveller Returns," William Ziff, "The Rape of Palestine," all found in Rafaeli Collection; Rafaeli, *Dream and Action,* 112.

35. Saidel, "Revisionist Zionism," 119–21.

36. Zaar, *Rescue and Liberation,* 58. On preparations for sending delegations abroad, see U.S. State Department to Steinhardt, 3 Sept. 1943, and Steinhardt to State Department, 7 Sept. 1943, Documents of the War Refugee Board (hereafter DWRB), Roosevelt Library.

37. *New York Times,* 7 Oct. 1943. For the vice president's reaction, see *Time,* 18 Oct. 1943, 21.

38. Wyman, *Abandonment,* 152–53.

39. *New York Times,* 1 Nov. 1943.

40. Phillip Monypenny, "Political Science and the Study of Groups: Notes to Guide a Research Project," *Western Political Quarterly* 7, no. 2 (June 1954): 198. Quoted in Halperin, *Political World,* 300.

41. On this conference, see Halperin, *Political World,* 219–51.

42. For an interesting description and analysis of ultra-Orthodox activity on behalf of rescue, see Joseph Friedenson and David H. Kranzler, *Heroine of Rescue* (New York: Meso-

rah, 1984). Notwithstanding the book's clear Agudath Israel bias, nonetheless it provides insight into ultra-Orthodox activity on behalf of rescue during the Holocaust.

43. David S. Wyman, "The American Jewish Leadership and the Holocaust," in *Jewish Leadership During the Nazi Era*, ed. Randolph L. Braham (New York: Social Science Monographs and Institute for Holocaust Studies of the City of New York, 1985), 24.

44. *Save Human Lives: Report of Activities and Financial Statement of the Emergency Committee to Save the Jewish People of Europe*, 1944, The Emergency Committee to Save the Jews of Europe, 1/1, JAI. Charles Levine ("Propaganda Techniques of the Bergson Group," 1974, 83) claims that the final figure was $423,252.68. See also Ferman, *Analysis of an Interest Group*, 91–93.

45. Rafaeli-Baumel interview, 17 Oct. 1994.

46. Halperin, *Political World*, 198–99. The financial data is cited by Ferman, *Analysis of an Interest Group*, 101.

47. "The Bergson Group," *Washington Post*, 3, 6, 7, 8 Oct. 1944, David Niv Collection, 2/5, JAI.

48. Meeting of the American Jewish Conference Interim Committee, 15 Dec. 1943, C7 1378, CZA.

49. Monsky, telegram to American Jewish Conference, 23 Dec. 1943, C7 1378, CZA.

50. Harold Ickes to Stephen S. Wise, 5 Jan. 1944, Z7 1378, CZA.

51. Moshe Shertok, telegram to Lipsky, 30 July 1944; memorandum by I. L. Kenen, public relations director of the American Jewish Conference, 11 May 1944, C7 1378, CZA.

52. Rafaeli-Baumel interview, 17 Oct. 1994; Ben-Ami, *Years of Wrath*, 296.

53. U.S. House of Representatives, Hearings before the Committee on Foreign Affairs, 1943, Rafaeli Collection.

54. Eri Jabotinsky, *My Father*, 162, quoted in Wyman, *Abandonment*, 200. An accusation using those very words appeared in a letter to him published in the *Jewish Times*, 24 Dec. 1943, quoted in David Morrison, *Heroes, Antiheroes and the Holocaust: American Jewry and Historical Choice* (Jerusalem: Milah Press, 1995), 235–36.

55. Peter Bergson to Henry Morgenthau, Jr., 26 Aug. 1943, The Emergency Committee to Save the Jews of Europe, 1/1, JAI; Morgenthau to Bergson, 3 Sept. 1943, DWRB, Roosevelt Library; "Report to the Secretary of the Acquiescence of This Government in the Murder of the Jews," DWRB, Roosevelt Library.

56. Executive Order 9417 Establishing a War Refugee Board, DWRB, Roosevelt Library.

57. Robert Silverberg, *If I Forget Thee O Jerusalem: American Jews and the State of Israel* (New York: William Morrow, 1970), 207; *New York Times*, 31 Dec. 1943, quoted in Wyman, *Abandonment*, 202; Statement of the American Jewish Conference, 15 Dec. 1943, C7 1378, CZA.

58. See FBI file on Peter Bergson, S. S. Alden memo to Mr. Ladd, 12 May 1943, quoted in Saidel, "Revisionist Zionism," 126–27. Saidel also cites an FBI document that argued that Hillel Kook had sought diplomatic immunity at one point, *evidently* as a means of avoiding the draft. But as he was found to be physically unfit to serve, this request must have served some other, probably diplomatic, purpose. FBI office memoran-

dum from E. A. Tamm to D. M. Ladd, Subject: Hillel Kook, 23 May 1944, 3, Rafaeli Collection.

59. Rafaeli, *Dream and Action,* 117; Rafaeli-Baumel interview, 17 Oct. 1994.

60. Barker et al., *Groups in Process,* 67; Eri Jabotinsky to Aryeh Altman, 9 July 1943, The Committee for a Jewish Army, 4/35, JAI.

61. Emergency Committee to Save the Jewish People of Europe—Special Release, Monday, 6 Dec. 1943, The Emergency Committee to Save the Jews of Europe, 1/6, JAI.

62. *Washington Post,* editorial, 13 Oct. 1944.

63. Regarding this debate, see Ferman, *Analysis of an Interest Group,* 145–50.

64. Ibid., 152.

65. Emergency Committee circular, Mar. 1944, Hillel Kook Collection, JAI ; Hillel Kook to Alexander Rafaeli, 27 June 1985, Rafaeli Collection.

66. Moshe Kolodny, Agudath Israel archivist, interview by Judith Tydor Baumel, New York, 22 June 1985.

67. See Morgenthau diaries, July 1943, Franklin Delano Roosevelt Library, Hyde Park, New York.

68. Zaar, *Rescue and Liberation,* 69; membership data taken from Halperin, *Political World,* appendix A, 317–20, and Penkower, "In Dramatic Dissent," 82; Moshe Arens, telephone interview by Judith Tydor Baumel, 7 Jan. 1996; Activity Report of the New England District to the New York Betar Headquarters, 18 Nov. 1946, Betar America Files, unnumbered, JAI.

69. Niv, *Battle for Freedom,* 274. David S. Wyman (*Abandonment,* 149n) notes that in March 1945 the FBI investigated the Bergson group in an effort to uncover evidence of an Irgun connection. Even though they found none, they thought there was a possibility that Ben-Eliezer had sent a few hundred dollars to the Irgun.

70. Ben-Ami, *Years of Wrath,* 300.

71. Ibid., 302–3.

72. On the condition of the LHI at that time, see Heller, *The Stern Gang;* Ben-Ami, *Years of Wrath,* 305–6.

73. Ben-Ami, *Years of Wrath,* 307.

74. State Department telegram to Ankara, 4 Oct. 1943, and Ankara to State Department, 7 Oct. 1943, and additional correspondence from Feb. 1944; Ira Hirschmann to John Pehle, 22 Apr. 1944; Henry Montor to John Pehle, 19 June 1944; John Pehle to Henry Montor, 27 June 1944; Steinhardt, telegram to State Department, 30 June 1944; and Henry Morgenthau, Jr., to Dr. Hans Cohen, 17 Aug. 1944, all in DWRB, Roosevelt Library.

75. Aryeh Morgenstern, "The Jewish Relief Committee" (in Hebrew), *Yalkut Moreshet* 13 (1971): 60–103; Dalia Ofer, "Relief and Rescue Activity by the Palestinian Jewish Delegation to Istanbul, 1943" (M.A. thesis, Hebrew Univ., 1972).

76. Report by Eri Jabotinsky to the Emergency Committee to Save the Jewish People of Europe, Ankara, 14 June 1944, DWRB, Roosevelt Library.

77. Eri Jabotinsky to Hillel Kook, 20 Nov. 1944, The Emergency Committee to Save the Jews of Europe, 3/4, JAI; Monty N. Penkower, *The Jews Were Expendable* (Urbana: Univ. of Illinois Press, 1983), 173–75.

78. Dalia Ofer, "Independent Revisionist Movement Aliyah" (in Hebrew), in *Ha-apala: Studies in the History of Illegal Immigration into Palestine, 1934–1948*, ed. Anita Shapira (Tel Aviv: Am Oved, 1990), 44–60; Dalia Ofer, "Illegal Immigration During the Second World War: Its Suspension and Subsequent Resumption," *Studies in Contemporary Jewry* 7 (1991): 239–40; Eri Jabotinsky to Joseph Klarman, 1 Nov. 1944, The Emergency Committee to Save the Jews of Europe, 4/3, JAI.

79. "Arrest of Jew by Turkey Laid to British Trick," *New York World Telegram*, 6 Mar. 1945; Stettinus to John Pehle, 22 Jan. 1945, DWRB, Roosevelt Library.

80. Douglas, *Groups*, 14.

81. Data taken from Wyman, *Abandonment*, 213–14.

82. John Pehle to Stettinus, 15 Feb. 1944, DWRB, Roosevelt Library.

83. "25 Square Miles or 2 Million Lives, Which Shall It Be?" *Washington Post*, 29 May 1944; *Islands, Free Ports, Haven for Refugees*, Emergency Committee pamphlet, early 1944, The Emergency Committee to Save the Jews of Europe, 3/2, JAI; Sharon R. Lowenstein, *Token Refuge: The Story of the Jewish Refugee Shelter at Oswego, 1944–46* (Bloomington: Indiana Univ. Press, 1986); presidential secretary William Hasset to Peter Bergson, 19 June 1944, The Hebrew Committee of National Liberation, 7/13, JAI.

84. American secretary of state to the American consulate in London, telegram, 3 June 1944, DWRB, Roosevelt Library.

85. Undated report of the American Jewish Conference [June 1944?], C7 28, CZA.

86. Penkower, "In Dramatic Dissent," 78–79; Rabbi Eliezer Silver, declaration of support for resolution calling for temporary shelters for refugees to be set up in Palestine, The Emergency Committee to Save the Jews of Europe, 1/6, JAI; John Pehle to Henry Morgenthau, Jr., 9 June 1944, Morgenthau Files, Roosevelt Library; "Summary of Steps Taken by War Refugee Board of Hungary with Respect to Jews," DWRB, Roosevelt Library.

87. Shmuel Ben-Zion, "The Musy Train: Negotiations with Heinrich Himmler Through Dr. Jean-Marie Musy to Rescue Jews from German Concentrations Camps (Fall 1944-Spring 1945" (in Hebrew), *Dappim LeHekker HaShoah* 8 (1990): 135–61; Reuven Hecht-Baumel interview, 22 Aug. 1990; Isaac Sternbuch to Monsignor Bernardini, 4 Oct. 1945, Hecht Archives, 10/1/K/124; Stettinus, telegram to the American embassy in Berne, 28 Nov. 1944; Grew, telegram to Harrison and McClleland, 2 Mar. 1945, DWRB, Roosevelt Library.

88. Hecht-Baumel interview, 22 Aug. 1990; McClleland to General William O'Dwyer, 17 Apr. 1945, DWRB, Roosevelt Library.

89. Napier and Gershenfeld, *Groups*, 148–50, 201.

90. Ferman, *Analysis of an Interest Group*, 80; Penkower, "In Dramatic Dissent," 77.

91. Eri Jabotinsky, *My Father*, 163.

92. Louis Rappaport, "The Hoskins Affairs," *Jerusalem Post*, 23 Nov. 1984, 5.

93. Frances Gunther to the members, 14 May 1945, The Emergency Committee to Save the Jews of Europe, 13/1, JAI.

94. "A Final Message from the Emergency Committee to Save the Jewish People of Europe to its Co-fighters for a Decent Humanity," The Emergency Committee to Save the Jews of Europe, 12/1, JAI.

95. For example, Ferman; Wyman, *Abandonment;* Penkower, "In Dramatic Dissent"; Feingold, *Politics of Rescue;* and Feinstein, "The Irgun Campaign."

96. Douglas, *Groups,* 49–50.

97. Halperin, *Political World,* 300–301.

98. Dorwin Cartwright and Alvin Zander, eds., *Group Dynamics: Research and Theory* (Evanston: Univ. of Illinois Press, 1960), 487–88; Edward Lehman, "The Macrosociology of Empowerment" (in Hebrew), in *State and Society: Problems in Political Sociology,* ed. Samuel N. Eisenstadt (Tel Aviv: Am Oved, 1976), 49–62.

99. Bauer, *American Jewry;* Dina Porat, "Palestinian Jewry and the Jewish Agency: Public Response to the Holocaust," in *Vision and Conflict in the Holy Land,* ed. Richard I. Cohen (New York: Palgrave MacMillan, 1985), 268.

100. Penkower, "In Dramatic Dissent," 82; Halperin, *Political World,* 317–20.

101. Niv, *Battle for Freedom,* 133; Wyman, *The Abandonment,* 328, 285.

102. Penkower, "In Dramatic Dissent," 79–85.

103. Feingold, *Politics of Rescue,* 238–39.

104. Halperin, *Political World,* 279.

105. *New York Times,* 27 Sept. 1981.

106. Yehuda Bauer to Seymour Maxwell Finger, 26 Apr. 1982, Rafaeli Collection.

107. *New York Times,* 4 Jan. 1983, 20 Jan. 1983; Seymour Maxwell Finger, ed., *American Jewry During the Holocaust (A Report for the American Jewish Commission on the Holocaust)* (New York: Holmes and Meier, 1984), 237–60.

108. Samuel Merlin to Seymour Maxwell Finger, 27 May 1982, Rafaeli Collection.

109. Lucy Dawidowicz, "Indicting American Jews," *Commentary* 75 (June 1983): 36–44.

5. A Time to Build

1. Hecht, *A Child,* 553–54.

2. Uri Greenberg, *Collected Works* (in Hebrew), vol. 5, *Rechovot ha-Nahar,* ed. Dan Meron (Jerusalem: Mossad Bialik, 1992), 53. ("Would that our martyrs could raise our blinds, look directly into our windows, and see how we live our lives: It is hell for them and heaven surrounds us . . .")

3. For a treatment of the parachutists' mission in historical perspective, see Judith Tydor Baumel, " 'Parachuting to Their People': The Operation of the Parachutist-Emissaries During World War II in Historical Perspective," *Yad Vashem Studies* 25 (1996): 137–80.

4. Heller, *The Stern Gang,* 61–126.

5. Niv, *Battle for Freedom,* 102.

6. Eri Jabotinsky, *My Father,* 160; "Memorandum on the Activities of the Free Palestine Committee in the United States of America 1941–1943," The Committee for a Jewish Army, 3/21, JAI.

7. Yitzhak Ben-Ami to Peter Bergson, 13 Aug. 1943, The Committee for a Jewish Army, 3/21, JAI.

8. Bergson to Bergson [*sic*], 16 Sept. 1943, The Committee for a Jewish Army, 3/21, JAI; protocols of a meeting of the Free Palestine Committee, 3 Apr. 1944, The Hebrew Committee of National Liberation, ´, JAI.

9. G. Zifroni, "The Embassy That Wasn't" (in Hebrew), *Maariv*, 9 Oct. 1977, 26; report by the league's founding committee, 24 Apr. 1944 and 8 May 1944, both in The Hebrew Committee of National Liberation, ´, JAI; Roberts and McInnes to the Commissioner of the District of Columbia concerning purchase of the "embassy," 13 June 1944, The Hebrew Committee of National Liberation, 2/3, JAI.

10. Press release from the 9 May press conference marking the founding of the HCNL, The Hebrew Committee of National Liberation, 3/1, JAI. See also Halifax memo to the British Foreign Office, 19 May 1944, FO 371/40131, PRO.

11. On Gurevitch and his thought, see Porath, 119–57; see also Ya'akov Shavit, *The New Hebrew Nation: A Study in Israeli Heresy and Fantasy* (London: Frank Cass, 1987).

12. Merlin interview, OHD, (67)1.

13. Marie Syrkin, "Bombs in Haifa, Bombast in New York," *Jewish Frontier*, May 1944, 20–22.

14. Rafaeli-Baumel interview, 22 May 1995.

15. "The Bergson Boys," David Niv Collection, 2/5; "Hebrew Committee for National Liberation Established: Attacked by Jewish Groups," *Jewish Telegraphic Agency*, 19 May 1944, 1; "National Council Warns Against Compromise on Palestine: Takes Adverse Stand Toward Hebrew Committee," *Zionnews Magazine*, 16 July 1944, 4–5.

16. Ben-Ami, *Years of Wrath*, 355–56.

17. *New York Post*, 26 June 1944.

18. Kook interview, OHD, (55)b.

19. Zaar, *Rescue and Liberation*, 107–8.

20. See, for example, Aviva Halamish, *The Exodus Affair: Holocaust Survivors and the Struggle for Palestine* (Syracuse, N.Y.: Syracuse Univ. Press, 1998).

21. Ben-Ami, *Years of Wrath*, 372.

22. Rafaeli, *Dream and Action*, 148.

23. Ben-Ami, *Years of Wrath*, 355.

24. Ibid., 356.

25. Ibid., 357.

26. See, for example, Yechiam Weitz, "The Role of *Sheerith Hapleta* in Jewish Agency Executive Deliberations (May-November 1945)" (in Hebrew), *Yalkut Moreshet* 29 (May 1980): 53–80; Yechiam Weitz, "The Yishuv and *Sheerith Hapleta*, 1944–45" (M.A. thesis, Hebrew Univ., 1981); Yechiam Weitz, "The Zionist Movement Facing the Surviving Remnants at the End of World War II" (in Hebrew), *Dappim LeHeker HaShoah* 3 (1984): 139–58.

27. Memo, Washington to Halifax concerning the principles of the HCNL, 19 May 1944, FO 371/40131, PRO; Zaar, *Rescue and Liberation*, 128–32.

28. Zaar, *Rescue and Liberation*, 132; Niv, *Battle for Freedom*, 188–89.

29. Peter Bergson to Chaim Weizmann, 2 Apr. 1945, Chaim Weizmann Archives, Rehovot, quoted in Penkower, "In Dramatic Dissent," 81–82.

30. Saidel, "Revisionist Zionism," 208–9.

31. Niv, *Battle for Freedom*, 186–87.

32. Rafaeli, *Dream and Action*, 154–55.

33. Ibid., 150–51.

34. Zaar, *Rescue and Liberation*, 149.

35. Stanley Rothman and S. Robert Lichter, *Roots of Radicalism: Jews, Christians, and the New Left* (New York: Oxford Univ. Press, 1982), 98–99.

36. Halperin, *Political World*, 214–15, 258–59.

37. Ben-Ami, *Years of Wrath*, 406.

38. Zaar, *Rescue and Liberation*, 217.

39. Score of *A Flag Is Born*, Rafaeli Collection.

40. Quoted in Chancery to Eastern Department Foreign Office, 5 Dec. 1946, FO 371/52571, PRO.

41. Ben Hecht, *A Child*, 571–75.

42. Rafaeli, *Dream and Action*, 160–62.

43. Niv, *Battle for Freedom*, 191–93.

44. Ibid., 185. On the British administration's attitude toward this delegation, see Henderson to Baker, 28 Nov. 1945, CO 733/461, PRO.

45. Ben-Ami, *Years of Wrath*, 381–83; Zipporah Levy Kassel-Baumel interview, 6 Feb. 1996; author's correspondence with Harry Selden.

46. Johan Smertenko to G. M. Martin, Office of Colonial Affairs, 21 Dec. 1945, CO 733/461, PRO. See also "Statement of the American League for a Free Palestine Policy on the Declaration of His Majesty's Government's Regarding Palestine," CO 33/461, PRO.

47. Hecht-Penkower interview, Hecht Archives, Haifa.

48. Ben-Ami, *Years of Wrath*, 404–5.

49. Douglas, *Groups*, 29–30.

50. Rafaeli-Baumel interview, 22 May 1995.

51. Ben-Ami, *Years of Wrath*, 435–37.

52. Douglas, *Groups*, 41–50, Barker et al., *Groups in Process*, 63–64.

53. Zaar, *Rescue and Liberation*, 210–12.

54. Halifax to Foreign Minister Eden, 20 Oct. 1944, FO 371/40132, PRO; Henderson to Baker, 28 Nov. 1945, CO 733/461, PRO; Russell to Foreign Office, 5 Mar. 1945, FO 371/50972, PRO.

55. Russell to London Foreign Office, 5 Mar. 1945, FO 371/50972, PRO; Chancery to Foreign Office, 6 Aug. 1945, FO 371/45349, PRO.

56. Chancery to Foreign Office, 7 July 1945, FO 371/45349, PRO.

57. Hecht, *A Child*, 576.

58. "Hebrew Committee for National Liberation Established: Attacked by Jewish Groups," *Bulletin of the Jewish Telegraphic Agency*, 19 May 1944.

59. Goldman to Roux, 28 Dec. 1944; A. Lourie to M. Cohen, 24 Nov. 1944; Goldman to Mead, 28 June 1944; Release of the AZEC regarding rabbis, 1 June 1944; American Jewish Trade Union Committee for Palestine release, 2 June 1944; all found in Z5 395, CZA.

60. Wyman, *Abandonment,* 345–47.

61. "The Bergson Group," David Niv Collection, 2/5, JAI.

62. Moshe Arens, telephone interview by Judith Tydor Baumel, 7 Jan. 1996. See also Arens's correspondence with Betar officer A. Propes regarding activist activity, Arens to Propes, 20 July 1946, Betar America Files, unnumbered, JAI; *Tzofe Betar II* 2, 25 Nov. 1948; *New York Herald Tribune,* 20 Apr. 1947; "Betar in Action," *Tel-Chai,* 9 Mar. 1950, Betar America Files, unnumbered, JAI.

63. Ben-Ami, *Years of Wrath,* 390.

64. Kook interview, OHD, (55)b.

65. Katz, *Days of Fire,* 71–72.

66. Kister, 145–49.

67. Tavin, *The Second Front,* 111.

68. Rafaeli-Baumel interview, 17 Oct. 1994.

69. Yaakov Meridor to Menachem Begin, undated, quoted in Tavin, *The Second Front,* 129.

70. Ibid., 128–29.

71. Heller, *The Stern Gang,* 157–58; Ben-Ami, *Years of Wrath,* 360–63.

72. Rafaeli, *Dream and Action,* 157.

73. Ibid.

74. Harry Louis Selden, correspondence with Alex Rafaeli, 26 Jan. 1996, Rafaeli Collection.

75. On this historiographical debate, see Niv, *Battle for Freedom,* 267–68; Yehuda Slutsky, *History of the Hagana* (in Hebrew), vol. 3, part 2, *From Resistance to War* (Tel Aviv: Am Oved, 1973), 1540–58; Zerubavel Gilead, ed. *Book of the Palmach* (in Hebrew), vol. 2 (Tel Aviv: Hakibbutz Hameuchad, 1956), 553–55; Uri Brenner, *Altalena: A Political and Military Study* (in Hebrew) (Tel Aviv: Hakibbutz Hameuchad, 1978).

76. Tavin, *The Second Front,* 259–60; Yonatan Shapiro, *Chosen to Command: The Road to Power of the Herut Party—A Socio-political Interpretation* (in Hebrew) (Tel Aviv: Am Oved, 1989); Arnold Sherman, *The Kindling: A Biography of Arieh Ben-Eliezer* (in Hebrew) (Jerusalem: Edanim, 1986), 164.

77. Napier and Gershenfeld, *Groups,* 467.

78. Halperin, *Political World,* 312.

79. Ben-Ami, *Years of Wrath,* 470; Harry Louis Selden to Louis Rappaport, 8 Dec. 1982, Selden Collection.

80. Katz, *Lone Wolf,* 117–18.

81. Aryeh Altman interview, OHD, 67(5).

82. Ben-Ami, *Years of Wrath,* 334.

83. Feingold, *Politics of Rescue,* 280–81.

84. Berman, *Nazism, the Jews,* 131.

85. Ibid., 133.

86. Frank W. Brecher, " 'The Western Allies and the Holocaust': David Wyman and the Historiography of America's Response to the Holocaust, Counter-considerations," *Holocaust and Genocide Studies* 5 (1990): 423–46.

87. Penkower, "In Dramatic Dissent," 84.

6. A Time to Evaluate

1. Kook-Baumel interview, 26 July 1990; Ben-Ami, *Years of Wrath,* epilogue; Eri Jabotinsky, *The Sakarya Expedition;* Sherman, 78–96; Samuel Merlin to Alexander Rafaeli, 27 Mar. 1990, Rafaeli Collection; Rafaeli-Baumel interview, 17 Oct. 1994.

2. John Keegan, *Battle for History: Re-Fighting World War II* (New York: Vintage Books, 1995), 28.

3. Stanley Payne, *A History of Fascism, 1914–1945* (Madison: Univ. of Wisconsin Press, 1995), 3.

4. Hans Rogger and Eugene Weber, eds., *The European Right: A Historical Profile* (Berkeley: Univ. of California Press, 1965); Ze'ev Sternhel, *Neither Right nor Left: Fascist Ideology in France* (in Hebrew) (Tel Aviv: Am Oved, 1984); Shavit, *Jabotinsky.*

5. Rogger and Weber, *The European Right,* 7.

6. Sternhel, 19; Rogger and Weber, *The European Right,* 2; Shavit, *Jabotinsky,* 1–3; Seymour M. Lipset and Earl Raab, *Jews and the New American Scene* (Cambridge, Mass.: Harvard Univ. Press, 1995), 151.

7. Shavit, *Jabotinsky,* 23–41.

8. Bergson to Bergson [*sic*], 16 Sept. 1943, H 13/4/35, JAI; undated report (late 1947), David Niv Collection, 2/5, JAI.

9. Oscar Handlin, *Race and Nationality in American Life* (Boston: Little, Brown, 1948), 250.

10. Eri Jabotinsky to Aryeh Altman, 9 June 1943, The Committee for a Jewish Army, 4/35, JAI.

11. Jonathan Boyarin, ed., *Remapping Memory: The Politics of TimeSpace* (Minneapolis: Univ. of Minnesota Press, 1994), 23.

12. Hayden White, "Narrativity in the Representation of Reality," in *The Content of the Form* (Baltimore: Johns Hopkins Univ. Press, 1987), 21–25; Hayden White, "Historical Emplotment and the Problem of Truth," in *Probing the Limits of Representation: Nazism and the Final Solution,* ed. Saul Friedlander (Cambridge, Mass.: Harvard Univ. Press, 1992), 39.

13. Glazer, *Ethnic Dilemmas,* 234; Donald L. Horowitz, *Ethnic Groups in Conflict* (Berkeley: Univ. of California Press, 1987), 29; Hubert M. Blalock, Jr., *Race and Ethnic Relations* (Englewood Cliffs, N.J.: Prentice Hall, 1982), 22; Esman, *Ethnic Conflict in the Western World,* 387; Robert A. LeVine and Donald T. Campbell, *Ethnocentrism: Theories of Conflict, Ethnic Attitudes and Group Behavior* (New York: John Wiley, 1972), 7; Charles Frederick Marden and Gladys Meyer, *Minorities in American Society,* 4th ed. (New York: Van Nostrand, 1973), 2.

14. Ferman, *Analysis of an Interest Group,* 155.

15. Barbrook and Bolt, *Power and Protest,* 65–67; 106–7.

16. Esman, *Ethnic Conflict,* 388–89.

17. Ferman, *Analysis of an Interest Group,* 158–59; Esman, *Ethnic Conflict,* 388; Blalock, *Race and Ethnic Relations,* 109; LeVine and Campbell, *Ethnocentrism,* 32, 118; Cynthia Enloe, *Ethnic Conflict and Political Development* (Boston: Little, Brown, 1973), 9;

Judith Tydor Baumel, "The IZL Delegation in the USA, 1939–1948: Anatomy of an Ethnic Interest/Protest Group," *Jewish History* 9, no. 1 (1995): 79–89.

18. Horowitz, *Ethnic Groups in Conflict*, 396–97; Rothschild, *Ethnopolitics*, 192–202; Bayard Rustin, *Strategies for Freedom* (New York: Columbia Univ. Press, 1976), 26, 38–39.

19. Rafaeli-Baumel interview, 5 Oct. 1990.

20. Fallows, *Irish Americans*, 54–55; Con Howard, David Noel Doyle, and Owen Dudley Edwards, eds., *America and Ireland, 1776–1976: The American Identity and the Irish Connection* (Westport, Conn.: Greenwood, 1980), 117–32.

21. William Orbach, *The American Movement to Aid Soviet Jewry* (Amherst: Univ. of Massachusetts Press, 1979), 10–180.

22. Ibid., 199.

23. Robert Friedman, *The False Prophet* (London: Faber and Faber, 1990), 83–85; Shlomo Mordechai Russ, "The 'Zionist Hooligans': The Jewish Defense League" (Ph.D. diss., City Univ. of New York, 1981), 26–28.

24. Friedman, *The False Prophet*, 9–10.

25. Meir Kahane, *The Story of the Jewish Defense League* (Radnor, Penn.: Chilton, 1975), 141; Friedman, *The False Prophet*, 33; Ehud Shprinzak, "Kach and Meir Kahane: The Emergency of Jewish Quasi-Fascism II: Ideology and Politics," *Patterns of Prejudice* 19, no. 4 (1985): 4.

26. Kahane, *The Story*, 86; Friedman, *The False Prophet*, 122.

27. *Jewish Press*, 6 Sept. 1968; Kahane, *The Story*.

28. Betar booklets (Betar America Files), JAI; Hasia R. Diner, *In the Almost Promised Land: American Jews and Blacks, 1915–1935* (Westport, Conn.: Greenwood, 1977); Thomas J. Cottle, *Hidden Survivors: Portraits of Poor Jews in America* (Englewood Cliffs, N.J.: Prentice Hall, 1980).

29. *Jewish Press*, 2 Jan. 1970.

30. Friedman, *The False Prophet*, 120.

31. Kahane, *The Story*, 227.

32. Friedman, *The False Prophet*, 122.

33. Esther Ashkenazi, *Betar in Eretz Yisrael, 1925–1947* (in Hebrew) (Jerusalem: Sifriya Tzionit and Mossad Bialik, 1997).

34. Meir Kahane, *Never Again* (Los Angeles: Nash, 1971), 143–44.

35. Kahane, *The Story*, 86.

36. Kahane, *Never Again*, 155–58; Kahane, *The Story*, 133.

37. Kahane, *The Story*, 99–100.

38. Meir Kahane, "Jabotinsky," *The Jewish Press*, 17 July 1970. Kahane lauded Irgun militarism as part of "the righteous Jewish National Liberation Movement." Kahane, *Never Again*, 186–87; Meir Kahane, *Our Challenge; The Chosen Land* (Radnor, Penn.: Chilton, 1974), 104.

39. Kook interview, OHD, (55)b; Rafaeli-Baumel interview, 17 Oct. 1994.

40. Kahane, *The Story*, 80–84.

41. Chaim I. Waxman, "An American Tragedy—Meir Kahane and Kahanism: A Review Essay," *American Jewish History* 78, no. 3 (1980): 433; Kahane, *Our Challenge*, 94.

42. The bombings at Intourist and Aeroflot took place on 23 December 1970, and those at other Soviet targets in January, March, April, and June 1971. For more about the merger between Betar and the JDL, see Friedman, 119. See also Joyce Lee Malcolm, *To Keep and Bear Arms: The Origins of an Anglo-American Right* (Cambridge, Mass.: Harvard Univ. Press, 1994).

43. Friedman, *The False Prophet,* 93.

44. Ibid., 10–111; Orbach, 19–58.

45. *New York Times,* 26 May 1970.

46. Friedman, *The False Prophet,* 124.

47. Judith Tydor Baumel, "Right-wing Ideologies Among American Jews: The Seductive Myth of Power in Crisis," *Nationalism and Ethnic Politics* 4, no. 4 (1998): 75–109.

48. Simon Schama, *Landscape and Memory* (New York: A. A. Knopf, 1995), 12.

Glossary

aliyah: immigration to Palestine or the State of Israel

aliyah bet: illegal immigration to Palestine during the mandatory period

Canaanites: a school of thought that attempted to historically merge the Jews of Palestine into a pan-Middle Eastern framework

conversos: Spanish and Portuguese secret Jews living as Christians for fear of the Inquisition

landsmanshaft/en: a Jewish organization of *landsleit* (people from a particular town, city, or area) organized especially for social and philanthropic purposes

Netziv Betar: Betar commander

rashomon: A story told from different perspectives by a number of people involved (based on the title of the movie by Akira Korasowa)

sheerith hapleta: Jewish displaced persons

Yishuv: the Jewish settlement in Palestine in the pre-State era

Bibliography

Primary Sources

Archival Materials

Public Record Office, London (PRO)
Franklin Delano Roosevelt Library, Hyde Park, New York
    Documents of the War Refugee Board (DWRB)
    Morgenthau Diaries
    Morgenthau Files
Jabotinsky Archives in Israel (JAI)
    Zeev Jabotinsky Collection
    Betar America Files
    The Committee for a Jewish Army
    The London Committee for a Jewish Army
    The Hebrew Committee of National Liberation
    The American Friends of the League for a Free Palestine
    The Emergency Committee to Save the Jews of Europe
    Yirmiyahu Helpern Collection
    Hillel Kook Collection
    David Niv Collection
Central Zionist Archives, Jerusalem (CZA)

Personal Collections

Selden Collection: Harry Louis Selden's personal papers, New York
Rafaeli Collection: Dr. Alexander Rafaeli's personal papers, Jerusalem
Hecht Archives, Haifa
Wise Papers, American Jewish Historical Archives, Waltham, Massachusetts

Interviews

Interviews by Author

Arens, Moshe. Telephone interview, 7 Jan. 1996.
Hecht, Reuven. Haifa, 22 Aug. 1990.
Kassel, Zipporah Levy. Jerusalem, 6 Feb. 1996.
Kolodny, Moshe. 1985. New York, 22 June 1985.
Kook, Hillel. Telephone interview, 26 July 1990.
Rafaeli, Alexander. 5 Sept. 1990, 17 Oct. 1994, 22 May 1995, 12 Oct. 1995.

Interviews at Oral History Documentation Center,
Institute for Contemporary Jewry, Hebrew University (OHD)

Altman, Aryeh. (67)5.
Kook, Hillel. (55)b.
Merlin, Samuel. OHD (67)1.
Rafaeli, Alexander. (67)4.

Interviews by Marsha Feinstein

Ben-Ami, Yitzhak. New York, Apr. 1971.
Kook, Hillel. New York, Apr. 1971.
Merlin, Samuel. New York, Apr. 1971.

Interviews by Monty N. Penkower

Hecht, Reuven. Hecht Archives, Haifa.

Newspapers

Chicago Sun
Congress Weekly
Philadelphia Evening Bulletin
Jerusalem Post
Jewish Chronicle
Jewish Frontier
Jewish Press
Jewish Telegraphic Agency News Bulletin
Jewish Times
New York Herald Tribune
New York Times

New York World Telegram
Pittsburgh Post Gazette
PM
Time
Washington Post
Zionnews Magazine

Congressional and Parliamentary Records

Congressional Record. Vol. 87, 77th Congress. Washington, D.C.: U.S. Government Printing Office, 1941.

Congressional Record. Vol. 88, 77th Congress. Washington, D.C.: U.S. Government Printing Office, 1942.

Hansard 1942. *Hansard Parliamentary Debates (Commons),* 5th ser., vol. 383. London.

Hansard 1944. *Hansard Parliamentary Debates (Commons).*

U.S. House of Representatives. "Hearings before the Committee on Foreign Affairs." House of Representatives, 78th Congress, H. Res. 350 and 352, 26 Oct. Washington, D.C.: U.S. Government Printing Office, 1943.

Published Sources

Alfasi, Isaac, ed. *Irgun Zvai Leumi: Collection of Archival Sources* (in Hebrew). Vol. 1. Tel Aviv: Jabotinsky Institute in Israel, 1980.

Ashkenazi, Esther. *Betar in Eretz Yisrael, 1925–1947* (in Hebrew). Jerusalem: Sifriya Tzionit and Mossad Bialik, 1977.

Banks, Dean. "Creating an American Dilemma: The Impact of Nazi Racism upon American Intergroup Relations, 1933–1940, with Special Reference to Jewish Americans, German-Americans and the Free Speech Movement." Ph.D. diss., Univ. of Texas, 1975.

Barbrook, Alec, and Christine Bolt. *Power and Protest in American Life.* New York: St. Martin's Press, 1980.

Barker, Larry L. et al., eds. *Groups in Process: An Introduction to Small Group Communication.* 2d ed. Englewood Cliffs, N.J.: Prentice Hall, 1983.

Bauer, Yehuda. *American Jewry and the Holocaust: The American Joint Distribution Committee, 1939–1945.* Detroit, Mich.: Wayne State Univ. Press, 1981.

———. *From Diplomacy to Resistance: A History of Jewish Palestine, 1939–1945.* Translated by Alton M. Winters. Philadelphia: Jewish Publication Society, 1970.

————. "Jewish Foreign Policy During the Holocaust." *Midstream*, Dec. 1984, 8–11.

————. *My Brother's Keeper: A History of the American Joint Distribution Committee, 1929–1939.* Philadelphia: Jewish Publication Society, 1974.

Baumel, Judith Tydor. "The IZL Delegation in the USA, 1939–1948: Anatomy of an Ethnic Interest/Protest Group." *Jewish History* 9, no. 1 (1995): 79–89.

————. " 'Parachuting to Their People': The Operation of the Parachutist-Emissaries During World War II in Historical Perspective." *Yad Vashem Studies* 25 (1996): 137–80.

————. "Right-wing Ideologies Among American Jews: The Seductive Myth of Power in Crisis." *Nationalism and Ethnic Politics* 4, no.4 (1998): 75–109.

————. *Unfulfilled Promise: Rescue and Resettlement of Jewish Refugee Children in the United States, 1934–1945.* Juneau, Alaska: Denali Press, 1990.

Ben-Ami, Yitzhak. *Years of Wrath, Days of Glory: Memoirs from the Irgun.* 2d ed. New York: Shengold, 1983.

Ben Yerucham, Ch. [Merchavia, Chen-Melech]. *Sepher Betar. Book of Betar: History and Sources* (in Hebrew). Vol. 1, *From the People.* Jerusalem: Publishing Committee of Sepher Betar, 1969.

————. *Sepher Betar* (in Hebrew). Vol. 2, *From the People.* Jerusalem: Publishing Committee of Sepher Betar, 1976.

Ben-Zion, Shmuel. "The Musy Train: Negotiations with Heinrich Himmler Through Dr. Jean-Marie Musy to Rescue Jews from German Concentration Camps (Fall 1944-Spring 1945)" (in Hebrew). *Dappim LeHeker HaShoah* 8 (1990): 135–61.

Berman, Aaron. *Nazism, the Jews and American Zionism, 1933–1948.* Detroit, Mich.: Wayne State Univ. Press, 1990.

Berne, Eric. *The Structure and Dynamics of Organizations and Groups.* New York: Ballantine Books, 1974.

Blalock, Hubert M., Jr. *Race and Ethnic Relations.* Englewood Cliffs, N.J.: Prentice Hall, 1982.

Boyarin, Jonathan, ed. *Remapping Memory: The Politics of TimeSpace.* Minneapolis: Univ. of Minnesota Press, 1994.

Brecher, Frank W. " 'The Western Allies and the Holocaust': David Wyman and the Historiography of America's Response to the Holocaust, Counter-considerations." *Holocaust and Genocide Studies* 5 (1990): 423–46.

Brenner, Uri. *Altalena: A Political and Military Study* (in Hebrew). Tel Aviv: Hakibbutz Hameuchad, 1978.

Carroll, Eber M. *American Opinion and the Irish Question, 1910–23: A Study in Opinion and Policy.* Dublin, Ireland: Gill and Macmillan and St. Martin's Press, 1978.

Cartwright, Dorwin, and Alvin Zander, eds. *Group Dynamics: Research and Theory.* Evanston: Univ. of Illinois Press, 1960.

Cohen, Naomi Wiener. *Not Free to Desist: The American Jewish Committee, 1906–1966.* Philadelphia: JPS, 1972.

Cottle, Thomas J. *Hidden Survivors: Portraits of Poor Jews in America.* Englewood Cliffs, N.J.: Prentice-Hall, 1980.

Dawidowicz, Lucy S. "Indicting American Jews." *Commentary* 75 (June 1983): 36–44.

Diner, Hasia R. *In the Almost Promised Land: American Jews and Blacks, 1915–1935.* Westport, Conn.: Greenwood, 1977.

Douglas, Tom. *Groups: Understanding People Gathered Together.* London: Tavistock, 1983.

Elam, Yigal. "The Development of Defensive and Underground Organizations: The Underground and Military Aspects of the Jewish Yishuv under the Mandate" (in Hebrew). In *The History of Eretz Israel.* Vol. 9, *The British Mandate and the Jewish National Home.* Jerusalem: Keter, 1990.

Elazar, Daniel Judah. *Community and Polity: The Organizational Dynamics of American Jewry.* Philadelphia: JPS, 1976.

Enloe, Cynthia. *Ethnic Conflict and Political Development.* Boston: Little, Brown, 1973.

Erikson, Robert S., and Norman R. Luttbeg. *American Public Opinion: Its Origins, Content, and Impact.* New York: John Wiley and Sons, 1973.

Eshkoli, Hava W. "The Transnistrian Plan: An Opportunity for Rescue or a Deception." In *American Jewry During the Holocaust (A Report for the American Jewish Commission on the Holocaust),* edited by Seymour Maxwell Finger, 237–60. New York: Holmes and Meier, 1984.

Esman, Milton J., ed. *Ethnic Conflict in the Western World.* Ithaca, N.Y.: Cornell Univ. Press, 1977.

Everson, David E. *Public Opinion and Interest Groups in American Politics.* New York: Franklin Watts, 1982.

Fallows, Marjorie R. *Irish Americans: Identity and Assimilation.* Englewood Cliffs, N.J.: Prentice Hall, 1979.

Feingold, Harry L. *The Politics of Rescue: The Roosevelt Administration and the Holocaust.* New Brunswick, N.J.: Rutgers Univ. Press, 1970.

Feinstein, Marsha. "The Irgun Campaign in the United States for a Jewish Army." M.A. thesis, City Univ. of New York, 1973.

Ferman, Yonah. "Analysis of an Interest Group: The Emergency Committee to Save the Jewish People of Europe, July 1943-August 1944." Ph.D. diss., Hebrew Univ., 1965.

Finger, Seymour Maxwell, ed. *American Jewry During the Holocaust (A Report for the American Jewish Commission on the Holocaust)*. New York: Holmes and Meier, 1984.

Foreign Relations of the United States (FRUS) Diplomatic Papers 1931, III, The British Commonwealth, the Near East and Africa. Washington, D.C.: U.S. Department of State, 1954.

Friedenson, Joseph, and David H. Kranzler. *Heroine of Rescue*. New York: Mesorah Publications, 1984.

Friedman, Robert I. *The False Prophet*. London: Faber and Faber, 1990.

Friedmann, Saul. *No Haven for the Oppressed: United States Policy toward Jewish Refugees, 1938–1945*. Detroit, Mich.: Wayne State Univ. Press, 1973.

Friesel, Avyatar. *The Zionist Movement in the United States, 1897–1914* (in Hebrew). Tel Aviv: Tel Aviv Univ., 1970.

Gal, Allon. *Brandeis of Boston*. Cambridge, Mass.: Harvard Univ. Press, 1976.

Gelber, Yoav, *Jewish Palestinian Volunteering in the British Army During the Second World War.* Vol. 1, *Volunteering and Its Role in Zionist Policy, 1939–1942* (in Hebrew). Jerusalem: Yad Izhak Ben-Zvi, 1979.

———. *Jewish Palestinian Volunteering in the British Army During the Second World War.* Vol. 2, *The Struggle for a Jewish Army* (in Hebrew). Jerusalem: Yad Izhak Ben-Zvi, 1981.

Gibb, Cecil A. "Leadership: Psychological Aspects." In *International Encyclopedia of the Social Sciences.* Vol. 9, edited by David L. Sills. New York: Macmillan and the Free Press, 1968.

Gilead, Zerubavel, ed. *Book of the Palmach* (in Hebrew). Vol. 2. Tel Aviv: Hakibbutz Hameuchad, 1956.

Glazer, Nathan. *Ethnic Dilemmas, 1964–1982*. Cambridge, Mass.: Harvard Univ. Press, 1983.

Greenberg, Uri Zvi. *Collected Works* (in Hebrew). Vol. 5, *Rechovot ha-Nahar*, edited by Dan Meron. Jerusalem: Mossad Bialik, 1992.

Halamish, Aviva. *The Exodus Affair: Holocaust Survivors and the Struggle for Palestine*. Syracuse, N.Y.: Syracuse Univ. Press, 1998.

Halperin, Samuel, *The Political World of American Zionism*. Detroit, Mich.: Wayne State Univ. Press, 1961.

Handlin, Oscar. *Race and Nationality in American Life*. Boston: Little, Brown, 1948.

Hecht, Ben. *1001 Afternoons in New York*. New York: Viking Press, 1941.

———. *A Child of the Century*. New York: Ballantine, 1970.

Heller, Joseph. *The Stern Gang: Ideology, Politics, and Terror, 1940–1949*. London: Frank Cass, 1995.

Helpern, Irma. "The Jewish Brigade" (in Hebrew). *Hamashkif,* 12 Jan. 1945.

Holmes, Jack E. *The Mood/Interest Theory of American Foreign Policy*. Lexington: Univ. Press of Kentucky, 1985.

Horowitz, Donald L. *Ethnic Groups in Conflict*. Berkeley: Univ. of California Press, 1987.

Howard, Con, David Noel Doyle, and Owen Dudley Edwards, eds. *America and Ireland, 1776–1976: The American Identity and the Irish Connection*. Westport, Conn.: Greenwood, 1980.

Jabotinsky, Eri. *My Father, Ze'ev Jabotinsky* (in Hebrew). Tel Aviv: Hadar, 1981.

———. *The Sakarya Expedition*. Johannesburg: Newzo, 1945.

Jabotinsky, Vladimir [Zeev]. *The Jewish War Front*. London: G. Allen and Unwin, 1940.

Kahane, Meir. "Jabotinsky." *Jewish Press,* 17 July 1970.

———. *Never Again*. Los Angeles: Nash, 1971.

———. *Our Challenge: The Chosen Land*. Radnor, Penn.: Chilton, 1974.

———. *The Story of the Jewish Defense League*. Radnor, Penn.: Chilton, 1975.

Kaplan, Jonathan. "Rescue Efforts by the Irgun Delegation in the United States During the Holocaust" (in Hebrew). *Yalkut Moreshet* 30 (1980): 115–38.

Katz, Shmuel. *Days of Fire*. Jerusalem: Steimatzky, 1980.

———. *Lone Wolf: A Biography of Vladimir (Ze'ev) Jabotinsky*. Vol. 2. New York: Barricade Books, 1996.

Kaufman, Menachem. *An Ambiguous Partnership: Non-Zionists and Zionists in America, 1939–1948*. Jerusalem: Magnes and Wayne State Univ., 1991.

———. *Non-Zionists in America and the Struggle for Jewish Statehood, 1939–1948* (in Hebrew). Jerusalem: Hassifriya Haziyonit, 1984.

Keegan, John. *Battle for History: Re-Fighting World War II*. New York: Vintage Books, 1995.

Kister, Joseph. *Etzel (I.Z.L.)* (in Hebrew). Tel Aviv: Ministry of Defence, 1993.

Lehman, Edward. "The Macrosociology of Empowerment" (in Hebrew). In *State and Society: Problems in Political Sociology*. Edited by Samuel N. Eisenstadt, 49–62. Tel-Aviv: Am Oved, 1976.

Levine, Charles. "Propaganda Techniques of the Bergson Group, 1939–1948." M.A. thesis, Univ. of Texas at Austin, 1974.

LeVine, Robert A., and Donald T. Campbell, *Ethnocentrism: Theories of Conflict, Ethnic Attitudes and Group Behavior.* New York: John Wiley, 1972.

Lipset, Seymour M., and Earl Raab. *Jews and the New American Scene*. Cambridge, Mass.: Harvard Univ. Press, 1995.

Lipstadt, Deborah E. *Beyond Belief: The American Press and the Coming of the Holocaust, 1933–1945*. New York: The Free Press, 1986.

Lowenstein, Sharon R. *Token Refuge: The Story of the Jewish Refugee Shelter at Oswego, 1944–46*. Bloomington: Indiana Univ. Press, 1986.

Lubar, Gloria, and E. F. van der Veen. "Functions of Various Groups Backed by Bergson Explained." *Washington Post,* 8 Oct. 1944.

Malcolm, Joyce Lee. *To Keep and Bear Arms: The Origins of an Anglo-American Right*. Cambridge, Mass.: Harvard Univ. Press, 1994.

Marden, Charles Frederick, and Gladys Meyer. *Minorities in American Society*. 4th ed. New York: Van Nostrand, 1973.

Medoff, Rafael. *The Deafening Silence: American Jewish Leaders and the Holocaust*. New York: Shapolsky, 1987.

Meyer, Michael A. *Response to Modernity: A History of the Reform Movement in Judaism*. Oxford: Oxford Univ. Press, 1988.

Morgenstern, Aryeh. "The Jewish Relief Committee" (in Hebrew). *Yalkut Moreshet* 13 (1971): 60–103.

Morrison, David. *Heroes, Antiheroes and the Holocaust: American Jewry and Historical Choice*. Jerusalem: Milah Press, 1995.

Napier, Rodney W., and Matti K. Gershenfeld. *Groups: Theory and Experience*. Boston: Houghton Mifflin, 1985.

Niv, David. *Battle for Freedom: The Irgun Zvai Leumi* (in Hebrew). 6 vols. Tel Aviv: Klausner Institute, 1965–81.

Ofer, Dalia. *Escaping the Holocaust: Illegal Immigration to the Land of Israel*. New York: Oxford Univ. Press, 1990.

———. "Illegal Immigration During the Second World War: Its Suspension and Subsequent Resumption." *Studies in Contemporary Jewry* 7 (1991): 220–46.

———. "Independent Revisionist Movement Aliyah" (in Hebrew). In *Haapala: Studies in the History of Illegal Immigration into Palestine, 1934–1948*. Edited by Anita Shapira, 44–60. Tel Aviv: Am Oved, 1990.

———. "Relief and Rescue Activity by the Palestinian Jewish Delegation to Istanbul, 1943." M.A. thesis, Hebrew Univ., 1972.

Orbach, William. *The American Movement to Aid Soviet Jewry*. Amherst: Univ. of Massachusetts Press, 1979.

Paassen, Pierre van. *The Forgotten Ally*. New York: Dial Press, 1942.

Payne, Stanley. *A History of Fascism, 1914–1945*. Madison: Univ. of Wisconsin Press, 1995.

Penkower, Monty N. "Eleanor Roosevelt and the Plight of World Jewry." In *The Holocaust and Israel Reborn: From Catastrophe to Sovereignty*. Urbana: Univ. of Illinois Press, 1994, 271–88.

———. "In Dramatic Dissent: The Bergson Boys." In *The Holocaust and Israel Reborn: From Catastrophe to Sovereignty*. Urbana: Univ. of Illinois Press, 1994, 61–90.

———. *The Jews Were Expendable*. Urbana: Univ. of Illinois Press, 1993.

Perl, William R. *Operation Action: Rescue from the Holocaust*. New York: F. Ungar, 1983.

Porat, Dina. "Palestinian Jewry and the Jewish Agency: Public Response to the

Holocaust." In *Vision and Conflict in the Holy Land*. Edited by Richard I. Cohen, 246–73. New York: Palgrave MacMillan, 1985.

Porath, Yehoshua, *The Life of Uriel Shelah (Yonathan Ratosh)* (in Hebrew). Jerusalem: Mahberot Lesifrut, 1989.

Rafaeli, Alexander. *Dream and Action: The Story of My Life*. Jerusalem: Achva Co-operative Press, 1993.

Robinson, Mike. *Groups*. Chichester, UK: Wiley, 1984.

Rogger, Hans, and Eugene Weber, eds. *The European Right: A Historical Profile*. Berkeley: Univ. of California Press, 1965.

Rogov, Faith. *Gone to Another Meeting: The National Council of Jewish Women, 1893–1993*. Tuscaloosa: Univ. of Alabama Press, 1994.

Rosenblum, Chanoch [Howard]. "The New Zionist Organization's American Campaign, 1936–1939." *Studies in Zionism* 12 (1991): 169–85.

Rothman, Stanley, and S. Robert Lichter. *Roots of Radicalism: Jews, Christians, and the New Left*. New York: Oxford Univ. Press, 1982.

Rothschild, Joseph. *Ethnopolitics: A Conceptual Framework*. New York: Columbia Univ. Press, 1981.

Russ, Shlomo Mordechai. "The 'Zionist Hooligans': The Jewish Defense League." Ph.D. diss., City Univ. of New York, 1981.

Rustin, Bayard. *Strategies for Freedom*. New York: Columbia Univ. Press, 1976.

Sachar, Howard Morley. *A History of the Jews in America*. New York: A. A. Knopf, 1992.

Saidel, Joanna M. "Revisionist Zionism in America: The Campaign to Win American Public Support, 1930–1948." Ph.D. diss., Univ. of New Hampshire, 1994.

Schama, Simon. *Landscape and Memory*. New York: A. A. Knopf, 1995.

Schechtman, Joseph B. *The United States and the Jewish State Movement*. New York: Herzl Press, 1966.

Schechtman, Joseph B., and Yehuda Benari. *History of the Revisionist Movement*. Vol. 1. Tel Aviv: Hadar, 1970.

Shapiro, Yonatan. *Chosen to Command: The Road to Power of the Herut Party—A Socio-political Interpretation* (in Hebrew). Tel Aviv: Am Oved, 1989.

Shavit, Ya'akov. *The New Hebrew Nation: A Study in Israeli Heresy and Fantasy*. London: F. Cass, 1987.

———. *Jabotinsky and the Revisionist Movement, 1925–1948*. London: F. Cass, 1988.

Shaw, Marvin E. *Group Dynamics: The Psychology of Small Group Behavior*. New York: McGraw Hill, 1971.

Sherman, Arnold. *The Kindling: A Biography of Arieh Ben-Eliezer* (in Hebrew). Jerusalem: Edanim, 1986.

Shpiro, David H. *From Philanthropy to Activism: The Political Transformation of American Zionism in the Holocaust Years, 1933–1945*. Oxford: Pergamon Press, 1994.

Shprinzak, Ehud. "Kach and Meir Kahane: The Emergence of Jewish Quasi-Fascism II: Ideology and Politics." *Patterns of Prejudice* 19, no. 4 (1985).

Silverberg, Robert. *If I Forget Thee O Jerusalem: American Jews and the State of Israel*. New York: William Morrow, 1970.

Slater, Leonard. *The Pledge*. New York: Simon and Schuster, 1971.

Slutsky, Yehuda. *History of the Hagana* (in Hebrew). Vol. 3, part 2, *From Resistance to War*. Tel Aviv: Am Oved, 1973.

Sternhel, Ze'ev. *Neither Right nor Left: Fascist Ideology in France* (in Hebrew). Tel Aviv: Am Oved, 1984.

Stevens, Richard P. *American Zionism and United States Foreign Policy, 1942–1947*. New York: Pageant Press, 1962.

Strong, Donald Stuart. *Organized Anti-Semitism in America, 1939–1940*. Washington, D.C.: American Council on Public Affairs, 1941.

Tannenbaum, Arnold S. "Leadership: Sociological Aspects." In *International Encyclopedia of the Social Sciences*, vol. 9, edited by David L. Sills. New York: Macmillan and the Free Press, 1968.

Tavin, Eli. *The Second Front: The Irgun Zevai Leumi in Europe, 1946–1948* (in Hebrew). Tel Aviv: Ron, 1973.

Tzur, Eli. *The Second World War: The War That Changed the World* (in Hebrew). Jerusalem: Ministry of Education, 1995.

Urofsky, Melvin I. *American Zionism from Herzl to the Holocaust*. New York: Doubleday Anchor, 1975.

Waxman, Chaim I. "An American Tragedy—Meir Kahane and Kahanism: A Review Essay." *American Jewish History* 78, no. 3 (1980): 429–35.

Weitz, Yechiam. "The Role of *Sheerith Hapleta* in Jewish Agency Executive Deliberations (May-November 1945)" (in Hebrew). *Yalkut Moreshet* 29 (May 1980): 53–80.

———. "The Yishuv and *Sheerith Hapleta*, 1944–45" (in Hebrew). M.A. thesis, Hebrew Univ., 1981.

———. "The Zionist Movement Facing the Surviving Remnants at the End of World War II" (in Hebrew). *Dappim LeHeker HaShoah* 3 (1984): 139–58.

White, Hayden. "Historical Emplotment and the Problem of Truth." In *Probing the Limits of Representation: Nazism and the Final Solution*. Edited by Saul Friedlander. Cambridge, Mass.: Harvard Univ. Press, 1992.

———. "Narrativity in the Representation of Reality." In *The Content of the Form*. Baltimore: Johns Hopkins Univ. Press, 1987.

Winkler, Allan M. *The Politics of Propaganda: The Office of War Information, 1942–1945*. New Haven, Conn.: Yale Univ. Press, 1978.

Wyman, David S. *The Abandonment of the Jews: America and the Holocaust, 1941–1945*. New York: Pantheon Books, 1984.

———. "The American Jewish Leadership and the Holocaust." In *Jewish Leadership During the Nazi Era*. Edited by Randolph L. Braham. New York: Social Science Monographs and Institute for Holocaust Studies of the City of New York, 1985.

———. *Paper Walls: America and the Refugee Crisis, 1938–1941*. Amherst, Mass.: Univ. of Massachusetts Press, 1968.

Zaar, Isaac. *Rescue and Liberation: America's Part in the Birth of Israel*. New York: Bloch Publishing Company, 1954.

Zifroni, G. "The Embassy that Wasn't" (in Hebrew). *Maariv,* 9 October 1977.

Index

Friedman-Yellin (Yellin-Mor), Nathan, 13, 175, 239

Galili, Yisrael, 241
Gallipoli, 59
Garibaldi, Guiseppi, 197
Gelber, Yoav, xxvii, 86
"General Government," 57
George Washington Legion, 226
Germany, 5, 55, 87, 183, 198, 209, 212
Gershenfeld, Matti K., 186
Gestapo, 6, 55, 224
Gibb, Cecil A., 45
Gillette, Guy M., 88, 164, 167, 186, 205, 217, 218, 221, 222, 223, 243
Giurgiu, 57
Glazer, Nathan, 129, 131
Goldberg, Arthur, 194, 196
Goldberg Commission, 194, 195, 196
Goldman, Nahum, 208, 209, 232
Goldstein, Israel, 232
Golumb, Eliyahu, 175, 176
Great Depression, 30, 31
Great Migration, 26, 27, 29
Greece, 38, 55, 81, 136, 205, 216
Greenbaum, Colonel, 113
Greenberg, Hayim, 123
Greenberg, Uri Zvi, 198
Griffel, Jacob, 178, 179
Grigg, Sir James, 110
Grossman, Meir, 21, 22, 94, 97, 255
Gruner, Dov, 60, 234
Gruss, Joseph, 276
Gunther, Frances, 17, 41, 51, 82, 154, 164, 262
Gunther, John, 16, 41, 51
Gurevitch, Adolf (Ben-Horin), 203

Haboker (newspaper), 11
hadar, 254, 271, 273
Hadassah, 30, 32, 33, 162, 172, 192
Hadassah Hospital, 8
Hagana, 11, 19, 175, 199, 200, 207, 208, 209, 211, 212, 219, 225, 241
Hagana B, xvi, 8, 11, 19
Haifa, xi, 60, 225, 240, 241
Hakohen, David, 208
Halperin, Rose, 125
Halperin, Samuel, xvii, 78, 143, 158, 160, 162, 190, 193, 203, 215, 218, 244
Handlin, Oscar, 259
Hannah, Ian (MP), 110
Harper, Fowler, 221
Hearst, William Randolph, 88, 148
Hebrew Committee of National Liberation, xii, xxiv, 96, 188, 197, 200, 201, 202, 204, 205, 206, 210, 212, 213, 214, 215, 216, 217, 218, 219, 220, 221, 222, 223, 224, 227, 228, 229, 230, 231, 233, 234, 235, 236, 237, 238, 239, 240, 242, 243, 244, 246, 247, 248
Hebrews, 180, 202–5, 228, 229, 233, 234, 236, 238, 244, 245, 247, 259
Hebrew State Party, 68
Hebrew University (Jerusalem), xxii, 194
Hecht, Ben, 17, 49, 88, 89, 90, 96, 97, 103, 114, 115, 117, 152, 182, 197, 206, 219, 220, 231, 243
Hecht, Reuven (Rudi), 58, 59, 71, 184, 185, 186, 224
Heidelberg, 58, 184
Heilperin, Uriel (Yonathan Ratosh), 22, 23, 24
Heller, Joseph, xxiv, xxvii, 22, 239
Helpern, Yirmiyanu (Irma), 17, 18, 88, 89, 91, 107, 108, 109, 111, 112, 129, 133, 141, 202, 243
Herald Tribune (newspaper), 100
Herut Party, 68, 177, 196, 242, 243, 249
Herzl Institute for the Study of Zionism, xxvii

Heyman, Miriam, 82, 262
Hill (colonial affairs minister), 221
Hirschmann, Ira, 178, 179
Histadrut, 19
Hitler, Adolph, xii
Hobsbawn, Eric, xxiv
Holland, 36
Hollywood, Calif., 90, 103
Honduras, 216
Honelein, Malcolm, 276
Hoover, Herbert, 144, 146
Hoover, J. Edgar, 78
Horthy, Miklos, 183
Hoskins, Harold, 187
Hull, Cordell (secretary of state), 144, 155
Hungary, 26, 54, 58, 183, 195, 198
al-Husseini, Haj Amin (mufti of Jerusalem), 213
Hyde Park, N.Y., xxiii

Ickes, Harold, 162
Intergovernmental Committee on Refugees, 137, 138
Iraq, 71
Irgun Zvai Leumi (IZL), xi, xv, 4, 7, 8, 21, 24, 199, 207, 239, 242
Israel Defense Forces, 241
Istanbul, 179
Italy, xii, 164, 181, 183, 216, 223

Jabotinsky, Aviva, 212
Jabotinsky, Eri, 13, 14, 16, 19, 24, 48, 54, 55, 56, 57, 59, 60, 61, 62, 66, 70, 72, 84, 88, 91, 101, 103, 108, 123, 129, 143, 144, 147, 166, 170, 171, 177, 178, 179, 180, 181, 186, 189, 200, 202, 203, 210, 228, 229, 236, 240, 243, 249, 250, 260
Jabotinsky, Joanna (Anna), 65
Jabotinsky, Karni, 129

Jabotinsky, Vladimir Zeev, xi, 3, 13, 14, 16, 18, 19, 20, 21, 22, 23, 24, 25, 37, 38, 39, 45, 62, 64, 65, 66, 67, 68, 70, 71, 72, 73, 76, 80, 84, 85, 86, 89, 95, 203, 222, 239, 273, 274
Jabotinsky Archives (Israel), xxii, 7, 47, 87
Jackson, Henry (senator), 279
Jarvik, Laurence, 195, 196
Jerusalem, xi, xv
Jewish Agency for Palestine, 34, 50, 73, 111, 112, 125, 133, 197, 200, 208, 221
Jewish Army, 69, 80, 83, 85, 91, 104, 111, 126, 141, 150, 225
Jewish Army Committee, 17, 71, 93, 94, 96, 98, 100, 103, 104, 107, 109, 110, 111, 112, 113, 118, 119, 124, 126, 127, 128, 129, 131, 132, 133, 134, 139, 141, 152, 189, 190, 200, 206, 233
Jewish Brigade, xii, xix, 85, 132, 133, 134, 206
Jewish Chronicle (newpaper), 108
Jewish Defense League, xxi, 261, 266, 268, 269, 270, 271, 272, 273, 274, 275, 276, 277, 278
Jewish Fairy Tale, A (Hecht), 206
Jewish Labor Committee, 32, 39
Jewish Legion, 103
Jewish National Fund, 73
Jewish Press (newspaper), 269
Jewish Standard (newspaper), 108
Johnson, Edwin C., 105, 139, 145, 187, 218
Joint Distribution Committee, 143, 172, 181
Joseph, Dov, 208

Kach (political party) xxi, 271
Kahane, Charles (Yehezkel Shraga), 97, 268, 269